SIMPSON

IMPRINT IN HUMANITIES

The humanities endowment
by Sharon Hanley Simpson and
Barclay Simpson honors
MURIEL CARTER HANLEY
whose intellect and sensitivity
have enriched the many lives
that she has touched.

The publisher gratefully acknowledges the generous contribution to this book provided by the Simpson Humanities Endowment Fund of the University of California Press Foundation.

The Decline of Sentiment

The Decline of Sentiment

American Film in the 1920s

LEA JACOBS

University of California Press

BERKELEY   LOS ANGELES   LONDON

University of California Press, one of the most distinguished university presses in the United States, enriches lives around the world by advancing scholarship in the humanities, social sciences, and natural sciences. Its activities are supported by the UC Press Foundation and by philanthropic contributions from individuals and institutions. For more information, visit www.ucpress.edu.

Parts of this book were previously published in different form as "The Seduction Plot: Comic and Dramatic Variants," *Film History* 13, no. 4 (2001): 424–42, and "Men without Women: The Avatars of *What Price Glory*," *Film History* 17, nos. 2–3 (2005): 307–33, and are reprinted here by permission of Indiana University Press.

University of California Press
Berkeley and Los Angeles, California

University of California Press, Ltd.
London, England

Library of Congress Cataloging-in-Publication Data

Jacobs, Lea.
    The decline of sentiment : American film in the 1920s / Lea Jacobs.
        p.   cm.
    Includes bibliographical references and index.
    ISBN 978-0-520-23701-8 (cloth : alk. paper)
    ISBN 978-0-520-25457-2 (pbk. : alk. paper)
    1. Motion pictures—United States—History.   2. Silent films—United States—History.   3. Melodrama in motion pictures.   I. Title.
PN1993.5.U6J198   2008
791.43'75—dc22   2007025657

Manufactured in the United States of America

17   16   15   14   13   12   11   10   09   08
10   9   8   7   6   5   4   3   2   1

To Ben

Contents

Preface

For anyone who enjoys even a cursory familiarity with American film of the 1930s and 1940s, with *How Green Was My Valley* or *Going My Way* or *The Little Colonel,* the idea that sentiment declined in the 1920s may seem implausible. But this book does not maintain that Hollywood ceased to produce films that might be considered moving or, by some, excessively pathetic. Rather, it seeks to delineate the moment when journalists and reviewers first began to criticize films on the grounds that they were cloying, foolishly optimistic, or too intent on achieving big dramatic effects. It argues that the rejection of sentimentality was a relatively new phenomenon within the American cinema of the period following World War I, although such a position already had currency in elite literary circles.

This work is proposed as a history of taste. While there are precedents for it in art history, I do not know of any in the field of film studies. I should make clear, therefore, that this investigation does not encompass the film spectator as such. I do not attempt to document the vagaries and eccentricities of individual viewing preferences, fascinating though these can sometimes be, nor do I embark upon a more properly sociological account of taste considered as the aggregate of individual preferences. Insofar as taste can be said to have a history, it seems to me to consist in the systematic alteration or, more conservatively, preservation of criteria of judgment. Commentary in the film industry trade press, as well as less specialized reviews, provides a good way to observe the articulation and institutionalization of such criteria. Films themselves are also crucial in that they responded to, and sometimes shaped, this critical discourse. I shall attempt to demonstrate the importance of key films that provided models for both critics and filmmakers and whose narrative and stylistic innovations led the way in the transformation of taste.

When I began studying film history almost three decades ago, the field of early cinema (cinema prior to 1915) had just opened up, a terra incognita. In contrast, the Hollywood cinema of the 1920s seemed almost depressingly familiar. In undertaking this project I have become much less certain of our knowledge of the latter period, more aware of the gaps and lacunae in the historical record, and excited by the opportunities for further research. It is my hope that this work will contribute to a reconsideration of some of the films we thought we knew and a rediscovery of many that have been forgotten.

I am grateful for a fellowship from the John Simon Guggenheim Foundation that provided the boon of uninterrupted time. I would also like to thank the Graduate School at the University of Wisconsin–Madison, and especially Judith Kornblatt, and the College of Letters and Science for their support.

Many archives and archivists made this work possible. Michael Pogorzelski and his staff at the Pickford Center of the Academy of Motion Picture Arts and Sciences accessed many obscure films from the 1920s and taught me much about the status of the prints. Barbara Hall guided me to documents in Special Collections at the Academy's Margaret Herrick Library. Schawn Belston, of Twentieth Century Fox, paved the way for my seeing rare prints and papers. I spent several weeks taxing the staff of the Film Division of George Eastman House; Paolo Cherchi Usai, then its director, patiently interrupted his work to answer queries and helped me through a formidable March blizzard in Rochester. Special thanks are due to Madeleine Matz and Zoran Sinobad of the Motion Picture, Broadcasting and Recorded Sound Division of the Library of Congress, where I spent a blissful month at the viewing tables. Both Ned Comstock, at Special Collections, Doheny Library, University of Southern California, and Eddie Richmond, of the UCLA Film and Television Archive, were most helpful. Closer to home, Maxine Ducey and Dorinda Hartmann of the Wisconsin Center for Film and Theater Research located stills and pulled films on short notice.

I received help at various stages of this project from colleagues past and present in the Department of Communication Arts at the University of Wisconsin, among them Tino Balio, Kelley Conway, Mary Anne Fitzpatrick, Scott Higgins, Michael Newman, J. J. Murphy, Sara Ross, Ben Singer, Jeff Smith, and Kristin Thompson. Three remarkable research assistants worked through the trade press of the 1920s with me: Jane Greene, Katherine Spring, and Rebecca Swender. Members of my seminar on the 1920s, Maria Belodubrovskaya, Jennifer Chung, Eric Crosby, Rachel Fischler, Lisa Jasinski, Pearl Latteier, Brad Schauer, and Tom Yoshikami, really did teach me more than I did them, as their names in several back-notes attest.

David Bordwell's rigor, wit, and omnivorous viewing habits are matched only by his mania for recording off air. I am very grateful for the movies he sent my way, and also for his editorial suggestions, which, I am afraid, were more honored in the breach than in the observance. Vance Kepley saved me from many stylistic infelicities and, at a crucial juncture, volunteered a much needed bottle of gin. Janet Bergstrom provided a home away from home in Los Angeles and expert editorial advice on an early version of chapter 4. I am indebted to James Naremore and Mathew Bernstein for their careful and astute readings of the manuscript, detailed commentary, and great generosity.

In an interview Mack Sennett once spoke of the necessity of employing a "cloud man," a writer who could walk into a room of stymied fellow gag men and, with an unexpected idea, "you take this cloud, see . . . ," inspire new avenues of invention. This book is dedicated to Ben Brewster, who, in addition to being editor, translator, computer wizard, and inveterate companion at the movies, is my cloud man.

1   Toward a History of Taste

The real war had been fought during the decade before 1920, when
almost every new writer was a recruit to the army against gentility,
and when older writers like Dreiser and Robinson were being
rescued from neglect and praised as leaders. In those days, Mabel
Dodge's salon, the Provincetown Playhouse and, in Chicago, the Dill
Pickle Club were the rallying grounds of the rebel forces. The
Masses (1911), *Poetry* (1912), and the *Smart Set* (of which the
greatest year was 1913) and the *Little Review* (1914) were its
propaganda organs. Every new book was a skirmish with the
conservatives, and some were resounding victories—as notably
"Jennie Gerhardt" (1911), "American's Coming-of-Age" and "Spoon
River Anthology" (1915), "Chicago Poems" (1916), "The Education
of Henry Adams" (1918), "Winesburg, Ohio" and "Our America"
(1919). In that same year, Mencken began publishing his collected
"Prejudices." The appearance and suppression and eventual re-issue
of "Jurgen" were a major triumph. Then, in 1920, came the success
of "Beyond the Horizon," the first play by a member of the group to
be produced on Broadway, and the vastly greater success of "Main
Street." By that time, the genteel critics were fighting rearguard
actions to protect their line of retreat. The "young intellectuals"
were mopping up territory already conquered.

MALCOLM COWLEY, *After the Genteel Tradition* (1937)

In the years prior to and immediately following World War I American literary culture may be said virtually to have defined the term *culture wars*.
Fueled not only by disagreements about what constituted literary merit
but also by attempts at censorship, the debates were vociferous and prolonged. This study is concerned with how these perturbations within the
field of letters affected Hollywood film. Of course the American cinema is
often said to have altered during the 1920s. Historians frequently charac-
terize the decade in terms of the development of the stereotype of the flapper—epitomized by the stars Clara Bow and Colleen Moore—and of a new
sexual permissiveness, both reflected in films and, perhaps, reinforced by
them.[1] Some historians have explained the new representations of sexuality seen in the films with reference to the emergence of a culture of consumption.[2] It seems to me that these by now standard interpretations of
the period do not account for the nature or full extent of the cinema's

transformation. In what follows I shall describe a decisive shift in taste that was manifested in critical discourse, in filmmaking technique, and across a broad spectrum of film genres. I will contrast the films that came to be identified as "sophisticated," on the edge of what censors or more conservative viewers would tolerate, with others that were dismissed as sentimental or simply old-fashioned.[3]

The changes that occurred within the cinema were congruent with, and to some extent parasitic upon, other cultural trends. The assimilation of jazz and blues by the Tin Pan Alley composers prompted a radical reworking of the sentimental ballad.[4] America's spectacular confrontation with modern art in the Armory Show of 1913 was moderated by a more gradual diffusion of modernist and protomodernist graphic elements into advertising and interior and industrial design.[5] But while the new forms of popular song and of graphic design certainly influenced filmmaking, it seems to me that the literary upheavals of the 1910s and 1920s provide the best context for explaining how taste altered. Dissident critics and journalists were articulate about what they admired and what they despised. Their writings, as well as the history of more or less successful attempts at literary and theatrical censorship, provide a vivid record of a transformation that eventually extended well beyond the literary sphere. This is not to propose that film critics and the mass audience for the movies straightforwardly adopted the positions and preferences of advanced literary intellectuals. Many aspects of elite literary taste remained quite remote from popular culture. Moreover, the cinema was distinct from literature both as an institution and as a medium. It had its own critical organs, most importantly the trade press, which figures prominently here as a guide to the industry's evaluation of its own products. In addition, the cinema had its own narrative and stylistic traditions. Thus it absorbed and reprocessed the ramifications of the literary rebellion of the 1910s and 1920s in distinctive ways. Nonetheless, the culture wars of the early twentieth century had a decisive impact on the ways in which reviewers judged films, on the novels and stage plays chosen for adaptation by the studios, and on the narrative models available to both screenwriters and directors. Before turning to an examination of the cinema, we need therefore to explore the debates that characterized the literary institutions of the period in more detail.

THE CHANGE IN LITERARY TASTE

The literary history of the 1910s and 1920s has been analyzed and described in many ways. In terms of the history of ideas it has been characterized by the entrance onto the American scene of Nietzsche, Freud, and Marx, and the consequent questioning of older assumptions about the inevitability of progress and absolute moral values. In terms of the history of institutions it has been associated with the demise of the older organs of genteel culture, the staid monthly magazines and publishing houses, and the ascent of the little magazines and new and more adventurous publishers.[6] In terms of urban history it has been depicted as the time of the formation of the first real American communities of bohemians: the Greenwich Village community that included such disparate types as Emma Goldman, Theodore Dreiser, Floyd Dell, and Randolph Bourne; and also the Chicago community that included Dell (at an earlier point in his career), Carl Sandburg, Margaret Anderson of the *Little Review,* and famously cynical newspapermen of the likes of Ring Lardner and, later, Ben Hecht.[7] In terms of the history of literary forms the period has been frequently celebrated as the point of a radical break with the past: the explosion of modernist experiments in poetry, the novel, and the short story in the United States and abroad.

But, of most importance here, this period may also be understood in terms of a profound questioning of what had formerly been considered the acme of literary achievement, a reevaluation of both the canon and the criteria of literary judgment. Henry May describes William Dean Howells's birthday dinner in 1912, at which guests included President Taft among other luminaries, as the culmination of a certain kind of progressive ideology and literary culture. Howells was being vilified by 1920. And as Howells's stock went down, Twain's went up. Melville, more thoroughly forgotten than Twain had ever been, was rediscovered. Whitman was revivified.[8] This reevaluation of nineteenth-century authors was accompanied by much more vitriolic debates about more recent ones. Although the 1920s are thought of as the time when modernism proper flowered—the time of Pound, Eliot, and Joyce—the change in taste that made it possible to appreciate, even to publish, these authors began much earlier, in the years prior to World War I. This change concerned writers who, from our vantage point in history, are considered more old-fashioned: the naturalists and, most notoriously, Theodore Dreiser as portrayed and promoted by H. L. Mencken. It may well be, as Henry May has argued, that European naturalism had its American advocates at the turn of the century; that Zola, Flaubert, Turgenev, and Ibsen were acceptable to the "most tolerant of the arbiters of American taste," men like Howells and Henry James.[9] But this acceptance was limited to a small number of critics, and, as May explains, their liberality was at least in some cases a function of "their confident assumption that American society was, and would remain, different from that of Europe. Not life, but the

Second Empire was being terribly described by Zola. There was little danger that a young American, reading Flaubert's *Sentimental Education,* would start looking for a fashionable married woman willing to become his recognized mistress. If even Turgenev was a pessimist, it must be because things were sad in Russia."[10]

Another reason why the European naturalists did not fundamentally disturb the turn-of-the-century American literary scene is that they were not considered seriously as part of the canon. As Kermit Vanderbilt has shown, for most American literary scholars that canon was largely comprised of British authors until the 1910s. Even American letters were not regularly taught within the academy. Referring to Van Wyck Brooks's experience at Harvard during the years 1904–07, Vanderbilt evokes an atmosphere of Anglophilia and "spiritual toryism," noting: "Brooks remembered that the academic mood of the period was to equate Americanism with philistinism, following Matthew Arnold's view that American life and culture were, frankly and simply, not interesting."[11] Vanderbilt's history of the creation of the American canon commences with the *Cambridge History of American Literature,* published in four volumes from 1917 to 1921.[12] Discussion about Dreiser becomes heated at just this point: Mencken's well-known attack on the critic Stuart P. Sherman and defense of Dreiser appears in *A Book of Prefaces* in 1917. Thus, although there had been naturalist writers in America at least since Frank Norris, and defenders of naturalism among even such traditional critics as Howells, the way in which this movement upset the hierarchy of traditional tastes did not become apparent until the 1910s, amid debates about the American literary canon.

Writing in the *Smart Set* in 1912, on the occasion of the translation of some short stories by Zola, Mencken explained why, in his view, naturalism remained important: "Zola, I am aware, did not invent naturalism—and naturalism, as he defined it, is not now the fashion. But it must be obvious that his propaganda, as novelist and critic, did more than any other one thing to give naturalism direction and coherence and to break down its antithesis, the sentimental romanticism of the middle Nineteenth Century—*Uncle Tom's Cabin, David Copperfield, La Dame aux Camélias*—and that his influence today, even if he has few avowed disciples, is still wide and undeniable."[13] This is more than an assessment of Zola, for Mencken himself, as critic and propagandist, would use naturalism in precisely this way, as an attack on what he took to be the sentimental qualities of American literature.

The assault on "sentimentality" in the literary discourses of the 1910s, often conjoined with criticism of the "genteel," presents a complicated problem in the history of taste. The negative valuation of sentimentality is as old as the eighteenth-century literature of sentiment itself.[14] Further, within the context of America in the 1920s, the New Humanists Irving Babbitt and Paul Elmer More, among the most intellectually formidable enemies of journalists such as Mencken, surely despised sentimentality in equal measure. Randolph Bourne, for example, speaks of More's dislike of "sentimental humanitarianism," while the idea of "uplift" and progressive political rhetoric was also repugnant to Mencken.[15] And both ends of this literary spectrum would have frowned upon most popular culture as sentimental "mush for the multitude," as Mencken dubbed it in one of his *Smart Set* book reviews.[16] Nonetheless, the discussion about the place of naturalism within the canon gave a new energy and vigor to the rejection of sentiment, an energy that reverberated throughout the culture and eventually affected even the assessment of popular culture made by some intellectuals in the 1920s.

Sentimentality, for the young intellectuals of the 1910s and 1920s, was often associated with a highly moralized view of literature and life. Mencken's 1917 essay on Dreiser provides a particularly clear instance of this point of attack. Mencken compares Dreiser to Conrad, quoting from Hugh Walpole's assessment of that author:

> Conrad is of the firm and resolute conviction that life is too strong, too clever, and too remorseless for the sons of men. . . . It is as though, from some high window, looking down, he were able to watch some shore, from whose security men are forever launching little cockleshell boats upon a limitless and angry sea. . . . From his height he can follow their fortunes, their brave struggles, their fortitude to the very end. He admires their courage, the simplicity of their faith, but his irony springs from his knowledge of the inevitable end.

Mencken goes on to write:

> Substitute the name of Dreiser for that of Conrad, and you will have to change scarcely a word. Perhaps one, to wit, "clever." I suspect that Dreiser, writing so of his own creed, would be tempted to make it "stupid," or, at all events, "unintelligible." The struggle of man, as he sees it, is more than impotent; it is gratuitous and purposeless. There is, to his eye, no grand ingenuity, no skilful adaptation of means to end, no moral (or even dramatic) plan in the order of the universe. He can get out of it only a sense of profound and inexplicable *dis*order.[17]

Indeed, according to Mencken, the only problem with Dreiser's view of the unintelligibility of the universe is that he is still too wide-eyed about it—he insists too much, because the discovery remains something of a shock to his Hoosier soul.[18]

In contrast to Mencken's celebration of Dreiser's amorality, those who rejected naturalism often did so on the grounds of an adherence to fundamental moral values. A prototypical, if rather extreme, example from 1913 is theatrical doyen William Winter's attack on Ibsen:

> It is easy to say, as was said by the despondent, hysterical, inflammatory Jeremiah, in the Bible, that the heart of man is deceitful above all things and desperately wicked. But what good have you done when you have made that statement? As a matter of fact it is only half true. There are in the world many kind, pure hearts and noble minds; not a day passes without its deed of simple heroism; not an hour passes without some manifestation of beautiful self-sacrifice, splendid patience, celestial fidelity to duty, and sweet manifestation of unselfish love. There must be evil to illustrate good, but in art, and emphatically in dramatic art, it must be wisely selected. The spectacle of virtue in human character and loveliness in human conduct will accomplish far more for the benefit of society than ever can be accomplished by the spectacle of imbecile propensity, vicious conduct, or any form of the aberrancy of mental disease.[19]

If Winter's position strikes us as sentimental, it is no doubt because the literary intellectuals of the 1920s won this particular culture war. The kind of affirmation made here in rebuttal of naturalist pessimism itself became a target, and the value of this kind of moral suasion as literary judgment came to be contested.

Mencken's rebuttal to Sherman's assessment of Dreiser provides a notorious example of the debunking of moral criteria in the evaluation of art:

> I single out Dr. Sherman, not because his pompous syllogisms have any plausibility in fact or logic, but simply because he may well stand as archetype of the booming, indignant corrupter of criteria, the moralist turned critic. A glance at his paean to Arnold Bennett at once reveals the true gravamen of his objection to Dreiser. What offends him is not actually Dreiser's shortcoming as an artist, but Dreiser's shortcoming as a Christian and an American. In Bennett's volumes of pseudo-philosophy—e.g., "The Plain Man and His Wife" and "The Feast of St. Friend"—he finds the intellectual victuals that are to his taste. Here we have a sweet commingling of virtuous conformity and complacent optimism, of sonorous platitude and easy certainty—here, in brief, we have the philosophy of the English middle classes—and here, by the same token, we have the sort of guff that the half-educated of our own country can understand.[20]

Although Randolph Bourne had his differences with Mencken, he makes a similar argument, and with almost the same targets:

Read Mr. Brownell on standards and see with what a bewildered contempt one of the most vigorous and gentlemanly survivals from the genteel tradition regards the efforts of the would-be literary artists of today. Read Stuart P. Sherman on contemporary literature, and see with what hurt panic a young gentleman, perhaps the very last brave offshoot of the genteel tradition, regards those bold modern writers from whom his contemporaries derive. One can admire the intellectual acuteness and sound moral sense of both these critics, and yet feel how quaintly irrelevant for our purposes is an idea of the good, the true, and the beautiful, which culminates in a rapture for Thackeray (vide Mr. Brownell), or in a literary aesthetic (vide Mr. Sherman) which gives Mr. Arnold Bennett first place as an artist because of his wholesome theories of human conduct. Mr. Sherman has done us the service of showing us how very dead is the genteel tradition in our hearts, how thoroughly the sense of what is desirable and absorbing has shifted in our younger American life.[21]

Thus, for Mencken, and for the slightly younger generation represented by Randolph Bourne, the taste for naturalism encompassed both a rejection of morality as a key component of literary judgment and a rejection of those literary works that had the cock-eyed optimism to posit a morally comprehensible universe.

The advocates of naturalism questioned aesthetic as well as moral principles of judgment. Naturalism overturned the rules of decorum that had governed nineteenth-century literature and the nineteenth-century stage. This was, first of all, an issue of censorship: the naturalists took up subject matter considered unfit even to be mentioned in mixed company. One gets a sense of the infraction of decorum by the outrage expressed on the occasion of the first American performance of *Mrs. Warren's Profession*, eleven years after the play first caused censorship controversies in England.[22] The reviewer for *The New York Herald* wrote: "'The limit of indecency' may seem pretty strong words, but they are justified by the fact that the play is morally rotten. It makes no difference that some of the lines may have been omitted and others toned down; there was superabundance of foulness left. The whole story of the play, the atmosphere surrounding it, the incidents, the personalities of the characters are wholly immoral and degenerate. The only way successfully to expurgate *Mrs. Warren's Profession* is to cut the whole play out. You cannot have a clean pig sty."[23] Revolted as the reviewer was, he quoted extensively from the speech made by the producer Arnold Daly (who also played the role of Frank) in defense of the play. Daly attacked efforts at censorship, singling out Anthony Comstock, the director of the New York Society for the Suppression of Vice. He defended the play on the grounds of realism: "We have many theatres . . . devoted to plays appealing to the romanticist or child—New York has even provided a hippodrome for such. But surely there should be room in New York for at least one theatre devoted to truth, however disagreeable truth may appear."

The terms of this debate were to be repeated throughout the decades that followed. The story of Dreiser's difficulties with publishers, and the pressure brought to bear by the Society for the Suppression of Vice to inhibit publication of his novels even as late as 1916, are too well known to need recounting here, at least in part because Mencken conducted such a vigorous public relations campaign against censorship in general, and the censorship of Dreiser's writings in particular.[24] Joyce is not usually classified as a naturalist, although one of the many critics who objected to *Ulysses* considered him as such.[25] But the banning of the 1920 issue of the *Little Review* containing the "Nausicaa" episode from *Ulysses* raised issues similar to those surrounding Shaw and Dreiser about the province of literature and the boundaries of good taste.[26] Patrick Parrinder points out that Joyce's representations of bodily functions offended not only literary conservatives and, in New York, watchdogs for the Society of the Suppression of Vice but also English novelists from H. G. Wells to Virginia Woolf and Rebecca West; Pound himself was eventually put off by the "cloacal" aspects of the work.[27]

These and other censorship battles represented more than just a debate over the limits, if any, that could legally be imposed on the novel or the stage. They also represented a decided shift in what was considered appropriate or fitting subject matter. In the United States in the 1910s the naturalists, preceded by muckraking journalists such as Lincoln Steffens (with whom they shared some affinities),[28] were the first to open up the terrain of the novel: big city corruption, prostitution, life in a gold-mining camp, work in the meat stockyards, and, one of Dreiser's specialties, the straitened horizons and ugly surroundings of the lower middle class. I imagine that this departure from the canonical subject matter of the novel imbued writers and literary intellectuals of the period with a tremendous sense of freedom. One gets this impression from Bourne:

> The other day, reading "My Literary Friends and Acquaintances," I shuddered at Howells's glee over the impeccable social tone of Boston and Cambridge literary life. He was playful enough about it, but not too playful to conceal the enormity of his innocence. He does not see how dreadful it is to contrast Cambridge with ragged vagabonds and

unpresentable authors of other ages. To a younger generation which feels that the writer ought to be at least a spiritual vagabond, a declassed mind, this gentility of Mr. Howells and his friends has come to seem more alien than Sologub. We are acquiring an almost Stend-halian horror for those correctnesses and tacts which wield such hypnotic influence over our middle-class life.[29]

Thus, what came to be stigmatized as "sentimental" or "romantic" or "genteel" was, in part, a refusal to accept subject matter that violated middle-class correctness and tact: explicit descriptions of sexual urges and encounters; an interest in the body and emphasis on the primacy of the instincts; exploration of the modern city or ugly industrial milieux that bore down upon and sometimes controlled the naturalist protagonist.

With the change in subject matter, the naturalists also abandoned the idea of a polite or refined style. Mencken spends a whole section of his 1917 essay on Dreiser documenting that author's brutal accumulation of detail and the unfinished quality of his language. Dreiser's awkwardness as a writer is used as a scourge against the taste for elegant and polished prose.[30]

The reaction against genteel stylistic conventions may help to explain why it was Dreiser, and not Henry James, who became the canonical pre-War American writer for the literary intellectuals of the 1910s and 1920s. For present-day critics, James certainly ranks higher, and he is considered to have broken new ground as a stylist. Writing in 1966, Richard Bridgman argued that despite the obvious differences in their respective styles, Henry James and Mark Twain shared an innovative tendency to incorporate collo-quial language into both dialogue and narrative prose, thereby loosening the more formal and rigid characteristics of the literary style they had inherited.[31] In a 1975 study comparing James's style with that of popular Victorian novelists such as Susan Warner, Fanny Fern and E. D. E. N. South-worth, William Veeder concluded that James's language, at least after the period of his apprenticeship, typically qualified the superlatives in which the best-selling novelists so frequently indulged, and that the resulting compli-cations of his style helped to prepare the way for his essentially modern representation of characters' mental processes.[32] But this was not at all the evaluation of James during the 1920s. Veeder refers slightingly to the "Brooks-Parrington thesis that Henry James was an ivory tower émigré aloof from the turmoil of his times."[33] This was, however, the predominant 1920s view of James, and it encompassed a judgment not only about his life choices and the restriction of his novels to middle- and upper-class charac-ters of the Northeast and their European counterparts but also about his style.[34] In his monograph on James, one of the few works on the author to be published in the period, Van Wyck Brooks acknowledged that James had good reasons for feeling alienated from the American scene, among others, "the little tales, mostly by ladies, and about and for children, romping through the ruins of the language in the monthly magazines."[35] For Brooks, the prose of the mature Henry James was the opposite of this, too perfect: "His sense, like Adam Verver's, had been kept sharp, year after year, by the collation of types and signs, the comparison of fine object with fine object, of one degree of finish, of one form of the exquisite with another; and type and object and form had moulded his style. Metaphors bloomed there like tropical air-plants, throwing out branches and flowers; every sound was muted and every motion vague."[36] James's prose thus registered as different from the despised models of the lady novelists, but it did not provide what the intellectuals of the 1920s considered a viable alternative. For them the models were Whitman and, above all, Twain.

One gets great insight into the transformation of literary tastes by considering the reevaluation of Twain. In part this was a function of the rediscovery of *The Mysterious Stranger* and the belated publication of *What Is Man?* which enabled critics to see his atheism and pessimism and thus assimilate his work to the world view of a Conrad or Dreiser. Predictably for Mencken, this is to Twain's credit, while for Sherman it is the object of a gentle remonstration.[37] But in addition to revising the biographical view of Twain as genial humorist, literary intellectuals came to a new appreciation of his language. In a 1911 *Smart Set* review, "Twain and Howells," Mencken refers to the "straightforward, clangorous English of Clemens and the simpering, coquettish, overcorseted English of the later Howells."[38] In his 1920 study of Twain, Van Wyck Brooks bemoans the restrictions placed on Twain's language by his contemporaries. He cites a memorandum by Twain, in the form of a dialogue with his wife, written when they were going over the manuscript of "Following the Equator":

> Page 1,020, 9th line from the top. I think some other word would be better than "stench." You have used that pretty often.
> But can't I get it in *any*where? You've knocked it out every time. Out it goes again. And yet "stench" is a noble, good word.
> Page 1,038. I hate to have your father pictured as lashing a slave boy. It's out, and my father is whitewashed.
> Page 1,050, 2nd line from the bottom. Change "breech-clout." It's a word that you love and I abominate. I would take that and "offal" out of the language.
> You are steadily weakening the English tongue, Livy.

Both Mrs. Clemens and William Dean Howells come in for criticism for this bowdlerization of Twain's language. Van Wyck Brooks concludes:

> We can see from this that to Mrs. Clemens virility was just as offensive as profanity, that she had no sense of the difference between virility and profanity and vulgarity, that she had, in short, no positive taste, no independence of judgment at all. We can see also that she had no artistic ideal for her husband, that she regarded his natural liking for bold and masculine language, which was one of the outward signs of his latent greatness, merely as a literary equivalent of bad manners, as something that endangered their common prestige in the eyes of conventional public opinion.[39]

Brooks's characterization of Howells's role in the process follows, and it accords with Mencken's description of Twain's friend and editor: "And in all this Mr. Howells seconded her. 'It skirts a certain kind of fun which you can't afford to indulge in,' he reminds our shorn Samson in one of his letters; and again, 'I'd have that swearing out in an instant,' the 'swearing' in this case being what he himself admits is 'so exactly the thing Huck would say'—namely, 'they comb me all to hell.'"[40] Van Wyck Brooks's monograph on Twain represents an angry protest against what he considered the genteel strictures on prose style: excessively polite, restricted in usage, and clearly (to poor Howells's detriment) identified as feminine.

Quite beyond their appreciation of the beauties of Twain's prose, the intellectuals of the 1910s and 1920s became interested in the literary appropriation of colloquial speech as a means of avoiding the constraint and formality of prior styles. For Van Wyck Brooks, Sherwood Anderson, Edmund Wilson, and others, Twain became the reference point to which they could compare other authors, such as Ring Lardner, who were experimenting in the vernacular.[41] Twain's language was also a crucial point of departure for Hemingway, whose alter ego in *Green Hills of Africa* asserts that "all modern American literature comes from one book by Mark Twain called *Huckleberry Finn.*"[42] The engagement with the vernacular is evident in H. L. Mencken's magnum opus, *The American Language: An Inquiry into the Development of English in the United States.*[43] Mencken excoriated the professional teachers of English and grammar for keeping alive what he claimed was, for most Americans, a dead language, one which could only "serve admirably the obscurantist purposes of American pedagogy and of English parliamentary oratory and leader-writing," as well as providing "something for literary artists of both countries to prove their skill upon by flouting it."[44] He discoursed at length on the felicities of the vernacular:

> Such a term as *rubber-neck* is almost a complete treatise on American
> psychology; it reveals the national habit of mind more clearly than any
> labored inquiry could ever reveal it. It has in it precisely the boldness
> and contempt for ordered forms that are so characteristically American,
> and it has too the grotesque humor of the country, and the delight in
> devastating opprobriums, and the acute feeling for the succinct and
> savory. The same qualities are in *rough-house, water-wagon, near-silk,
> has-been, lame-duck* and a thousand other such racy substantives, and
> in all the great stock of native verbs and adjectives.[45]

Many of Edmund Wilson's reviews from the latter half of the 1920s
indicate the ongoing fascination with the vernacular. In his 1927 "Lexicon
of Prohibition" Wilson lists one hundred and five words denoting drunk-
enness, arranged "in order of the degrees of intensity of the conditions
which they represent."[46] In addition to tweaking Prohibition, one of
Mencken's favorite pastimes, Wilson echoed the compilations of idiomatic
expressions found in Mencken's *The American Language,* as well as an
early 1913 essay in which Mencken had listed fifty American synonyms
for "whiskers."[47] In his drama reviews Wilson compared the stodgy and
pretentious language of the theatrical avant-garde with the racy vernacular of popular American stage successes. In 1925 he complained about the
slow and ponderous speech of the actors in the current crop of "serious
plays"—Joyce's *Exiles* at the Neighborhood Playhouse, Wedekind's *Erdgeist*
produced in New York as *The Loves of Lulu,* and *What Price Glory*—contrasting it with the swift pacing of the "musical shows" praised by Gilbert
Seldes.[48] Similarly, while criticizing the literary quality of George Abbott's
and Philip Dunning's 1927 play *Broadway* as "melodrama," Wilson
nonetheless praised the language, "written entirely in New York slang,"
for its flavor and color. In the same review he complained that T. S. Eliot's
play "Wanna Go Home, Baby?" published in the *Criterion,* lacked the linguistic resources exhibited by the authors of *Broadway:* "It is written in a
vernacular—part English and part American—which Mr. Eliot appears to
have acquired in somewhat the same fashion as Sanskrit."[49]

The changes in literary taste and culture of the 1910s and 1920s thus
included an affirmation of naturalism, a rejection of decorum in the selection of literary subject matter, sometimes to the point of courting legal
censorship, and an appreciation of the rough and inventive aspects of
American slang over more polished and formal rhetorical conventions.
This particular rapprochement provided some literary intellectuals with
the opportunity to engage seriously with popular culture and, indeed, to
set many of the terms by which we have appreciated it ever since. Edmund

Wilson's 1924 review of Gilbert Seldes's *The 7 Lively Arts* characterized it as "a genuine contribution to America's new orientation in the arts which was inaugurated by [Van Wyck Brooks's] *America's Coming of Age*, in 1915, and more violently promoted in 1917 by *A Book of Prefaces*."[50] Seldes's well-known essays on the Ziegfeld Follies, on vaudeville performers Fanny Brice and Al Jolson, on jazz, on George Herriman's *Krazy Kat*, and on the films of Charlie Chaplin and Mack Sennett argued for such works and artists as constituting an American vernacular culture, one free from the restrictions of genteel good taste and from pretentiousness and sentimental bunk.

The conjoining of the taste for naturalism with the taste for slapstick is perhaps most appropriately exemplified in the case of Sennett, for in addition to being lauded by Seldes, Sennett was praised and interviewed by Dreiser. In 1924 Seldes, looking back to the films Sennett made in 1914, wrote that he believed that slapstick was in danger, that in the intervening decade "the remorseless hostility of the genteel began to corrupt the purity of slapstick."[51] While he praised Chaplin's work after he left Sennett, and in addition the independent work of Ben Turpin, Al St. John, Mack Swain, and Chester Conklin, he remained suspicious of Harold Lloyd, who he suspected was "a step towards gentility."[52] His approbation of slapstick's vulgarity becomes clear in contrast to his evaluation of the most important polite comedians of the mid-teens:

> Let us . . . look for a moment at the comedy which was always set against the slap-stick to condemn the custard-pie school of fun—the comedy of which the best practitioners were indisputably Mr. and Mrs. Sidney Drew. In them there was nothing offensive, except enervating dullness. They pretended to be pleasant episodes in our common life, the life of courtship and marriage; they accepted all our conventions; and they were one and all exactly the sort of thing which the junior class at high school acted when money was needed to buy a new set of erasers for Miss Struther's course in mechanical drawing. The husband stayed out late at night or was seen kissing a stenographer; the wife had trouble with a maid or was extravagant at the best shops; occasionally arrived an ingenuity, such as the romantic attachment of the wife to the anniversaries contrasted with her husband's negligence—I seem to recall that to cure her he brought her a gift one day in memory of Washington's birthday. These things were little stories, not even smoking room stories; they were acted entirely in the technique of the amateur stage; they were incredibly genteel, in the milieu where "When Baby Came" is genteel; neither in matter nor in manner did they employ what the camera and the projector had to give. And, apart from the agreeable manners of Mr. and Mrs. Sidney Drew, nothing made

them successful except the corrupt desire, on the part of the spectators, to be refined.[53]

In contrast with such polite one-reel films, Seldes held up the unpretentious and, he claimed, more cinematic, 1910s features of Douglas Fairbanks and Charles Ray. But, most important, he opposed the films of the Drews to those of Keystone:

> It is equally bad taste, presumably, to throw custard pies and to commit adultery; but it is not bad taste to speak of these things. What is intolerable only is the pretense, and it was against pretentiousness that the slap-stick comedy had its hardest fight. It showed a man sitting down on a lighted gas stove, and it did not hesitate to disclose the underwear charred at the buttocks which were the logical consequence of the action. There was never the slightest suggestion of sexual indecency, or of moral turpitude, in the Keystones; there was a fuller and freer use of gesture—gesture with all parts of the human frame—than we are accustomed to. The laughter they evoked was broad and long; it was thoracic, abdominal. . . . The animal frankness and health of these pictures constituted the ground of their offense. And something more. For the Keystone offended the sense of security in dull and business-like lives. Few of us imagined ourselves in the frenzy of action which they set before us; none of us remained unmoved at the freedom of fancy, the wildness of imagination, the roaring, destructive, careless energy which it set loose.[54]

This praise of anarchic comedy is now familiar, having been elaborated in numerous subsequent scholarly works on both silent and sound film comedy.[55] But it is important to note both the originality of Seldes's argument with respect to film in 1924 and the way that his argument came out of prior literary debates about the canon. In appreciating Sennett, Seldes defied both the strictures of genteel taste regarding the subject matter fit for representation and the preference for a polite and polished style.

Dreiser's interview with Mack Sennett was published in *Photoplay* in 1928, and since presumably he would not have been paid for an article that was derogatory to the movies one must be wary. Nonetheless the grounds for praise of Sennett seem both typical of Dreiser and of Seldes's earlier defense of slapstick. Dreiser began the interview:

> My admiration for Mack Sennett is temperamental and chronic. I think it dates from that long ago when he played the moony, semi-conscious farm hand, forsaken by the sweetly pretty little milkmaid for some burlesque city slicker, with oiled hair and a bushy mustache. . . . For me he is a real creative force in the cinema world—a master at interpreting the crude primary impulses of the dub, the numbskull, the weakling,

the failure, clown, boor, coward, bully. . . . Positively, if any writer of this age had brought together in literary form—and in readable English—instead of upon the screen as has Sennett—the pie-throwers, soup-spillers, bomb-tossers, hot-stove-stealers, and what not else of Mr. Sennett's grotesqueries—what a reputation! The respect! The acclaim![56]

The interview turned repeatedly to ideas of genre. Sennett's "burlesque," described as "grotesque" by Dreiser and by Sennett himself as "rough," is opposed to the "sentimental" or "melodramatic" tendencies of the drama. Sennett recounted the origins of his own comedies at Biograph in contradistinction to the genres that he claimed were then made at the studio (conveniently forgetting the Mr. and Mrs. Jones comedies directed by Griffith): "They didn't make comedies then, just sentimental romances and very meller melodramas and tragedies—what tragedies! These were awfully funny to me; I couldn't take them seriously. I often thought how easy it would be, with the least bit more exaggeration—and they were exaggerated plenty as it was—to turn those old dramas into pure farce."[57] Sennett also described his own failure to make a convincing melodrama: despite his best efforts, audiences found it funny.

After discussing the famous comedians that were trained at Keystone, the two men speculated on the absence of comediennes, with Sennett citing the exceptions of Mabel Normand, Louise Fazenda, and Polly Moran.

> "I was just thinking of a nice woman we had out there at the studio." He laughed at this point. "Good actress, too. Played crazy parts that we created for her, but did it under protest sometimes because she didn't always like it. . . . Well, we got up a part in which she had to wear a big red wig and a cauliflower ear." And here he went off into another low chuckle that would bring anyone to laughing.
>
> "What a shame!" I said, thinking of the hard-working, self-respecting actress.
>
> "I know," he replied. "It was sort of rough." And he laughed again. "But we couldn't let her off." And into that line I read the very base and cornerstone of that ribald Rabelaisian gusto and gaiety that has kept a substantial part of America laughing with him all of these years. Slapstick vigor—the burlesque counterpart of sentiment—the grotesquely comic mask set over against the tragic.[58]

Like the dirty joke as discussed by Freud, this interchange takes as its object the unnamed actress, identified with good taste and, perhaps, vanity, who is undone by the Rabelaisian vigor of slapstick. While casual and semicomic in tone, the interchange brings together several aspects of advanced early-twentieth-century literary taste: the misogyny (quite remarkable in *Photoplay*, which was essentially a woman's magazine) attendant upon the simultaneous rejection of sentimentality and celebration of the vulgate.

The intellectual appreciation and approbation of slapstick by the likes of Seldes and Dreiser came at a cost. The system of taste that admitted these films excluded others. This is most apparent in the case of *The 7 Lively Arts*, in which Seldes made clear his distaste for most serious and ambitious Hollywood feature filmmaking of the 1910s, which he scornfully typified as "Elinor Glyn–Cecil De Mille–Gilbert Parker" or "le côté Puccini."[59] Even Griffith, after *The Birth of a Nation*, was thought to be overly dignified and genteel.[60] Seldes failed to find value in works justly lauded today: Cecil B. DeMille's dramas and society comedies of the late 1910s, Griffith's *Way Down East* and *Broken Blossoms*, Maurice Tourneur's lovely *Victory*, and Frank Borzage's *Humoresque*.[61] In making judgments like these, Seldes produced and helped to promote a very selective definition of popular culture, one that highlighted artists whose works could be valorized as inventive, masculine, and genuinely vulgar. This view of authentic popular culture is also reinforced, it should be noted, when Sennett, in his interview with Dreiser, dismisses Biograph films other than his own as sentimental romances, exaggerated "meller melodramas" and tragedies.

One can see why Seldes, one of the most perceptive critics of the 1920s, was predisposed to dismiss most film drama of the late 1910s and early 1920s. Many early narrative films emulated nineteenth-century models. *Uncle Tom's Cabin*, for instance, one of Mencken's hated triumvirate of works characteristic of "the sentimental romanticism of the middle Nineteenth Century," has had a long and important history of silent film adaptation beginning as early as 1903.[62] After 1914, once feature filmmaking was the industry norm, the adaptation of well-known plays and novels became the mainstay of an industry seeking higher ticket prices, longer runs, and greater cultural respectability. The films of Griffith, of Tourneur, and of Cecil B. DeMille and William C. deMille, among others, can be seen as more or less self-conscious efforts to emulate the norms of the official culture and to claim an elevated status for the cinema (although it seems to me that Cecil B. DeMille's efforts, in particular, always resulted in such bizarre and sensational works that they can hardly be characterized as "genteel"). I have no doubt that the best dramatic features of the 1910s provided little, if any, ammunition for the advocates of naturalism and the critics of America's congenital optimism and sentimentality. Seldes's judgments had their own logic and necessity.

The problem is that the intellectuals of the 1920s set an agenda that is still with us. While few would now accept the claim boldly made by Seldes in "An Open Letter to the Movie Magnates" that most film drama of the 1910s represented an imposition of bogus, middle-brow taste upon a genuinely popular form, the best present-day scholarship continues to look back to the prefeature cinema, and to the preclassical cinema, when it tries to imagine film's relationship to the rebellions and cultural perturbations that presaged modernism. Noël Burch's important work on early cinema, for example, posits an affinity between primitive and avant-garde film.[63] Tom Gunning and Ben Singer, while engaging a very different account of the nature and origins of modernism than Burch's, still turn to preclassical examples, the cinema of attractions and the early crime serial, respectively, as instances of a genuine vulgate informed by the ethos of modernity and bearing the traces of modernist aesthetics.[64] But I think it is important to begin to question the very idea of the vulgate as rough and shocking, anarchic and masculine. I would insist that the enthusiasm for the sentimental or pathetic—*Uncle Tom's Cabin* if not *La Dame aux Camélias*—was just as profound an aspect of popular taste as that for slapstick or burlesque. The older traditions of stage melodrama and the illustrated story papers give ample evidence of this, and I hope to show that the films of the 1910s and early 1920s were no exception in this regard. If we are to understand how changes in literary taste and in the canon rebounded upon the institution of the cinema, it will not do to accept blinkered definitions of "authentic" popular culture elaborated in the 1920s, definitions that already presuppose a rejection of sentiment as bogus or middle-class. We must get an independent sense of how the canons of popular taste were configured and how they changed over time.

A HISTORY OF POPULAR TASTE

Taste, however capricious, always depends on more than taste. Any aesthetic system, however loosely held together, is inextricably bound up with a whole series of forces, religious, political, nationalist, economic, intellectual, which may appear to bear only the remotest relation to art, but which may need to be violently disrupted before any change in perception becomes possible. Dealers and artists, historians and clergymen, politicians and collectors, may all at one time or another have different motives for wanting to change or to enforce the prevailing aesthetic hierarchy. Enforcement can indeed be just as dominant an urge as change.[65]

There are clear models for writing the history of elite taste in art. Francis Haskell examines changes in the canon of Old Master paintings in England

and France in the period after the French Revolution by considering how what he calls rediscoveries in art were affected by "the availability or otherwise to the collector or connoisseur of recognized masterpieces; the impact of contemporary art; the religious or political loyalties that may condition certain aesthetic standpoints; the effects of public and private collections; the impression made by new techniques of reproduction and language in spreading fresh beliefs about art and artists."[66] Haskell has the advantage of being able to study concrete artifacts that were bought and sold, exhibited or not, under conditions he can specify. The question of how to conduct a study along similar lines in the case of the cinema has not really been posed. Most film scholars have been concerned with either the history of exhibition or the history of reception; the latter has been most successfully approached via the study of specific viewing communities such as Lexington, Kentucky, or Sacramento, California.[67] Work of this kind has some bearing on the history of taste, but it is primarily aimed at reconstructing the reactions of groups of actual spectators. What interests me above all is something more abstract: the systematic assumptions and categories that structured film preferences. According to what logic were films ranked? What was their cultural status? How were they grouped together?

This book uses two basic strategies to explore alterations in the system of taste. The first is the discursive analysis of the industry trade press, augmented to some degree by other journalistic sources. The second is the examination of the historical development of films directly influenced by literary naturalism, as well as four popular narrative types—the sophisticated comedy, the male adventure story, the seduction plot, and the romantic drama. All four types elicited discussion about what was old-fashioned and what was not. They provide a spectrum of comedic and dramatic forms. They also permit a contrast between films that were supposed to appeal to men and films that were supposed to appeal to women. By examining successive iterations of these plots, it is possible to hypothesize a sort of feedback loop between reviewing and film production and to chart alterations in both the critical judgments made by reviewers and the ways filmmakers handled precisely circumscribed sets of narrative conventions.[68]

My use of the trade press requires some comment, since it differs from that of histories of reception, which take it as evidence of how audiences might have actually reacted to films. Here the trade press is considered as *producing* a discourse on films and on audiences, not as a *reflection* of what real spectators did with the movies they watched. Many of the critical judgments found in the trade press were framed in terms of a film's potential profitability and appeal in the market. The nature of this market gives us some insight into the way in which the trade press constructed its idea of the audience. As Richard Maltby has insightfully pointed out, while those involved in film distribution and exhibition did not do audience research in the 1920s, they did know a great deal about theaters.[69] By the early 1920s three major film companies, Paramount, First National and Loew's, were vertically integrated, encompassing film production units, distribution exchanges, and theater chains. Ticket sales for affiliated theaters would have been carefully monitored by distribution personnel. All theaters were classified according to their location and the population they served and were on this basis assigned a "run" and a minimum ticket price, and thereby a place in the distribution hierarchy. Reviewers for the trade press, particularly *Variety*, tried to estimate where a film would fit within this hierarchy: in the major downtown picture palaces, in the subsequent-run theaters in urban neighborhoods (the "nabes" in *Variety* parlance), or in small towns and rural areas. The reviewers also made some estimate about how long a film would play—whether it would last only week or be "held over" on Broadway, whether a film was appropriate for a split week (three or four days) in a neighborhood theater or, even worse, only a single day in what was called a "grind" house.[70] Some films were deemed fit only for the second half of a double bill. There was frequently an estimation of the budget spent on the film and its worth relative to this: *Variety* sometimes praised a cheaply made independent film on the grounds that it was a "good independent" and able to hold an audience despite its low cost. Similarly, the reviewer would make an estimation about whether a high-budget film was worth roadshowing at special prices—what was called a "$2 special." Sometimes studios were chastised for trying to sell an ordinary big budget film as a special; at other times they were praised for refraining from trying to elevate a simple "programmer" to this status.

Variety's judgments about where a film would play, how long it would play, and at what cost were linked to judgments about its potential audience. For example, *Variety* reviews often assume that audiences in neighborhood theaters are working class and less educated than those in downtown theaters. In the case of *Hook and Ladder No. 9*, a drama about firemen, the *Variety* reviewer wrote (December 21, 1927: 25): "This picture will be most appreciated by unsophisticated customers. Best for the neighborhoods and small towns. In the best places it would encounter tough sledding." However, on some occasions the neighborhood theaters were connected with female, as opposed to working-class, viewers, as in this review of *Three Hours* (March 9, 1927: 16):

> Corinne Griffith's last for Asher, Small & Rogers and First National
> hints at being one of those pictures that will roll off the laps of men but
> which women may like. The male population at the Strand Sunday
> afternoon wasn't overly interested, but the symbolized death of a child
> had a few of the girls blowing their noses. . . . Neither great nor bad,
> and on its feminine appeal apparently a better matinee picture than as
> after-dinner entertainment. Which brings about the conclusion its
> sphere is in the neighborhoods, where the Griffith name should mean
> something and where mothers predominate. A woman's picture.[71]

Presumably women were associated with the neighborhood theaters
because these tended to be located in suburban shopping districts where
housewives ran their errands.[72] The biggest picture palaces on Broadway in
New York, or in the Loop in Chicago, were presumably too remote and too
expensive for all but the wealthiest women to use regularly, as a place to
drop in casually after shopping.

The trade press thus provides a subtle, professional estimate of the market for a given film: as urban or rural, male or female, for the "classes"
or the "masses."[73] Trade press reviews do not comprise direct, empirical
evidence about the composition of a film's audience. Nor is a single, isolated review necessarily trustworthy in its forecast about how well an individual film will perform either in the market as a whole or in particular
sectors of the market. Nonetheless, reviews provide a record of an informed
reporter's tastes and preferences. Moreover, read *en bloc* for a given genre
or plot type, they permit us to understand how the industry assessed its
audience and understood the appeal of particular sorts of films. What follows derives from an examination of two industry trade papers, *Variety*
and, as a point of comparison, *Film Daily* (called *Wid's Daily* until 1922). I
also refer to the trade papers *Moving Picture World* and the *Exhibitor's
Trade Herald,* to the fan magazine *Photoplay* and the more refined *Exceptional Photoplays,* and to the *New York Times* and *Life.* I believe that *Variety* is the single best source for understanding how the industry evaluated
its product. *Film Daily, Moving Picture World,* and the *Exhibitor's Trade
Herald* were largely for the exhibitor: they published advice about how to
advertise and exploit the coming films, tried to anticipate audience
response, and occasionally gave warnings about films to be avoided. *Variety* seems to have been directed to the interests of producer-distributors
(although, of course, exhibitors read it). It tended to make more careful
judgments about genre, to write about plot in more detailed terms, and frequently to assess a film's technique. It also usually gave the best general
account of where a film fit in the distribution hierarchy.

For the most part I cite trade papers rather than critics, as most reviews in the trade press—including, for example, those in *Moving Picture World* and *Exhibitor's Trade Herald*—were published anonymously. Presumably many of the reviews in *Wid's Daily* in the late 1910s and early 1920s were by the editor Wid Gunning, but it seems unlikely that he was responsible for all of the films discussed. *Variety* reviewers were identified by three- or four-letter "dog-tags." Only some of those working in the 1920s can be named on the basis of an article by Robert J. Landry published in that paper in 1974.[74] The decision to refer to journals rather than individuals seems appropriate given that the trade press sought impersonal evaluations of film. As Landry noted, "Nobody is hired by *Variety* as a critic. Instead as a reporter. Criticism is on the side, hopefully not too bad, but surely in a wide range of quality."

While *Variety* reviewers, like others working for the trade press, were not encouraged to cultivate distinctive profiles, they collectively invented a highly distinctive house style. According to H. L. Mencken, the lexicographer W. J. Funk, writing in 1933, identified the *Variety* editor Sime Silverman as one of the ten "most fecund makers of American slang." Walter Winchell credited the *Variety* reporter Jack Conway with finding *palooka*, *belly-laugh*, *S.A.* (sex appeal), *high-hat, pushover, baloney* (bunk), and felicitous verbs such as *to scram* and *to click*.[75] In addition to providing what is, in my view, the best account of a film's genre and market among the trade papers of the 1920s, *Variety* is also, indubitably, the most fun to read.

The film industry trade press provides not only evidence of how films were evaluated in relation to the distribution hierarchy of theaters but also of how they had fared or would be likely to fare under the restrictions of political censorship as administered by the states. Discussions about censorship, or films likely to cause outcry in rural communities, provide important additional clues for the historian of taste. To an even greater degree than novelists or dramatists, film producers could not ignore the strictures of the moral guardians of decency. With the backing of a producer or publisher willing to fight, authors such as Shaw, Dreiser, and Joyce were able to challenge the dictates of the Society for the Suppression of Vice. When their work was subject to regulation, there was a public debate about its censorship; by 1933 even *Ulysses* was granted constitutional protection by the courts. However, the Mutual decision of 1915 excluded film from the category of "speech" as defined by the First Amendment. State censor boards operated in Florida, New York, Massachusetts, Kansas, Ohio, Pennsylvania, Virginia and Maryland, and in the city of Chicago a board was run by the police. The sphere of influence of these boards actually extended beyond their geographical boundaries, since distribution was run through exchanges that served more than one city or state: thus prints altered for one state board would have been distributed to the entirety of the area served by the exchange.[76]

To avoid having state censors cut their films, producers had to make concessions to what Randolph Bourne called middle-class tact and correctness. In my view, the problem censorship posed for the industry was not simply one of enforcing a particular moral agenda but also, and more importantly, of negotiating very different sets of assumptions about the subject matter deemed fit for inclusion in a film and the manner in which it could be represented: it was an issue of decorum as much as of morality. The difficulty was exacerbated by the wide range of Hollywood's audience. Films would play in rural districts or conservative sections of large towns that would never have been exposed to the latest *succès de scandale* on Broadway. Writing in 1926 about the film *The Far Cry,* an exhibitor in Melville, Louisiana, complained to the *Moving Picture World:* "Here it was a case of 'another lemon from the First National orchard.' These pictures may have gone over big in the large cities, but the average country patron does not enjoy eight reels of a cigarette smoking heroine, who makes unchaperoned visits to the hero's studio."[77] The industry was clearly aware of the disparities in taste with which it had to deal. The Formula, one of the first self-regulatory policies adopted by the film industry in 1924, states: "The members of the Motion Picture Producers and Distributors of America, Inc., in their continuing effort 'to establish and maintain the highest possible moral and artistic standards of motion picture production' are engaged in a special effort to prevent the prevalent type of book and play from becoming the prevalent type of picture."[78] But it was not simply a matter of ignoring current literary and dramatic productions: Broadway was a more important market than Melville, Louisiana, and it was in major metropolitan centers that the vertically integrated producer-distributors owned their theaters. Film producers thus had to steer a course between the minority whose tastes might be epitomized by the hip and irreverent *Smart Set* and the vast majority who remained loyal to Norman Rockwell and the *Saturday Evening Post.* The trade press estimates of the kinds of films that were likely to be censored or provoke offense provide an extensive record of the attempt to negotiate this passage and show the distinctions made between what was held to be old-fashioned or sentimental and what was deemed more up to date or too far outside of mainstream tastes.

The trade press also allows us to broach the complicated question of the relationship between gender and taste. Any analysis of the reconfiguration of taste in the 1920s must deal with this issue, since women were held to epitomize gentility in the literary discourses of the 1910s and 1920s and are still assumed to have a preference for sentimental, sad, and stirring tales. In *Variety*, assumptions about gender often took the form of a comparison between a particular film and the works of one of a number of lady authors, most commonly E. D. E. N. Southworth or Laura Jean Libbey. Sometimes a film's plot was said to have originated in *True Confessions* magazine or to be of that ilk. Nonetheless, it is important to note that *Variety* assumed a predilection for sentiment among diverse sectors of the audience. Films criticized by *Variety* for being soppy were said to appeal sometimes to women, sometimes to lower-class viewers, and sometimes to small-town audiences. For example, a *Variety* review of a low-budget independent release, *Tessie* (September 23, 1925: 39), complained about the preponderance of lachrymose tales in the nabes: "The important thing about *Tessie* is that it is the first of many features lined up by Arrow for the new season and that it is mercifully free from the pathos and bunk which have permeated so many features from the independent market. This one is a breezy and ingratiating little comedy able to hold up the feature end of a program in the intermediate and neighborhood houses."[79] There was also sometimes a confusion between the presumed sentimentality of female viewers and working-class ones. Noting that *Hearts of Youth* was adapted from a novel by E. D. E. N. Southworth, the *Variety* reviewer posited a sentimental feminine appeal for the original novel (May 20, 1921: 41): "If you ask your 'living ancestors' of the feminine sex about it they will tell you how they wept over the tribulations of Ishmael Worth" and a working-class audience for the film: "It is rather well done in approved 10–20–30 fashion and should appeal to the proletariat."

Moreover, contrary to our present-day conceptions, the trade press in the 1920s was far from assuming a universal feminine taste for lachrymose tales. The industry lore on this question is far better summed up in a *Variety* article of 1931 headlined "Dirt Craze Due to Women" (June 16, 1931: 1 and 24): "Women love dirt. Nothing shocks 'em. They want to know about bad women. The badder the better. . . . Women who make up the bulk of the picture audiences are also the majority readers of the tabloids, scandal sheets, flashy magazines and erotic books. It is to cater to them all the hot stuff of the present day is turned out. . . . Women are far more interested in anything with sex interest to it than are men." The reporter's statistics are dubious: there is no solid evidence that women made up either the bulk of motion picture audiences or the bulk of the readers of "flashy magazines and erotic books."[80] But, as I will argue in chapter 6, patterns of filmmaking and reviewing in the 1920s help us to understand how this could have been a plausible depiction of feminine viewing preferences for someone in the industry who had been keeping up with the latest trends in filmmaking and carefully reading the trade press.

Examples such as these lead me to investigate the process by which certain plots, whether dubbed "sentimental" or "sophisticated," came to be associated with women. In addition I shall consider the problem of gender in differential terms, contrasting what was considered "masculine" with what was considered "feminine" taste in film within the trade press discourse and the genre conventions of the 1920s. Rather than assuming that women have always liked weepies, I pose the question of how films were sorted by gender and by whom, and at what point this occurred in the history of the decline of sentiment.

2   Hollywood Naturalism

The basic backbone of all stage or screen performance is action, be
it dramatic, comedy, hokum, but it must be action. Thus "Wild
Geese" is a little more exciting than one of Mencken's "Prejudices"
scenarized. . . . Tiffany-Stahl's ambassadorial entry into the Roxy
is by no means a handicapping try. Very likely "Wild Geese" will
do business here for the Roxy is just the type house a picture of
this nature will please. The sophisticated downtown film fan that
contributes to the Roxy's staggering grosses will rather fancy the
deft treatment of each character. . . . "Wild Geese" is conversely
questionable for mass appeal in relation to its artistry. Somewhat
subtle and generally sluggish, the mob of hinterland fans might
not cotton to it as much as it deserves.

Review of *Wild Geese, Variety*, December 7, 1927

Although this book is primarily concerned with popular film genres, it
seems necessary to take account of the fact that, along with its impact on
the American literary establishment, naturalism had an effect on the mar-
gins of Hollywood filmmaking. Given its pessimism, its depiction of protagonists overwhelmed and acted upon by their environment, and its
open-ended and dilatory plots, literary naturalism would seem to be the
antithesis of the classical Hollywood narrative based on a goal-oriented
protagonist, a rising curve of action, and a well-calculated articulation of
suspense. That at least some directors sought to reconcile such seemingly
antithetical modes of storytelling is a testament both to the growing prestige of naturalism in the 1920s and to the relevance of the literary debates
it inspired for the institution of the cinema.

It should be noted that aestheticism, like naturalism usually considered
an important precursor to modernism, also influenced some Hollywood
films of this period. Kristin Thompson discusses two 1918 adaptations of
Symbolist works by Maurice Tourneur, *The Blue Bird*, from Maeterlinck's
allegorical fantasy (figures 1 and 2), and *Prunella*, from a play by Granville
Barker. She also makes reference to Alla Nazimova's *Salome*, 1923, with
sets by Natacha Rambova, based on Aubrey Beardsley's drawings for the
original edition of Oscar Wilde's play.[1] *Salome* was not only visually stylized, but assimilated the sexual decadence frequently associated with aestheticism. Echoes of both exotic visual motifs and sexual decadence also

1   2

3   4

occur in more mainstream Hollywood fare, often to represent villainy, or motivated historically, as when a film represents a period as decadent. An example of the first may be found in the decors associated with Satan Synne in DeMille's *Affairs of Anatol* (1921); the second can be seen in the Babylon story in Griffith's *Intolerance* (1916). By the early 1920s what I would consider a less overt form of aestheticist mise en scene had also begun to develop. Fantastical set design, like that found in *The Blue Bird* and *Salome,* gave way to decorative effects achieved less obtrusively, with lighting, soft focus, and composition. See, for example, the highly stylized use of landscape in Tourneur's luminous *The Last of the Mohicans* (1920) (figures 3 and 4), as well as in many of his other films. The films produced after 1924 by Rex Ingram's unit in Nice are similarly characterized by deliberate artifice and self-conscious pictorialism, apparent in the use of landscapes and, for scenes shot in the studio, diffused lighting and atmospheric effects.

Aestheticism did influence directors, such as Josef von Sternberg, who were associated with naturalist-inspired filmmaking in the 1920s. Within the framework of the cinema, at least, aestheticism and naturalism should not be considered as opposed, or even completely distinct, tendencies. Nonetheless, I think it would be fair to argue that aestheticism's impact in Hollywood was largely exercised at the level of visual design, whereas naturalism's was more acutely felt, and rendered problematic, at the level of plot. My concern here is with the latter's effect on narrative conventions and particularly with the way in which naturalism eventually provided a framework for filmmakers who sought to depart from sentimental narrative prototypes.

The prime example is, of course, Erich von Stroheim's *Greed,* adapted from Frank Norris's *McTeague* and premiered in December 1924. Although *Greed* was a commercial failure, it was followed by a number of films in the same vein, some highly budgeted and publicized, that still retain a prominent place in the silent film canon—among them *The Crowd, The Docks of New York,* and *The Wind.* However, naturalism was well established as a literary movement before the commencement of narrative filmmaking, and its effects can be seen as early as the 1910s. In this chapter I will consider protonaturalist filmmaking before *Greed* in some detail. I find these films important for two reasons. First, they helped to establish the taste for simple stories about ordinary people, a preference that will be at issue for almost all of the films and film genres discussed in this study. Second, the radical nature of von Stroheim's experiment, its especially virulent antisentimental tendencies, becomes readily apparent against the backdrop of these prior works.

The variety programs of one- and two-reel films, which predominated in the nickelodeons between 1908 and 1913, were composed of films in a range of genres: comedies, dramas, scenics, Westerns. As scholars of early cinema have shown, the variety format allowed for some experimentation with narrative form, because a film with a sad, or even a rather inconclusive ending, could immediately be followed by another with more traditional closure. A relatively open-ended film such as Griffith's *The Country Doctor* seems reminiscent of a short story by O. Henry or Guy de Maupassant. A family is introduced in an idyllic country setting. The little girl becomes ill, apparently with diphtheria, but her father, the doctor, is called away to attend to the child of a poor neighbor, stricken with the same disease. The film cuts between the two families as the doctor moves back and forth between them. Finally the doctor successfully operates on the daughter of the poor family, only to return home and find his own daughter dead. Tom Gunning has noted, "As happens more often in Biograph films than clichéd views of Griffith would indicate, the rush to the rescue fails, and we are confronted with the grim image of a child's death and a family's despair. Parallel editing does not always announce a victory over time. Family order does not always defeat the forces that threaten it."[2] For Gunning, two "empty" shots, pans over the landscape that open and close the film, assimilate it to naturalism: "This landscape, unchanged after the child's death and reflecting none of the family's loss, operates in naturalistic counterpoint to the grief behind the closed door." In my view, it is also the lack of a providential outcome that places this film within the compass of naturalism, evoking that "sense of profound and inexplicable disorder" that Mencken found so characteristic of Dreiser's work. Of course, there are many films by Griffith and others in this same period in which the unjust are punished and the virtuous rewarded; indeed, as Gunning argues, the development of a panoply of techniques for establishing moral judgments on characters and actions is one of Griffith's great accomplishments in the early years at Biograph. Yet the very structure of the one-reel film, and of the variety program in which one-reel films were exhibited, allowed for less moralized and more open narrative forms. Prominent Biograph examples in addition to *The Country Doctor* include *The Broken Doll, Just Gold,* and even to some extent *A Corner in Wheat,* in which the greedy and unscrupulous wheat king is deservedly killed, suffocated by his own wheat, but the people who have been most harmed by his manipulations of the stock market do not know this, and their life goes on as before.

In the early feature period many films were drawn from naturalist or naturalist-inspired sources. Steven Ross has written of the 1914 adaptation of Upton Sinclair's *The Jungle,* about a strike in a meatpacking plant.[3] In 1916, well before *Greed,* Norris's *McTeague* was adapted as *Life's Whirlpool,* directed by Barry O'Neill and distributed by World.[4] DeMille's 1915 *Kindling,* taken from a play by Charles Kenyon, dealt with life in the slums of Hell's Kitchen and used sets and cinematography modeled on Jacob Riis's photographs of the poor.[5] Raoul Walsh's *Regeneration,* also released in 1915, was based upon a play derived from a memoir by Owen Kildare, which recounted his experiences as a youth in an urban gang in the Bowery. Although these and similar films occupied the terrain of the naturalist novel, most followed the narrative formula of the social problem film, identifying problems that were more or less successfully resolved by the film's end.[6] Even if the characters faced an unhappy outcome, the plots provided moral and narrative closure, and in this respect were quite different from a film like *The Country Doctor.* For example, although Jurgis Rudkus, one of the striking workers in *The Jungle,* is sent to jail and loses his wife and child, the film ends hopefully with his discovery of socialism. *Regen-*

eration is not so explicitly radical a film, but it follows the same pattern: reformed by his love for a settlement worker, the gang leader Owen resolves not to take revenge when she is accidentally shot during a gun fight between gang members and the police. *Life's Whirlpool* seems to have been an exception in this regard; although one cannot be sure, since no print has so far been recovered, the summary in *Moving Picture World* (January 1, 1916: 146) suggests that the film remained faithful to the pessimistic tone and ending of the original novel.

Classical Hollywood narrative patterns and genre norms were well established by the time filmmakers began to experiment with naturalism in the 1920s. Thus directors and screenwriters actually faced more resistance than Griffith and others had in the one-reel period. The *Variety* review of *Young Nowheres* (October 9, 1929: 38), an obscure film starring Richard Barthelmess, indicates some of the areas of difficulty. The film was thought to be artistically ambitious but unlikely to do well at the box office: "It requires a certain courage, coupled with confidence, to attempt such a fragile and homely story. It is remarkable, too, that a star deliberately chooses to impersonate anyone so deficient in glamor as an elevator boy and so submerges the personality of the actor that the audience sees only the eventlessness of an existence that is a dull ache and a haircomb only a lift engineer would wear." The humdrum characters and setting are said to pose difficulties for the actor, in that Richard Barthelmess does not have a typical "star" part, but also for the plot. *Variety* formulated the problem as one of sustaining interest for the length of a feature film: "Running but 65 minutes, 'Young Nowheres' is the cinema equivalent to a short story as distinguished from a full-length many-episoded novel. It deals with a situation rather than a plot and bases appeal entirely on humanity."[7] The kinds of debates that naturalism inspired in the literary arena—debates about moral comprehensibility and optimism, the subject matter fit for representation, decorum and formal polish—did not become relevant for Hollywood filmmakers until the release of *Greed* and von Sternberg's *The Salvation Hunters*. Instead, during the first half of the 1920s, the critical response to naturalist-inspired filmmaking dealt largely with the problem of making compelling narratives about ordinary people in everyday settings, and films were blamed or praised for the slightness of their plots.

Most of the films made prior to 1925 that essayed reduced or dilatory plots took place in the country and adopted a nostalgic view of rural America. In this sense they were quite sentimental. Griffith's *A Romance of Happy Valley*, released in January 1919, provides a clear example. It was considered a "small" feature compared to the director's films immediately preceding it, the spectacular *Hearts of the World,* which was a road-show release in 1918, and *The Great Love* and *The Greatest Thing in Life* of the same year, made on smaller budgets but nonetheless, like *Hearts of the World,* dealing with the weighty theme of World War I. *Wid's Daily* (February 2, 1919: 23) discussed *A Romance of Happy Valley* as a return to an earlier form of filmmaking: "The war is over. Griffith has demobilized his soldiers, converted his trenches into corn fields and stacked his guns in an armory. He is back again among simple, peaceful folk, whose problems and struggles are in their own hearts. He is doing more superbly than ever, what he has done so surpassingly well in the past." For Wid Gunning the film was one of the pastoral Biograph one-reelers writ large. *Exhibitor's Trade Review* (February 1, 1919: 715) expressed a similar opinion:

> This time the genius of D. W. Griffith has been turned to the country, the farm section of Ohio [actually Kentucky], and about the people of a little village he has woven a romance that for sheer interest, homely pathos and a deep understanding of human nature has never been approached on the screen before. There are no "big" scenes in this picture, no thrills, no massive sets or anything of that nature. It's just about as different from Mr. Griffith's late pictures as darkness is from day, but it is one of the most human documents ever filmed.

Despite the claims of *Exhibitor's Trade Review* that the plot abjures "thrills," *A Romance of Happy Valley* actually combines a bucolic, semi-comic romance with a murder mystery that comes to the fore at the film's end. Part of the interest of this example lies in the fact that almost all of the critics preferred the romance, which they regarded as realistic, to what they perceived as the "melodrama" of the ending.

John L. Logan, Jr. (Robert Harron), lives in rural Kentucky, assisting his parents in the running of the local inn, the Happy Valley Cottage. Despite the opposition of his parents and his sweetheart, Jennie (Lillian Gish), he resolves to go and make his fortune in New York. His resolve is shaken briefly by his rebirth into the Sanctificationist Church, but, after a bitter argument with his father, he does leave, promising Jennie to return in a year's time. Once in the big city, John takes a job in a toy factory and spends his spare time trying to design a toy frog that will swim. Years pass, the frog fails to swim, and he does not return, but Jennie remains true. The inn falls on bad times, and, just as the frog does at last swim, John's father is forced to go to the nearby town to try—unsuccessfully—to borrow money from an old friend. While there he notices a rich stranger, whom he follows back to his own inn. Meanwhile, a gang is surprised attempting to rob the bank in the town; one of the robbers is shot and wounded, and the sheriff's posse pursue him to Happy Valley. John's father, finding himself alone in the Happy Valley Cottage with the rich stranger, resolves to rob him. Feeling for the sleeping stranger's wallet in the darkened bedroom, he accidentally wakes him, and, after a brief struggle, finds that the man is dead. He takes the body down the back stairs and dumps it in a field.

John's mother has a sudden intuition that her long-lost son has returned. Discovering a token in the guest's room that confirms this, she joyfully announces the return of their son to John's father, who is stricken to think he has killed his own son. John himself suddenly enters from the back stairs, unharmed. He says he had heard shooting outside and gone out to investigate but could find nothing. The posse arrives, and as the sheriff begins to interrogate John and his father, the bank robber is found dead in the field. John's father realizes that the wounded robber must have sought refuge in the Cottage and died from his wounds when aroused by the attempt to find the wallet. John proposes to Jennie, who accepts him. At the Sanctificationist Church service, John's father admits the error of his ways.

As Ben Brewster has argued,[8] the resolution of the story depends on a double enigma. The first enigma concerns the identity of the rich stranger; the film is staged to obscure the hero's face until he arrives back in his old bedroom, although of course many spectators would have guessed his identity before this moment. The second and more obscure enigma concerns the substitution of the bank robber for John Logan, a mystery that is established by blocking the face of the criminal as he struggles with John's father and by withholding John's action of leaving his room and the thief's subsequently entering it (this information is provided in flashbacks when the solution to the mystery is explained).

Most reviewers commented on the way the ending shifted the tone of the piece. *Variety* (January 31, 1919: 52) described the film as "a simple story of bucolic life" that "progresses sweetly until the last reel, when it takes a morbid, tragic twist, the curse of which is taken off by a surprise climax." *Moving Picture World* (February 8, 1919: 804) was more critical of the ending: "The first half of the story is a study in character that delights by its quaintness and truth. Then comes a change in the mood of the picture that is as unexpected as a snow storm in June. And to many spectators it will be as unwelcome. From a well balanced and consistent tale it suddenly turns into a highly colored melodrama with a convenient bank robbery, the mortgage-on-the-farm motive and an attempt on the part of the elder Logan to murder and rob a stranger who turns out to be his own son." *Wid's* argued that "the struggles of the would-be inventor are handled in a way that works up quite a bit of suspense and when the frog actually swims, a real climax in the picture has been reached, in fact a more natural climax than that prepared for the melodramatic ending."

A number of films that followed the release of *A Romance of Happy Valley* were discussed, and sometimes advertised, as simple stories of country life. Griffith's *True Heart Susie* was compared to the earlier film in *Wid's* (June 8, 1919: 25) and *Motion Picture Classic* (August 1919: 60). In *True Heart Susie* Griffith eliminated the "melodramatic" elements and focalized the film around the heroine; he did so perhaps partly in response to the trade press's praise for the bits of comic business Lillian Gish had performed as Jennie in *A Romance of Happy Valley.*[9] Susie is a plain girl in love with William. William's father cannot afford to send him to college. When a rich man's promises of help prove to be empty, Susie sells some of her farm animals to raise the necessary capital. She sends a letter to William, ostensibly from the rich man, promising to pay his tuition. After four years of college William returns to take up a position as minister in the local church. Although he tells Susie that men do not actually marry girls who use paint and powder, he is ensnared by Bettina, a milliner from a nearby town and one of the "paint and powder brigade." William is rapidly disillusioned with his wife's slovenly ways and bad cooking, and she is bored and lonely. One night she sneaks out to join some former associates at a party. On the way home she is caught in the rain and finds she has lost her house key. She appeals to Susie to give her shelter for the night and to lie to William about the reason for her absence from home. After some resistance, the kind-hearted Susie backs Bettina up. But exposure to the rain leads to Bettina's falling ill and dying, and after William learns of Susie's sacrifices for him, and of Bettina's activities on the night that led to her death, he proposes to Susie.

Variety (June 6, 1919: 49) called *True Heart Susie* a "comedy-drama," and considered it likely to appeal to women because clothes and make-up figure as vital strategic elements in the plot. Most of the other reviews stressed the twin ideas of realism and simplicity. In response to the film's first intertitle, "Is real life interesting? Every incident of this story is taken from real life," the *New York Times* critic responded (June 2, 1919: 20): "He might have said that the photoplay holds a mirror up to life, for in it is reflected what has happened, not once, but thousands and thousands of times, is still happening and will happen always." After a summary of the plot, deemed "simple," the review continued, "These human beings, with their virtues and shortcomings, making their mistakes and going wrong blindly, are the essence of 'True Heart Susie,' and the environment in which they move, the rural scenes and characters of the background, have been represented with such care and faithfulness that the photoplay as a whole is a unit, harmonious throughout." Both *Moving Picture World* and *Motion Picture News* recommended exploitation schemes keyed to the ideas of realism and country life. *Moving Picture World* (June 14, 1919: 1679) proposed the advertising catch phrase "Another D. W. Griffith Masterpiece in Which He Tells a Simple Story of Everyday Life in a Highly Artistic and Satisfying Manner"; and *Motion Picture News* (June 7, 1919: 3813) suggested, "Now this is a simple little story with every scene laid in a country town and the nearest villain that we have is a sort of amateur near-vampire and the only violence a rather comic fight between the hero and another of the boys at college. Simplicity is the point to stress the greatest at the same time telling your patrons that it is the art of Griffith that makes this so delightful."

But praise for *True Heart Susie* was by no means universal. A later issue of *Motion Picture News* (June 14, 1919: 4029), while continuing to advise exhibitors to sell the film as a "plain story of plain folks," contained this complaint from Peter Milne: "It is a see-sawing Griffith that we meet these days. Right after we have seen in 'Broken Blossoms' what is probably the highest form of the motion picture art, we find him stretching a two-reel story out to feature length in his latest Artcraft, 'True Heart Susie.'" *Wid's* (June 8, 1919: 25) had voiced the same complaint:

> The trouble here is that there is not enough plot substance to balance properly a production of this length. At times the picture drags, not through any deficiencies on the part of the players, or any shortcomings in the direction, rather owing to a lack of variety in the action. The thinness of the plot makes necessary the too frequent repetition of scenes that in their meaning and expression of emotion are virtually the same. In more abbreviated form, "True Heart Susie" might easily have become a masterpiece of screen character fiction. At present, it suggests an ideal short story expanded to novel length.

No doubt *True Heart Susie,* released in June 1919, and one of six program features made for Paramount-Artcraft, suffered in comparison with *Broken Blossoms:* the latter, released only one month earlier, was Griffith's first film for United Artists, made at a much higher budget, and given road-show distribution and an elaborate publicity campaign.[10] Still, one cannot help being struck by the disparity between the reception of *A Romance of Happy Valley,* criticized for an overly contrived ending that departed from the pastoral tone of the romance, and the reception of *True Heart Susie,* rendered more consistent in tone and criticized for being monotonous and thinly plotted.

Joseph de Grasse's *The Old Swimmin' Hole*, which featured actor Charles Ray, exemplifies a film with an extremely reduced plot that managed to finesse the ambivalence with which the trade press typically viewed "plain stories of plain folks." Ray, who had been very successful in a series of 1910s program features produced by Thomas Ince, usually played juvenile parts, in many ways the male equivalent of Pickford's girl-woman roles, except that Ray was more consistently associated with rural types than was Pickford.[11] In its review of *The Old Swimmin' Hole*, *Wid's* (February 20, 1921: 2) noted that Ray was "best known and liked for his 'Rube' country boy portrayals." Indeed, the Charles Ray films made prior to *The Old Swimmin' Hole* may well have provided a model for Griffith's features about country life. *The Hired Man*, released in 1918 and made before *True Heart Susie*, dealt with a similar situation: Ezry Hollins, a hired hand on a New England farm, longs to go to college and is in love with the farmer's daughter. *The Busher* (1919) plays up the opposition between small-town and big-city life. Ray plays a minor-league pitcher who makes the majors, the St. Paul Pink Sox, becomes a snob, and deserts his small-town girl for a city woman. When he loses his skill he is sent back home, where he wins a game for the home team and gets back his sweetheart.

In 1920 Ray formed his own production company, distributing through First National. *The Old Swimmin' Hole* (1921) was perhaps the most ambitious of the First National films and is certainly the best known. The film was made without intertitles and was widely regarded as experimental at the time of its release. Summary is difficult since the main line of action is slight, with a wealth of anecdote only peripherally related to it. The film follows Ezra Hull (Ray), a schoolboy, in the days leading up to the Settler's Day Picnic. Ezra is enamored of Myrtle, who seems to favor Skinny (played by the rotund Lincoln Stedman). Esther, ignored by Ezra, desires his attentions. At the picnic Ezra fights with Skinny, is spurned by Myrtle, and consoled by Esther. This action is paralleled by the shoe motif. Barefoot for much of the film, Ezra early on pleads with his mother for a pair of shoes and then "borrows" his father's on the day of the picnic. However, they prove to be as much of a disappointment as is his encounter with Myrtle, for they make it impossible to run or climb fences. When Esther unpacks a lunch for Ezra at the film's close, he contentedly removes shoes and socks and puts his feet in the river.

Much of the plot is taken up with incidental boyish pranks played by Ezra and his friends. The sequence that gives the film its title has nothing to do with the burgeoning romances described above. When Ezra gets home at the end of the school day, his mother gives him money to go to the store for her and tells him to take the baby. He is pulling the baby's wagon when he meets Skinny, who carries a note addressed to Mrs. Hull from their teacher, explaining that Ezra has been temporarily expelled from school for bad behavior. The boys "fight"—they step on one another's feet, strike postures, and, after Ezra draws a line in the dirt, flail their fists at a safe distance from one another. Ezra trades his sling shot for the teacher's note. Skinny forges Mrs. Hull's response: "Ezra says he will be a good boy from now on."

While the other boys play at the swimming hole, Ezra takes the baby to the store. He gives the storekeeper the order, then goes to watch the shoe-maker next door, leaning up against the glass and peering longingly inside. He gets a package of goods, including a bag of flour, from the storekeeper. As he leaves, he notices some watermelons and manages to purloin one.

He takes the baby's wagon over a rough plank bridge to the swimming hole and falls over a log, splitting the melon. He shares the melon with the other boys. Meanwhile his mother goes looking for him with a switch, her actions intercut with those of the boys. Ezra enters the water and the boys get into a mud-slinging fight. One boy takes the package out of the baby's wagon and starts throwing the flour. The baby is dirtied by both mud and flour. His mother approaches. Ezra hides under water while the boys assure her that her son is not with them. After she leaves they convince Ezra that he needs to go on hiding, and while he is under water they steal his clothes. He wraps himself in the baby's blanket and takes the wagon back over the plank bridge.

Several other sequences resemble this one in their tenuous relationship to the main line of the plot. The opening, for example, establishes Ezra's intention to invite Myrtle to the picnic (he writes this information in his diary), but on the way to her house he is distracted by the boys, who convince him to steal some apples from a farmer's orchard. His misadventures with the stolen apples and pursuit by the irate farmer dominate the film's beginning, even though these actions have no consequence for what follows. The film is unified, then, not so much by a strong causal development as by restricting story time to the days leading up to the picnic and by focalizing on Ezra.

The press uniformly praised the film and connected the absence of intertitles to the simplicity of the plot. *Wid's* (February 20, 1920: 2) advised exhibitors, "Maybe you won't believe it but there are no sub-titles in it. The pictures tell the story and you understand it perfectly. There isn't any plot or 'intrikut' business. It's just a series of incidents in the life of a country boy but they're important enough to keep you interested all the time."

Burns Mantle in *Photoplay* noted, "Of course it is not a story that demands titles." In an interesting inversion of the frequent correlation between simple plots and the form of the short films of the 1910s, he noted that the film "could go on and on for sixteen as easily as for six reels."[12] The point is telling: the film works by the accumulation of incidents, a structure that allows for expansion just as readily as contraction (although obviously boredom becomes a problem in the expanded forms). *Variety* (February 25, 1921: 42) thought *The Old Swimmin' Hole* was well made, if inexpensive, but noted that the lack of plot made it easy to produce a film without intertitles: "In some respects it is hardly a fair test, inasmuch as there is little or no story to the picture, merely a series of incidents in the life of a bucolic youth." The *New York Times* (February 28, 1921: 2) defended the experiment: "It may be pointed out that a story more complex in plot and characterization would not lend itself to wordless treatment as 'The Old Swimmin' Hole' does. And this is all true. . . . But there's more to the matter than this. The photoplay remains significant and promising. For, in the first place, no matter how easily its story may be told without words, 999 directors out of every 1,000 would have done the usual thing and used words."

Although it was not stated in the press at the time, it seems to me that one of the most radical aspects of Ray and De Grasse's experiment is their willingness to allow a story of everyday people and events to proceed without the narrational intervention of subtitles. In contrast, both of Griffith's experiments in this vein depend heavily upon intertitles. The opening title of *A Romance of Happy Valley* distances the spectator from the rural world depicted, which is given a fairy tale aspect:

> What better place for a romance
> Than Old Kentucky—
> In the County of MAKE-BELIEVE
> On the Pike THAT NEVER-WAS?

A second title introduces two incidental characters symbolizing pessimism and optimism, respectively. It also prepares one for the church scene and the small-town atmosphere that John finds so hostile to his aspirations: "A bit of dream life, atmosphered by a religion, still clinging to the doctrine of complete sanctification; where Vinegar Watkins and Old Lady Smiles wage an unseen battle." The film often resorts to irony in the intertitles dealing with the heroine. A good example occurs in an early scene where Jennie plans to make a new dress: "Jennie struggling between duty to her father, who wants her clothes patterned after Mother's, and the terrible fear that unless she follows a more up-to-date model, Kentucky will lose John."

During the scene in the church, Jennie prays, "Save him from the Devil—and New York." Such titles juxtapose our own understanding of events with what are supposedly old-fashioned, rural values.

True Heart Susie goes even further than *A Romance of Happy Valley* in using titles to set up an ironic distance between the spectator and the world of the characters.[13] For example, the sequence in which Susie decides to fund William's college education begins with a narrative title: "Susie confides her sorrows to sister Daisy." This is followed by a shot of the heroine seated in a field beside a cow. Susie explains, "—and I want him to go to school—I MUST marry a smart man." She hugs the cow and cries over it. After Susie tells her aunt that she will sell the cow and other things to send William to college, there is a shot of a turkey in the farmyard. A narrative title follows: "The various stepping stones upon which William is to rise to fame." We see more ducks and hens in the farmyard. There is no doubt that the spectator is meant to admire the sacrifice that Susie makes for William's sake, but humor comes from the fact that we do not share her sentimental attachment to the cow and from the mock-heroic description of the impending fate of the turkeys, ducks, and hens.

By eschewing intertitles, *The Old Swimmin' Hole* provides more direct access to the diegetic world. The foibles and eccentricities of rural types are not self-consciously presented to the spectator as they are in the Griffith examples. The narration does not intervene to point out the significance of ordinary events or to mark the distance between the rural world and our own. It would be easy, for example, to miss the significance of the shoe motif, as its importance is not built up either through narrative or dialogue titles. The relative opacity of the narration in *The Old Swimmin' Hole* moves it closer to a naturalistic mode of storytelling than is the case in previously discussed examples of bucolic romance.

Yet all of the examples discussed thus far may be considered sentimental in that they partake of a nostalgia for a rural past. Most are also highly moralized, with the possible exception of *The Old Swimmin' Hole,* which glories in the naughtiness of the boys, and in which the children's cruelty to each other is not punished. A few films made in the period prior to the release of *Greed* are more critical or pessimistic. Most were adaptations of contemporary literary works, and in such cases it is important to consider the source material in some detail, as that perhaps best indicates the changes in taste under consideration here.

William deMille's 1922 version of Zona Gale's *Miss Lulu Bett* provides a good contrast to the nostalgic stories of rural life already discussed. Most of the press coverage at the time of the film's release was concerned with deMille's adaptation of the play, which Zona Gale had derived from her original novel and which was well known in literary circles, having garnered the Pulitzer Prize for drama in 1921.[14] Despite the differences imposed by the lack of spoken dialogue, the *New York Times* (sec. 6, December 25, 1921: 2) and *Wid's* (December 25, 1921: 49) praised the film's rendering of the main characters. As with previous stories of rural life, the plot was considered slight. *Variety* (December 23, 1921: 35) called it a "first-rate, non-sensational, program feature" and "a well-wrought, closely-knit, straightaway, cumulative domestic drama of rural life." *Wid's* found it "a quite delightful entertainment that consists mostly of characterization, though there is a consistent plot that is developed smoothly and interestingly to an effective climax." In *Representative Photoplays Analyzed,* Scott O'Dell warned, "A brief analysis of *Miss Lulu Bett* might make it appear that it was a story of very simple development. It was really a story exceedingly hard to write, for the reason that almost the entire burden of interest was thrown upon Lulu's characterization and such contrasting bits of characterization of other members of the cast as would always keep Lulu the figure of dominant interest."[15] It was clearly considered a simple story in which characterization played a more important role than plot. Yet just as clearly, in my view, the source material and consequent film adaptation pushed it in a rather different direction than films such as *A Romance of Happy Valley* and *The Old Swimmin' Hole.*

Upon its publication in 1920, the novel *Miss Lulu Bett* was hailed by critics as a welcome departure from what they considered Gale's overly sentimental Friendship Village stories. These popular stories, originally published as magazine fiction, were very much in the vein of Griffith's *A Romance of Happy Valley* and may indeed have been an influence upon it. *Friendship Village*, Gale's first collection of stories about an imaginary Wisconsin town, appeared in 1908. Four more published collections followed, the last appearing in 1919, as did the one-act play *The Neighbors,* produced by the Wisconsin Players in 1920. Writing in the *New Republic* in 1920, Constance Rourke praised *Miss Lulu Bett* in relation to these previous works:

> The typical Friendship Village story is also a typical American story. Calliope Marsh, who is made to do most of the telling, is an own sister of those many dealers in maxims who have adorned our literature. Uplift is her purpose; she wants improvement. But her tone is the familiar tone of content with our American life. The stories which she often quite unnaturally sets forth are full of a factitious optimism, with an occasional dash of native wit, and a general air of provincial blessedness overspreading all. Calliope always finds the sweet and wholesome and good.[16]

Although Rourke finds some hints of injustice and unresolved social conflicts in the later Friendship Village stories, she nonetheless argues that "one is wholly unprepared for Miss Lulu Bett. This last story of Zona Gale's teaches no lesson and holds no brief. It is written almost bitterly." She concludes, "It would be interesting to know the road by which Miss Gale traveled out of Friendship Village and into the greater world in which this last story lives; but this is her own affair. Whatever its antecedents, the book stands as a signal accomplishment in American letters." An article published in *Bookman* in 1923 echoed Rourke's argument:

> There was a time, not so many years ago, when the sweet sentimentalism that ran through Zona Gale's work was like to shove her over the cliffs to disaster. She was so sickeningly dear and precious that it hurt—almost as good and cream puffy as the author of "Pollyanna." But of course her stories had more relation to art; and when one thought of her early promise, in several lovely poems, one was inclined to weep for her going rapidly the way of the popular magazine writer, making money out of a stupid optimism, preaching an all's-right-with-the-world doctrine, when her common sense must have told her often enough that all was not right.[17]

The reviewer argued that Gale salvaged her literary reputation with the more realistic and pessimistic novels *Birth* (1918) and *Miss Lulu Bett*.[18]

Despite the fact that the theatrical version of *Miss Lulu Bett* was criticized for having a weak dramatic structure, and the author for making a concession to popular taste in the form of a revised, happy, ending, the play was viewed as a contribution to an emerging naturalist canon.[19] In the pages of the *Nation*, Ludwig Lewisohn compared it to Eugene O'Neill's *Beyond the Horizon*, and in the *New Republic* it was classed as "a part, if you like, of that wonderful Discovery of America which is now being made by Willa Cather, Sherwood Anderson, Sinclair Lewis, Floyd Dell, Edith Wharton."[20] *Literary Digest* compared it to the "small-town stuff" found in Sinclair Lewis's *Main Street* and Floyd Dell's *Moon-calf*.[21] Alan White, cited in Heywood Broun's column in the *New York Tribune*, noted, "The old-fashioned 'hick' farce of reuben melodrama, which went to the country town to expound the beauties of the simple life and homely virtues, has no relation to these new expressions of small-town life. Small-town life is used to-day not to lure us 'Back to Mother's Knee,' but rather because small-town life is a plastic medium. It is used in the drama and the novel and free verse to tell big necessary things with compelling, artistic vigor. And Zona Gale in *Miss Lulu Bett* has led the back-to-the-earth movement."[22]

The story is fundamentally the same in novel, play, and film, with some differences to be described below. Lulu and her aged mother live with her sister Ina, who is married to Dwight Deacon, a dentist and the town magistrate. The household includes two children: Diane, who has just finished high school, and the young Monona (although the author does not specify the location of Warbleton, the small town in which the action takes place, the youngest daughter is named for one of the lakes in Wisconsin's state capital). Lulu is a household drudge and the helpless butt of Dwight's teasing. When she buys a potted tulip for the house, he first pretends to think it is a gift from a suitor, to her great embarrassment, then chastises her for spending his money on luxuries.

Dwight's brother Ninian, a traveling salesman, visits after an absence of twenty years. Although he is crude and egotistical, he perceives the inequities in the household division of labor. He joins Lulu when she does the dishes in the kitchen after dinner, and he invites her to join the family and their guests in the parlor, a breach of precedent. Since Lulu is never invited anywhere, Ninian takes her, along with his brother and sister-in-law, to the city for dinner and a show. During a lull in the conversation after dinner, partly out of boredom and partly to torture Lulu, Dwight playfully dares them to reenact the marriage ceremony. After they have done so, Dwight recalls that he is a magistrate and that the ceremony is binding. Ninian tells Lulu that he is willing to let the marriage stand, and she shyly agrees. They depart for Savannah, Georgia, where Ninian has business.

Upon their return home, Ina and her mother realize that they will be seriously inconvenienced by Lulu's departure. Neither one of them can cook a decent meal, nor do they relish doing the housework. In the film version, this point is made viscerally as dishes pile up in the sink and ants take over the kitchen counters. Lulu returns home unexpectedly. She explains that Ninian had confessed that he had been married eighteen years before and later deserted by his wife. Unsure whether or not his wife was still living, Ninian hoped that Lulu would go on with him all the same. But, given doubts about the legality of the marriage, Lulu opted to return to Warbleton.

The novel, play, and film diverge slightly at this point, although all turn upon the fact that Dwight and Ina want above all to protect the family name and prevent gossip about Ninian's bigamy. They ask Lulu to keep quiet about her reasons for having left Ninian, which leaves the townsfolk to conclude that she has been rejected by her husband. In the novel, this is seconded by Dwight's convenient assumption that this is, in fact, what has happened. He confidentially assures Lulu that Ninian's claim to have been married before was just a ruse to get rid of her. Lulu resumes her old place and her old chores, but she is not as passive as before. Determined to know where she really stands with her erstwhile husband, she threatens to tell everyone her version of events, thereby forcing Dwight to write to Ninian and ask for proofs.

Ina and Dwight depart for a few days, leaving Lulu in charge of the children. Dwight gives Lulu strict instructions not to open "his" mail, including any letter that might come from Ninian. During their absence, the letter containing proof of Ninian's marriage arrives and is opened by Lulu's mother, who does not seem to have registered Dwight's prohibition. A family friend, Neil Cornish, witnesses the contents of the letter, as well as Lulu's predicament with regard to its opening.

Meanwhile, the older daughter, Diane, elopes with her high-school sweetheart. Lulu follows them to a neighboring town, where the girl, at least, hopes to get married (the boy is the more reluctant partner). As she argues with Diane about the wisdom of the elopement, Lulu realizes the kinship between them: Diane wants to get married because she longs to escape from the family as much as her aunt does. Lulu brings Diane home and helps her to keep her parents, who have returned from their trip, ignorant of the episode.

Dwight is furious at finding the letter open. However, he and Ina convince Lulu that she needs to keep silent about Ninian's bigamy for the sake of the girls, and Dwight "forgives" her. Lulu decides to leave the Deacons, even though her prospects of employment—making cakes for a local bakery, working as a chambermaid in a hotel—are not promising. When a second letter arrives from Ninian, which confirms that his first wife is still alive, Neil Cornish proposes marriage. He admits that he is not likely to be very successful as a businessman, but Lulu accepts him. Ina and Dwight view this sudden marriage with alarm, realizing that they will now have to make the news of Ninian's bigamy public.

The first version of the play has a more severe ending than the novel, one reminiscent of *A Doll's House*, in which Lulu refuses Neil's offer of marriage and departs to an uncertain future.[23] In the revised version Ninian returns to town with evidence that his first wife is dead, which not only provides a happy end but obviates the scandal of the week Lulu spent with him in Savannah. In the film the romance plot is both "happier" and better integrated than in the other two versions. The character of Neil Cornish is introduced much earlier in the plot, and he witnesses Lulu's mistreatment by her family before Ninian's arrival. When she returns from Georgia he treats her sympathetically in the face of the town gossips who assume that she has been rejected by her husband. He is also made a more respectable suitor, a schoolmaster, and is acted by the handsome Milton Sills, who was known for playing stalwart types.

Despite having the most conventional romance plot of the three versions, the film retains those elements of the play and original novel that break most definitively with the nostalgic representation of rural life: the negative characterization of the various Deacons and the evocation of an oppressive domesticity. These were the points most widely praised by literary critics writing of the play in the 1920s. For example, Ludwig Lewisohn: "That Deacon family group on its front porch is magnificent and memorable. The preaching and blustering and nagging of Dwight, the prattling and posturing of his wife, the cold and weary resistance of Lulu, the crafty little rebellions of the child Monona, the sentimentalized scorn and detachment of Diana—these things that project the strain and tug and essential hollowness and maladjustment of the lives involved, mark an enormous advance in the American drama."[24] The reviewer for the *New Republic* singled out the character of Dwight Deacon as the butt of the play's satire:

> He is a small-town dentist, but of a self-sufficiency that would fit him for the Cabinet and with a line of pontifical axioms that would get him re-appointed at the renewal of the term. In addition to this insufferable pomposity there is his insufferable good-nature, his great American habit of "kidding," with no idea as to the point at which attention to personality becomes invasion of personality and the sin of sins. He is a provider, possibly a good provider, but he provides the tribal morals and manners as well as the canned salmon and the oatmeal wallpapers and the rocking chairs and the chandelier.[25]

Heywood Broun particularly approved of Monona: "Generally a child is treated by a dramatist as unbelievably saintly, and the effect is wearing on both actor and audience. Monona, on the contrary, is studiously bad and unlovely in thought and word."[26] Robert Benchley praised Gale for her "almost phonographic reproduction of the vocal processes of the average American in a state of domesticity." He approved of the way the author captured the banality of everyday speech and quoted several passages from the novel, including this one:

> "Baked potatoes," said Mr. Deacon. "That's good—that's good. The baked potato contains more nourishment than potatoes prepared in any other way. The nourishment is next to the skin. Roasting retains it."
> "That's what I always think," said his wife pleasantly.
> For fifteen years they had agreed about this.[27]

The film has its own techniques for evoking the banality of domestic life and Dwight's bluster. These techniques, as well as the slow pacing noted in the film industry trade press, are clearly apparent in the opening. Monona comes into the dining room, where the table is set for dinner. She steals food and hides under the table to eat it. Dwight enters and compares his pocket watch, which indicates that it is after six o'clock, with the clock on the wall, which shows ten minutes to. He changes the time on the wall clock. Meanwhile, Monona steals out from under the table and goes onto the back porch. She innocently reenters the room. Her father shows her his watch and chides her for being late. The two sit at the table. Ina approaches and, seeing her husband seated, apologizes for her lateness. She then looks at the clock on the wall and indicates that it is fast. Dwight disagrees, showing her his pocket watch as proof. When Diane arrives, she, too, is reprimanded. She checks her wrist watch, asserting that she has a different time. Her father resolutely points to his pocket watch as final arbiter. Mrs. Bett finds the family seated and puts on her glasses to read the time on the wall clock. Dwight stands and addresses her, "Has the Queen of our Household such pressing business that she can't be on time for supper?" Mrs. Bett takes offense and goes off into the kitchen. Lulu brings in the dinner and is confronted with Dwight holding his pocket watch. As she, too, questions the time on the wall clock, the film cuts to a factory whistle, blowing, to indicate that it is six o'clock. Lulu assures her brother-in-law that the clock is fast, to the great pleasure of the assembled company.

The point is to show not only Dwight's unwarranted exercise of paternal authority but also the way in which everyone in the family automatically responds to the ritual of the six o'clock dinner hour: Ina has only to see her husband waiting to know she is late, Mrs. Bett only to see the family seated to put on her glasses and check the time. The relatively trivial question of whether the clock on the wall is accurate assumes inordinate importance within the life of the family. This point is restated in the film's opening title, which proposes the moral "The greatest tragedy in the world, because it is the most frequent, is that of a human soul caught in the toils of the commonplace."

Unlike Zona Gale's play, which was criticized for its lack of conventional dramatic structure, the film version of *Miss Lulu Bett* builds to a clear-cut climax that involves Lulu's renunciation of her family. Although from the point of view of naturalist dramaturgy the final decisive confrontation may be seen as a defect and a concession to popular taste, it sustains the film's satirical treatment of the Deacons and its forceful evocation of an oppressive domesticity.

After Lulu has prevented Diane's elopement, Cornish drives them home from the train station. Lulu is shaking Neil's hand in thanks when Dwight and Ina come home. A shot from their point of view shows the couple talking, framed by the doorway, Lulu still holding the suitcase with her niece's things. Neil says, "If you were only free—" and Dwight comes to the conclusion that they are eloping. He enters and accuses Lulu of once again disgracing the family. After Neil leaves, Dwight and Ina confront Lulu, while Diane and Monona sneak down the stairs to listen to the quarrel going on in the parlor. In the course of the following scene, every character in the family, at one time or another, attempts to send the recalcitrant Monona back upstairs. Dwight insists on knowing what Lulu was doing with a suitcase. Having promised to keep Diane's secret, she cannot speak in her own defense. Dwight sees the girls and motions for Monona to leave the room, telling Lulu she is not fit to be under the same roof with his innocent children. Lulu agrees to leave and goes to say goodbye to her mother. Dwight, Ina, and the girls then confer. Each acts in his or her own self-interest, without concern for Lulu. Diane says nothing. Ina asks who will do the work if Lulu goes. Monona pleads, "Oh, papa, let Aunt Lulu stay! She cooks lots better than mama." This point infuriates her mother, who orders her upstairs, but it registers with her father, who decides to countermand his request. Diane then upbraids her sister, who retreats only partly up the steps.

In the kitchen Dwight tells Lulu he cannot turn his wife's sister out into the streets, so he has decided to forgive her. Lulu loses her temper, upsetting the pots on the stove and breaking the crockery. She throws the scrubbing brush at her sister and mother, saying, "Now do your own dishes!" She denies Dwight's right to exercise authority over her, even in the guise of forgiveness. A short epilogue shows Lulu, now working at a local bakery, bringing Neil Cornish a letter from Ninian indicating that his first wife is still alive and thus opening the way to their courtship. But the force of the ending lies in Lulu's rebellion against domestic tyranny and in the almost bitter satire of familial relationships that prepares the way for her outburst. In this regard, deMille's film remains quite close to those aspects of the play praised by literary intellectuals in the 1920s.

Critics classed Zona Gale with other novelists writing about the Midwest, particularly Sinclair Lewis, whose *Main Street*, published in 1920, and *Babbitt*, published in 1922, were critically acclaimed by contemporaries for their merciless dissections of American small-town life. Warner Brothers produced adaptations of both novels under the direction of Harry Beaumont. Neither film seems to have survived. The reviews of *Main Street* indicate that, like many of the other films already discussed, critics found the plot slight. *Variety* (May 3, 1923: 22) wrote, "A consensus of opinion would indicate that the producers took a chance on making a picture out of the story, for the book's principal attribute was the penmanship of the author in drawing his characterizations of the small-town inhabitants. That left little action upon which to build interest for filming." *Film Daily* (June 17, 1923: 3) simply advised exhibitors, "You'll have to cut this one." The reviews in the trade press also suggest that the film might have had difficulty finding a market. *Variety* thought that it would not be able to draw the crowds to sustain it at the highest prices in the major metropolitan theaters. But *Film Daily* surmised that the film's only chance would be in the big cities: "When cut to moderate length will doubtless have big appeal in the big cities because of popularity of the book, but small town folk may object to caricatures of Main Street types which are enormously exaggerated." Indeed, the description of the film in the *New York Times* (June 12, 1923: 22) suggests a comic treatment of small town manners and cultural aspirations. Carol Milford moves from a large city to Gopher Prairie when she marries the town doctor.

> The party given for her [Carol] at which Dave Dyer officiates as master of ceremonies is interesting, especially when a Gophir [*sic*] Prairie girl recites, her gestures being amusing and quite true to the type. When another individual has consented to sing the gathering is obviously restless, and it is with great relief that they hear: "This way for the eats." Mr. Beaumont paints a very hungry lot of people in Gophir Prairie, and their manners need correction. They are eager to pass dishes of food, but they appear to be more eager to get other dishes. Carol is pictured as a person utterly dismayed by the constant interchange of dishes. One arm crosses her from one side and then another from the other, so much so that she has no time for conversation or to eat.

According to the *Times,* the film included an equally amusing "Chinese" party, replete with its own poetic oration, which Carol gives in an attempt to lift the cultural tone of the town.

The script for *Babbitt* suggests that the filmmakers backed away from the most controversial aspects of Lewis's novel, which is set in Zenith, described as a small Midwestern city. In the film script the description of shot 3 is "*PAN SHOT. LARGE MIDDLE WESTERN CITY, such as Detroit or Toledo.* This shot is inserted as essential coloring to the characterization of Babbitt; it should impress the audience that it is a big city which produced Babbitt, that he is not in any sense the product of Main Street."[28] Based upon the evidence of the script, the filmmakers do not seem to have sought out equivalents for the novel's meticulous, semiparodic descriptions of Babbitt's real-estate dealings or his participation in local fraternal organizations. Rather, as *Variety* (July 16, 1924: 22) pointed out, the film becomes "the time-worn tale of the middle-aged fairly successful business man, tired of home surroundings and the wife who has reared his three children. He is ripe for the first vamp who makes up her mind to ensnare him." The film was also apparently played for comedy. *Variety* noted, "It is all told in a human vein with an eye on the main chance for laughs, and the latter are plentiful." *Film Daily* (July 20, 1924: 9), which preferred *Babbit* to *Main Street*, recommended to exhibitors that they run a trailer showing some of the "comedy bits." The *New York Times* (July 15, 1924: 9) complained that the film's comedy was "handled with the bludgeon rather than with the rapier."

The tendency of Hollywood filmmakers to push naturalist or quasinaturalist treatments of small-town life toward comedy is evident in all of the examples cited above, from Griffith's gentle parody of the Sanctificationist Church meeting in *A Romance of Happy Valley* to deMille's ironic undermining of Dwight Deacon in the opening of *Miss Lulu Bett*. It seems also to have been a feature of Beaumont's adaptations of Sinclair Lewis. Mal St. Clair's 1925 *A Woman of the World* is the logical extension of this trend. The plot, loosely based on Carl Van Vechten's novel *The Tattooed Countess*, focuses on an Italian countess (Pola Negri) who is disappointed in love and comes to visit relatives in Maple Valley, a town in the Midwest. Featuring slapstick comedian Chester Conklin in a major supporting role, the film has no pretensions to naturalism. However, the attack on small-town notions of propriety and lack of tolerance bears comparison to *Miss Lulu Bett* and the descriptions of *Main Street*. Many of the jokes revolve around the differences between the cosmopolitan aristocrat and the denizens of the town. Running gags concern reactions to her clothes and her habit of smoking in public, as well as the unrelenting gossip inspired by rumors about the tattoo that she keeps hidden. When the leading citizens of the town gather to meet the Countess, her shocked reaction to their manners, eating habits, and narrow view of the world echoes Carol's reaction in the party scene in *Main Street* as recounted in the *New York Times*. The tendency to push the criticism of rural life in the direction of comedy is worth noting, since the tone of naturalist depictions of rural America becomes much more grim in the second half of the 1920s, as I will show.

Writers such as Frank Norris and Theodore Dreiser who inaugurated naturalism in America were much more concerned with urban experience and urban types than the later generation represented by Sinclair Lewis and Zona Gale. But aside from the social problem films of the 1910s discussed above, most of Hollywood's experimentation with reduced plots and everyday characters prior to the release of *Greed* in 1925 dealt with rural life. The 1923 film adaptation of Eugene O'Neill's *Anna Christie* is distinctive in that it essayed a story about the life of immigrants in the city.[29]

The play *Anna Christie,* first performed in 1921, was one of O'Neill's early successes. It garnered him his second Pulitzer Prize and was popular enough to run for 127 performances on Broadway.[30] The play recounts the familiar story of a prostitute redeemed by love, a variant of the seduction plot that I will discuss in more detail in chapter 5. However, O'Neill's play is distinguished in part by its emphasis on the lower-class surroundings of a sailor, Chris Christopherson, and his daughter, Anna. Writing at the time of the play's first production, Burns Mantle called it "a rough play in that it is a story of rough characters."[31]

Chris, who deserted his family years ago, is delighted to receive a letter from his daughter, Anna, announcing an impending visit. Upon her entrance it is clear that she is a prostitute down on her luck, but Chris is oblivious to this fact and takes her to live with him on the coal barge of which he is the captain. At sea some weeks later they pick up four stokers, the sole survivors of a wreck. One of them, Mat, makes a play for Anna. When she rebuffs him and refers to the presence of her father, Mat assumes she is "decent" and begins to court her. Chris attempts to interfere. He blames the sea for everything bad that has happened to him, or that he has done himself, and he does not want Anna to marry a sailor. A particularly vehement argument between the men motivates Anna to reveal that she is not what they both suppose: she has worked in a brothel just like the ones Mat and Chris visit when they arrive in a new port. Disillusioned, both men disappear on drinking sprees. Chris, who returns first, tells Anna that he is going to "help" her by shipping out as bosun on the *Londonderry* and making his wages over to her. Anna clearly thinks that Chris is simply running out again, as he has always done, but she has her own brand of fatalism. The dialogue here and throughout the scene implies that though she regards herself as a "bad" woman she does not think she could have helped it, any more than Chris could help either his attraction to the sea or his tendency to hold it accountable for his actions. Mat then returns and quarrels with Anna, who alternates between attempts to assure him that love has made her "good" and a tougher stance in which she tells him that if he cannot accept what she was, he can leave. He finally allows himself to be convinced that she has reformed. He, too, is shipping out on the *Londonderry,* but the couple plan to be married before he goes.

According to Christine Dymkowski, O'Neill was disturbed by the reception of the play. When critics congratulated him for finally catering to popular taste, he complained in a letter to the New York Times: "A kiss in the last act, a word about marriage, and the audience grows blind and deaf to what follows."[32] O'Neill's reference is to the play's end, in which Chris curses the old devil sea, presumably implying that the sea is about to claim both of the men who love Anna. In addition to this pessimistic note, the idea of redemption is only fitfully articulated at the play's close, largely confined to the character of Mat. A similar clarity of moral judgment cannot be ascribed either to Chris, for whom the sea figures as an all-encompassing symbol of fate, or to Anna, who, like him, considers the circumstances that made her "bad" as well as "good" to be beyond her control. These elements of the play, which are clearly an inheritance of naturalism, were retained in the film adaptation and help to account for its reception.

Anna Christie was a "prestige" production that earned the producer, Thomas Ince, credit for realism and seriousness. Indeed, George Pratt indicates that Ince chose to adapt the play to improve his reputation as a producer.[33] In the National Board of Review magazine *Exceptional Photoplays*, Ince and the director, John Griffith Wray, were congratulated for "picturizing the first play of our greatest living dramatist" and for hewing closely to the outlines of the original without distorting the work into "standardized movie product."

> Here certainly is a play which at first blush seems far removed from the smugness of the movies and their tricky moralising. Mr. O'Neill's honesty, the realism of his dialogue, the incisiveness of his character drawing, and above all his method of establishing the fundamental morality of his theme without sentimental concessions, were so many more obstacles to deter the conventional scenario writer and director. Anna is not a girl who is made good or who turns out to be a misunderstood model of virtue. She is simply that rarest thing in the movies or, for that matter, in the theatre too—a convincing human being.[34]

Exceptional Photoplays was not alone in celebrating the film version. The *New York Times* (December 10, 1923: 20) wrote, "This photodrama, now at the Strand, is an example of progress in film history, and let us hope, one which will help to deter some producers from putting forth money into nonsensical contraptions. It sheds light on the way directors can strengthen their productions." *Variety* (December 6, 1923: 23) reported that the film deserved the honor of being the first of the 1923–24 season to be chosen for a special showing before the membership of the National Board of Review: "It is a picture that is interesting. It is a picture that is as different to the regular runs of screen productions as the Eugene O'Neill plays are to the majority of hits and near-hits that come to the spoken stage; but, still, there is going to be a question whether or not it is going to pull money to the picture theatre box offices the country over." *Variety* thought that the problem was not that the film would be found offensive but rather that the author and play were not well known to exhibitors or audiences outside New York. There is at least one piece of evidence that *Variety* was correct in its estimation of the film's lack of box office appeal. When the film played in repertory in New York in 1928, the *New York Times* (December 23, 1928: 7) reported that upon its first release it was "by no means a howling success." Nonetheless, *Anna Christie* is an important early example of filmmakers' banking on the prestige of literary naturalism. It is quite different in scale and aspiration from the deliberately "small" and unpretentious films about country life directed by Griffith or De Grasse, and it was also accorded much more prominence in the trade and popular press than the more or less comedic adaptations of *Miss Lulu Bett* and *Main Street*. Assimilation of naturalism into the serious, prestige picture was to be carried much further with Erich von Stroheim's adaptation of *McTeague*.

When Erich von Stroheim was shooting *Greed*, he gave an interview to the *New York Times* (August 5, 1923: 10) in which he called for greater realism in films. He made the familiar distinction between stories that rely on plot, "thrilling, romantic or amusing situations," and those that rely on character. For von Stroheim, realism emphasized character development over plot, and he mentioned Dickens, De Maupassant, Zola, and Frank Norris as exemplifying this kind of storytelling. He argued, "Little realism has been seen on the screen. There are 'Miss Lulu Bett,' some of Will Rogers's pictures, 'Grandma's Boy' and 'The Kid' in comedies. Certain moments in Marshall Neilan's pictures have possessed the spark, as did the two-reel production of O. Henry's 'The Cop and the Anthem' and other O. Henry stories. There was realism in Rex Ingram's 'The Conquering Power,' and that to my mind is about all." Thus, realism in film was for him primarily identified with comedy—*Miss Lulu Bett*, Will Rogers, Harold Lloyd's *Grandma's Boy* and Chaplin's *The Kid*—and with the short film, Vitagraph's 1917 adaptation of "The Cop and the Anthem" to which he refers.[35] It is a mark of its originality and importance that *Greed* broke definitively with both of these trends. It was much darker in tone than any of the previous 1920s experiments. And, as originally conceived by its author, its meticulous accumulation of detail and painstaking character development accrued over many reels: *Greed* was infamously long.

The vexed textual history of *Greed* necessitates comment. Richard Koszarski's account of the production cites two early reports of the length of the rough cut, one indicating forty-five reels with a nine-and-a-half-hour running time, the other forty-two reels. In the initial round of editing, von Stroheim reduced the film to twenty-two reels, but it was still too long for any exhibitor of the period to cope with. With the help of editor Grant Whytock, von Stroheim cut the film down further, to a version alternatively described as eighteen and fifteen reels.[36] He hoped that MGM would release this version in two parts, to be shown on successive nights. When the studio took over, the film was given to Joseph Farnham, a respected title writer, who drastically reduced the exposition in the opening sections, completely excised two major subplots, and shortened the main story about Mac and Trina, writing titles to fill in the gaps he had created.[37] This 133-minute, ten-reel version was premiered in December 1924 and released in January of the next year. As is well known, the excised footage has never been found. But in 1999 Rick Schmidlin produced a virtual reconstruction on video, using extant production stills of the missing scenes, creating new titles based on von Stroheim's script and Norris's novel, and eliminating some of the original titles, presumably those he attributed to Farnham. Because Schmidlin's version is too far removed from the historical *Greed*, i.e., from the version that reviewers and audiences saw in the 1920s, I have drawn the following summary from the release print and the published version of the complete script, which identifies the footage that survives in the 1925 version, and includes the titles added to that version to cover narrative gaps.[38]

The young McTeague works in the Big Dipper gold mine in Placer, California.[39] His mother aspires to better things for him and sends him off with an itinerant dentist of dubious training to learn the trade. Some years later McTeague has established a small dental practice on Polk Street in San Francisco, living in the room he uses for his office.[40] Mac's friend Marcus Schouler brings in his cousin and sweetheart, Trina Sieppe, for a series of treatments. One day his drilling causes her pain and he administers ether. He finds himself attracted to the unconscious woman and, despite a struggle with his conscience, kisses her. When she awakes, he proposes marriage, which she refuses.

Learning that his friend is glum because he is in love with Trina, Marcus offers to let Mac "have" the girl. The two men take the train to Oakland to meet Trina and her family. Mac begins to visit Trina regularly, and they become engaged. When Trina and her family repair to Mac's room for a celebratory dinner, a representative of a lottery company informs Trina that her ticket has won $5,000. Alone after the celebration, Marcus curses his luck: if he had kept Trina, he would have had the $5,000.

A month later Mac and Trina are married in the rooms across from the dental office that Mac has taken for their new home. After a large supper with the family, the Sieppes move permanently to Southern California, leaving a frightened Trina alone with her new husband. In the early months of their married life, Trina's stinginess becomes apparent. Mac hopes to rent a little house where they can be by themselves, but Trina considers the rent too high.

Mac and Marcus quarrel when Marcus demands a share of the lottery money and is refused. Marcus becomes violent, throwing a knife at Mac. Sometime later Marcus visits the McTeagues in their rooms and tells them that he is leaving permanently to work on a ranch. After his departure Mac receives a letter from the State Board of Dentistry, forbidding him to practice without a license. Trina realizes that it was Marcus who reported them. Mac's business drops away, and he swears vengeance on his former friend.

Without an income from Mac's practice, Trina sells their nicest things and begins to earn money whittling toys so as not to touch her $5,000. She hides the gold coins in a trunk, taking them out in secret and polishing them. When Mac is fired from a job at a surgical instrument factory, Trina demands that he look for another job immediately, and she takes away his severance pay, refusing him a nickel for carfare. Drenched while walking home in the rain, Mac is invited into Joe Frenna's saloon by his former mates and treated to several drinks. Drinking and idleness become habitual to him. One day, after promising his mates in the bar that he will return with some money, he attacks Trina, pinching her shoulder and biting her fingers until she gives him a couple of dollars. Shortly thereafter he abandons his wife.

Trina becomes a scrubwoman, living in the school that she cleans. As Trina prepares for bed, pouring her gold pieces onto her mattress, Mac, now a bum, comes to her window. He rouses her and begs for money for food. He says he "wouldn't let a dog go hungry." She replies by showing him her hand, which is now missing two fingers, and says: "Not if he'd bitten you?" She closes and locks the window as he utters threats. He returns on Christmas and kills Trina in a struggle for the key to her trunk. He takes her gold.

Some weeks later a reward is posted for McTeague's arrest and apprehension. Marcus, now a cowboy, reads this notice and joins the posse being assembled to follow the culprit into Death Valley. Mac leads his mule deep into the desert and fills his canteen at the last watering hole. While the rest of the posse elect to circle around the desert, Marcus insists on following Mac's trail directly. His horse dies, and he runs out of water, but he continues the pursuit on foot, eventually finding Mac and pulling a gun on him. The mule carrying Mac's canteen begins to run off, and Marcus shoots and kills the animal. The two men discover that Marcus has inadvertently shot a hole in the canteen, squandering the last of their water. Mac nonetheless decides to push on and indicates that he wants his saddle bags, which contain the gold. Marcus claims the money, and the men fight for it. While Mac bludgeons Marcus to death with the revolver, Marcus manages to secure handcuffs on one of Mac's wrists. Sitting handcuffed to the corpse, Mac waits.

Two of the film's stylistic features not captured by this plot summary are important, as they account more fully for its debt to literary naturalism. In 1925 the film was notable for its departure from the decorum that actors in serious drama typically maintained. In its mildest form, this departure consists in a predilection for low comedy. On the trip to the picnic grounds, Chester Conklin as Pappa Sieppe carefully lines up first his children and then the adults, briskly marches up and down the line himself, and then gives the order to advance. When Jean Hersholt as Marcus comes to collect Trina from Mac's office, he makes an entrance that looks like a ham-fisted arabesque, giving a little jump and closing the door with his foot. Then, in an effort to amuse Trina, he rotates his hat and turns up the brim, pulls up his collar, and strikes the familiar "Napoleon" pose, with hand resting in the lapel. As he exits with Trina, he waves breezily to Mac and then flicks his coat tails as he goes out the door, exposing his behind. In other scenes, crude or indecorous gestures are introduced with little or no comic effect but merely as an indication of the lower-class milieu. In the scene in which Marcus first introduces Trina to Mac, for example, he nudges her repeatedly with his elbow, sticks his finger in his ear to scratch it, and picks his nose. When Mac descends from the train at the Oakland station, Trina greets him and almost immediately pulls back her upper lip, displaying her dental work. At the wedding dinner the guests are shown eating in a gross manner: Mr. Sieppe gnaws on a calf's head, the skull already visible, and uses his napkin to wipe the sweat from his face; Mrs. Sieppe pulls meat off a carcass with her teeth; at their table the children, besmeared with food, quarrel over a tidbit; Heise, with a large and very dirty napkin tucked into his shirt, eats, drinks, and belches.

The emphasis on uncouth bearing and demeanor sometimes approaches the grotesque, as in the shot from the wedding dinner of Chester Conklin with the calf's skull in hand. Similarly, the shot of the stranger from the lottery company who brings Trina the news of her winning is gratuitously ugly. The man has a boil or open wound covered by plaster. He stands at the top of the stairs, framed in a low angle so that he looms toward the camera, the use of a wide angle lens further distorting his features. Even with the cuts made by the studio in the released version, one senses how von Stroheim planned Tina's gradual transformation from a neat and pretty girl to yet another grotesque figure—hair falling in disarray, ragged clothes, a mutilated hand with the remaining fingers covered in bandages. It is a process brilliantly enacted by Zasu Pitts, who manages to alter both her carriage and her range of facial expression in the course of the film.

A second innovation is in the titling of the film. Most of the dialogue titles were not written by Farnham but derive from the original script and remain in the 1925 release print. They were designed to evoke vernacular speech. Finally enraged by Marcus's attack on him in Joe Frenna's saloon, McTeague says, "—he can't make small o' me," a phrase he repeats when he is drunk and quarrelling with Trina. Marcus complains, "All I know is . . . that I've been soldiered out of my girl an' out o' my money." The use of slang by the American-born characters is complemented by the indicated Swiss-German accents of Mr. and Mrs. Sieppe. As she says goodbye to her daughter after the wedding dinner, Mrs. Sieppe tells McTeague, "Doktor . . . pe goot to her! Pe vairy goot to her . . . von't you?" The inarticulate McTeague's efforts to communicate are conveyed by multiple, fragmentary titles. For example, take the scene at the Cliff House in which Mac and Marcus first discuss Trina (each iteration of the character name represents a distinct title card, separated by shots of the interlocutors):

> MAC: "It's . . . it's . . . Miss Sieppe!"
>
> MARCUS: "You mean . . . that you, too—"
>
> MAC: "She's been the first girl I've ever known. I couldn't help myself."
>
> MAC: "—I was so close to her—"
>
> MAC: "—an' smelled her hair—"
>
> MAC: "—an' felt her breath!"
>
> MAC: "Oh! . . . you don't know."

Mac's difficulty is conveyed by the large number of titles, the use of sentence fragments, and the dashes and ellipses suggesting the speaker's hesitations. The radical nature of von Stroheim's experiment in the treatment of dialogue titles becomes apparent if we contrast *Greed* with Ince's *Anna Christie*. Although some of the dialogue titles for Chris suggest that he speaks with an accent, the dialect is much less marked than that spoken by the Sieppes, or, indeed, than that in the written text of O'Neill's play. Thus Chris says, when he first sees Anna: "You're grown up, and you're so purty." And, later in the same scene: "Anna, on the sea, in my ship, will be as good for us as on land." Anna initially speaks in a prose that would be considered rough for a woman in 1923. When Martha tells her that Chris is at sea, she says, "Damn. That means I got to find somebody again. Lousy dump!" But she usually speaks in complete sentences with only a hint of slang: "I got to get a roof over my head, and somethin' to eat. I need a rest. I'm knocked out."[41] By contrast, von Stroheim's dialogue titles distort spelling much more radically in the case of accented speech. They are also much more fragmentary and informal. Von Stroheim's use of slang and his attempt to replicate the speaking rhythms of largely inarticulate characters seem to have been inspired by Norris's own attempts to reproduce working-class speech. More generally, he adheres to the naturalist tendency to abjure a polished style in favor of an exploration of the vernacular.

A certain obviousness attaches to the debate over *Greed.* Everyone agreed that the film lacked popular appeal, that it was, to use the Shavian term, "unpleasant" and unlikely to prove a financial success. *Film Daily* (December 7, 1924: 4) commented, "As a great picture, a big picture, one which took over a year to make and therefore developed certain anticipations, 'Greed' is one of the keenest disappointments of the season. It may interest certain peculiar types to the box office but as an outstanding attraction for even the average theater-goer 'Greed' will not do." *Moving Picture World* (December 20, 1924: 726) outlined the reasons for its unacceptability: "'Greed' which consumed many months in the making and a great outlay of money, fails to measure up to expectations. Despite its good points, it is deficient in the basic requirement for success; it does not entertain, for it leaves one with the impression in which a sordid theme, a morbid tone, the stressing of the unpleasant and a gruesome ending are dominant and outweigh the excellent acting, fine direction and undoubted power of the story." *Variety* (December 19, 1824: 34) wrote in a similar vein:

> Nothing more morbid and senseless from a commercial picture stand-point has been seen on the screen in a long long time than this picture. Long awaited, von Stroheim having utilized two years and over $700,000 of Goldwyn and possibly some Metro money in the making, it came as a distinct shock to those viewing it.
>
> Never has there been a more out-and-out box office flop shown on the screen than this picture. Even D. W. Griffith's rather depressing "Isn't Life Wonderful?" is a howling comedy success when compared to "Greed." Metro-Goldwyn will never get the money that was put in this picture out of it, and the exhibitors that play it will have a heck of a time to get back via the box office route what they pay out in rentals for the picture.

Pointing out, however, that von Stroheim was not entirely to blame for the fiasco, since the film exhibited was not his version, the *Variety* reviewer thought that both von Stroheim's final cut and the studio's should have been exhibited to the trade for evaluation and that MGM had been hasty in ruling out a longer version to be shown over two successive nights.

Some of the major newspaper reviewers agreed with the assessment in the trade press that *Greed* was likely to offend the sensibilities of the average viewer. While recognizing the importance of the film, the *New York Times* (December 5, 1924: 28) cautioned, "It is undeniably a dramatic story, filled with the spirit of its film title, without a hero or a heroine. The three principals, however, deliver splendid performances in their respective roles. Gibson Gowland is unusually fine as McTeague: but from beginning to end this affair is sordid, and deals only with the excrescences of life such as would flabbergast even those dwelling in lodging houses on the waterfront."

Greed was by no means universally condemned, however. A number of important reviewers came to the defense of the film on grounds reminiscent of the earlier literary debates about naturalism. The film was held to be a welcome corrective to the sentimental bunk that dominated Hollywood filmmaking. The reviewer for *Exceptional Photoplays* argued:

> Most emphatically there is and should be a place for a picture like *Greed.* It is undoubtedly one of the most uncompromising films ever shown on the screen. There have already been many criticisms of its brutality, its stark realism, its sordidness. But the point is that it was never intended to be a pleasant picture. It is a picture that is grown up with a vengeance, a theme for just those adults who have been complaining most about the sickening sentimentality of the average film. Nobody can complain of being deceived when he goes to see it; Zola did not compete with Gautier and Frank Norris would never have sent any story of his to *True Romance.*[42]

Writing for the *Spectator* in London, Iris Barry echoed this argument:

> Nothing could have been sweeter to the cinema enthusiast's ear than the mingled noise of hissing and clapping which greeted the new film, *Greed,* on its first night at the Tivoli, Strand. The sheep and the goats were expressing their different points of view at last. There were those present who genuinely disliked it: those—no doubt the majority— who frankly prefer the usual type of film, with its hero and heroine suffused with meaningless virtue, its scenes of gilded boudoirs and ballrooms, its false but flattering psychology, and its soothing "happy endings." Such people need not be alarmed, there will always be plenty of what they like. But among the millions of people who every night of the year frequent picture palaces are reckoned a good many hundred thousands who appreciate a degree of realism, of imagination, or of wit.[43]

Robert Sherwood, writing in *Life,* began his review: "Ferocity, brutality, muscle, vulgarity, crudity, naked realism and sheer genius are to be found—great hunks of them in Von Stroheim's production, 'Greed.' It is a terribly powerful picture—and an important one."[44] Carl Sandburg, who reviewed the film twice in the Chicago *Daily News,* informed readers, "Among the best pictures which have come to our city within the last year—standing by itself for the low percentage of bunk and hokum—is the photoplay named *Greed,* now in its second week at the Roosevelt Theater."[45]

Even the critics who defended the film found it sometimes overstated or exaggerated, however. The review in *Exceptional Photoplays* praised Gibson Gowland's and Zasu Pitts's acting but concluded, "Jean Hersholt's impersonation of Marcus Schouler, McTeague's false friend, is hardly less skillful though it, together with the other characters, shows some of the exaggerations of low comedy into which the actors were undoubtedly pushed by Stroheim's over-direction. There are times when Stroheim squeezes the lemon a little too hard." In addition to this complaint about overacting, which was blamed on the director, there were objections to the film's heavy-handed symbolism. Both Robert Sherwood and Iris Barry complained about the yellow stencil-tinting of objects such as Trina's dental bridge, the watch Marcus gives her at the wedding, and her coins, which made them stand out against the more neutrally tinted and toned background. Sherwood thought that the underlining of the film's theme marred the effect of realism. Barry complained about "unnecessary symbolism," referring to the nondiegetic insert of emaciated hands and arms fondling gold coins that appears at intervals. She also disliked the intercutting between Marcus and a cat stalking the McTeagues' pet birds, which occurs in the scene in which Marcus visits Mac and Trina to say good-bye. This use of animals foreshadows the next scene, where the letter arrives from the State Dental Association forbidding Mac to practice dentistry without a license (at this point in the plot the cat actually pounces on the bird cage). The criticisms of *Greed* by reviewers sympathetic to von Stroheim's project point to its anomalous stylistic status. While the film was, I think rightly, considered to be one of the most radical experiments in naturalist filmmaking produced by the Hollywood studios, its grotesque characterizations and emphatic symbolism represented a departure from the dedramatized narratives and abjuration of strong effects found in previous films such as *Miss Lulu Bett,* or *The Old Swimmin' Hole. Greed* proposed a spectacular, deliberately overwrought naturalism—it may have been about "simple folk," but it was about as far as one can imagine from a "simple story."

The extent to which *Greed* altered the tone and temper of naturalist-inspired filmmaking becomes evident when it is contrasted with Griffith's *Isn't Life Wonderful*, which also appeared in December 1924. There is evidence to suggest that Griffith's film was made in response to von Stroheim's. Koszarski informs us that von Stroheim arrived in San Francisco to begin location shooting early in January 1923. The production was highly publicized both locally and nationally; it would not have escaped Griffith's notice.[46] Moreover, it is at least possible that Griffith was aware of the 1916 adaptation of *McTeague. Life's Whirlpool* was released while von Stroheim was working as an assistant director for Griffith at Fine Arts. Koszarski concludes that von Stroheim had seen it, since he referred to this version while making his own, and it seems plausible that Griffith would also have gone to see such an important new release.[47] Griffith did not start production on *Isn't Life Wonderful* until after Stroheim had finished shooting *Greed* and was working on the editing. He purchased the rights to Geoffrey Moss's story "Isn't Life Wonderful" in June 1924 and sailed to Germany to begin location shooting in July of the same year.[48]

The story concerns a family of Polish refugees in Berlin in the period of rampant inflation following World War I. Ina, who has been adopted by the Professor's extended family, lives with all of them in two small rooms. They subsist on meager rations of potatoes. She eagerly awaits the return of Paul, one of the two sons, from the War. Paul returns ill, having been gassed at the front. Ina tenderly nurses him, giving him portions of her food as well as his own until his strength returns. The young couple want to get married, but the family counsels against it since there is neither enough food nor housing available to them. At the shipyard where he works Paul is given an allotment and plants potatoes. He begins building a house for Ina with his own hands. In addition to a job as a salesclerk, Ina works in a used furniture store where she is paid in kind, allowing her to build up a supply of household items for her dowry. Because of inflation, food becomes even more scarce, and the family is reduced to a diet of turnips. Ina tries to buy some meat for the ailing grandmother, but as she waits in line at the butcher's, the price is raised beyond what she can afford to spend. A run of good luck follows. A neighbor leaves some hens for Ina to look after, and one lays an egg. Theodore, the other son, is given a gift of liverwurst in the nightclub where he works as a waiter. Paul brings home part of the potato crop. They share their bounty with neighbors, and, amidst the general celebration, the family agree to Paul's and Ina's marriage. But when Paul and Ina go to dig up the potato crop that will feed the family for a year and permit their marriage, they run afoul of a mob of unemployed and hungry laborers. The men had been stealing food from war profiteers, but, even after Ina has convinced them that Paul is a workingman like themselves, they knock him out and take the potato crop. At first Ina thinks that Paul has been killed. When he recovers, Ina assures him that all is not lost as long as they have each other. An epilogue shows the family accompanying Paul and Ina to their cabin the following year, this time with "enough potatoes for all!"

The trade press considered *Isn't Life Wonderful* a worthy and realistic film but a difficult sell. *Variety* (December 3, 1924: 27) wrote, "The story is too realistic. It is a page torn from life. Those who rave about 'the finer things in pictures' may not come to the box office in sufficient numbers to offset the out and out fans who will stay away. After all the latter are the ones to be catered to. Fans like naught but the sweetened pap fed to them day after day on the screens of this country." *Film Daily* (December 1, 1924: 1) warned, "Exhibitors—especially those who do not have limousine trade—had better see this first." But the film was praised, and in terms quite reminiscent of the reviews of *A Romance of Happy Valley* and *True Heart Susie.* Although *Moving Picture World* (December 13, 1924: 624) thought that the film would not have much appeal to "the masses," the reviewer noted, "It is a story which is simplicity itself, a page from life which depends upon its absolute realism, its remarkable character delineation and superb handling. He [Griffith] has steered clear of melodrama or the familiar devices of the drama to heighten the effect." *Exhibitors Trade Review* (December 13, 1924: 55) agreed, "In 'Isn't Life Wonderful' he has disregarded all the recognized rules of plot values, carefully built-up suspense, etc., and given us another innovation—a picture of straight narrative simplicity, just the plain record of a few humble lives, devoid of melodramatic complications, but starkly realistic and irresistibly compelling in its power of awakening emotional response." *Motion Picture News* (December 13, 1924: 3077) explained that Griffith had "departed from the era of big sets and crashing climaxes, eliminated storms and ice-jams and rides-to-the-rescue, and told a simple compelling human story about the privations of a family of Polish refugees in a German village. . . . Stressing characterization, rather than the mechanics of plot, Griffith has contrived to tell an extremely human story in a very human way. There is a total absence of 'hokum.'"

Although the critical reception of *Isn't Life Wonderful* dubbed the film a page torn from life and a challenging example of realistic filmmaking, the tone of the film differs considerably from that of *Greed.* This difference was registered in the *Variety* review of the latter, already cited, which found Griffith's film to be a "howling comedy success" in comparison to von Stroheim's. In my view the more far-reaching pessimism of *Greed* is a function of the conception of character and the motivation of the action. Von Stroheim seems to have been well aware that naturalist writers typically used heredity or environment to motivate character action. Thus in the scene in McTeague's dental office in which he tries and fails to resist the urge to kiss the unconscious Trina, a title explains, "But below the fine fabric bred of his mother, ran the foul stream of hereditary evil . . . the taint of generations given through his father." This title, given in the complete script as well as in the 1925 release print, refers back to an earlier sequence, excised by the studio, that dealt with Father McTeague's cruelty toward his wife, his alcoholism, and his relations with other women. But references to inherited vice seem less important in the film as a whole than the irrationality and self-destructiveness of the major characters. This is most strikingly the case for Trina, whose growing miserliness makes less and less sense as the McTeagues descend into ever more miserable circumstances and she increasingly alienates the husband whom the film is at pains to show she actually loves. At the nadir of her descent, when she climbs into bed with her money, her relationship to gold is explicitly represented as perverse. Although there is a certain logic to Marcus's envy of McTeague's luck in getting Trina and her money, his decision to report McTeague to the State Dental Association is a purely gratuitous act of spite; he does not thereby recoup his fortunes. The final scene in Death Valley when, despite recognizing their impending doom, the men waste what little energy they have left fighting over money, presents a similarly bleak view of human nature. If *Greed* seems pessimistic, it is not only because many of its characters seem incapable of altruism and real generosity, a point that could be made about a much less radical film such as *Miss Lulu Bett*, but, more important, because the protagonists seem incapable even of rationally pursuing their own self-interest.

Given the likelihood that Griffith was familiar with *Life's Whirlpool* and anticipated von Stroheim's adaptation of Norris's novel, it is tempting to see *Isn't Life Wonderful* as a kind of refutation. The opening title asserts a moral:

> This simple story shows:
> That LOVE makes beautiful all that it touches;
> That when we LOVE, no trials are ever grim;
> No disappointments make us morbid;
> Our struggles, however tense, are never depressing;
> For where there is LOVE there is HOPE
>   and TRIUMPH—which is what
>   MAKES LIFE WONDERFUL

This title is followed by another, which sets up the film as a kind of thought experiment: "Time: From the Armistice until 1923. The story is laid in Germany only because conditions there were most favorable for showing the triumph of love over hardship. It concerns a family of Polish refugees." It should be clear that this assertion of a human spirit existing apart from material circumstances runs counter to the tenets of literary naturalism. Moreover, in decided contrast with *Greed, Isn't Life Wonderful* presents no hint of gratuitous cruelty or self-destructive impulses. Even the stealing of food by the gang of unemployed laborers is instigated by a scene in which the gang leader sees his wife trying to force herself to eat rotten stuff taken from the garbage. Later, when the leader is in a position to take Paul's and Ina's potatoes, his motivation is emphasized by a dissolve that indicates that he is thinking of his starving wife. As the men take the food they cry that they have been made to act like "beasts," but it is clear that their actions are purely a function of dire circumstances and that they experience some degree of remorse.

Both *Isn't Life Wonderful* and *Greed* were considered realistic films by the trade press in 1924, and of the two, Griffith's was certainly better received. But there can be no doubt as to which film ultimately left a greater mark on the development of naturalist-inspired filmmaking in Hollywood. Passive protagonists overwhelmed by harsh social conditions or natural surroundings, families riven by tyranny or jealousy, sexuality rendered as a predatory and violent force—the path led out of Happy Valley.

Three of the principal examples of urban naturalism in the late silent period, Josef von Sternberg's *The Salvation Hunters* and *The Docks of New York* and King Vidor's *The Crowd*, may be distinguished from both *Greed* and *Anna Christie* in that they are not adaptations of well-established literary works. *The Salvation Hunters* and *The Crowd* are from original stories by von Sternberg and Vidor, respectively, while the screenplay for *The Docks of New York* was written by Jules Furthman and inspired by a story by John Monk Saunders. These examples suggest a more thorough-going assimilation of naturalist literary trends by Hollywood directors and screenwriters.

Both *The Salvation Hunters* and *The Docks of New York* were dubbed "sordid" at the time of their release, and, perhaps because of their tone and subject matter, historians often identify them with *Greed*.[49] However, von Sternberg's films cannot be solely, or even primarily, ascribed to naturalist influences. He began his career as a laboratory technician and then assistant director working for World, where there was a great deal of interest in stylistic experimentation and the influence of French émigré directors was strong. In addition to Maurice Tourneur, the group at World included

George Archainbaud, who had worked for the French company Éclair both in Paris and Fort Lee; Albert Capellani who was a veteran of Pathé Frères; and Émile Chautard, cited in von Sternberg's autobiography as a mentor, who had been an actor on the Paris stage and then a director for Éclair.[50] Von Sternberg is likely to have been familiar with the symbolist experiments of Maurice Tourneur, *The Blue Bird* and *Prunella;* these, although distributed by Famous Players-Lasky, were made at production facilities in Fort Lee, New Jersey, which was also the production center for World.[51] Starting with the first films over which he could exert control, von Sternberg demonstrates a marked interest in highly stylized camerawork and mise en scene that is much closer to aestheticism than to naturalism. In the case of *The Salvation Hunters,* this emphasis is conjoined with a symbolism even more marked than that for which von Stroheim was criticized.

The Salvation Hunters was released in February 1925, just two months after *Greed.* It was independently produced and directed; in 1965 von Sternberg recalled that he had had a budget of $6,000 and that shooting was completed in three and a half weeks.[52] The film impressed Charlie Chaplin and Mary Pickford, and it was picked up by United Artists. However, reviews were generally hostile, and it does not seem to have been widely distributed. The status of the surviving copies is not entirely clear. Of the two prints that are at the Library of Congress, one, in 35mm, has been drastically cut for what appears to be reasons of censorship. The 16mm print is more complete but may not be the version released by UA, although one cannot determine this definitively from the published reviews. Given the uncertainty as to what was actually seen in the 1920s, I have based the following summary on the longer version.

In keeping with the abstraction typical of symbolist drama, none of the characters have proper names. The Boy, the Girl, and the Child, all destitute, live on a dredge that pulls mud and sand from the waterfront.[53] The Boy, who has been unsuccessful in his attempts to find employment on the waterfront, dreams of something better for himself and the Girl. The Brute, the man in charge of the dredge, makes an advance to the Girl, which she rejects with contempt. The Boy and Girl watch as the Brute admonishes the Child and then beats him. When the Boy does nothing to help, the Girl calls him a coward. Finally the Boy helps the Child out of the Brute's grip, and they find a hiding place on the rig. Later the Boy tries to convince the Girl that they should "get away from the mud." She is dubious: "There's mud all over." The film does not motivate her change of mind very clearly, but finally she joins the Boy and the Child in their departure from the dredge.

All three walk in the city, tired and hungry.[54] They meet a pimp, the Man, who offers them lodging with the aim of getting the girl to work for him. The Man cautions the Woman, a whore who lives with him, not to feed the three young people so as to make the Girl more tractable. The next day the Boy is not successful in finding work. He comes back with only a stick of chewing gum for them to share, but in an attempt to amuse his companions he spins a fantasy in which they are wealthy and riding in a fancy car. The Child insists that he is hungry. The Girl makes up and goes out onto the street. She is followed home by a john, the Gentleman (the pick-up and much of the following action inside the flat are not in the Library of Congress's 35mm print). When he sees the Boy and the Child in the apartment, the Gentlemen decides to withdraw, offering them money, which the hungry Child promptly accepts. The pimp stops the Gentleman in the hallway and offers to fix things up for him. He then enters the flat and tries to convince the Girl to oblige. She watches the effect of these negotiations on the Boy, who does nothing. She finally closes the door on both the pimp and the Gentleman waiting in the hall. The Man tells the Woman that he will take the Girl out into the countryside and try to soften her up with some romance.

All five characters travel by car to a grassy hillside with a real estate agent's sign: "HERE 'Your Dreams Come True.'"[55] The Man takes the Girl away to talk to her, while the Woman distracts the Boy. The Child comes between the Girl and the Man, and the Man begins to beat him. The Boy is finally roused to fight and beats up the Man. The Girl, the Boy, and the Child walk off together.

The naturalist influences on the film are evident from the plot summary: a story about derelict characters, much of it shot in real urban locations, which frankly depicts the sexual and monetary negotiations around the act of solicitation. However, the film also shows evidence of symbolist influences. It begins with three titles evoking the power of thought, which conclude, "Our aim has been to photograph a thought—A thought that guides humans who crawl close to the earth—whose lives are simple—who begin nowhere and end nowhere." Evoking an ideology very close to that espoused by Griffith in *Isn't Life Wonderful,* the film explores the capacity of the characters to rise above their environment. The Boy is introduced with the title "This boy was a failure because he believed in failure—a coward because his soul was unripe—only his dreams saved him from destruction, and his blind unreasonable faith in a better day." The film differs from the Griffith example, however, in its radical insistence on the power of the environment to determine the character of the Boy and the Girl, both of whom are fundamentally passive. For most of the film he longs to change his circumstances but proves incapable of actually bettering them. She watches him, hardly daring to expect that things will improve.

The dredge, and especially the movement of its giant claw, are visually dominant in the opening scenes (figures 5 and 6). A title informs us: "The huge claw was a symbol of the boy's faith. He believed that all mud could be brought up into the sun." However, the claw's movement is also linked to the futility of human endeavor. A title explains, "For every load of mud the claw dislodged, the earth laughed and pushed in another." Neither of these titles fully accounts for the way the motif of the dredge functions, however. The Boy's attempt to convince the Girl to leave for the city is articulated in terms of "getting away from the mud," and the claw in the background of so many of the shots in the opening sequences helps to construct the dredge, as well as the mud it carries, as a symbol of all that they seek to leave behind. In Carl Sandburg's interpretation, "The big clamshell shovel, moving, closing, opening, is an incessant figure or symbol in the movement of the first two-thirds of the play. It is ruthless, ironic, necessary, hard to get away from."[56] Less complex and of less visual interest are the shots that pose the pimp beneath a pair of horns that hang inside his apartment. The connotations of priapism seem inescapable, although the reviewer for the *New York Times* (February 2, 1925: 14) thought the pose merely gave him a "diabolical aspect."

In conjunction with the highly explicit symbolic structure of the film, certain shots of the waterfront utilize soft focus imagery to convey a much more amorphous sense of atmosphere. Note, for example, the extreme softness of the edges of the shot of the Boy walking along the edge of the harbor (figure 7). This kind of aestheticized cinematography, seemingly out of place in a realistic treatment of urban derelicts and their haunts, is even more pronounced in *The Docks of New York*.

Von Sternberg's distinctive use of actors in *The Salvation Hunters* elicited much commentary at the time of the film's release. Von Sternberg seems to have opted for an acting style entirely unlike the grotesque postures and facial expressions adopted by the principals in *Greed*. His actors move very little and employ facial expressions only sparingly. Take, for example, the extremely dedramatized presentation of the interaction between the Girl and the Boy, when the Man (for clarity described as the pimp in what follows) tries to convince her to oblige the Gentleman. Although this particular scene, taken from the Library of Congress's 16mm print, may have been censored from the version released by United Artists, it has been chosen because it is indicative of von Sternberg's tendency to

5

6

7

restrain his actors even in a scene that would seem to call for highly wrought emotions and big gestures:

1. Medium long shot of the Gentleman standing in the hallway. The pimp enters from the apartment shared by the children. He approaches the man, nods and mouths "I fixed it." The man nods.

2. Extreme long shot of the apartment interior. The Girl walks to the open door.

3. Medium shot, frontal view, of the Boy sitting on the couch, looking down.

4. Medium long shot of the girl, in left profile. She turns slowly to look behind her.

5. Medium long shot, her point of view, of the Boy on couch, showing the back of his head and a quarter view of his face. He does not look back at her.

6. The Girl as before, looking in his direction.

7. Medium shot of the Boy on the couch in a frontal view, i.e., not from her point of view. He rubs his hands and his face works.

8. The Girl as before, looking in his direction.

9. Medium long shot of the Gentleman, and behind him the pimp, waiting beside the apartment door. The pimp turns and looks into the apartment, then looks back at the Gentleman.

10. The Girl as before, looking in the direction of the Boy. She turns more in his direction and shrugs slightly, raising her hands. She closes the door.

11. Medium long shot of the door hitting the pimp, who stands beside it. He steps away from it and looks in the direction of the door.

12. Long shot of the apartment. The Girl walks over to the couch and sits next to the Boy.

13. Medium long shot of the pimp. He opens the door and looks in.

14. Long shot of the apartment, the pimp now inside, holding onto the open door. He says something to the Girl. She shakes her head very slightly. The pimp withdraws.

There are no dialogue titles and very little in the way of facial expression to signal the interior states of the characters. The one shot in which the Boy clearly registers distress with his face and hands is not seen by the Girl, whose point of view only reveals the back of his head. Georgia Hale, as the Girl, displays neither chagrin nor shock at the proposition made to her. She watches the Boy dispassionately, waiting for a signal that does not come. Her refusal of the pimp's offer is indicated by relatively small actions— shutting the door, shaking her head—and her solidarity with the Boy is indicated by the simple act of sitting down beside him. In this scene, as throughout the film as a whole, the spectator must intuit the characters' feelings and motivations on the basis of a limited number of small gestures and the direction and object of the actor's look, often specified through point-of-view editing. The restraint of the acting strikes me as much more modern than that employed in *Greed,* and, with the possible exception of the reduced style adopted in sophisticated comedy, to be discussed in chapter 3, it has few precedents in the American cinema of the early 1920s.

The reception of *The Salvation Hunters* was by no means uniform. *Variety* (February 4, 1925: 33) found the film pretentious, apparently largely because of its symbolist, as opposed to its naturalist, aspirations:

"'The Salvation Hunters' is nothing more nor less than another short cast picture to express an apparently Teutonic theory of fatalism. The derelicts of the world are the characters and a flock of freshman philosophy the theme. The idea of the whole thing is that, although we're born in the mud, we can lift ourselves by our own bootstraps until we see the sun. That's the alleged original idea." The *New York Times* reviewer objected to the depressing tone of the film, which he characterized as "mud, indolence and depravity, with a ray of sunshine thrown in at the end." This reviewer also recommended that the director alleviate tedium by "picturing natural movements with his characters," complaining that the actors "move their heads very slowly when talking to one another."

The reviewers who praised the film tended to construct it as a naturalist work of art. The review in *Exceptional Photoplays* explained the film's premise as "the effect of environment upon a young boy and girl," and the deployment of actors was understood to express this theme:

> How real is the battering on two souls of the constant fall and rise of the dredge, all day long, day after day. How dulling and killing this effect is on these two young minds is disclosed to the audience by the slow moving, often motionless, poses of the girl and the boy on the scow. The slow tempo is far from the nervous action popularly supposed to represent motion picture art. And yet, these quiet, monotonous scenes often reveal in an insistent manner the dull unhappiness of two persons imprisoned by circumstances.
>
> There are other touches, too—such as when in the squalid room in the slums the two feel defeat creeping up the stair. They sit and look. That is all. But in the director's hands what does this almost motionless motion picture scene not tell us?[57]

Thus the film's most notable stylistic eccentricities, the visual prominence of the dredge and the impassivity of the actors, were explained as the director's way of representing the weight of material circumstances upon the human spirit.

Other positive reviews stressed the film's simplicity, in terms reminiscent of those employed in many of the reviews already discussed. *Film Daily* (February 8, 1925: 10) called *The Salvation Hunters* "a bit of life" as opposed to a "drama" or "melodrama." The review continued, "There's practically nothing to the story and there's not much more to the production. Sternberg didn't have to spend a fortune on sets to make a fine picture. But he's shown a wealth of understanding, an abundance of human interest and realism—even if it isn't always pleasant—plus a quantity of deft touches that can not help but make his effort outstanding." *Moving Picture World* (February 14,

1925: 701) assessed the director's treatment of the theme of faith's conquering adverse circumstances: "How does his treatment of this theme differ from the accustomed handling? By the employment of symbolism, exceptional simplicity and straightforwardness in direction and unusual restraint in the acting of his players; by reducing his sets to a minimum, discarding the obvious as far as possible and avoiding the theatric." This astute review notes both the symbolist predilections of the film and the pared-down quality resulting not only from the low production budget but from the handling of the actors and the deliberately flat presentation of events.

While historians often class *The Docks of New York* with *The Salvation Hunters*, it actually emerged at a very different point in von Sternberg's career and was very differently assessed by the trade press. *The Docks of New York* was released in September 1928, after von Sternberg had experienced commercial success working in the genre of crime melodrama (not yet then called the "gangster film"). *Underworld,* with George Bancroft playing the head of a crime syndicate, had been released in August 1927.[58] Another crime film, now lost, *The Dragnet,* appeared in May 1928, this one with Bancroft playing a tough urban cop. *The Docks of New York* provided yet another rough and tumble part for the star.

Bill Roberts, a stoker on a commercial vessel, has one night ashore in New York. He rescues Mae, who has attempted suicide by drowning, and takes her to a room in a waterfront dive, the Sandbar, stealing some clothes out of a pawnshop for her. At the same time one of the officers on the same vessel, the Third Engineer, discovers the wife he had deserted three years before working as a prostitute in the dive. During the course of the evening in the Sandbar, the two men quarrel and almost fight over Mae. Bill marries Mae on a lark, to the delight of the drunken denizens of the establishment. Immediately after the wedding he tells a pal that he is more or less serious, "Who says I want to get rid of her?" However, at breakfast the next morning he informs the Third Engineer that it was all in fun and he intends to ship out as usual. After Bill's departure, the Third Engineer makes advances to Mae, whereupon his embittered wife kills him. Bill returns briefly to help Mae, who stands accused of the crime. But when the wife's confession frees the girl, Bill shoves off again. His ship departs, and he is back at work in the boiler room when he has a change of heart. He jumps ship and returns to find that Mae has been arrested for possession of stolen clothes. He takes the sentence the judge would have imposed on her and asks her to wait for his release.

This plot has extensive debts to naturalism. It reworks, and perhaps improves upon, the story of *Anna Christie*. Suspense revolves not around the man's discovery of the woman's shady past, as in O'Neill's play, but rather around whether the man will prove reliable. The parallel between Mae and the Third Engineer's wife is stressed at several points. For example, when the minister calls for the ring during the impromptu wedding ceremony, the wife lends hers to the bride, remarking, "I hope it does you more good than it did me." The next morning, after the murder, the wife repeats the sentiment: as the police lead her away, she tells Mae, "I hope you have better luck than me—but I doubt it."

Notwithstanding the naturalist underpinnings of its plot, the film represents one of the acmes of aestheticism in the late silent period. Both the boiler room and the night scenes on the docks are dominated by low-key lighting, augmented by prodigious amounts of smoke and fog. The elliptical sequence of Mae's attempted suicide and Bill's rescue makes striking use of reflections and silhouetted figures. Exquisitely tawdry, the Sandbar set provides an exceptionally dense mise en scene. Large numbers of extras fill several spatially distinct areas, among them a bar with tables around it and a dance floor with a raised platform that holds a player piano (and later the minister). The camera frequently tracks through this crowded space, the movement revealing nautical motifs such as nets and a ship's wheel that protrudes into the frame. These techniques are far removed from the location shooting and simple, pared down sets of *The Salvation Hunters*.

Most of the contemporary reviewers did not comment on the highly stylized mise en scene of *The Docks of New York*, although *Variety* (September 19, 1928: 12) compared the "foggy mystic water shots" on the waterfront to the visual quality of Borzage's *Street Angel*. But the same reviewer found the Sandbar set to be "a faithful replica of the barrel houses that used to dot the waterfront." Despite the putative realism of the setting, *Variety* did not consider the plot to be an instance of naturalism but placed it, rather, in the context of the previous crime films that von Sternberg had made with Bancroft: "The sense of conflict which existed in 'Underworld' and 'The Drag Net' is absent here." Although *Motion Picture News* (September 22, 1928: 928) found a "hint" of the realism of *The Salvation Hunters* in the atmosphere and background of *The Docks of New York*, it praised the film largely for its underworld elements: "Von Sternberg knows what he's shooting at since he directed 'Underworld,' and his newest essay along the paths of crime once again indicates that he knows his slums and his boys 'who take 'em for a ride.'"

Only one review saw *The Docks of New York* as a calculated departure from conventional plot formulae. Richard Watts, writing in the *Film Mercury*, argued, "In *The Docks of New York*, von Sternberg has a story that is essentially a melodrama in story, background and characterization. His hero is one of those hard-boiled he-men, given to smashing up waterfront dives at the slightest opportunity. His heroine is one of those sad-eyed sentimental prostitutes so often encountered in the works of Mr. Eugene O'Neill and his lesser colleagues." Following a summary of the plot, which included references to Bill's rescue of Mae, the bar-room brawls, and the shooting, he notes, "To all of this potentially sensational material, Mr. von Sternberg adopts the most casual attitude imaginable. His plot always seems a distinctly side issue with him. He starts just as if he were all set to build up to a vigorous climax and then he calmly refuses to get excited, while his narrative, all set for something smashing, slides off into semi-placidity. In many a director, you would say that this neglect of the climactic was the result of an inability to accomplish it. But in *The Docks of New York* it is so obvious that this truncated manner of melodramatic narration is intentional, that you realize it comes from the intent of a man who knows just what he is doing."[59] Von Sternberg's abjuration of the highly dramatic and overwrought is evident, for example, in the decision to elide the shooting of the Third Engineer. It may also be found in the well-known scene that follows. Mae, deeply regretting Bill's imminent departure, remains largely stoical, a tear evident only when she attempts to sew the pocket of his shirt: we see a blurred point-of-view shot of a needle that she is unable to thread. The understated acting style and avoidance of dramatic climaxes in *The Docks of New York* recalls the more extreme experimentation with dedramatized narrative found in *The Salvation Hunters*. And, despite the film's aestheticized mise en scene, it provides one of the most convincing connections between *The Docks of New York* and the tradition of naturalist-inspired filmmaking that, at least since *A Romance of Happy Valley*, had been characterized by the avoidance of "melodrama."

While *Greed, The Salvation Hunters,* and *The Docks of New York* were considered sordid, a "lower-depths" model of naturalism, films such as Vidor's *The Crowd* and Paul Fejös's *Lonesome* concerned themselves with the lives of everyday working people in the city. *The Crowd* traces the life of John Sims, an ambitious boy with great expectations for his future. His father dies when he is but a youth, and at the age of twenty-one John goes to work for an insurance company in New York City. Through a coworker, Bert, he meets and marries Mary, whose more prosperous brothers look down on him. Husband and wife struggle to survive on his meager income and have a spat about their cramped living quarters. When his son is born, John feels a renewed impetus to become "somebody." Then a second baby arrives, a girl. John has remained at the insurance company and received only a small increase in his pay, in contrast with the more forceful Bert, who has risen in the company ranks and become John's boss. Husband and wife quarrel over his failure to make good. John enters an advertising slogan contest and wins $500, but the toys he buys for the children with the money prove a misfortune. Running across the street to receive her gifts, his little girl is struck by a truck and dies. Grief-stricken, John gives up his job. He is unable to obtain another, and Mary goes to work to keep the family. After a violent quarrel with Mary, John walks to the railway yard and considers jumping off a bridge, but he does not have the courage to carry through with the suicide. His son's faith in him raises his spirits. He gets a job as a sandwich-board man promoting a restaurant: he walks up and down the street juggling, wearing a clown costume. Mary, under the influence of her brothers, prepares to leave him. With money from his new job John brings her small gifts, including tickets to a vaudeville show that evening. She cannot bring herself to leave. The family attends the vaudeville show, notices John's advertising slogan in the theater program, and laughs at the show.

Vidor describes having shot seven endings due to uncertainty about how to conclude the film, and he recalls that MGM distributed it giving exhibitors a choice between the ending described above and an alternate, less "realistic" one.[60] MGM script files contain a fragment of a cutting continuity in which the film concludes as follows: Mary decides to stay with John, a title covers an ellipsis of many years, and the final scene shows the family, with a new baby, gathered around a Christmas tree. John, now a successful advertising executive, is admired by Mary's mother and brothers.[61] Both *Variety* (February 22, 1928: 20) and Welford Beaton in the *Film Spectator* describe the film being shown with two different endings at its premiere.[62]

The *New York Times* (February 20, 1928: 14) praised the virtuoso cinematography, which utilized a highly mobile camera, singling out the well-known shot in which the camera appears to mount a skyscraper and then penetrates the open-plan office of the insurance company, lined with rows of identical desks, coming to rest on John. Gilbert Seldes in the *New Republic* likewise expressed admiration of Vidor's technique. But in addition to the flashy cinematography, he valued the simplicity of the plot. Arguing that the film broke "completely with the stereotype of the feature film," he wrote, "There is virtually no plot; there is no exploitation of sex in the love interest; there is no physical climax; no fight; no scheduled thrill. The characters, all commonplace people, act singularly unlike moving picture characters and singularly like human beings; there is no villain, no villainy, no success."[63] Like Seldes, *Exceptional Photoplays* considered *The Crowd* a welcome relief from the "fairy tale" diet usually accorded

motion picture fans and noted: "The picture has next to no plot. There are
no fights in it and no big moments."[64] This observation does not seem to
me entirely accurate for a film in which a baby is run down by a truck in
front of her parents' eyes, but it would be fair to say that much of the plot
is systematically anticlimactic. The narrative is structured by the failure of
John's career despite his early ambitions. Individual scenes are similarly
built around anticipated big moments that fail to materialize: the suicide
attempt that simply peters out, the separation between husband and wife
averted through John's simple gifts, and Mary's habitual care for him.

Vidor's use of the anticlimax as a structuring principle points to one
aspect of his narrative that differentiates it rather strongly from comparable films of the early 1920s. In *A Romance of Happy Valley* Griffith may
have poked fun at John Logan's aspirations for a big city career but, at the
crucial moment, the frog swims. Reviewers of *The Crowd* were strongly
divided over the merits of a story in which an ambitious young man ends
up walking the street in a clown costume. *Exceptional Photoplays* was
impressed by Vidor's daring: "A picture so drab, so devoid of our national
optimism, so unmindful of the 'send them home smiling' slogan of our
popular directors who are so sure of knowing what the public wants, must
have some outstanding virtues to carry it to success." Welford Beaton
thought that both the director and the studio deserved credit for attempting a film that was out of the ordinary, but that it was ill-advised to frus-
trate spectators' expectations for their screen surrogates:

> The discouraged stenographer is inspired by the fact that the stenogra-
> pher in the picture marries the boss, and the traveling salesman is given
> fresh hope when he sees Dick Dix or Bill Haines, playing a salesman,
> cop the millionaire's daughter in the final reel. . . . But what does any-
> one get from *The Crowd*? . . . With extraordinary vigor and conviction
> it plants the utter futility of endeavoring to battle one's way to success.
> It shows that the crowd is too powerful to be combatted, and it breathes
> hopelessnesss and despair. All these drawbacks are accentuated by the
> excellence of the production from a motion picture angle.

I presume that similar reasoning underlay the *Variety* review, which
found the film "a drab actionless story of ungodly length" and an unlikely
prospect for release as a "special" on Broadway. The reviewer commented
that the only character who showed any spirit was Mary: "Casting aside
his permanent desk job through mental strain over the death by a truck of
his little daughter, the young husband tries other jobs in vain, until his
wife, disgusted, finally slaps him in the face and walks out. That is the sole
bit of action." Both positive and negative reviews point to what was most

unusual about the plot of *The Crowd* in relation to its precursors: its emphasis on a relatively passive and hapless protagonist. This construction of
character allies the film with both *Greed* and *The Salvation Hunters,* despite
the fact that Vidor's characters are less spectacularly "low," and despite his
predilection for a much more sentimental treatment of the family.

As already noted, in the latter half of the 1920s naturalist or quasi-
naturalist treatments of small-town life undergo a decided shift in tone.
The bucolic rendering of village life in the films by Griffith and Charles
Ray, and even the relatively cheerful satire of provincial domesticity found
in such films as *Miss Lulu Bett* and *Main Street,* give way to explorations
of deeply exploitative families, predatory sexuality, and weak or guilt-ridden
protagonists. Although most of the innovations in rural naturalism appeared
after 1927, well after the release of *Greed* and *Salvation Hunters,* Victor
Sjöström's first American film, *Name the Man,* anticipates this trend. An
adaptation of a best-selling Hall Caine story set in the Isle of Man, the film
went into production about the same time as *Greed* and was released
before it in January 1924.[65] The story concerns the seduction of a peasant
girl by the son of the island's deemster or chief justice. According to tradition, the son inherits his father's post, and he is called upon to pass sentence upon the girl for the infanticide of the child he himself had fathered.[66]
Apparently in the same vein as *Name the Man,* Sjöström's 1925 *The Tower
of Lies,* adapted from a novel by Selma Lagerlöf, and starring Norma
Shearer and Lon Chaney, remains a lost film. While press accounts of the
plot seem garbled, there can be no doubt that it was a tale of sexual betrayal
and male guilt set in the Swedish countryside.

Karl Brown's *Stark Love,* released in late February 1927, was shot in the
Great Smokey Mountains of North Carolina with a nonprofessional cast
drawn largely from the village where the action was set. The film undertakes a seemingly anthropological documentation of the way the moun-
taineers live and work. We see wheat being milled into flour, the dividing
of the spoils after the men have finished hunting, women preparing meals
over an open fire, and sleeping quarters being organized for a large family
living in a one-room cabin. A "funeral feast," a yearly celebration for generations of past dead, coincides with the arrival of the circuit preacher,
and all "wild marriages" are legalized in a single ceremony. Following a
funeral, the film demonstrates the building of a typical burial mound. The
documentary aspects of the film led both *Variety* (March 2, 1927: 16) and
the *New York Times* (February 28, 1927: 22) to compare it to Flaherty's
Nanook of the North. But the plot, obviously a dramatic construct, engages
with the traditions of naturalist-inspired filmmaking.

The people of Wolf Trap Creek live isolated from the world in a community that treats women as the property of men and as their beasts of burden. Rob Warwick has been reading about the polite ways of the world and tells his friend Barbara Allen about the conventions of chivalry. Rob asks her if she would like to be treated with love and respect, to be taken care of and protected. She informs him that she can protect herself and is surprised when he offers to carry her sack of flour home from the mill. Later, at the Warwick cabin, Rob's father reacts with sarcasm when the boy offers to help his mother, who is ill, by chopping wood.

Rob tells Barbara that he will accompany the itinerant preacher to the city and sell his horse so that he can afford to go to school. She encourages him to go and says that Rob should not have told her about all the "beautiful things," because she is now dissatisfied. He promises to send her to school and to take her away with him to the city.

Rob and the preacher travel to the city and sell the horse. In the village Barbara dreams of better things while chopping wood. She pretends to shake hands with the axe and talks politely to imaginary interlocutors. Later, realizing that she has resin on her shift from the pine she has been cutting, she goes into the house to change clothes. Her father and brothers watch her, and we see her naked from behind. A title explains that there is no privacy in the cabin. She looks off wistfully in response to the men's laughter. At the school Rob enrolls Barbara in his place. He is told to walk home by an alternate route, as the river is flooding and he no longer has a horse to ford it.

While Rob is away his mother dies. Jason, in need of someone to clean and take care of the children, asks Barbara's father, Quill, if the girl may come and live with him. He promises to legalize the marriage at the next visit of the itinerant preacher. Barbara is sent with Jason against her will.

Rob arrives home first. By the time Jason and Barbara walk home, the foot bridge is out, and they have to wade through the water to cross the river. Rob is appalled when Jason, pinching a bit of Barbara's exposed midriff, announces that she is the new mother. He explains that he has enrolled Barbara in school and pleads with his father to let her go. When Jason refuses, the men struggle. The more powerful Jason beats his son severely and deposits him outside by the river bank. When Jason returns, Barbara picks up the ax that once belonged to Rob's mother. He seems to be afraid that she will kill him, but she merely hacks her way through the lock on the door and warns him not to follow.

Outside, Barbara discovers that the river has risen still further and that Rob is now floating in it. Barbara joins him, and together they grab a log and float downstream. They go through some rapids and finally make it to a point of dry land. A title informs us that a new life starts the next morning. They walk through fields and are last seen with their arms around each other, looking down a hill to the highly lit city beyond.

In decided contrast to the films of the early 1920s, *Stark Love* avoids any trace of nostalgia for a rural past. The city represents the only hope of a decent life, whereas the village in the Great Smoky Mountains is characterized by harsh working conditions and the sexual exploitation of women, a point emphasized in what is perhaps too blatantly Oedipal a scenario. The plot recalls *The Salvation Hunters* in its depiction of a young couple trapped by intolerable social conditions who manage to escape to an uncertain future at the film's close. The relative impassivity of the actors, possibly a function of the use of nonprofessionals, further recalls von Sternberg's film. With the exception of the scene in which Barbara threatens Jason with the ax, the film avoids overt emotional display. In emotionally important scenes such as when the couple courts, Rob tells the preacher he has sacrificed his place at school for Barbara, or Jason speaks a rough eulogy for his dead wife, facial expressions remain neutral and gestures are restricted to functional, everyday tasks like smoking a pipe or hefting a bag of flour. The similarities between *The Salvation Hunters* and *Stark Love* help to position the latter as a relatively modern reworking of rural naturalism. Perhaps this accounts for *Variety's* judgment that "if there are any high-brows in the neighborhood they are going to rave over it," although the film was also thought to contain enough "raw melodrama" to attract the "low-brows."

The release of *Stark Love* was followed by a number of films in the same vein. *Wild Geese*, which, as noted at the beginning of this chapter, *Variety* found exceedingly dull, was released by Tiffany-Stahl in November 1927. To my knowledge no print has survived, but the novel by Maria Ostenso upon which it is based concerns a Canadian farm family ruled by an autocratic and land-hungry patriarch who works his children without mercy for the benefit of the farm. The *New York Times* (December 5, 1927: 26) found the scene in which a rebellious daughter throws an ax at her father reminiscent of *Stark Love*.[67]

The best-known example of Sjöström's naturalist work in America, *The Wind*, an adaptation of Dorothy Scarborough's novel, appeared in November 1928. This film provides a clear illustration of the extent to which rural films of this period depart from a pastoral rendering of the countryside; the landscape is shown to be hostile, or at best indifferent, to human needs and aspirations. Coming from Virginia to live with her cousins on the plains,

Letty confronts cyclones and wind storms that, along with the social isolation attendant upon ranch life, increasingly frighten her and endanger her
fragile mental equilibrium. As in *Stark Love* and *Wild Geese,* Letty finds
herself at the mercy of a hostile family. The warm reception given her by her
cousin and his children provokes jealousy on the part of Cora, her cousin's
wife. Cora eventually drives Letty from the house, effectively forcing her
into marriage with Lige, a rough rancher whom she had previously refused.
Despite his lack of fine manners, Lige behaves kindly when he discovers
Letty's distaste for him. He decides not to consummate their marriage and to
try to earn enough money to send her away. When a wind storm arises most
of the ranchers, including Lige, depart, hoping to corral some wild horses.
The cattle dealer Roddy takes advantage of Letty's fear of being alone, and of
the wind, and rapes her. She shoots him the next morning and tries to bury
him in the blowing sands. This dramatic climax recalls Barbara's confrontation with Jason in *Stark Love,* although it could not have been taken from
that film, as it derives from a novel published in 1925. The confrontation in
The Wind is obviously more extreme, both in its representation of the man's
sexual aggression and the violence of the woman's response.

Several endings were considered for *The Wind.* The synopsis of the original novel in the MGM script files recounts Scarborough's ending, in which
the wind uncovers Roddy's corpse, and Letty, driven mad, runs off into the
raging storm. The studio reader continues, "A first-rate tragedy, done with
fine honesty and truth. It would be immensely effective on the screen, but
would probably be a box-office failure. However, it could be made into
another 'Greed.'"[68] This ending does not seem to have been seriously considered, for it does not figure in any of the versions of the script by Francis
Marion. Rather, Marion seems to have essayed different ways to motivate a
reunion between Lige and Letty. The phantom horses that figure Letty's
horror of the wind in the finished film are doubled in several script versions
by real wild horses that stampede and threaten the fleeing girl until she is
rescued by her husband. In several early variants of the plot Roddy, though
wounded, survives the murder attempt.[69] In the ending finally selected, Lige
returns to find Letty at home, and the two are reconciled with only minimal
discussion about the circumstances of Roddy's death. It is the simplest and,
in my view, the most effective of the proposed endings.

Reactions to *The Wind* were lukewarm at best. *Variety* (November 7,
1928: 15) acknowledged the film's technical excellence but considered the
story "poison for screen purposes." While it is not surprising that this grim
story would have been considered a dim prospect, more interesting is the
opinion expressed by a number of reviewers that the film was too explicit

in its evocation of the threatening landscape. *Exceptional Photoplays* complained: "Its atmospheric chord is twanged too often."[70] The *New York Times* (November 5, 1928) agreed, "Victor Seastrom hammers home his points until one longs for just a suggestion of subtlety."[71] *Photoplay*, which praised Lillian Gish's performance as Letty, took a humorous tack in describing the setting: "Out where men are men and weather is weather."[72] Although highly esteemed by present-day critics, *The Wind* seems to have been considered overwrought in the 1920s. Its reception stands in sharp contrast with that of the more restrained, documentary-like *Stark Love*, which garnered much more positive reviews.

It seems clear, then, that following the release of *Greed* in 1925 both the urban and rural strains of film naturalism assume a more full-bodied pessimism and make a decisive break with the bucolic romances of simple folk that had predominated in the first half of the decade. The films also became more ambitious than the modest stories made by Griffith, Charles Ray, and William deMille, a change reflected in the production budgets of the films. *True Heart Susie, The Old Swimmin' Hole,* and *Miss Lulu Bette* were program pictures made at relatively low cost, a situation that changed with Ince's *Anna Christie*, and even more decisively with *Greed*. Despite the fact that von Stroheim's film as well as many of those that followed were judged bad commercial bets by the trade press, they commanded long production schedules, high budgets, often top-flight technical personnel, and, less frequently, stars. In addition to *Greed*, relevant examples include Sjöström's early films *Name the Man* and *The Tower of Lies,* and *The Crowd* and *The Wind*. Although it was not completed as originally planned, Murnau's *City Girl* may also be added to this list. *Variety* (April 9, 1930: 39) noted that this film, about a Chicago waitress who marries the son of a ruthless and domineering Minnesota wheat farmer, was scheduled to be released in 1928 as a "potential two-buck topper," i.e., a special. However, Fox decided to add dialogue sequences and reshot some of the footage, and the resulting severely truncated and altered print was not released until 1930, when *Variety* judged it to be only fit for the "grinds."[73]

In addition to the high budgets accorded to the naturalist films of the late 1920s, the films were stylistically more ambitious, self-conscious, and flashy than those of the first half of the decade. Indeed, some films became vulnerable to criticism at this level. *Variety* chastised Josef von Sternberg, for example, for the "freshman philosophy" enunciated in the opening titles of *The Salvation Hunters*. The overt symbolism of *Greed* and *The Wind* disturbed even sympathetic critics. But on the whole the films were well received in venues such as *Exceptional Photoplays, Life,* and the *New*

York Times, and garnered praises from intellectuals such as Gilbert Seldes, Iris Barry, and Carl Sandburg. It would be fair to say that by the late 1920s naturalism provided the framework for most serious, intellectually ambitious filmmaking within the classical Hollywood cinema.

Yet despite the vitality and importance of this tradition, these films occupied a marginal status within the industry. The trade press, and particularly *Variety*, consistently described them as drab and downbeat and unlikely to appeal to a mass audience. Studio executives also seem to have entertained doubts about their commercial viability. That is why so many of these projects suffered extensive interference—consider the hatchet jobs done on *Greed* and *City Girl*, the multiple endings filmed for *The Crowd*, the multiple endings scripted for *The Wind*. Moreover, it seems likely that *The Salvation Hunters*, arguably more important than *Greed* in its influence on rural dramas such as *Stark Love* and *Wild Geese*, would never have been made at all had it not been produced completely outside the parameters of the studio system. Given the tenuous position occupied by the naturalist films and filmmakers, how are we then to understand their influence outside the confines of the prestige picture? How, if at all, did they affect the vast bulk of Hollywood's output?

This study is primarily concerned with popular Hollywood genres: the sophisticated comedy, the male adventure story, the seduction plot, and the romantic drama. Although individual films within these categories were certainly directly influenced by naturalism in its literary or filmic variants, I would not maintain that many were, nor that Hollywood films *en bloc* became in some sense more "naturalist." I would argue, however, that some of the most prominent stylistic and narrative features of the naturalist films recurred in other generic contexts. Thus, in discussions of films otherwise quite remote from naturalist concerns, one finds praise for simple over complex plots, for dedramatized scenes and situations, and for restrained modes of storytelling. It would be decades before the Hollywood cinema readily accepted (and could prevent the censorship of) the sort of frankly salacious material to be found in *Greed* or *The Salvation Hunters*. But across a wide spectrum of Hollywood filmmaking in the 1920s one finds a rejection of blatantly didactic or highly moralized narratives. It became an insult to describe a film as "Pollyannaish," and critics came to value films that engaged a darker or more cynical view of sexuality and of marriage. The kind of "low" gestures employed in *Greed* had always been acceptable in comedy, and, as Seldes notes, been de rigueur in slapstick. But over the course of the 1920s a premium came to be placed on the actor's informal carriage and bearing in dramatic contexts as well, where this style was prized for its realism. Experimentation with intertitles included efforts to mimic vernacular speech, as von Stroheim had done in *Greed,* as well as a more general movement to reduce the number of intertitles and to make them more "snappy." I will argue that the net effect of these alterations in filmmaking conventions, and in the criteria for judging films, was a diminution of sentimentality and the taste for sentiment.

3   Sophisticated Comedy

A weak little drab of a vacuous, aimless woman, too puerile to be
moral, and almost too cowardly to be brazenly immoral, pitted
against two lovers—one a type of the bestial Broadway booze-
feeder, representing immorality, the other the figure of a vigorous
Lothario, suggesting non-morality—made out a sensational case at
the Stuyvesant Theatre last night, in a play called *The Easiest Way*.
It purported to sketch the familiar picture of the theatre-woman,
struggling for her virtue amid the alleged temptations of
Broadway—temptations that are popularly supposed to begin at
the lobster-palace and end at the devil, but which last night began
at the devil and ended at the lobster-palace. It did sketch this
picture, with daubs of color, splashes of verity and a dazzling
varnish of candor at which a sophisticated audience laughed last
night, at which a less sophisticated audience might feel impelled
to grieve.

ALAN DALE, "Eugene Walter's 'The Easiest Way'"

The definition of sophisticated comedy is usually taken for granted:
opposed to slapstick, akin to the high comedy of manners or to farce, and
best epitomized by the silent films of Ernst Lubitsch. But the idea of
sophistication went well beyond the boundaries of comedy as such, as is
suggested by this 1909 review of Eugene Walter's drama *The Easiest Way*.[1]
I shall seek to illuminate the more general distinction between sophisticated and naïve taste as a prelude to understanding how the genre became
recognized in the trade press during the 1920s and to explaining its importance for filmmakers throughout the industry.

Throughout the decade, and for most of the popular press as well as
the trade press, sophisticated taste is attributed to the clientele of the big
first-run theaters on Broadway and other metropolitan centers, whereas
more naïve tastes are attributed to the neighborhood and small-town
theaters. This opposition is augmented by one between adult and family
audiences. These oppositions are so stable that they make the historian
wary. Surely some families attended first-run theaters in New York? Surely
there were adventurous exhibitors and filmgoers in rural America? The
latter would seem to be indicated, for example, by the apparent success of
E. A. Dupont's *Variety* in rural districts. This German film was described as

out of the ordinary and a welcome departure from typical Hollywood fare by small-town exhibitors who reported doing good business with it in *Moving Picture World*'s "Straight from the Shoulder" column.[2] Moreover, as Jennifer Chung has pointed out in a study of the small-town reception of sophisticated comedy, many local newspapers even in medium-sized cities did not have access to prints early enough for a reporter to write about a film before it played. By the 1920s reviews in local small-town papers were most frequently syndicated (and thus, most commonly, from a reviewer situated in a large city), derived from studio-produced press releases, or drawn from papers in New York.[3] To some extent, then, the barometers of taste in Appleton, Wisconsin, were set in New York. This is not to suggest that small-town film culture was identical to that found in the key cities but rather that the trade press discourse probably exaggerated the differences between big cities and small towns, differences that, in any case, have just begun to be systematically documented.[4] I do not intend to compare actual rural film-going habits with urban ones on the strength of the trade press discourse but propose, rather, to use the discussion of hick or naïve taste to get a sense of what was considered old-fashioned and morally or stylistically conservative. Such an investigation should help us to understand the formal innovations of sophisticated comedy in a new light.

Naïve taste was held to be conservative in sexual matters, mindful of a film's suitability for children, and easily offended. An early example of this assessment may be found in the reviews for the Olive Thomas comedy *Upstairs and Down* (1919).[5] The film was adapted from a stage play described by *Wid's Daily* (June 15, 1919: 22) as "a cynical smart set comedy that scored on Broadway largely because it gained a reputation of being risque [*sic*]." The reviewer cautioned, "It strikes me as being essentially a city show, or at any rate one best adapted to please a moderately sophisticated audience. There is not much that can be called heart interest and the worldly-wise attitude of the characters may not exactly fit in with the ideas of a family group."

Naïve audiences were also thought to be attached to a highly moralistic, if not overtly religious, tone, qualities deemed old-fashioned by *Variety* as early as 1921. *Variety* (November 25, 1921: 43) describes the conclusion of the George Loane Tucker melodrama *Ladies Must Live* as follows:

> Before the tragedy an aeroplane has brought two men from the clouds to the house party. Both are presumably wealthy, so the women set their traps for them. One of them is a roughneck, so grabs the lady he wants and rushes off with her in a motor, followed by Anthony and Christine. Anthony's idea is, of course, to prevent "the worst," but he

has hard luck and ends up by having to spend the night in a mountain shack alone with Christine. At this point alarmed exhibitors will catch their breath—but no! The two come out as pure as they went in. In fact, there is enough purity in this film to suit a woman censor in Kansas.

The reviewer concludes that "while this picture may not suit the sophisticated, it is well to remember New York is not all America. In a country where novels by Harold Bell Wright sell to a million, 'Ladies Must Live' may still make money."[6]

Many similar assessments are made by *Variety* reviewers later in the decade. Writing in 1925 of the Fox adaptation of Channing Pollock's *The Fool,* a play about a minister who is pilloried for trying to live out Christ's precepts, *Variety* (April 15, 1925: 36) cautions, "'The Fool' is not primarily a New York special run picture. In the medium-sized cities and the small towns, especially the latter, where there are communities, churches and schools, this one should tie up so closely with people who never go to movies that business is almost assured. In some of the cities it is altogether more than likely that the reviewers will treat this one with scant courtesy. They will be bored to tears at the moralizing and preaching of Daniel Gilchrist, the minister who tried to live like Christ." *Variety* (June 1, 1927: 24) also thought that *Paying the Price* would have a rural appeal: "Because the picture is so very moral and because it oozes over with sweet sentiments and Godly people it may be figured as good for the lesser communities, but a pain in the neck for the big towns." The *Variety* reviewer of *Captain Salvation* (June 29, 1927: 19) approved of its vindication of religion, the "dignified treatment of a theme commonly touched upon in a spirit of cynicism," but also noted, "Whether it will exert an exceptional pull from the generality of screengoers in New York is a question."

Film Daily was not so quick as *Variety* to sneer at old-fashioned stories, but it seems to have accorded with the opinions of the *Variety* reviewers about the kinds of films likely to do best in the neighborhoods and small towns. For example, *Laddie,* from Gene Stratton Porter's best-selling novel of 1913, concerned the relationship between two Indiana farm families initially at odds. The courtships of the older siblings are enabled by Little Sister, whom *Film Daily* (August 22, 1926: 7) described as "a Pollyanna sort of youngster whose philosophy of happiness is contagious." *Film Daily* thought that the film was "likely to prove especially appealing to the small town audience." *Variety* (November 3, 1926: 17) judged that "it is a certainty that the picture will make its best score in the neighborhoods and add further to its lustre in the theatres outside the big cities."

Naïve taste was assumed to encompass a taste for strong effects as well as for an overt moral. In the trade press this was referred to as "hoke" or "hokum."[7] In an essay on stage terminology from 1926 Percy White defines the term:

> Briefly, *hokum* may be defined as any old, time-worn line, gag, or piece of business which has been found by experience to be absolutely sure-fire before any kind of audience. It is something which may be depended upon to get across and wow 'em. Comedy hokum is usually of the simple, slap-stick variety; for instance, the waiter bearing the tray heavily laden with dishes who suddenly trips over nothing and falls with the dishes crashing to the floor in a thousand pieces. Hokum is not always comedy; sometimes it borders on pathos. In the old "ten-twenty-thirty" days it was hokum when the poor factory girl defied the immaculately dressed villain from the upper crust of society to do his worst.[8]

In a 1927 essay on Broadway slang Walter Winchell concurs: "'Hokum,' in case you haven't heard, is low-down stuff. Actors who redden their noses, and wear ill-fitting apparel, and take falls to get laughs, are 'hokum comics' *a la* 'Skid' in Mr. Arthur Hopkins' successful play *Burlesque*."[9] The *Film Daily* (November 29, 1925: 6) review for *Hogan's Alley* is headlined "East side story crammed with heart interest and dizzy melo. Good old hokum gets popular vote as usual." The reviewer comments, "The outstanding fact is that the author is well posted on all the box-office hokum that appeals to average audiences. And so he used most of it—sob stuff, love stuff, slapstick haw-haw, thrills. . . . A Broadway audience guffawed at the slapstick and gulped hard at the meller. . . . Made for the uncritical audience that wants its laughs and thrills laid on broad and heavy. As such—a cleanup. Not for a high-grade clientele." As Winchell's definition of the term indicates, old slapstick gags were thought to appeal to this kind of naïve taste. Within the film industry trade press, however, highly sentimental films were more likely to be dubbed hokum than slapstick. *Variety* (January 21, 1925: 36) wrote of John Ford's *Hearts of Oak*:

> James A. Herne has contrived a plot in which the nobility of sacrifice is stressed to the limit. As a result it becomes difficult at times to swallow the heroic hoke in its entirety. But the suspense is perpetuated and the pathos at the finale is certain to start fountains of tears. . . . It's hokum, but when the little daughter whispers "Goodbye Daddy, dear; I love you very much," in the microphone, and Bosworth is seen thousands of miles away doing a really remarkable piece of acting, it's a mighty hard-boiled egg that won't loosen up for a couple of sniffles. At the Circle they sobbed in unison, women, men, ushers and even assistant managers.[10]

Thus *Variety* reviewers were not always adamantly opposed to hoke. They also found it appropriate in many programmers destined for the neighborhood houses, including *The Closed Gate* (June 1, 1927: 16) and *His Buddy's Wife* (September 8, 1925: 39), although the latter was criticized for employing "the most prolific collection of old lady close ups yet shown" in a scene of a dying mother. The reviewer of *The Thirteenth Juror* (November 23, 1927: 24) praised the film with moderation:

> For the not inconsiderable portion of the fan public who take their drama straight and unsmiling, "The 13th Juror" ought to prove first-rate entertainment. To the sophisticated the play takes itself rather seriously and absurdities creep in, but the story is direct and absorbing in its naive way, working up to a melodramatic climax that for theatric effect is not without its kick. . . . Of course, it's old stuff, but here presented with intensity and obvious aiming for effect that carries it through. A Sunday afternoon crowd at the Roxy might giggle at it, but the sentimental customers of a Washington Heights neighborhood will love its emotional splurge.

There were times, however, when the *Variety* reviewers, at least, thought that filmmakers had gone too far in their attempt to create strong emotion.[11] This was the case for *Burning Words* (June 7, 1923: 25):

> Some of these story makers and directors must think the human race is extremely obtuse. They are never content to picture emotion, sentiment or action in convincing proportion. Everything has to be superlative. . . . That's what happens in "Burning Words." Not content with working up a situation of moderate pathos—briefly, the meeting in a cell between a condemned murderer and his aged mother—they work endless variations on the theme, such as having the mother asking the boy to repeat a childhood prayer learned at her knee, etc. The idea presumably is that emotional appeal must be spread on so thick that it will bore through the densest grade of fans. If it is Universal's deliberate campaign to specialize in pictures for the lowest class of audiences, this is the way to go about it. Only it's rather a cynical notion that the majority of fans are boneheads.

Variety deemed *Pride of the Force* (October 21, 1925: 35)

> one of the hokiest films ever. Combines the tear jerkers of every show that ever played the Stair and Havlin time; its hero is as pure a hero as any one ever created; its mother bears what sorrows Job left over, while the errant son is not only errant but equipped with a backbone of muffin-like consistency. . . . For a bunch of police reporters who haven't laughed in years this is one of the best things ever made. Maybe in the country towns they'd accept it as a great moral preachment, but in the

cities where people know wooden nickels when they see them, it doesn't stand a chance.[12]

The criticism of films for being too moralistic or too obvious or both was not confined to anonymous low-budget productions. Some of the most esteemed filmmakers of the 1910s came to be seen as old-fashioned on these grounds. As Richard Koszarski notes, Lois Weber, praised for her early social problem films, came to be considered passé in the 1920s, in part because of her propensity for didacticism.[13] Pearl Latteier, in a study of Weber's critical reputation in the 1920s, dates the decline in her reputation from such films as *Home* (1919), *Forbidden* (1918), and *To Please One Woman* (1920), although *Variety* (November 23, 1917: 43) objected to moralizing in her films as early as *The Price of a Good Time* (1917).[14] By 1927 *Variety* (November 2, 1927: 18) writes of *Angel of Broadway*, "For New York this title is a dud, but in the hinterland it may well be esteemed box office. Pathe has, in fact, a very good commercial property for the territory west of Hoboken. It's weepy with religion and socky with night club stuff. It's the sort of story Harold Bell Wright might author. . . . Lois Weber, one of the two women directors in the business, has done exceptionally well. Aiming at the tear ducts of the great sentimental American public, she will probably be rewarded with quite a gush."

Although D. W. Griffith's critical reputation did not decline as swiftly as Weber's, and although he made highly successful and well-regarded films in the first half of the 1920s, he too was criticized on occasion for being either overly melodramatic or overly emphatic. The *Variety* review of *Dream Street* (April 15, 1921: 40) is respectful but does not foresee much of an audience in the metropolitan first-run theaters: "This new production will have its Broadway triumphs, although it may not reach the proportions of 'Way Down East,' but in less sophisticated communities, both in New York and elsewhere, its smashing melodrama will give it a following probably as great if not greater than anything the film producer has done. Its second half is tremendously absorbing with a succession of surprises and telling dramatic situations equaled by no straight-away film story that comes to mind." The *New York Times* (April 13, 1921: 25) also praised the film but noted, in the context of a discussion of overacting in the film, "And for this, perhaps, Mr. Griffith, rather than the actors, should be held chiefly responsible, for with all of his sureness and unequaled skill in many things, Mr. Griffith does not seem to know the meaning of restraint. Many of his best scenes lose force because they are too intense, too long continued, too often repeated or too explicitly described in words and pictures. 'Dream

Street' suffers from this lack of subtlety and suggestion as have other Griffith works." The reviewers made similar observations near the end of Griffith's career. *Variety* (October 17, 1928: 16) criticized *The Battle of the Sexes* for "suggestiveness too obvious for the sophisticated," while the *New York Times* (October 15, 1928: 16) wrote, "Mr. Griffith has not left enough to the imagination in depicting the attack of a gum-chewing gold-digger on the bank roll of the susceptible husband and parent."

Complaints about overly moralized or emphatic forms of filmmaking often focused on the use of intertitles. Consider *Variety*'s review of the American version of Lubitsch's *Anna Boleyn,* in which both Griffith and Cecil B. DeMille came in for reproach: "The action is developed with good crescendo and the captions are few and simple. Which simplicity is a welcome relief from the bunk philosophy, bunk psychology, bunk poetry, bunk economics, and, worst of all, bunk moralizing, which have become prevalent of late. With all due respect to their other excellent qualities, De Mille and D. W. G. might do well to consider these captions carefully. When one reviews the downgrade from the splendid pantomime of 'The Birth of a Nation' through the half-baked sophomoric philosophizing of 'Intolerance' to the underdone moralizing of 'Way Down East,' there's stuff for thought."[15] Ample evidence in the pages of *Variety* seconds this criticism of the discursive intertitle. In the case of a rather obscure low-budget film, *Mine to Keep, Variety* (August 30, 1923: 27) complained, "The very first titles start out with a discourse on the marriage theme and the third of the lengthy leaders concludes with something like this: 'Our advice is, etc.' This stamps the production right off the bat, although it does not become too preachy, which is something to be thankful for, anyway." In contrast, a reviewer in the same issue of *Variety* complimented Clyde A. Bruckman, who wrote pithy and humorous titles for *Rouged Lips* (August 30, 1923: 27). The reviewer singles out the title that introduces the erstwhile hero, James Patterson III, "whose main ambition is to yawn without stretching." The intertitles written by *Variety* reporter Jack Conway for *Knockout Reilly* (April 20, 1927: 17) and humorist Robert Benchley for *Paradise for Two* (January 26, 1927: 20) were also praised in the magazine for being both funny and unobtrusive. By the end of the 1920s *Variety* was regularly indicating that films could have been improved by the addition of "snappy" titles.[16]

Variety's observation in 1921 that Griffith and DeMille were similar in their use of didactic intertitles is significant. It raises the questions of DeMille's critical reputation in the 1920s and of his position relative to the distinction between sophisticated and naïve taste so far elucidated. In *Screening Out the Past* Lary May argues that DeMille's society dramas and comedies of the late 1910s made a radical break with previous filmmaking traditions, represented for May by Griffith. May argues that deMille's films put in place a more modern idea of marriage, one based upon an overtly sexualized image of the ideal marriage partner, especially the wife, and an endorsement of the consumption of fashionable clothes and beauty products.[17] Scholars such as Charles Musser and Sumiko Higashi have singled out *Old Wives for New, Don't Change Your Husband,* and *Why Change Your Wife?* as instantiating a new, more liberal, attitude in American culture toward divorce. Musser also sees these films as the progenitors of the screwball comedy of remarriage of the 1930s and, by implication, of the farces dealing with marital infidelity directed by Lubitsch, Mal St. Claire, and others during the 1920s.[18] In my view, however, DeMille's divorce films cannot be easily assimilated to either the idea of sophisticated taste or the genre of sophisticated comedy as it developed in the mid-1920s. The reception of DeMille's films was complicated and calls for further analysis. His society dramas and comedies often dealt with sexually scandalous subject matter and for this reason were sometimes dubbed "sophisticated" by the trade and popular press. However, the same films were thought to be highly moralistic and were occasionally criticized for being overemphatic; thus they also bore the stigma attached to naïve taste.

Old Wives for New needs to be distinguished from the later sex comedies, for it was quite differently received. The film derived from a social problem novel by David Graham Phillips that advocated the liberalization of divorce laws. Both novel and film effectively compare the situations of two friends and partners. Charles Murdock (Elliott Dexter) feels repulsion for his wife of many years, who has grown fat and sloppy, and he falls in love with Juliet Raeburn (the transcendentally beautiful Florence Vidor). He asks his wife for a divorce on the grounds of incompatibility and is refused. Murdock's partner, Berkeley (Theodore Roberts), takes the more traditional route for dealing with marital dissatisfaction: he maintains a mistress, Jessie (Julia Faye). Both novel and film propose that Murdock's approach is ultimately preferable to Berkeley's.

The contrast between the two men, and between the two strategies for dealing with marital dissatisfaction, comes to a head in the scenes that lead up to Berkeley's murder. Murdock, having been spurned by Juliet after she discovers that he is married, goes with Berkeley to a louche café. The men are accompanied by Jessie and the equally disreputable Viola, who hopes to become connected with the wealthy Murdock. At the café, Berkeley begins a flirtation with yet another woman. Later, Jesse discovers her lover in the midst of a rendezvous with this other woman and shoots him. Murdock is called upon to hide the circumstances of the murder and to protect Berkeley's name: his double existence is maintained even after death.

The plot is resolved when Murdock's wife, Sophie (Sylvia Ashton), becomes interested in his secretary, Blagden (Gustav Seyffertitz), and herself initiates a divorce. Murdock and Juliet are eventually reconciled. After Blagden puts Sophie on a reducing plan, she buys new clothes and marries her husband's former secretary.

Although the ending, and especially the interplay between Sophie and Blagden, is decidedly comic, the café and murder scenes are quite dramatic and in my view led to the *New York Times's* characterization of the film (May 20, 1918: 9) as "not much more than a rather highly colored melodrama." Most reviewers found the film scandalous, without qualifying their judgment by types of theaters or audiences. This may be because it was assumed that the film ran the risk of offending even metropolitan audiences, but since vertical integration was not in place as early as 1918, I think it more plausible that most reviewers did not yet try to place films in terms of the distribution hierarchy of metropolitan first-run theaters, suburban theaters, and small towns. In any case, it is clear that *Old Wives for New* was found to be titillating but potentially problematic. *Photoplay* wrote that it "is extremely difficult to build up a pleasing romance upon a foundation of divorce" and objected to "scenes of disgusting debauchery." The reviewer thought that DeMille "seemed to revel in the most immoral episodes."[19] *Wid's Daily* (May 26, 1918: 27) liked the film but warned exhibitors that it might run into trouble in some communities, referring to "a sequence of cafe and bed room incidents which was handled with finesse so far as class and true to life details were concerned but oh boy!—it was rough!" *Moving Picture World* (June 8, 1918: 1470) wrote, "The cabaret scene is too insistent in establishing the moral laxity of its female guests, and other scenes of the same nature would stand cutting without the slightest danger of the spectator not comprehending their meaning."[20]

At the same time that DeMille's film was widely criticized for being scandalous, the advertising campaign for the film stressed its supposedly moral character. In a two-page spread devoted to advertising strategies for *Old Wives for New, Exhibitor's Trade Review* (June 1, 1918: 2080) recommended that exhibitors boost the film as "a real object lesson for wives, who are taught by the story that merely being virtuous is not, as it may have been at one time, enough in these days."[21] *Moving Picture World* (May 25, 1918: 1191) proposed exploitation along the same lines: exhibitors were advised to put up advertisements in beauty shops cautioning wives to see the film to learn what happens to the woman who is not well groomed. Yet the "moral" proposed for the film seems to have very little to do with what reviewers actually found scandalous: the way the film forces a confrontation between the sexual activities of Berkeley, and to some extent Murdock, and their status as husbands and respectable businessmen. But *Motion Picture News* (June 8, 1918: 3453), at least, seems to have found that the advertising campaign provided a plausible interpretation of the film, for, although the review noted some risqué situations, it nonetheless dubbed the film a "powerful sermon."

The divorce and remarriage comedies that follow *Old Wives for New, Don't Change Your Husband,* and *Why Change Your Wife?* are further removed from the social problem novel that served as the source of the first film and less aggressively in favor of divorce. In these films it is remarriage to the original partner, now beautified, that provides the narrative resolution. No reviewer objected to *Don't Change Your Husband* on moral grounds; most found it instructive. *Moving Picture World* (February 8, 1919: 803) wrote that *Don't Change Your Husband* "teaches wives that 'out of the frying pan into the fire' is often true of the divorce court. This is told with the saving grace of humor, but the lesson is driven home none the less." *Variety* (February 7, 1919: 61) wrote that the film was "Clean and wholesome, sustained in interest" and that "its moral must be far reaching." The review in *Wid's Daily* (January 26, 1919: 5) suggested the film was "most suitable to a sophisticated audience." At the same time, it presented the film as highly didactic, speculating that the scriptwriter, Jeanie Macpherson, "started out to give reasons why it is better to put up with a few disillusionments than to make matters worse by choosing another partner." Exploitation ideas addressed to wives along these lines were proposed.[22]

Critical opinion was much more divided on *Why Change Your Wife?* than it had been on *Don't Change Your Husband. Moving Picture World* (March 6, 1920: 1678) called the film "truth itself" and praised the intertitles as "replete with homely philosophy, the kind that strikes every married man or woman, every lover or sweetheart." *Motion Picture News* (March 6, 1920: 2389) praised the plot and the "satirical" subtitles and judged that the film would be "a huge money-maker for exhibitors everywhere, for it will appeal to both men and women of all classes." *Photoplay,* on the other hand, characterized the film as an over-seasoned dish with a bogus moral: "Mr. DeMille and his studio associates know that the 'moral' they have tacked on to this picture—that, in effect, every married man prefers an extravagant playmate-wife, dressed like a harlot, to a fussy little home body who has achieved horn-rimmed spectacles and a reading lamp—is not true of normal husbands anywhere in the world, however true it may be of motion picture directors."[23] The reviewer expected that the film would raise protests "somewhere out in the middle west, where the clean prairie winds blow across the brows of a native Anglo-Saxon multitude."

Unlike *Photoplay*'s Burns Mantle, the reviewer for *Wid's Daily* (May 2, 1920: 3) was not offended by *Why Change Your Wife?*, but hedged on the question of how the film would be received in neighborhood theaters. The film's appeal was thought to rest not on the plot, dubbed "nil," but on "lingerie, bare backs and limbs glimpsed through filmy things." *Wid's* assumed that the film's biggest audience would be on Broadway: "Its spice, its gorgeous displays of clothes and of extravagance in setting, its interesting detail are things which will bring it success in such houses." It cautioned exhibitors in the neighborhoods to use their own judgment based upon their own experiences with their patrons. At the same time that the reviewer considered the film best suited to metropolitan taste, however, he noted its blatant reaching for effect: "Of course De Mille is capable of better things than this. At times herein he insults intelligence while catering to the supposed mob demand for the exotic and the sensuous and the forbidden." The *Variety* review (April 30, 1920: 43) was largely in agreement with *Wid's*, finding the film a good business bet but too heavy-handed: "DeMille is too obvious a workman to touch the high points of the imagination." The *Variety* reviewer also, I think correctly, identified the film's particular mix of didacticism and sexual titillation: "What he [DeMille] has done is to preach a good everyday sermon in story form. Using the 'Wanderer' and other religious trick dramas as a guiding star, he has also worked in good sex stuff camouflaged carefully for the benefit of the censor. His moral may be chocolate coated with women undressing, but it will get by just the same." The same strategy was noted by the *New York Times* (April 26, 1920: 18), which found that the film gives "one the impression that he [DeMille] isn't seriously preaching at all" and typified DeMille's style in general as both "sophisticated" and "persistently homiletic."

In general, DeMille's divorce films got a mixed reception. In the case of *Old Wives for New*, highly controversial subject matter—the film was extremely adventurous for its time in its representation of louche sexual behavior on the part of supposedly upstanding, and largely sympathetic, characters—was marketed in terms of a more or less contrived "moral" that some reviewers, at least, seemed to accept. *Don't Change Your Husband* retreated from some of the more offensive aspects of *Old Wives for New*, and the reviewers took its didacticism at face value and approved it. Reviewers considered *Why Change Your Wife?* potentially more offensive, because of its outré clothes and sets and blatant display of the female figure. While they did not all use the term, reviewers for *Photoplay, Wid's, Variety,* and the *New York Times* might be said to have found the film "sophisticated" in the sense that it was sexually daring. But they identified other elements in the film that corresponded more closely to what was considered unsophisticated taste. *Wid's* referred to DeMille's blatant appeal to popular conceptions of the exotic and the sensuous, while both *Variety* and the *New York Times* referred to the sermonizing tendency.

I have tried to show that the idea of "sophistication" circulating in the trade press in the 1920s extended beyond the assumptions that big-city audiences preferred a racy or daring representation of sexuality and small-town audiences did not. The term encompassed other qualities which cannot be applied so readily to DeMille's films of the period. Indeed, his films can be assimilated to naïve taste in two important ways. First, his films were didactic. The sermonizing may or may not have been regarded as bogus, but it was an important aspect of his style and was recognized as such. The bombastic use of intertitles came in for particular criticism here.[24] Second, and contrary to Gilbert Seldes's characterization of the director cited in chapter 1, the trade press did not consider DeMille's films restrained or genteel. While the word "hokum" was not to my knowledge used in relation to DeMille, I can think of few directors who better deserve the term. Throughout his directorial career DeMille sought to create big effects at the levels of both spectacle and plot. The tendency is evident in his increasingly fantastic and bizarre mise en scène, which *Variety* discussed in connection with *Forbidden Fruit* (January 29, 1921: 39), *The Affairs of Anatol* (August 26, 1921: 36), and *The Golden Bed* (January 21, 1925: 34).[25] The preference for big effects is evident as well in his preference for extreme narrative situations, what the *Times* called "highly colored melodrama," in scenes such as the murder of Berkeley in *Old Wives for New* or the cat fight between the first and the second Mrs. Gordon in *Why Change Your Wife?*[26] These aspects of DeMille's style served to differentiate him from the directors who pioneered the canonical sophisticated comedies of the 1920s.

The emergence of sophisticated comedy as a genre, and its recognition as a type by the trade press, occurs in the mid-1920s, well after the release of DeMille's divorce comedies. The plots of these films were not new; they were familiar from nineteenth-century operetta and farce and were, in any case, usually considered slight.[27] But the films were held to be the acme of stylistic refinement, understated and restrained, and thus in opposition both to hokum effects and to slapstick, which was understood to be a subset of hokum. For example, the *Variety* review of James Cruze's *Is Matri-*

mony a Failure? (April 21, 1922: 40), an adaptation of Leo Ditrichstein's farce, itself taken from a German original, describes the film as "sophisticated funmaking" and "a conspicuous example of enlivening entertainment sustained through five reels without resort to slapstick or custard pie." A much later review makes a similar contrast but is less sanguine about the economic chances of understated comic fare. *Variety* (July 20, 1927: 19) writes of *The World at Her Feet,* an adaptation of *Maître Bolbec et son mari* by Georges Berr and Louis Verneuil:

> These French triangle stories never seem to bull's-eye at the box office, though this one is a first-rate sophisticated comedy with excellent wise humor and a lot of sparkle. It has much elegance of atmosphere and a brisk play of wit.
>
> The answer seems to be that the fans run to either low comedy in domestic stories or high intense drama, and the graduations between the extremes don't register. There have been a score of suave comedies of this sort on the Broadway screen, but not one of them sticks in memory as a commercial success. . . .
>
> It's all very smooth and casual, without theatrical parade, and perhaps the screen public wants its dramatic punch delivered with more force than grace. . . . The French are a discriminating, fastidious people, sipping their pastimes like old wine. This American people gulp their screen and stage sensations like straight redeye.

Sophisticated comedy would thus seem to be at the opposite extreme from the "sensations like straight redeye" of the Keystone comedies so appreciated by Seldes and other intellectuals of the 1920s. Yet I hope to demonstrate that those involved with the cinema perceived the formal strategies developed within the genre as innovative. While, according to *Variety,* the films were not wildly financially successful, for a generation of filmmakers and critics, these films charted the possibilities of an indigenous and fully modern style.

As already noted, films based upon theatrical farce such as *Upstairs and Down* and *Is Matrimony a Failure?* were termed "sophisticated." But *A Woman of Paris,* released in October 1923, definitively altered the way such comedies were made. While this film is difficult to place generically, and is only partly comic in tone, it established new strategies for adapting theatrical farce to the medium of silent film and paved the way for the cynical amorality and nonemphatic presentation of jokes characteristic of films such as *The Marriage Circle, Forbidden Paradise,* and *So This Is Paris. A Woman of Paris* was generally well received by intellectuals and was deemed influential by directors as different as Lubitsch, Eisenstein, and Ozu.[28] But what interests me here is that critics in the trade and popular press also praised this film's technique and held it up as a model for other filmmakers to emulate. In an interview with Chaplin in *Motion Picture Magazine* in 1925, Harry Carr claimed, "It was the picture that changed the entire motion picture business."[29]

A Woman of Paris was not labeled a comedy. The subtitle of the film is "A Drama of Fate." The first intertitle, signed by Chaplin and directly addressed to the public, likewise stresses the film's status as a drama: "In order to avoid any misunderstanding, I wish to announce that I do not appear in this picture. It is the first serious drama written and directed by myself." The *Variety* review (September 27, 1923: 25) also stresses this idea, calling the film "a serious, sincere effort." The plot summary in the *Variety* review, which the reviewer claims was taken from a press release written by Chaplin himself, makes the film sound as if it has no comic elements at all. The reviewer notes, however, that the "broad and keen farce touches" that have distinguished Chaplin's slapstick films are "just as effective when applied to lighter humor and to drama—even to tragedy." He commends Adolphe Menjou's "brilliant dramatic and comedy strokes that will draw applause and laughs," and further reports, "Before an audience the comedy will be more easy to judge, but in the cold silence of a 42nd street projection room it drew audible howls at times and titters whenever the seriousness was relieved." As *A Woman of Paris* deals with a young girl who misses her chance to marry and becomes the mistress of a Paris roué, it is not surprising that the film was called a drama, or even a tragedy. Despite changes in taste, this was not a topic that could be treated purely and simply as a comedy in 1923 (or, indeed, later, in the sound period). The film nonetheless contains surprising comedic elements, most importantly in its treatment of what in earlier versions of this plot would have been the part of the villain, here played by Adolphe Menjou.

In a town in the French provinces, Marie St. Clair is planning to elope to Paris with her young man, Jean. He fails to meet her at the railway station because, unbeknownst to her, his father has suddenly been taken ill. She departs for Paris alone.

Months later Marie, now ensconced in Paris as the mistress of the wealthy Pierre Revel, discovers Jean and his mother living in the Latin Quarter in reduced circumstances since the death of his father. He is working as a painter, and she arranges to have him paint her portrait. After finishing the portrait of Marie, Jean proposes marriage, telling her that he loves her "in spite of everything." Marie quarrels with Pierre and tells him they must part. Meanwhile, Jean quarrels with his mother, who opposes the match. Jean finally swears to his mother that he never really intended to marry Marie. Marie overhears this conversation as she enters the open door of Jean's studio. Jean is immediately penitent and attempts to make amends, but she rejects him coldly and leaves. That night she is reconciled with Pierre. Disconsolate, Jean confronts Marie and Pierre in a fashionable café and, when he is rebuffed, shoots himself in the foyer. Later that night Jean's mother finds Marie mourning beside Jean's body in his studio, and they are united in grief.

There is a short epilogue: Sometime later, Marie and Jean's mother maintain a house in the provinces where they adopt orphaned children. Setting out to pick berries, Marie and one of the children catch a ride in a farmworker's cart. The cart is passed by a motorcar carrying Pierre and a friend in the opposite direction. The friend asks Pierre what has happened to Marie and he shrugs. The ex-lovers do not see each other.

The dramatic—I am tempted to say "melodramatic" and the *Variety* reviewer used "tragic"—dimension of this plot is most pronounced in the episodes that concern Jean: the missed connection at the railroad station, the quarrel with his mother, and his own ambivalence about Marie, leading to his final disappointment in love and suicide. These are indeed the elements of the plot emphasized in the summary presented in *Variety,* where the film is portrayed as a drama pure and simple. But all of the scenes concerning Marie and her life with Pierre are comic. In the exposition about Marie's status as Pierre's mistress, for example, the film cuts from the scene at the provincial railway station, where she is about to board the train, to an elegant restaurant in Paris. Two couples make an entrance and are seated for dinner: a richly dressed elderly woman with a handsome young man, followed by Pierre and Marie. After they are seated the young man asks his companion about Pierre and is told that he is "the richest bachelor in Paris." In response to Marie's question Pierre tells her the elderly woman is "one of the richest old maids in Paris." In response to her question "who's the man with her?" there is a close-up of Menjou, who pointedly shrugs, then smiles. The contrast between these two couples clearly works to Pierre's advantage: an old maid supporting a handsome young man is ridiculous, whereas a rich bachelor with his young mistress is viewed with admiration, if not moral approbation. Moreover, the parallel between the young man's position and Marie's undermines the potentially "tragic" dimension of her position as fallen woman. The nameless male gigolo cannot be viewed as anything but comic, and this sets the tone for how we are to understand Marie's position as well.

A scene in which Marie quarrels with Pierre, confronting him with her dissatisfaction about their mode of life, provides one of the most surprising shifts in tone. A narrative title informs us, "In the mind of Marie St. Clair is the problem—marriage or luxury." The title poses the problem as a serious choice for the heroine. But the scene that follows begins in her flat with Pierre playing a miniature tenor saxophone, a rather absurd prop, which immediately puts him in a comic realm, removed from her deep and obvious vexation. In response to her complaint, "I want a real home, babies and a man's respect," he sighs and goes to the window. He opens it. From his point of view we see the street below, where a family crosses the street: the man is laden with packages and his wife is pulling one of three fighting children by the hand. Pierre gestures for Marie to look out the window. She remains vexed, however, and complains that she gets nothing out of life. In response to this comment, he gestures to the string of pearls around her neck. In anger, she pulls off the pearls and hurls them out of the window, a dramatic gesture signaling her willingness to renounce material for emotional fulfillment. The pearls fall to the street, where a passing tramp picks them up. When Marie realizes what has happened she runs downstairs, retrieves the pearls from the tramp, and, belatedly giving him a tip, returns to the flat, actions punctuated by cut-aways to Pierre, laughing.

The comic tone here is unexpected in the context of what claims to be a "drama of Fate." Not only is Pierre an unconventional villain, if indeed he can be said to fit that category at all, but Marie's attempts to assume the role of the conventionally "wronged" woman are undercut as so much posturing. At the very moment one expects the film to lapse into melodrama—expectations reinforced by the opening title, which laid out the conventional choice between "marriage or luxury"—the plot gets turned in quite another direction by the gags: the saxophone, the view of the family on the street, the pearls. These gags effectively reinforce Pierre's amoral and resolutely unapologetic stance toward his mistress. While I do not think Marie's desire for marriage is itself ridiculed in this scene, and one may indeed retain the sense that she and Pierre are the "right" couple, it becomes difficult to interpret her unmarried status as the infliction of a grievous injury. This helps to explain the subdued tone of the ending; the woman's requisite "reformation" is there, but there is no recognition scene and no sense that either character is consumed with regret. This also helps to explain why the dramatic portions of the plot center around Jean. He is the only character who is undone by Fate and experiences irretrievable loss.

While some critics applauded the film's representation of the affair between Pierre Revel and his mistress, others voiced doubts. In *Motion Picture Classic*, Ted Le Berthon declared that Chaplin had brought Freud to the movies, stripping away the veneer of popular theories of right and wrong and debunking the notion that humans were accountable for their destinies.[30] Without invoking Freud, *The Storyworld and Photodramatist* voiced a similar appreciation of the characters' mixed motivations.[31] Other critics expressed hesitations about the treatment of the love affair. *Photoplay* deemed the film "sophisticated" and warned that "any fifteen-year-old child who appreciates it should be taken home and spanked."[32] In *Exceptional Photoplays,* published by the National Board of Review, the reviewer tried to reassure readers that the attachment between Pierre and Marie was "not excessively fleshly." Characterizing the film as "a plea for charity and understanding of such people by one who is charitable and understands them" and not as "a subtle stroke at the wholesomeness and desirability of marriage and lawful love," the reviewer nonetheless opined that many would find the plot cause for censure.[33] The more pragmatic *Film Daily* (October 7, 1923: 5) worried that it might not get past state censors without cuts.

Charles Wood, in a review entitled "With the Bunk Left Out," praised the film's subdued ending, in which Pierre and Marie pass each other on the road without recognition or comment. In his view the film was neither amoral nor immoral but simply refrained from overt moralizing:

> If Charlie had only had Jean almost kill himself and recover, he might have produced a regular picture. The least he could do, it would seem, would be to give Marie a halo of saintly sadness. She might pass out apples to the kids; but she ought in all conscience to have sighs of repentance while she was doing so, or gaze skyward with a serene and stony chill. But Charlie Chaplin managed to have her do much less than that. . . . Mr. Chaplin likewise found it unnecessary to hang his villain, or to get him pushed into a deep cavern just as he was about to execute some hellish plot. He didn't even make the villain leer and proclaim to all concerned, so that everybody above the intelligence of a heroine might easily perceive it, that all his ways were vile. . . . Charlie didn't seem to think it necessary to load vice down with any artificial handicaps in order that virtue might compete with it on even terms.[34]

According to Wood, *A Woman of Paris* was unusual not because of the love affair but, rather, because it refrained from moralizing about it. The ending is particularly important in this regard. Although the heroine's reformation in the epilogue may seem conventional, even sentimental, to present-day viewers, it did not apparently provide a strong sense of moral closure for any of the reviewers in the 1920s. This can probably be attributed to the missed meeting of the two protagonists and to the absence of intertitles commenting on Marie's suffering and change of heart.

Every review, even those that expressed concern about the story's morality, praised the film's technique. Carr explained, "'A Woman of Paris' is rather an old story, but his [Chaplin's] treatment of it is one of the most daring and revolutionary events in the history of motion pictures. . . . 'A Woman of Paris' is built upon a technique so breathlessly new and startling that it takes your breath away."[35] *Photoplay* characterized it as "a post-graduate course in the use of simplicity," while the reviewer for the National Board of Review praised its "restraint." The *New York Times* (October 2, 1923: 7) appreciated "touches" such as the wild party in the Latin quarter, which indirectly presents the disrobing of a painter's model: instead of seeing her unwind the sheet that covers her, we see it wound progressively around a fat and drunken male accomplice. Both the *New York Times* and *Film Daily* also regarded the massage scene as a characteristic Chaplin "touch": Marie, presumably nude, remains below the frame line while we see her masseuse at work. Charles Wood praised the film's indirect modes of representation more broadly: "Leaving out words is his [Chaplin's] speciality. Simplicity. The elimination of the unnecessary. One cannot even judge Charlie Chaplin by what he does. It is what he doesn't do that makes him great."[36] Both Wood and Scott O'Dell, in *Representative Photoplays Analyzed,* commented upon the use of ellipsis, especially the gap between Marie's departure from her village and her appearance, one year later, in Paris as Revel's mistress.[37]

One scene, which O'Dell praised for its subtlety, deserves closer analysis. It occurs just after Marie finds Jean living with his mother in the Latin Quarter. Having been invited to paint her portrait, he arrives at her flat for the first time. O'Dell was impressed by the end of the scene, in which Pierre comes into the living room and figures out that another man is being received in the bedroom. The two men never actually meet, and O'Dell notes, "The author has avoided the obvious. There are no exaggerated postures and gestures on either side. No breaking of furniture and glassware."[38] At issue here is not simply the absence of a direct, physical confrontation but the fact that the filmmaker deliberately underplays the typical farce situation of a man hidden in a woman's bedroom (or vice versa). Typical dramatic construction would have built suspense in the scenes preceding the discovery. Among the many possible examples are the stage and screen versions of *A Pair of Silk Stockings, The New York Idea, The Last of Mrs. Cheyney,* and *Lady Windemere's Fan;* in the last-named it is, of course, the woman who is hidden away. By contrast the discovery scene in *A Woman of Paris* is virtually thrown away. Pierre enters and apparently deduces Jean's presence from the maid's reluctance to admit him to the bedroom, although this is neither explicitly stated in dialogue titles nor vehemently acted out in gesture. When Marie joins him in the living room he politely offers her one of the chocolates he is eating, and when she declines he instructs the maid, "Ask the gentleman in the next room if he would care for some." Marie indignantly exclaims, "Why should I explain? You wouldn't understand." Laughing, he tells the maid to put down the chocolates and approaches his mistress: "You jump at conclusions. I understand perfectly." They kiss. The sophistication here is not only a matter of character—Pierre, a man of the world, is both self-confident and tolerant enough to accept the presence of another man in his mistress's bedroom—but, also, the deliberate courting of anticlimax: Pierre knows about Jean's presence immediately, but there is no suspense, and no real consequences follow from his knowledge. The situation develops "with more grace than force."

The conclusion of this scene was singled out for praise in the 1920s, but the scene's opening is worth considering as well, for it provides a telling instance of Chaplin's narrative technique. The simplicity and restraint that critics praised in this film are, in part, a result of the economy of the narration. Very few intertitles are used, exposition is terse and often advanced through a single object or motif, and the actors employ very small gestures, if any, to underscore changes in the hierarchy of knowledge. As the scene begins Marie is in the bedroom trying to select a dress to wear for her portrait. Jean enters the living room and sits, impassive, merely glancing to the right to indicate that he notices the expensive furnishings (figure 8). Marie's catty girlfriend Paulette leaves as he is admitted to the bedroom; her interest in this potentially scandalous situation is indicated in two shots without titles. In the long shot she turns and glances after him (figure 9). Her look is emphasized by a cut-in (figure 10). Inside the bedroom Marie greets Jean and displays a gown, then changes her mind and displays another. She asks her maid to fetch a scarf from the bureau nearby, and, as the maid pulls it from a drawer, an object drops to the floor (figure 11). A detail shot shows a man's shirt collar on the floor at the maid's feet (figure 12). Jean, still impassive, looks off left in the direction of the collar, then up at Marie, who is fussing with her clothes and has not noticed the incident (figure 13). Both the shot of Paulette looking after Jean and the shot of Jean looking at the collar tell us a great deal about what the characters know, or think they know. The glance at the shirt collar is also quite economical in that it obviates the need for a dialogue title explaining Marie's relationship with Pierre to Jean—thereby curtailing potentially cumbersome exposition and also helping to avoid censorship. Moreover, the tone of the film is restrained, the actor refraining from any pronounced

8   9

10   11

12   13

gesture: the object and the use of the eyeline match are enough to confirm Jean's suspicions for the spectator.

As the scene continues, Marie brings both dress and scarf over to Jean, and as he fingers the material she notices that he is wearing a black armband. She sits down and looks concerned (figure 14). A title follows: "Why,

14

15

16

17

Jean, who are you in mourning for?" Jean looks down right at his armband, then looks up, almost directly into the camera, but without expressing emotion (figure 15). "My father." Marie asks, "When did he die?" "The night you left." Jean, still impassive, exhales smoke from his cigarette (figure 16). Marie looks down and off left (figure 17). It is through the use of the armband and four rather spare dialogue titles that Marie comes to understand the circumstances underlying Jean's seeming abandonment of her. There is very little in the way of exposition, and, although her surprise and their mutual regret are unmistakable, the actors represent these emotions with small, contained gestures.

When *The Marriage Circle* was released four months after *A Woman of Paris* in February 1924, most reviewers compared the two films on the basis of their technique. *Film Daily* (February 10, 1924: 5) wrote, "A thread of a story but so skillfully handled; so full of unusual treatment, that it brings satisfaction with every frame of film. The handling of the production is the all important matter. Lubitsch shows a school of direction which may well be considered by important American directors. His touches, his ideas, the lack of heavy backgrounds . . . are all done with a master's hand. The simplicity of production is equaled only by Chaplin's 'A Woman of Paris.'"[39] *Moving Picture World* (February 16, 1924: 581) compared the two as follows:

> With a technique as revolutionary as Chaplin's in "A Woman of Paris" and resembling it in its subtlety, he [Lubitsch] has handled a rather daring and sensational theme with simplicity and directness; concentration of action, incident and even sets being always evident. For instance, he confines his scenes to the particular portion of the set in which the action occurs, puts over his points with a minimum of footage, having his characters portray whole situations in a gesture, a look and even by absolute inaction at times. It is an excellent example of finely handled pantomime; there is a minimum of subtitles, but few are needed, for the situations are so deftly handled as to render them unnecessary.

The critic for the National Board of Review likewise found the director innovative and the style similar to Chaplin's: "So slim a plot, so hackneyed, if you will, is told with a gaiety and a wit that lift the picture into the very first rank of screen comedy. Comparison with Chaplin's *A Woman of Paris* inevitably comes to the mind and eye." And later: "Everywhere we encounter this eloquence of the camera focusing our attention upon a handkerchief or a crushed flower, not in blatant close-ups but with a deceptive air of the casual which nevertheless builds up the story. Here again we are led into comparisons with *A Woman of Paris*. Both these films are really technical innovations in picture-making. They carry the method of significant suggestion to a point of perfection hitherto unknown to American picture audiences. Undoubtedly it is in this direction that the greatest improvement in the picture-making of the future lies."[40]

Like the *Moving Picture World* critic, several other reviewers noted the small number of subtitles in *The Marriage Circle,* singling out this aspect of the film as both central to its technique and related to Chaplin's. *Photoplay* commented, "It is becoming more generally recognized by producers that a story can be told on the screen with pictures, plus intelligence, and does not have to have a title every thirty or forty feet. Also it can be told clearly, concisely and straightforwardly, without 'flashbacks' or other nuisances. Mr. Chaplin did it with *A Woman of Paris,* and Ernst Lubitsch has done it again with *The Marriage Circle.*"[41] Writing in 1925, after seeing a revival of Griffith's *Broken Blossoms*, Robert Sherwood noted, "In just one way does 'Broken Blossoms' show its age; it lacks that form of pictorial expressiveness which came to the screen in 'A Woman of Paris' and which is now practiced by every worthy director on both sides of the Atlantic. Griffith did not know then how to tell a story in terms of moving pictures; he had to label every scene with a sub-title, using his pictures merely as illustrations for the text. Unfortunately, while Chaplin, Lubitsch, Vidor and many others have moved ahead with the times, Griffith has stood still."[42]

In her review of *The Marriage Circle*, headlined "The Cinema: Hope Fulfilled," Iris Barry referred to a "new subtle method of dramatic expression and of story telling." Referring to Sheridan, Molière, and Congreve in considering precedents for Lubitsch's film, she singled out only one cinematic precedent, *A Woman of Paris* (although she qualified this by noting that in his other films Chaplin's characteristic mixture of farce and pathos "has always been conceived too emotionally, too little cerebrally, to be right comedy"). Barry's review praised *The Marriage Circle* for finding visual equivalents of literary wit: "There is a minimum of subtitling, and the progress of the plot is not dependent on the letterpress."[43] In a volume of criticism published in 1926, Barry argued that filmmakers should aim for a small number of very concise titles: "The making of sub-titles might well be held to be a new form of literary style. The sub-title must be crystalline, packed with meaning, allusive, condensed—a work of art and elegance and simplicity, in fact." Her examples of good titling include Chaplin's early films (it is not clear to which period of his work she refers), Lubitsch's *The Marriage Circle*, Karl Grune's *The Street* (*Die Strasse*, 1923), and Constance Talmadge's comedies, some of which will be discussed below.[44]

The *Variety* review (February 7, 1924: 22) of *The Marriage Circle* is the only one I have seen that did not make reference to *A Woman of Paris*. But the reviewer found the film unusual in its subtlety: "Almost any director would have resorted to the obvious hoakum to get this one over. 'Jazzing it up' would have been the thing that most would have tried and ruined a fine piece of work." Indeed, this absence of hokum seems to have given the reviewer for *Moving Picture World* reason to pause; although he endorsed the film he worried that "its subtlety and wit" might be "over the heads of certain classes of patrons."

Lubitsch's film derives not from a farce but from Lothar Goldschmidt's *Nur ein Traum*, a 1909 drama described by Ben Brewster as a "naturalist-influenced problem play."[45] Lubitsch and scriptwriter Paul Bern took and elaborated upon a series of misunderstandings that, in the original play, involved one adulterous couple and one potentially adulterous couple. In the film this is softened so that neither couple commits adultery. Franz Braun (Monte Blue) is pursued by Mizzi Stock (Marie Prevost), his wife's best friend. Charlotte Braun (Florence Vidor) is worshipped from afar by the doctor who shares her husband's medical practice, Gustav Mueller (Creighton Hale). Mizzi is married to Professor Stock (Adolphe Menjou), a character who remains largely outside of the circuit of desire and deception that enmeshes the others; he wants only to find a way to divorce his wife.

The opening of the film establishes the discord between the Stocks by showing them get up and get dressed for the day. Cecil B. DeMille's influence is apparent here: the scene clearly echoes the bathroom scenes of marital discord with which DeMille opens both *Old Wives for New* and *Why Change Your Wife?* A misunderstanding is introduced almost immediately. Professor Stock looks out of the window and sees Mizzi get into a cab with another man in what he assumes is an assignation. It is made clear to us, however, that Mizzi, newly arrived in Vienna and on her way to visit her old friend Charlotte Braun, accidentally steps into a cab that is waiting for another client and that they decide to share it.

When Mizzi shares the cab with Dr. Braun, the two are not yet aware of their mutual connection with Charlotte. She flirts with him so aggressively that he flees, leaving behind the flowers he had intended for his wife. Mizzi presents the flowers to Charlotte as her own gift, and when Braun returns home they stand as a reminder of what happened in the cab: of what he and Mizzi know and Charlotte does not.

A subsequent dinner party scene depends crucially on Charlotte's misunderstanding of events. As she sets out place cards for the guests in preparation for the party, Franz notices that he has been seated next to Mizzi. He prudently switches Mizzi's card with that of a Miss Hofer. Charlotte notices this and, misinterpreting her husband's motives, switches them back. The circulation of the place card then becomes a means of escalating the situation. When Mizzi arrives Charlotte explains what happened and voices her suspicions of Miss Hofer. Mizzi secretly switches the place cards yet again, to throw further suspicions on Franz and the innocent girl.

After dancing, Mizzi inveigles Franz into a walk in the garden, an interlude that features the economical use of a motif both to advance the attempted seduction and further to mislead Charlotte. As Franz accompanies Mizzi out onto the veranda, he gallantly covers her shoulders with her wrap, then offers her a cigarette from his case. She tosses the case into the garden. When he goes to retrieve it, he finds her by his side. Later, seated on a garden bench and nervous about her advances, he suggests that they return to the house so that she will not be cold. She tosses off the wrap, implying that she is anything but cold. As the wrap blows away in the wind, she kisses him. Charlotte, worried that her husband is in the clutches of Miss Hofer, walks the garden with Mueller. Mizzi's wrap attaches itself to his foot. Charlotte notices it and calls for Mizzi, and Franz quickly makes his way back to the house unseen. As Charlotte returns the wrap to Mizzi, she asks for her husband; Mizzi denies having seen him. Then, much to Charlotte's dismay, she points to Franz talking to Miss Hofer on the veranda.

After the party Charlotte quarrels jealously with her husband concerning Miss Hofer, which motivates him to keep an assignation proposed by Mizzi. Mueller, who witnesses his departure, thereupon goes to sit in the Brauns' garden, somewhat dejected but not without hope. Mistaking Mueller for her husband (they wear identical straw hats), the repentant Charlotte taps on the window to invite him inside. Seated with her back to him, she does not see his face when he enters. She speaks to him affectionately and permits him to kiss her before she recognizes her mistake and shows Mueller the door.

Franz does not sleep with Mizzi, but his presence in her apartment is noted by the detective hired by Professor Stock, and he is named as correspondent in the professor's suit for divorce. Although Franz is eventually able to clear himself with his wife, she feels compelled to get her revenge by averring that she, too, had an assignation on the night of the party. The film ends, as Ben Brewster notes, with a misapprehension on the part of both husband and wife. Charlotte demands that Mueller recount to her husband the events leading up to the kiss. When Charlotte is not watching him, Franz laughingly pantomimes encouragement to Mueller to "confess." It is clear that Braun does not really believe this confession, although we know it to be true. Meanwhile, when Charlotte is watching him, Braun pretends to be outraged, giving her the mistaken belief that he accepts the veracity of her account.

Two scenes from early in the film, one showing Franz leaving for work and then a later scene in his office, provide a good example of how Lubitsch intensifies aspects of the style of *A Woman of Paris*. Mueller's place in the circle of confusion is established when he calls for Franz to go the office. Charlotte goes out onto the balcony to ask him to wait while Franz finishes breakfast. Gustav compliments her as she stands there, and she demurely pulls her wrap around her and looks inside, where Franz is finishing his meal. She turns to pick some roses from a planter on the balcony; as the previous point-of-view shot toward the interior indicates unmistakably, they are for Franz. A detail shot shows one rose that falls accidentally at Mueller's feet. He picks it up, interpreting it as a gift from the woman he admires. He takes off his hat in tribute, and she looks down and notices that he is inhaling the scent of her rose. She laughs. As Franz rushes out the door, she presents her husband with the bouquet of roses. He drops them carelessly as he kisses her goodbye. When Franz joins Mueller beside the car, Mueller hides his rose behind his back, as if it were a guilty secret. As the men depart, they raise identical straw hats in a gesture of farewell. Charlotte teases that she might show up at the office some day, a point Mueller assumes is addressed to him, although it is actually meant for Franz. Both men make gestures encouraging the visit. Mueller waves goodbye to Charlotte with the rose, again being careful that Franz does not see it.

The scene in which Mizzi and Charlotte visit the doctors' office simultaneously brings the two couples together in a tour de force of farcical complications built upon the continuation of the flower motif and the use of point-of-view editing, the latter device augmented by the arrangement of the set. The offices of the two doctors are side by side, with a door connecting them. Each doctor's office also has a door that leads into their common waiting room. Mizzi arrives, veiled, in Franz's office and proceeds to make advances: she rips up a letter he had written her declining to serve as her physician and then pulls a lock of his hair down and smoothes it back into place with her hand. In his office Mueller dismisses a talkative patient and then opens the door to Franz's room. A point-of-view shot shows Franz, back to camera, obscuring the face and body of the woman whose arms are around his neck (figure 18). Mueller's misinterpretation of what he sees is signaled by a dialogue intertitle congratulating his partner: "Lucky Devil—to be so loved by your own wife!" The woman waves Mueller away, Franz nods in agreement, and Mueller returns to his office. Then, opening the door to the waiting room, Mueller sees Charlotte making good on her promise of a visit (figure 19). The film is very discrete at this juncture. There is a medium shot of Mueller thinking (figure 20) but no title to confirm his revised interpretation of what he has witnessed—we must infer his suspicions on the basis of what he has seen.

When Mueller approaches Charlotte, she holds up the flowers Franz had dropped, saying, "I want to teach him not to throw my roses away." Mueller invites her into his office. Glance/object editing shows Charlotte looking at his rose carefully enshrined in a glass of water. This object suggests a complicated disparity of knowledge between the two characters, a disparity that has been carefully constructed across the course of two scenes. Charlotte knows that she did not make a gift of the rose and that Mueller mistakenly thinks she did. Mueller knows what Charlotte has told him, that Franz was careless with her flowers, and he also knows what Charlotte does not, what Franz is up to in the next room. The film lightly touches upon his sense of superior love and devotion in a medium shot in which Mueller looks in the direction of Charlotte, nods, and looks off left in the direction of the flower. No intertitles are employed.

18   19

20

But Lubitsch is not done with the flower motif. Cutting to Braun's office, we see the doctor beside a plant stand with a vase of fresh flowers. He looks grim. Mizzi approaches and grabs him by the lapel. A detail shot shows the vase falling to the floor and breaking. In the next room Mueller and Charlotte react to the sound. Mueller explains to her that it is a serious case (the doctors specialize in "nervous disease"). Charlotte, concerned for her husband, wants to check on him, and Mueller anxiously tries to keep her in her seat. Back in Franz's office, Mizzi, once again veiled, exits. When Mueller enters the room, he sees his friend bending over the broken vase. Franz laughs, putting on a front: "You see—how crazy my wife is about me?" Again the use of the motif is quite complex: Mueller has seen the flowers that indicate that Franz's wife is crazy about him, but these flowers indicate something quite different. Mueller exposes his friend's pretense by opening the door that joins their offices, revealing Charlotte's presence.

Husband and wife come together in Franz's office. She playfully refuses a kiss, showing him the roses and, in a repetition of Mizzi's gesture, smoothes back his hair. The subsequent quarrel between husband and wife is conveyed through two objects and two dialogue titles. Charlotte looks at the broken vase. Franz explains, "I—er—a nervous man knocked it over." She responds by taking up a pair of woman's gloves left on his desk. His response, that he has many patients, obviously fails to satisfy her.

The scene concludes with a misapprehension on the part of Franz that anticipates not only the ending but also an incident at the dinner party in which Charlotte, worried about Miss Hofer, begs an apparently reluctant Mizzi to dance with her husband. Called away to visit a sick patient, Franz enters the waiting room, where he is joined by Mueller. Both men react to the sound of Charlotte's weeping in Franz's office (a variation of the moment when Charlotte and Mueller responded to the breaking of the vase in that room). Franz asks Mueller, as his best friend, to comfort Charlotte. Assuming a noble posture Mueller assents. After Franz's exit he checks his hair and tie in the mirror before entering Franz's office to complete his mission. The last shot is of the door he closes behind him.

The plot of *The Marriage Circle* depends on deliberate deception and the misapprehension of events by the four principal characters in a way that *A Woman of Paris* does not. Complex hierarchies of knowledge—who knows what about whom and when—are enacted largely through point-of-view and glance/object editing. In the office scene, most of the shifts in knowledge are accomplished through Mueller. For example, when he opens the door to the waiting room to find Charlotte, his interpretation of what he has seen in Franz's office changes. Near the end of the scene, when he opens the door that reveals Charlotte to Franz, he lets Franz know what he now knows, or at least suspects. Such shifts in knowledge could of course also be represented or confirmed through intertitles, but in this film the director often eschews this option.

In contrast to Chaplin, Lubitsch employs narrational devices in highly formalized patterns. The scene in the office is scored with repeated elements: the contrasts between three sets of flowers, two moments in which characters in one room react to sounds in another, and two gestures of smoothing back Franz's hair. An analysis of the film in its entirety would reveal that the motif of the straw hat fulfills even more functions than do the flowers in the office scene. In addition, many parallel scenes on the order of Franz's asking Mueller to comfort Charlotte and Charlotte's asking Mizzi to dance with Franz would become apparent. The economy of the style, the effect of "simplicity" that was so remarked upon in the 1920s, is in fact established through intricate networks of repetition.[46]

At the time of their release, both *A Woman of Paris* and *The Marriage Circle* were hailed as inaugurating a new style and providing a model for other filmmakers. In exploring the extent and nature of their influence I shall proceed chronologically by season (release patterns in the 1920s were organized not by calendar year but for the period of September through May) and focus mainly on the films that critics held to be representative of the trend for subtle and understated humor. In the 1923–24 season, following the release of *A Woman of Paris* in October and of *The Marriage Circle* in February, Monta Bell's *Broadway After Dark* was released in May by Warners, the same studio that had produced *The Marriage Circle*. This is the first film in which Adolphe Menjou held an unambiguously heroic part, leading the *New York Times* (May 20, 1924: 15) to comment, "A leopard, according to reports, cannot change its spots, but in 'Broadway After Dark,' Adolphe Menjou, hitherto seen in numerous pictures as a deep-dyed cynical villain, covers up his pantomimic past and blossoms forth as a blasé hero." The critic goes on to explain that his "role is not intensely heroic, and therefore as might be expected he employs the same facial expressions in this new part as he did in his previous portrayals. He is tamer, but just as nonchalant." The story derives from a play of the same name by Owen Davis. Ralph Norton (Menjou), a wealthy Broadway swell, is jilted and abandons his set, going to live in a humble theatrical boarding house. There he becomes interested in Rose Dulane (Norma Shearer), who works in the house as a domestic until the fact that she has served a jail sentence comes to light and she is fired. Norton passes her off in society as his ward and eventually they are married. *Variety* (May 21, 1924: 26), describing the film as "just another version of the oft told Cinderella" and a "good old-fashioned melodrama," thought the picture would do well outside of New York: "The title seems sure-fire for out of town and the smaller the town the bigger the picture should go. It is a hokum tale, done with a lot of dash and pep." But *Film Daily* (May 25, 1924: 10) evaluated the film quite differently, advising exhibitors, "The title will bring them in. They'll surely figure melodrama but they will go out delighted even though they have not seen what they expected." This reviewer described the film as follows: "Monta Bell, once a newspaper man, whose directorial ability was discovered by Charles Chaplin, was given the script of a melodrama written by Owen Davis many years ago. He promptly forgot the story and wrote in a new one and it is almost as entertaining and delightful as 'The Marriage Circle,' and you see the same touches, the same charming sequences that made 'The Woman of Paris' stand out as a great directorial contribution to the screen." Far from seeing the film as a "hokum tale," the *Film Daily* reviewer cautions, "Story? There isn't a story, that is nothing to talk about, but where it lacks heart interest and could probably stand a dramatic kick here and there still it runs so quickly that you never know that an hour or more has gone and you're mighty sorry when the final title comes."

In the absence of a print, it is hard to reconcile these two quite different evaluations of the film. But both the *Variety* and *Film Daily* reviewers praise the comedy in the film, especially in the boarding house scenes. The *New York Times* critic also describes several gags, one of which takes place in the boardinghouse:

> In one humorous scene one observes the varied histrionic types [in the rooming house] eager for their morning tub. All are disappointed, as they stealthily open the doors of their respective rooms and see the bathroom door closed. Norton, ignorant of the custom of such places, emerges from his room and goes straight to the bathroom, opens the door and—finds it empty. The irritation on the faces of the other boarders is indeed comic. The director then cuts to a scene showing Norton's valet enjoying himself in his master's tub, reading a newspaper, with a glass of wine on a chair.

Another gag reported by the *Times* concerns one of Norton's high-society friends: "Mrs. Vance (Carmel Myers) flirts with Norton while her husband is away. Vance calls her up on the long-distance telephone, and with Norton at her elbow she tells her husband how lonely she is without him. Norton, strangely disappointed with the woman, leaves her and goes home. Mrs. Vance rings him up, and he, after listening to her for half a minute, puts his valet on the wire, while he sits down in a comfortable chair, enjoying a libation, laughing at his servant's nervousness." On the basis of the gags reported in the *Times*, it seems safe to conclude that *Broadway After Dark* was not a straight melodrama but rather a comedy. The gags, as described, depend upon deliberate shifts in levels of knowledge as well as, presumably, Menjou's understated, "nonchalant" performance style. *Variety*'s categorization of the film as hokum may have been skewed by the original source material, which was a melodrama. Moreover, the techniques associated with the Chaplin and Lubitsch films were still quite new and may not have been fully recognizable as such.

Three important examples were released in the 1924–25 season. *Forbidden Paradise* (November 1924) was directed by Lubitsch, with a script by his long-time collaborator Hans Kräly and a juicy role for Adolphe Menjou. Because the film has been discussed by other historians, notably Lewis Jacobs, and because I want to consider Lubitsch's influence on other filmmakers, I will focus on the other two, *Open All Night,* released in October 1924, and *Her Night of Romance,* released in January 1925.[47]

Open All Night was directed by Paul Bern, who had been Lubitsch's screenwriter for *The Marriage Circle.* It will come as no surprise that the film is set in Paris and there are two principal couples: the upper-class Thérèse Duverne (Viola Dana) is bored with her refined and restrained husband Edmond (Adolphe Menjou); the working-class Lea (Jetta Goudal) tends to the needs of the brutish cyclist Petit Mathieu (Maurice B. Flynn). Thérèse's friend Isabelle (Gale Henry) has taken charge of an American floorwalker, Igor Romanoff (Raymond Griffith), who has pretensions to becoming the next American movie sheik. Thérèse quarrels with her husband, whom she regards as overly tame. Isabelle proposes to cure her of her "cave man complex" by introducing her to Petit Mathieu, and sends Edmond off for the evening. Mathieu is in the course of a grueling six-day race (the cyclists alternate three-hour stints of riding and sleeping, hence the film's title). Mathieu's manager banishes Lea from Mathieu's tent for kissing the champion when he needs to sleep. When Mathieu and Thérèse are introduced, the champion insists that she stay with him, mesmerizing her with a display of his biceps. Meanwhile, Edmond picks up Lea in the Café des Boulevards; she is happy to have a flirtation, although her allegiance to Mathieu remains paramount. The plot is resolved when Mathieu not only loses the race but is revealed to be an ungentlemanly cheat. While rescuing his wife from the champion's brutal and now unwelcome attentions, Edmond loses his temper when she accidentally breaks his cigarette holder, an elaborate affair in the shape of a nude woman's torso. He shakes her, bruising her arm, and she is happy to be ordered home. Lea is restored to Mathieu, who was always her first choice.

Film Daily (September 21, 1924: 5) characterized the film as "similar in many ways to the type of material presented by Chaplin in 'A Woman of Paris,' Lubitsch in 'The Marriage Circle,' and Monta Bell in 'Broadway After Dark.' The story is slight but the excellent handling of the characters more than redeems this." Other reviewers do not seem to be as concerned with this connection. In discussing the film's comedy, *Variety* (September 10, 1924: 27) focused entirely on the work of Raymond Griffith, praising his "souse" act. The critic for the *New York Times* (September 9, 1924: 19) also focused on this aspect of the film: "Mr. Griffith is seen intoxicated, making the most absurd and witless mistakes. One can only groan at these scenes, knowing that in a flash or two they will be supplanted by others."

As early as *Moving Picture World*'s review of *The Marriage Circle,* the trade press had worried that sophisticated comedy was too subtle to be really successful with the general run of audiences. Although *Film Daily* praised *Open All Night,* it also cautioned, "While the excellent characterizations and the skillful direction is important it is a question whether or not the picture fans care sufficiently about this." The introduction of the Igor Romanoff subplot may have been an attempt to compensate for sophisticated comedy's supposed lack of mass appeal with Raymond Griffith's slapstick. For example, at the climax of the race Igor stumbles drunkenly onto the track. The floor of the track is sharply banked, and he has trouble keeping his balance, a problem exacerbated by the cyclists whizzing by. Of course, no one actually does crash into him, although such a catastrophe appears imminent. At one point his coat flies out of his hand and into a cyclist's face. On the next round the coat is flung back to him. This kind of humor may have been considered "low" by the sniffy *New York Times* reviewer and approved by *Variety* for exactly the same reasons.

Alongside the slapstick, however, Bern employed another strain of comedy, of the sort *Film Daily* associated with Lubitsch, Chaplin, and Monta Bell. This is most pronounced in the film's opening, which deals with the discord between husband and wife. As Edmond enjoys a smoke, he casually picks up a pair of binoculars and looks out of the front window. The man across the way lifts his belt, as if about to beat his wife with it. The couple moves out of sight before he can see the beating. He passes judgment on this scene, talking to the cigarette holder, "Ivory Lady, you can't beat your wife and hold her, too. A woman may be fascinated by a brute—but she can never respect him."

Thérèse is introduced in the bath, facing away from the camera, scrubbing her back with a long-handled brush. She is reading a novel that is propped up on the faucets. An insert, emphasized by a mask, shows us what she is reading, first in French, then with a dissolve into English:

"You brute," she moaned.

"You are hurting me—I love you."

After a close-up of Thérèse, the film returns to the original framing and shows the scrubbing brush beginning to move quickly on her back. Edmond enters his wife's room and notices her clothes laid out in preparation for dressing for a nine o'clock dinner engagement. He examines her dainty things with some amusement. In the bathroom Thérèse uses a large sponge to squeeze water over her shoulders. There is a second insert: "Now he was beating her—beating her. She moaned half in pain and half in ecstasy." Thérèse bites the sponge.

Edmond knocks on the bathroom door. She is startled, then exasperated. He tells her that they are an hour late. She tells him she is not going. Still standing outside the door, he says nothing, looking surprised. She tells him: "If you were a man you would make me go. You would break down the door. You would beat me—*beat* me!" He laughs. She cowers in the bath. He winks, blows a kiss at the door, and backs out of the shot. She raises her head, wondering. Downstairs, he gets his hat and stick and goes to the door. She waits nervously in the tub, panting. He opens the front door and shuts it, without actually leaving. She gets out of the tub and puts on a robe. He waits, arms folded, until she appears. They eye each other, and she begins to cry. He goes to embrace her, but she refuses: "Iceberg! If only once I could make you lose your temper!" She throws a photograph of her husband to the floor and stamps on it. He looks bored and contains a yawn.

The scene is constructed through a symmetrical deflation of each character. Duverne's knowing homily about how to handle women is juxtaposed with his wife's sexual fantasies. Her expectation of a beating, or at least of a good fight, is undercut by his amused, polite refusal to engage. In addition to the editing, which contrasts the husband's state of mind with that of his wife, the film plays up what had already become Menjou's signature "nonchalance." This film's affinity with the emerging genre of sophisticated comedy is also indicated by the fact that Lubitsch borrowed two devices—a wife's being aroused by the "cave-man" lovemaking of a sheik in a novel, and a character's looking through the windows at the shenanigans of neighbors across the way—and used them to much greater effect in the opening of *So This Is Paris*, released in 1926.

From the start the methods of indirect representation that were hallmarks of Chaplin's and Lubitsch's technique were used to treat erotic subject matter. But compared with, for example, the shots of the model unwinding her sheet in *A Woman of Paris*, or the use of Mizzi's wrap in the garden scene in *The Marriage Circle*, Bern's teasing framings of Viola Dana in the bath in *Open All Night* and the rather transparent metaphor of the scrubbing brush seem a bit coarse. Although the reviewer does not mention this scene in particular, *Variety* was concerned that "for some localities the picture will be a little too sophisticated and offend certain audiences." This becomes more of an issue in the 1925–26 season.

Her Night of Romance, directed by Sidney Franklin and starring Constance Talmadge, is of particular interest because it featured a star who had been turning out comedies long before Adolphe Menjou was even a gleam in Lubitsch's eye. Constance Talmadge began her career as a comedienne as the Mountain Girl in *Intolerance*. In the late 1910s she worked for Joseph Schenck (her sister Norma's husband), releasing through Lewis Selznick's company Select, and starred in a series of polite comedies, many adapted from the stage. In 1919 Schenck signed with First National, and thereafter her films, many labeled Constance Talmadge Productions, were released through that company. After she left Select, Talmadge worked with a range of directors, among whom Sidney Franklin and Victor Fleming were the best known, but her most frequent collaborators were John Emerson and Anita Loos. This team wrote eleven of the fifteen comedies that she made for First National prior to *Her Night of Romance,* and they were also frequently credited as supervisors or producers on her films. Talmadge often played a madcap heroine, sexually innocent but aggressive in pursuit of her man.[48] In *Mama's Affair,* for example, she plays Eve, under the thumb of her controlling mother and about to be married off to the son of her mother's best friend so that she can be kept near at hand. She finally has a nervous breakdown, and the handsome young doctor called in to consult separates her from her mother. Once her "cure" is effected she vigorously pursues the doctor, overcoming her mother's conniving as well as some scruples on the part of the doctor himself.

Her Night of Romance represents a break with the Emerson and Loos team. It was written by Lubitsch's scenarist Hans Kräly, who was to write two further screenplays for the star, *Her Sister from Paris* (August 1925) and *The Duchess of Buffalo* (August 1926). At the time of its release, *Her Night of Romance* was seen as a departure for the actress. *Variety* (January 14, 1925: 30, 43) wrote that "the last series of this ingenue's pictures have more or less fallen down at the box office, but this one bids fair to again raise the status of Constance as a drawing card. It is a good story with just enough touch of sex to get it over." The reviewer also hinted that the style of the film was new: "There is one thing, however, that might be desired in regard to this picture, and that would be to see the treatment that Lubitsch would have given this story in direction had he handled it. It is of the type built to order for him." In the *New York Times* (January 13, 1925: 16) Mordaunt Hall noted that Kräly had previously worked with Lubitsch and praised him for "giving opportunities for many novel touches, which have been aptly and adroitly handled by the director, Sidney Franklin."

Like Talmadge's previous films, *Her Night of Romance* is fundamentally inoffensive. It deals neither with seduction, as did *A Woman of Paris,* nor with adultery and divorce, as did *The Marriage Circle* and *Open All Night.* The rich heiress Dorothy Adams and her father, Sam, the scrubbrush king, arrive in London. In her first appearance before the newspaper cameras while still on board ship, she makes herself appear ugly in order to scare off any fortune hunters who might become interested in her. She trips as she debarks and is aided by Paul Menford (Ronald Colman), an impecunious aristocrat. Menford follows Dorothy and her father to their train, seeking to return a watch she has dropped. He is pleased and surprised to find a much more beautiful girl hidden in the train than he had seen on the pier.

Joe Diamond, an agent who is trying to sell Paul's estate to Sam Adams, proposes that he could also arrange a marriage for Paul to the wealthy Dorothy, whose horrible grimacing features have appeared in the newspaper. Diamond asks for ten percent of all the money that Paul would make on the deal. Seeing the picture, Paul laughs and says, "Get me *that* girl and you can have *one hundred* percent." Diamond takes this as a sign to proceed.

Meanwhile, in order to see Dorothy again, Paul impersonates his uncle, a doctor, who has been asked to treat Dorothy for a heart condition. Menford starts visiting his patient regularly, and her "heart condition" improves. When Joe Diamond completes the sale of Menford Manor, he brings the paperwork to Paul for his signature. Diamond explains the beauty of the arrangement, "Mr. Adams buys your house—you get the money—then you marry his daughter and get back your house." Repulsed by this piece of double dealing, Menford writes to Dorothy to explain that he is not really a doctor and that he cannot see her again.

Telling her father that her nervous illness has taken a turn for the worse, Dorothy goes to Menford Manor to be alone for the night. A portrait on the wall indicates the identity of the previous owner. Menford arrives at the estate drunk, having forgotten that he no longer lives there. He climbs into the room in which Dorothy is sleeping. It is a typical farce situation: he slowly undresses while she waits under the covers, wide-eyed and terrified, until modesty demands that she flee, at which point she screams and bolts. Paul follows her into the hallway to beg forgiveness, and, after some further comic business, she is returned to her bedroom, and he falls asleep in the hall.

As they breakfast the next morning, Paul promises to leave promptly. But before he can do so, a friend and neighbor turns up. To save her from embarrassment, Paul introduces Dorothy as his wife. The old family butler is overcome with joy at this news, which he relays to the mailman, who promises to spread the word to the village. Sam arrives at the manor and assumes that the "doctor" is simply in attendance on his daughter. When the villagers come to the manor demanding to see the bride and groom, Sam is delighted at the turn of events.

After dinner Sam is in his cups, and he roars with laughter when Paul tells him that he is not really married to Dorothy. The more Paul protests, the more Sam laughs, telling him, "One more drink and you'll deny being a doctor." Sam escorts Paul to Dorothy's bedroom and leaves him there. Paul proposes marriage and, after mistakenly drinking her nerve medication, falls into an innocent sleep.

When Joe Diamond shows up at the manor to claim his ten percent from Paul, Dorothy overhears their conversation. She calls off the wedding and sends them both back to town. It takes the combined machinations of her father and his old butler to bring the couple back together again.

The film places the characters in indecorous situations as the genre of farce requires, but both hero and heroine are fundamentally blameless, and the improprieties lead to a marriage that carries the paternal imprimatur. If *Her Night of Romance* can be considered sophisticated, it is not because of the story, which is very much in the vein of the Talmadge vehicles of the late 1910s and early 1920s, but rather for its style. There are many situations in which Sidney Franklin seems to be experimenting with Lubitsch's technique. For analytical purposes consider a scene early in the film, when Paul Menford, posing as the doctor, has been invited to dinner. At the dinner table Dorothy reproaches Sam for drinking too much wine, which will make him sleepy. To Sam's relief, the doctor concurs with his opinion that he can and should drink for his health. They move to the sitting room. I provide a shot breakdown of what follows, as the film is not commercially available and is not well known:

1. Narrative title: Wine and music are a drowsy combination.

2. Extreme long shot of Dorothy seated at the piano, right. A bunch of flowers rests on the piano, front center.

3. Medium shot from around the front of the piano. Dorothy peeks over the instrument and is seen framed by flowers (figure 21).

4. Detail shot that isolates the following elements: Sam's hand, arm and shoulder on the right; a wine decanter and two glasses on a table center; and Paul's hand on the left. Sam's hand holds a cigar. Paul's hand begins to refill Sam's empty glass. Sam's hand falls off the arm of his chair, and Paul refrains from pouring (figure 22).

5. Medium shot of Sam in his chair. His head nods, and his eyes are closed.

6. As 4. Only Paul's hand is visible as he puts the decanter back on the tray and puts in the stopper. He puts out his cigarette.

7. As 2. Dorothy lowers her eyes, looking down.

8. Detail shot of Dorothy's feet at the pedals. One is labeled "soft," the next "medium," and the third "forte." She depresses the "soft" pedal (figure 23).

9. Medium shot from around Dorothy's back. The sheet music on the piano is prominent in the center of the shot. Paul's profile, in shadow, becomes evident on the music (figure 24).

10. 180-degree cut. Medium close-up of Dorothy. She breathes heavily, and her eyes move (figure 25).

11. 180-degree cut. The sheet music is again prominent. The framing isolates her hand, reaching out to turn the page, and Paul's hand, arresting her motion (figure 26).

12. Close-up of Dorothy in profile. She looks up left.

13. Low-angle medium shot of Paul. He looks down right. He moves.

14. Long shot from behind the couple as Paul sits beside Dorothy on the bench. He is still holding her hand in his left, and he takes her other arm in his right hand. She withdraws her arm and gets up, nervous. She exits right.

15. Extreme long shot. Dorothy moves to an open, arched doorway that leads to a conservatory with potted plants. To the right of the door is a plant stand with a vase of cut flowers. Paul enters from the left and crosses to the right of Dorothy. She begins to fiddle nervously with the flowers in the vase. He approaches. She suddenly grabs the vase and turns to face him.

16. Medium shot of the couple, Dorothy left and Paul right, with the vase between then. He places his hands over hers. He speaks.

17. Medium long shot of Sam, sleeping in his chair.

18. 180-degree cut. Paul is now left and Dorothy right. He speaks again (figure 27).

19. Detail shot of their hands on the vase. He moves his hands off hers (figure 28).

20. As 18. He moves his hands up the vase and separates the flowers so that he can kiss her.

21. Detail shot of her hands on the vase, with the trunks of both actors visible but not their heads. He leans forward, and the vase slips down.

22. As 18. They are about to kiss; there are just a few roses between them (figure 29).

23. Detail shot of the vase hitting the floor and breaking at their feet (figure 30).

24. As 18. They separate, reacting to the crash.

25. As 17. Sam is startled awake and immediately begins to clap. He mouths "bravo."

26. Medium shot of the couple. The camera is farther back than in 18 and has also been moved 180 degrees so that Dorothy is on the left and Paul on the right. Paul is still holding the roses. Dorothy turns around to face right, in the direction of her father.

27. As 17. Sam stops clapping and looks suspicious. He looks down and to the right (figure 31).

28. Detail shot showing what Sam sees: the pedal stand beneath the piano, without feet (figure 32).

29. As 17. Sam looks off in the direction of the piano.

30. As 28. Dorothy's feet as she takes her place at the piano.

31. As 17. Sam leans back, smiles and nods.

32. Long shot of Dorothy seated at the piano. Paul, holding the flowers behind him, approaches her from the right. He stands to look over the piano, looking off left.

33. Dialogue Title: "Did you like that selection, Daddy?"

34. As 17. Sam smiles.

35. Dialogue Title: "Fine! Especially the thunder effect at the finish."

36. As 17.

37. As 32. Dorothy sits back down. She glances behind her at Paul, who gestures with the flowers he is holding behind his back. She smiles. Fade to black.

The subject matter of this scene, unlike the one in which Paul examines Dorothy's heart, or the one in which he undresses in her bedroom at Medford Manor, is not very risqué. It treats nothing racier than a kiss, which does not actually happen. The calculated effort to put Sam to sleep is slightly wicked, but since it has been established that he likes the doctor and wants to see his daughter married, the paternal prohibition so flouted is not severe. The suggestiveness of this scene lies almost entirely in the way

21

22

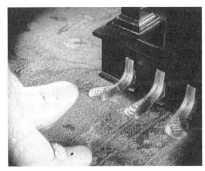

23

24

25

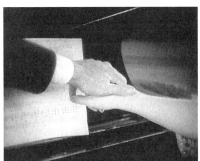

26

27

28

29

30

31

32

it is framed and edited. There are twenty-one distinct framings. Ten of them (shots 2, 3, 5, 14, 15, 16, 17, 18, 26, 32) are medium to long shots, while eleven (shots 4, 8, 9, 10, 11, 12, 13, 19, 21, 23, 28) are detail shots, not necessarily close-ups but framings that isolate one or more significant elements from the surrounding space. Unlike the office scene in *The Marriage Circle,* there are very few instances of glance/object editing or point-of-view editing that delineate shifts in characters' relative levels of knowledge. Only shots 27 through 30, when Sam notes the absence of his daughter's feet under the piano, perform such a function. Most of the detail shots play upon the spectator's knowledge and understanding of events, slyly leading us to make inferences about characters' motivations, and the events which occur in off-screen space. Shots 3–8 delineate the success of the conspirators in a series of discontinuous actions: Dorothy peeking at her father over the piano, the hand with the cigar going limp, the hand stopping up the wine bottle, Dorothy hitting the soft pedal. Shots 9–11, around the sheet music, refer to the initiation of amorous advances off-screen, and shots 19, 21, and 23, around the vase, similarly imply the initiation of the kiss, and subsequent interruption of Sam's nap. The use of detail shots to stand in for a more comprehensive depiction of the action is highly suggestive in itself. The charm of the scene derives, in part, from its simplicity; it was not necessary to maneuver the hero and heroine into a bedroom at night or have a heroine reading a spicy novel, naked, in the bath.

Although the large number of 180-degree cuts in the scene are a bit jarring and have no equivalent in Lubitsch, who, by the 1920s, was meticulous in his observance of continuity rules, Franklin's editing shows the influence of Lubitsch in its use of highly exposed symmetries and contrasts.[49] In shot 4 the hand holding the cigar goes limp, while in shot 6 a different hand purposefully extinguishes a cigarette. Dorothy's look at Sam in shot 3 and her use of the soft pedal in shot 8 are reversed by Sam's look in shot 27 and the absence of feet at the pedals in shot 28. The flowers from the vase, which foreclosed the kiss, come back to serve as a reminder of the attempt; Paul holds them behind his back (presumably to keep them from Sam's view) in shot 32, and from this position he manages to show them to Dorothy in the final shot of the scene. In addition to relying upon indirect methods of representation, Franklin seems to have assimilated the economical repetition of objects found in *The Marriage Circle.*

Monta Bell's *The Snob,* a lost film, was released in November 1924, during the same four months as *Forbidden Paradise, Open All Night,* and *Her Night of Romance.* Even though it is not possible to view a print, *The Snob* merits discussion because it was evaluated in similar ways. Ostensibly a drama about a small town social climber, the *Variety* reporter (December 17, 1924: 36) observed that the narrative had "a vein of comedy that continuously registers, and undoubtedly is the means of lifting this issue above what might be a drab classification." The film was dubbed "a well-conceived example of screen construction," and the reviewer alluded to the simplicity of the presentation: "Not given to pulse quickening nor calling for lavishness in settings, the film rests upon the story it has to tell and the manner in which it has been directed and played." According to *Variety,* much of the humor derived from scenes with the social climber's lower-class relatives and especially from one with his niece: "The passages in which this youngster is put through her recitation paces are classics as to cutting, through the manner in which the sub-titles have been inserted, treatment and characterization." *Film Daily* (November 2, 1924: 10) praised the film in much the same terms as *Variety:* "Monta Bell has put over another fine piece of direction and all the way through there are touches which stamp him emphatically as being in the advance of the directors who are blazing the way along new lines." The critic for the *New York Times* (24 December 15, 1924: 14) obviously saw the film as of the same ilk but an unsuccessful attempt at the style: "Monta Bell, the director, apparently fearful that some of his rather original touches might be missed, has overemphasized them to the extent that, instead of being mildly pleasing, these points become not a little irksome. . . . Mr. Bell drums home his ideas, when it would have been well for him to remember that Ernest [sic] Lubitsch is content to give only a few feet to a masterly stroke." This reviewer thought that the film would have been better if directed by "Lubitsch, Chaplin or Buchoweight [presumably Buchowetski]" and recommended cutting the "long-winded close-ups." The differences in critical evaluation here do not obviate the fact that, despite there being no association with Menjou or Hans Kräly, Monta Bell was thought to be attempting the style associated with *A Woman of Paris* and *The Marriage Circle.*

By the 1925–26 season the trade press seemed to have a clear sense of sophisticated comedy as a genre. The films were thought to run two risks: of being too subtle and of being too racy for the state censorship boards and conservative taste. The first problem seems to have been more worrisome than the second; but both certainly attracted comment.

Hobart Henley's *Exchange of Wives* (October 1925), adapted from a stage play by Cosmo Hamilton, again concerned two couples. In one the wife, an excellent cook, is unresponsive to her husband's sexual advances; in the other the husband fails to live up to his wife's expectations of aggressive, "cave-man" lovemaking. In the event of the "exchange" both men come to see the advantages of a really good lemon pie, but the original order of spouses is ultimately restored. Commenting on what had already become a cliché, *Film Daily* (October 18, 1925: 7) noted, "The plot lays no claim to outstanding originality in its situations nor any spectacular comedy gags but director Hobart Henley's deft touches and good development keeps it wholly interesting." The reviewer claimed that the film contained a moral, to the effect that one should not covet one's neighbor's wife, and judged that the film was within the bounds of censorship because during the exchange the husbands sleep in their original apartments and merely visit the women in theirs. *Variety* (October 7, 1925: 44) was more cautious than *Film Daily* in evaluating the film, speculating that Henley's rather blatant representation of the second wife, a sexually aggressive "Mizzi" type, would be likely to provoke censorship by the state boards in Ohio, Pennsylvania, and Maryland.[50]

Indeed, Sidney Franklin's *Her Sister from Paris*, released four months before *Exchange of Wives*, had been cut by state and local censorship boards. In that film Constance Talmadge, again teamed with Ronald Colman, has a double role. Helen Weyringer separates from her husband Joseph. When her twin sister, Lola, a famous dancer, visits her sister in Vienna, Joseph is smitten. With her sister's help, Helen impersonates Lola and fascinates her own husband, to the point of luring him to the same hotel and room in which they had spent their honeymoon.[51] *Film Daily* (August 30, 1925: 4) wrote, "This is Hans Kraely's first [*sic*] for the Schenck organization. Kraely came to this country with Ernst Lubitsch and has prepared all of the Lubitsch material, so you can easily imagine the type of story he presents, only this time he goes quite a bit further and some of the scenes are dangerously close to what the censors will kick at." The reviewer nonetheless praised the film, noting that his summary of the plot could not "possibly furnish an adequate idea of the delightful treatment and the splendid direction which results in a lovely piece of entertainment." While endorsing the film enthusiastically, *Variety* (August 26, 1925: 25) noted that it had been censored in Ohio.[52]

In addition to the concerns about censorship raised by *Her Sister from Paris* and *Exchange of Wives*, the trade press was preoccupied with the problem of the breadth of sophisticated comedy's appeal. Presumably the ideal film was explicit enough to make its meaning unmistakable and indirect enough to obviate the threats of censorship. This preference is indicated by *Variety*'s reaction to the lost Lubitsch film *Kiss Me Again* (August 1925), which had been loosely adapted by Hans Kräly from *Divorçons*, a farce by Victorien Sardou and Émile de Najac.[53] *Variety* (August 5, 1925:

31) seems to have hesitated in its judgment about the market, characterizing the film as "a picture that is designed principally for the sophisticated, but still broad enough in its humor to be appreciated almost by anyone. In the bigger towns it should be surefire at the box office." This reviewer also referred to a "touch" that he apparently considered just suggestive enough. At the end of the film, when the wife abandons her plans for divorce and a new husband and is reconciled with the old one, "there is a touch that will cause audiences to gasp when they get the suggestion of the two disrobing. It is cleverly done, and at the finish there is a touch that takes away all suggestiveness."

I have not been able to view Monta Bell's *The King on Main Street* (November 1925), but the trade press discourse indicates that it was similarly judged both comprehensible for all audiences and delicate enough in its handling of sexual matters. Under the threat of marriage to a rich but unattractive princess, the King of Molvania (Adophe Menjou) goes to America to borrow money. En route he stops in Paris to visit his mistress, Terèse (Greta Nissen), but once in the United States he falls in love with an American girl (Bessie Love). In the end he must return to his kingdom and his princess. The film was based upon a 1917 play, *The King,* starring Leo Ditrichstein, itself taken from *Le Roi* by Gaston Arman de Caillavet, Robert de Flers, and Emmanuel Arène. *Variety* (October 28, 1925: 36) referred to the 1917 production of the play: "It is a sophisticated comedy, or rather was as a play, and with Leo Dietrichstein [*sic*] in the title role just about suited the better classes, but the adaptation has broadened to such an extent that the high, the low and the in between are all bound to fall for it." *Moving Picture World* (November 7, 1925: 60) assured its readers, "It is told with a wealth of delightful incident that will appeal to everyone from the kiddies and the lowbrow to the intellectual who affects to despise comedy." The reference to children seems to have been motivated by an episode in which the king explores Coney Island in the company of an American boy. *Film Daily* (November 1, 1925: 5), which averred that a scene on a roller coaster in Coney Island was an enormous success with audiences, thought it had "sure-fire box office values" and told exhibitors, "Don't worry about this one." Although the film was thought to have wide appeal, it was also considered subtle and indirect. *Variety* refers to the king's stopover in Paris: "He has a sweetie in Paris and wants to spend the evening, the night and part of the morning with her first. He does that little thing and the way in which it is handled in the direction is complete. There isn't a single thing that anyone could take offense at, yet there isn't a single thing left to the imagination." *Photoplay* agreed with this judgment: "The picture is centered around a series of spicy and ultra-sophisticated situations which Monta Bell, the director, has logically developed with skill and freshness without shocking the censorious."[54]

Malcolm St. Clair's *The Grand Duchess and the Waiter* (February 1926) was intrinsically less offensive than *The King on Main Street*. The plot concerns a millionaire's efforts to woo the Grand Duchess Zenia, an exiled Russian aristocrat, by posing as a waiter in her service. Although the hero is shown with multiple assignations at the film's opening, he becomes devoted to the Duchess from the first moment he sees her. Neither character is married, so there is no suggestion of adultery. The duchess is obviously in need of help: she is attended by her highborn relations who, with no money and expensive tastes, remain charmingly oblivious to the reality of their new circumstances. Even when he goes so far as to kiss the sleeping Zenia's foot, the hero's attitude to his erstwhile employer can only be described as chivalrous. In the manner of a fairy tale, the marriage that closes the story is a foregone conclusion from the start. Both *Variety* (February 10, 1926: 40) and *Film Daily* (February 21, 1926: 6) assumed that the film would be widely successful and that it would not pose any problems at the level of censorship (*Variety* also noted that Menjou went through his role "like Sherman through Georgia"). *Moving Picture World* (February 27, 1926: 788) stressed that the film was not just for first-run metropolitan theaters: "Although the high standard of the wit will delight the most intelligent spectators it can hardly be called sophisticated for the humor of the situations and lines can be grasped by anyone." *Photoplay*, in contrast, admitted the film's sophistication, especially at the level of its sexual appeal: "A dramatic bonbon that will not improve your mind nor help you hold your husband nor solve how to pay the mortgage. But how it will delight you if you belong to that class which finds an uplifted eyebrow more stimulating than a heaving chest." However, the reviewer went on to reassure readers, "Sophistication and sex at their merriest are here. Yet so beautifully is it all handled it is safe for everyone from grandma down to the baby."[55]

Lubitsch's *Lady Windemere's Fan* (December 1925) provides an interesting contrast with most of the other films of that season. Most critics appreciated the film, and it was not considered a censorship risk, but some deemed it overly subtle. *Moving Picture World* (December 12, 1925: 575) commented favorably upon individual "touches," including the shot indicating Lord Augustus's pursuit of Mrs. Erlynne after the races, the development of the race track scene through "clever and extremely effective facial by-play" (and, it should be noted, point-of-view shots), and the "unexpected and amusing handling of Lord Darlington's declaration of love for Lady Windemere and the deft way he assists the Lord to retrieve an incriminating letter." *Variety* (January 13, 1926: 42) also singled out the scene at the race track, among other distinctive bits. But the reviewer for *Moving Picture World* thought that Lubitsch's "distinctly high-class rendition of Oscar Wilde's play" suffered from a "drawing room tempo," and he regretted that the "possibilities" of the racing scene had been ignored (i.e., the race was not shown in any detail). Due to this, and to Lubitsch's "method of handling," he estimated that the film's greatest appeal would be to "the highest class of patronage." *Film Daily* (December 6, 1925: 4) wrote, "Lubitsch with his masterful touch has turned this somewhat weak material for pictures into a very fine production replete with Lubitsch touches, but whether or not it is over the heads of the average picture audience remains to be seen." *Photoplay* dubbed the film unsuitable for children, although it is not clear if this was because of the scandalous situation at the film's close, or because the film was thought to be too difficult for them to understand.[56]

As late as Harry d'Abbadie D'Arrast's *A Gentleman of Paris, Variety* (October 5, 1927: 22) remained concerned about the extent of sophisticated comedy's appeal, commenting, "Graceful society comedy daintily done, but, of course, terribly thin fare for meat-eating picture fans." But if the stylistic traits of sophisticated comedy made the trade press leery about its commercial prospects, there was nevertheless a sense that these films represented an advance in filmmaking technique. This position was stated again and again in relation to *A Woman of Paris* and *The Marriage Circle*, as indicated above, but it was retained later in the decade as well. For example, *Variety* (August 18, 1926: 58) applauds *So This Is Paris* with the comment "Lubitsch has a snappy way of putting forward the laughs. He slams them over without unnecessary 'planting' or using any of the rigamarole of the stereotyped." *Variety* (December 14, 1927: 21) also described a "delightfully jaunty scene" in Allan Dwan's *French Dressing*, in which an American goes to Paris in search of his wife, who has run off and seeks a divorce. He meets the Frenchman who is courting her. "Frenchman and American measure each other. Each observes the other wears the red ribbon of the Legion of Honor, and they depart to conference. It takes two close-ups and one brief title to convey a world of unexpressed drama, where the ordinary 'movie' technique would have had two artificial actors generating high-power scenes all over the place." This analysis, directed toward a film that did not involve the best-known practitioners of the style, without the participation of Lubitsch, Adolphe Menjou, or even Hans Kräly, indicates that the techniques of sophisticated comedy had become generally available to American directors and that they were readily identifiable as such within the industry trade discourse.

To my knowledge, the literary intellectuals of the 1920s did not write extensively about this form of comedy as it unfolded before them. In a brief review of Lubitsch's *Lady Windemere's Fan*, Edmund Wilson praised the acting and cinematography but asserted that the film, in contrast to Wilde's play, was without wit.[57] In a 1932 essay on American humor, Gilbert Seldes characterized twentieth-century humor in terms of an opposition between sophisticated and popular varieties.[58] The *New Yorker* was described as the "semi-official organ of sophistication," and Seldes wrote both of the writers associated with the group, Franklin P. Adams, Robert Benchley, Donald Ogden Stewart, Frank Sullivan, and Dorothy Parker, and the cartoonists, Peter Arno and O. Soglow, applauded for their minimal use of words. The popular humorists discussed included George McManus, who composed the daily comic strip *Bringing Up Father;* the radio comics Freeman Gosden and Charles Correll, who played Amos and Andy; and Walt Disney's Mickey Mouse cartoons. Although in conclusion Seldes predicted that the division of American humor into elite and popular types would not endure, he nonetheless cast the mass media purely on the side of the popular: "The radio and the moving picture are specifically adapted to the small town citizen, the rustic, and the provincial—and, of course, all of these occur in great numbers in our larger cities." There was no hint that any Hollywood film had been described as sophisticated.

But I hope to have indicated that within the terms of the institution of cinema, films like *A Woman of Paris* and *The Marriage Circle* were considered sophisticated insofar as they presupposed a preference for subdued effects and eschewed didacticism and highly wrought climaxes in equal measure. Not only were the films appreciated for their wit and elegance, they were held as exemplars of modern filmmaking technique. I have argued that the hallmarks of this technique, an apparent simplicity and restraint, were generated by a rather complex system of narration, which limited the use of intertitles and employed devices such as point-of-view editing and motivic scene construction to convey characters' states of mind. Moreover, the seeming economy of the films, as well as many of the jokes, depended on careful preparation and sometimes quite elaborate structures of repetition. These principles of storytelling and scenography have, of course, been seen as typical of the classical Hollywood cinema as a whole, and from as early as 1917.[59] But in the 1920s filmmakers such as Chaplin and Lubitsch pushed these principles in the direction of increasingly reduced depictions of story events and an increasingly understated dramaturgy. And, their techniques were identified as new within the trade press, part of a coming trend, an efficient and streamlined approach to directing. This congruence between what most present-day film scholars regard as "classical" and what in the 1920s was regarded as "modern" is not as anomalous as it may seem. There are canonic examples of the affinities between modernism and classicism: Stravinsky, Le Corbusier. To these may be added the literary avant-gardists who advocated a lean and precise vernacular. Thus, in a 1916 letter to Iris Barry, Ezra Pound asserted that the art of writing was "concision, or style, or saying what you mean in the fewest and clearest words."[60] Given the tools of the medium and the constraints of a popular form, the sophisticated filmmakers worked out a classicism with its own debts to modernism.

4   The Male Adventure Story

> The current gyneolatry is as far outside his scheme of things as the
> current program of rewards and punishments, sins and virtues,
> causes and effects. He not only sees clearly that the destiny and
> soul of man are not moulded by petty jousts of sex, as the prophets
> of romantic love would have us believe; he is so impatient of the
> fallacy that he puts it as far behind him as possible, and sets his
> conflicts amid scenes that it cannot penetrate, save as a palpable
> absurdity. Love, in his stories, is either a feeble phosphorescence or
> a gigantic grotesquerie. In "Heart of Darkness," perhaps, we get his
> typical view of it. Over all the frenzy and horror of the tale itself
> floats the irony of the trusting heart back in Brussels. Here we
> have his measure of the master sentimentality of them all.
>
> H. L. MENCKEN, "Joseph Conrad"

Mencken's argument that the adventure story provided an escape from the
demands of the sentimental novel—the romance plot, the importance
accorded to the woman, ideas of sin and virtue, reward and punishment—
now has wide intellectual currency.[1] This argument has been applied retro-
spectively to nineteenth-century novelists like Cooper, Melville, and Twain
by Leslie Fiedler, and it survives even in contemporary feminist accounts of
the male adventure story, such as Jane Tompkins's *West of Everything.*[2] But
note that for Mencken writing in 1917 Conrad's adventure stories were
held to be unusual in their amorality and their refusal of "gyneolatry." This
suggests that stories of male adventure have not always been dissociated
from sentimentality and romance. A somewhat obscure example of a sentimental adventure story, *The Black Avenger of the Spanish Main* (Tom
Sawyer's favorite adventure story), is cited by Henry Nash Smith in a discussion of mid-nineteenth-century low-brow fiction.[3] The rather complex
plot concludes when the pirate Solanis, after outfighting his enemies in
many sea battles and killing some of the governor's best men, brings
together the governor who seeks his arrest and a nobleman who, like himself, had been deprived of his wife and child. Through a series of wordless
tableaux, clearly modeled on Diderot's *Entretiens sur Le Fils naturel,* the
pirate reenacts the separation and reunion of both families, thereby soften-
ing the governor's hard heart and bringing all together for a happy

end.[4] While boys' literature did not often borrow so directly from the proponent of the *comédie larmoyante*, it remained a sentimental genre well into the twentieth century. Franco Moretti's well-known essay on sentiment, "Kindergarten," often cited by film scholars interested in the creation of tears or pathos, is an essay on boys' literature, not women's fiction.[5]

For the American cinema the 1920s seems to be the decade in which sentimentality began to be judged to be inappropriate for masculine action stories, a process I will investigate here. Nonetheless, it should be established that many films of the 1920s that may be classified as male adventure, and were so seen by the trade press at the time, do not manifest the kind of "tough stories in a tough manner" that the critic Robin Wood has held to be epitomized by the work of Howard Hawks. Many low-budget action films, sometimes described as "action melodramas" by *Variety*, manifest a sentimental as well as a thrilling, "blood-and-thunder," melodramatic strain. Some of these are assumed to appeal to a juvenile audience. *Speed Madness*, independently produced, starring the stunt man Frank Merrill (whose stage name is itself taken from boys' adventure fiction) and distributed by Peter Kanellos, was described by *Variety* (December 2, 1925: 41) as "aimed at 11-year-old intelligences": "The dear old homestead mortgaged to the mustachioed, foreign villain. And the kindly but weak old mother who consents to her daughter's marrying the cur to save the farm. And finally the hero who says 'Nay' and nearly breaks his neck selling his auto valve patent, chasing the heavy all around the place and finally crushing the little lady to his athletic bosom."[6]

Such films were not only targeted at boys. *Hook and Ladder No. 9*, distributed by FBO Pictures, concerns two firemen in love with the same girl. Dan is shy, and by the time he proposes, Johnny has wooed and won her. The two men fight, and after Johnny marries the girl Dan refuses to accept the situation gracefully. But when the big fire inevitably occurs, Dan nobly rescues Johnny's wife and child (according to *Variety* there is some doubt about whether or not he dies in the attempt). *Variety* (December 21, 1927: 25) describes it as a "straightforward handkerchief melodrama" it presumes will "be most appreciated by unsophisticated customers." *Variety* (December 14, 1927: 23) also approves of *Shield of Honor*, distributed by Universal, which it claims has "no pretension to class, and for its purpose is an expert bit of work." The plot is summed up briefly: "A vigorous action drama of sure fire material, the high points made up of an airplane chase by the hero, a police aviator, who rounds up a gang of diamond thieves in a thrilling action fought in the clouds and on the ground." *Variety* comments that the story "is labored in parts, as usually happens in these he-man pictures," but that, in addition to some neat comic bits, "sentiment is laid on pretty thick, which is probably as it should be for the clientele it is addressed to." At least some of this pathos involves the aviator's policeman father, who is forced to retire from the force against his will. In addition to praising the emotional value of this situation, *Variety* notes that Universal made a similar film dealing with firemen.

Films featuring fistfights or boxing matches, usually considered a masculine genre,[7] were given to scenes of pathos and were frequently highly moralistic. The *Variety* reviewer reassures exhibitors that *April Showers* (November 22, 1923: 27) has fight scenes "full of action and not technical enough to bore the women and those not interested in boxing." The reviewer also notes that the director, Tom Forman, "has not wrung his pathos dry, but puts it across with a wealth of simplicity and comedy relief that make it not the ordinary screen pathos, but genuine poignant human interest." From the plot description given in the review, it is clear that these moments of human interest involve not only the hero's feisty Irish sweetheart but also his mother. The most cursory glance at the plot summaries of such major boxing films as *The Beloved Brute* (1924), *The Knockout* (1925), *Knockout Reilly* (1927), and *The Shakedown* (1929) reveals their sentimentality, at least according to present-day tastes. For example, *The Beloved Brute*, Victor McLaglen's first film in America, is a Western in which fight scenes predominate. Charles Hinges, a brutal boxer, experiences a spiritual transformation when he is bested in a wrestling match by his long-lost brother, who is a reformer in a Western town. He renounces his girlfriend, Jacinta, in his brother's favor and later takes the blame for a murder of which his brother is accused, only to be saved at the last minute by Jacinta, who fixes the blame on the real murderer (neither brother) and reveals her true love for Charles. In *The Shakedown*, an early experiment in deep staging directed by William Wyler, the protagonist is a street tough teamed with a group of shysters who set him up as a surefire win and then bet against him, cleaning up when he throws the fight. He moves to Boonton and, as part of an effort to make himself the local favorite, adopts an orphan boy. His growing love for the boy, who believes in his honesty and prowess, as well as for a local waitress, leads him to break with his partners; in the final fight, against the odds, he wins.

The action melodrama rubric included more than just films for the neighborhoods or subsequent-run theaters. *Variety* looked favorably upon Samuel Goldwyn's 1923 version of *The Spoilers*, adapted from Rex Beach's best-selling novel about claim jumping in Alaska (August 9, 1923: 26). The high point of the plot is a fistfight between the hero and the villain, and *Variety* compares at great length the fight staged between William Farnum and Thomas Santschi in the 1914 Selig-produced version with the fight staged between Milton Sills and Noah Beery in 1923. The *Variety* reviewer lauds both but thinks the 1923 version superior: "Boy, that is a fight! It's remarkable either one or both didn't go to the hospital. They broke little furniture, but went after each other like a couple of tigers." In addition to the action elements, *Variety* notes the presence of sentiment in the film, asserting that the triangle between the saloon girl, Cherry, the hero Glennister, and the good woman, Helen, is "very feelingly set out." In this sentimental subplot Glennister abandons Cherry, who nonetheless loves him and continues to look out for his interests. She warns him when the villains are about to engineer his arrest, stops him from drinking too much at a crucial moment, and finally sends him off to rescue her rival, Helen, when the girl has gone off alone with one of the minor villains and is threatened with rape. The film thus incorporates a subplot that, had it stood by itself, might well have been found old-fashioned. In this context, however, *Variety* praises both the subplot and the sympathy generated for Cherry, going on to assure its readers that when the film opened in Chicago "it had a run in the middle of the summer that bespoke its drawing qualities. It's one of those self-advertisers and sure-fire for money."

Variety (August 17, 1927: 21) classed *Wings*, one of the biggest hits of 1927, as having "vital and universal appeal" and belonging to an elite group that included only six other films: *Birth of a Nation, Way Down East, The Ten Commandments, The Covered Wagon, The Big Parade,* and *Ben-Hur.* This classification was based upon the spectacular aerial battle scenes. *Variety* found the story an "average tale" that "was human enough to make 90 per cent of the women in the house cry."

Two boys from the same town, Jack Powell (Charles Rogers) and David Armstrong (Richard Arlen), go through training school together and become fast friends and fliers with the Allied Expeditionary Force (AEF) in France. David is shot down behind enemy lines and steals a German plane in an attempt to get back to his base. Jack shoots down what he thinks is an enemy flier and then discovers what he has done when he lands and finds his friend, who dies in his arms. *Variety* singled out as affecting not only the death scene, which made the women cry, but also the scene near the beginning, in which David takes leave of his parents (Henry Walthall and Julia Swayne Gordon), and the scene near the end, in which Jack faces those parents, bringing them David's decorations and the toy bear that was his friend's good luck charm.

The film's romance subplots are equally sentimental. Both boys are in love with Sylvia (Jobyna Ralston), although it is clear from the start that

Jack's next-door neighbor Mary (Clara Bow) is really the girl for him. Before the big battle the boys quarrel over a locket with Sylvia's picture. Sylvia meant it for David and inscribed it to him on the back but, out of pity, gave it to Jack when he asked for it. When Jack drops the locket and the picture falls out, David, concerned that his friend might see the inscription and be hurt, tears it up, gallantly refusing to explain this seemingly hostile action. The inevitable sequence of the boys on leave in Paris is also quite tame and sweet. Mary has joined the ambulance corps and is in Paris when all leaves are revoked and all fliers ordered to report to the front. She searches for Jack, finding him drunk and still drinking champagne in the Folies-Bergère in the company of a French woman. Animated bubbles rise out of the wine glasses, containing women's bodies and other objects to indicate his state of mind. He is too drunk to recognize Mary in her ambulance driver's uniform and refuses to leave with her when she tells him he must report to the front. She finally borrows a seductive dress and gets him away from the French woman and back to his flat, where he passes out before he can kiss her. When the military police who are rounding up fliers come to his room, they find Mary undressing. They give her the eye but then send her home with a dialogue title that seems laughable today: "Put your clothes on! You can't get away with this sort of thing in the A.E.F. It's back home for you, sister." At the end of the film, when Jack and Mary are reconciled, he apologizes for the episode in Paris. Without knowing that she was the girl, he explains that he got drunk and "forgot himself." This insistence on the hero's boyish innocence and upright nature is integral to the film's sentimentality and almost takes it back into the realm of boys' fiction.

Consideration of a range of films from low-budget melodramas such as *Shield of Honor* and *Hook and Ladder No. 9* through moderately successful programmers such as *The Spoilers* to prestigious productions such as *Wings* reveals that a presumed masculine appeal and an emphasis upon action in a film did not necessarily preclude the inclusion of sentimental elements. But another aviation film, probably made to compete with *Wings* and released during the month of its première, does provide a hint that tastes were changing by the late 1920s. Charles Brabin's *Hard-Boiled Haggerty* starred Milton Sills and was distributed by First National. As usual, *Variety* (August 27, 1927: 23) provides a zesty plot summary: "Haggerty has a habit of popping off German planes, watching them fall and then flying on to Paris to dodge the M.P.s. Dodging himself into Germaine's (Miss O'Day) apartment the love interest is on, only to become complicated when the Irish boy's major tips him off that the girl isn't all she should be. Sock, and into the conference which will lead to a court-martial unless one

of the men speaks. The major finally gives in and the girl admits everything. Haggerty disillusioned." The plot is resolved when it is revealed that
Germaine has a twin sister, Go-Go, a notorious cabaret dancer. The major
had confused the good sister with the bad one, and Germaine had played
along with this for fear that her boyfriend would be court-martialed. All is
resolved after the Armistice, and "it looks as if Germaine will see the
Atlantic." *Variety* approves of the "rough and ready characterization holding situations where strong men stifle their emotions, but not so much that
the camera can't catch it." It judges the story to be an "all male affair" and
evaluates the star's appeal in a similar fashion: "Nothing doll-faced about
Sills. Probably why the men like him." It is obvious from the description
that the plot has many sentimental elements—the aviator protecting his
sweetheart's name, the girl sacrificing her reputation for the man she loves
(although *Variety* finds this part of the story overly "theatrical"), and
another scene, mentioned in the review as having quite a "kick," in which
the hero renounces his uniform before the board of inquiry. But the example is interesting because there is a complaint about its plot as well; the love
affair was apparently quite developed, too much so for *Variety*'s taste:

> That's "Haggerty," and it has a good chance to survive at the various
> box offices despite the anchors Brabin has tied to it every time a love
> port heaves in sight. Brabin, not the speediest director in the world has
> sprinkled this one with enough closeups to take care of two normal pic-
> tures. Don't tell a director where to place his closeups. They say. Well, if
> the ethics of the studios permit, somebody should take the subject up
> with Charles in a general way. No kiddin', there are enough heads of
> Molly O'Day in this one to make those Barthelmess "stills" in the
> Globe's lobby blush.

(This last reference is to another First National release, *The Patent Leather
Kid,* with Richard Barthelmess and Molly O'Day.) Thus, in *Variety*'s estimation, *Hard-Boiled Haggerty* was not quite hard-boiled enough. This is a
tantalizing hint of a change in taste, but it is difficult to elaborate further
and definitively to trace the development of the "tough" male adventure
story. Many different plot types are involved—Westerns, war films, sea stories, detective stories, stories of prospecting for gold or oil, and stories about
railroad men, policemen, and firemen. The literary influences on this development in the cinema are also correspondingly diffuse, including Kipling,
Wister, London, Conrad, Hecht, more remotely Nietzsche, and, later in the
1930s, Hemingway and Faulkner.[8] I propose to begin, then, by examining
the influence of a single text, the play *What Price Glory* by Maxwell Anderson and Laurence Stallings, which was produced by Arthur Hopkins at the

Plymouth Theatre in New York in September 1924. The play was an enormous success, running on Broadway for 299 performances and launching a touring company.[9] Hollywood attempted to capitalize upon the play's popularity in many films. The film adaptation by Raoul Walsh for Fox was roadshowed beginning in December 1926 and went into general release in August 1927. It was preceded in 1925 by MGM's *The Big Parade,* based on a story that King Vidor worked out with Stallings. Although very different in tone from *Wings,* both of the Stallings-influenced World War I films were big hits. *Variety* (December 2, 1925: 40) wrote of the New York opening of *The Big Parade,* "The first Sunday night (Nov. 22) saw them standing six deep in the Astor, and they've been on their feet to view it ever since. . . . it's a cinch Jeff McCarthy knew what he was talking about when he took one flash at this picture long before it was finished and said 'road show.'"[10] *What Price Glory* was similarly assessed. *Film Daily* (November 28, 1926: 12) called it "a box office knockout. One of the biggest of this year and of any other year." *Variety* (December 1, 1926: 12) concurred:

> The chances are that "What Price Glory" will be just as big at the box office as "The Big Parade" was, providing it is as deftly handled as a road show. One thing the Fox people do not want to do and that is to rush in all over the country with road shows right off the bat. The thing to do with this one is to lay back, pick the spots and play about six of the big cities this season. Philadelphia, Boston, Chicago added to New York and Los Angeles already opened, and possibly San Francisco should be all that are hit this season, and then late next August strike out with about 12 companies in the week stands and get the money.

These two films gave rise to many subsequent imitations and variants that, taken as a group, represented a sharp break with previous films about the War and stood apart from more traditional representations of male heroism and honor.

Kenneth MacGowan, a drama critic and producer in New York from 1910 to 1924, cites three plays from those years that epitomize the realist (as opposed to symbolist or expressionist) tendencies of the American theater: *What Price Glory,* O'Neill's *Anna Christie,* and Sidney Howard's *They Knew What They Wanted.*[11] These plays were considered realist in at least two senses. First, they made extensive use of the vernacular. Although comedic actors had always freely employed dialect, and plays set in the West, the South, or New England employed the accents and intonations of regional speech for secondary characters, the language of the principals in the plays cited by MacGowan was distinctly new. In *Anna Christie* the main characters are working-class Swedish and Irish immigrants who use accented English; in *They Knew What They Wanted* one principal has an Italian accent, while the rest use ethnically unmarked but nonetheless slangy and ungrammatical speech. In the Anderson and Stallings play, the accented and sometimes incorrect English of the French characters, and their extensive use of French, is set against the speech patterns of the Marines, full of slang, military and otherwise, and their debased, Americanized French. This passage is from the end of the first act:

CHARMAINE: *Le capitaine—il est parti?*

QUIRT: Just left. Don't cry, little one.

CHARMAINE: *Le nouveau sergeant. N'est-ce pas?*

QUIRT: *N'est-ce pas* is right.

CHARMAINE: I wanted to see the captain.

QUIRT: Just too late, sorry to say. You one piecie captain's fella boy? You captain's fella?

CHARMAINE: *Le capitaine? Mais non!*

QUIRT: I'll bet it's *mais non.* Say, ain't you Cognac Pete's daughter?

CHARMAINE: *Oui.* You stay at Pete's?

QUIRT: Sure. *Et vous?*

CHARMAINE: *C'est mon père.*

QUIRT: Uh-huh. I thought so. Well, baby, you better stick to me, and you'll have another papa.

It should be stressed that the departure from the norms of genteel English in *What Price Glory* and kindred works went far beyond the introduction of profanity—it amounted to a decisive shift away from formality and decorum in stage dialogue for principal characters. However, the 1920s debates about the use of the vernacular focused on oaths and swear words. Kenneth MacGowan tells a story, current in the period, of a dowager who, "as the curtain fell on *What Price Glory?,* muttered to her companion: 'Where the hell are my goddam overshoes?'"[12] When he published *Anna Christie* in the volume *The Best Plays of 1921–1922,* Burns Mantle warned that its dialogue might "prove offensive to playgoers of superfine sensibilities," and he reminded his readers that "it is the story of a coal barge captain, a prostitute and a steamship stoker. These do not speak the language of the drawing room."[13] In *The Best Plays of 1924–1925,* Mantle noted that four plays of that season, O'Neill's *Desire Under the Elms, What Price Glory, They Knew What They Wanted,* and Edwin Justus Mayer's *The Firebrand,* together revived a demand for the New York district attorney to institute play censorship as well as "a lusty, and effectively overwhelming protest, as it turned out, against such interference."[14] According to an item by Stark Young in the *New York Times* (September 28, 1944: 1), the language of *What Price Glory* had to be toned down (presumably as a result of negotiations with the district attorney's office), although Young, I think rightly, remarks that the play "does not depend on its somewhat startlingly frank and recognizable phrases. What ultimately gives that effect of life to the lines of the play is the rhythm and cadence of the writing and fine vitality behind it."

MacGowan gives a slightly different context for the language of *What Price Glory*. He compares it to such later produced comic plays as *Broadway*, by Philip Dunning and George Abbott, *Chicago*, by Maurine Watkins (both produced in the 1926–27 season), *Burlesque*, by George Manker Watters and Arthur Hopkins (1927–28), and *The Front Page*, by Ben Hecht and Charles MacArthur (1928–29). He describes it as a "particularly American kind of play," "fast and funny" and unlike either O'Neill's realist work *(Anna Christie)* or his more symbolist work *(The Emperor Jones, The Great God Brown, Strange Interlude)*.[15]

What Price Glory was considered realist not only because of its use of the vernacular but also because of its departure from conventional representations of the War. Burns Mantle wrote of the play that it had "most effectively cleared the stage forever of the type of war play that is no more than prettily heroic. It represents war, specifically the great war of ten years back, as it is in truth and in fact and there is pretty general agreement with the estimate of Heywood Broun who wrote that 'This is certainly the best use which the theatre has yet made of the war, and it is entirely possible that it is the best American play about anything.'"[16]

Stark Young evaluated the play in similar terms: "The chaos, the irrelevance, the crass and foolish and disjointed relation of these men's lives and affairs to the war shows everywhere, and the relation of the war to their real interests and affairs. This is a war play without puerilities and retorts at God and society, and not febrile and pitying, but virile, fertile, poetic and Rabelaisian all at once, and seen with the imagination of the flesh and the mind together."[17] MacGowan wrote most incisively that it "is unromantic about war and women. It is neither patriotic nor respectable."[18]

What Price Glory was clearly aligned with literary naturalism in its violations of stage decorum—its use of the vernacular, and of deliberately rough and crude characters—its abandonment of moral justifications for war, and its scabrous representation of sex. Despite its popularity the play posed enormous problems for film directors and studios interested in its adaptation.[19] It depended heavily on a new style of spoken dialogue which, quite apart from the profanity involved, was a challenge to translate to the medium of silent film. It was also, in contradistinction to the Hollywood cinema, "unromantic about war and women," "neither patriotic nor respectable." Although *What Price Glory* left a deep impression upon American film, most of the film adaptations or variations of it muted at least some of these elements. It is as if the play were a bitter tonic that no studio was prepared to swallow whole, but by dint of ingesting little bits of it, films were nonetheless transformed, and the male adventure story was moved in a decisively antisentimental direction.

The play and the two primary film variants are very similar in structure. The play is in three acts. The first is set in a provincial French town behind the lines, where two men, Captain Flagg and Sergeant Quirt, compete for the affections of a French girl, Charmaine. This act ends with the troops being called up to the front. The second act takes place in a disputed town in a deep wine cellar that provides shelter from the thick of battle. The act is highly episodic; men enter and exit, engaged in caring for the wounded and planning new assaults. In the last act the men return to the village of the first act, their competition for the girl escalates almost to violence, and they are then recalled to the front. MGM's *The Big Parade,* which, as already noted, preceded the Fox adaptation of the play, is bookended by scenes in the United States in which the protagonist takes leave of his family and returns to them (a structure similarly employed two years later in *Wings*). The film was planned with an intermission that, according to Vidor, was designed to break up the long 130-minute running time. The first part is set behind the lines in a French village, where the protagonist falls in love with a French peasant girl; like the end of act 1 of *What Price Glory,* this section concludes with the troops returning to the front. The second part is set in the trenches and is largely composed of scenes of battle. Like the two male protagonists of *What Price Glory,* the hero of *The Big Parade* returns to the village after the battle ends, but in this case he fails to find the girl. The film concludes with a brief epilogue following upon the wounded hero's return to his family in the United States: he revisits the French village and this time is successful in finding his sweetheart. The Fox adaptation of *What Price Glory* shows backstory events that the play evokes only in dialogue, but, with one important change, which I shall discuss below, the film follows the plot of the play quite closely.

Dissecting the differences between these closely related stories reveals the problems posed for the studios in adapting the controversial play. There were three principal areas of difficulty: the representation of sex and the character of the French girl, Charmaine; the play's pessimism about the War and antiauthoritarian attitude to the military; and the development of filmic strategies for evoking the vernacular language of the Anderson and Stallings play without venturing too far from the glamour typically associated with Hollywood protagonists and stars. As the film variants retreated from one or another of these areas of difficulty, or made compromises with the theatrical original, they became relatively more sentimental. But this sentimentality was, precisely, relative, and it remains the case that at the time of their release the MGM and the Fox variants were seen as realistic and uncompromising, a departure from more traditional, sentimental, representations of the War.

Female promiscuity and male sexual rivalry are crucial themes in the Anderson and Stallings play. When it opens Charmaine is already sleeping with Captain Flagg. She is described in the stage directions as a "drab" and discussed by one of the men in the company as "Pete's kid! The poor little tart! What could she do? Ain't the skipper billeted there? God! I guess even Lippy could make a kid if she slept on the other side of a paper wall."[20]

When Flagg's new top sergeant, Quirt, enters, it becomes apparent that he and Flagg have a history of enmity. They served in China together, where Quirt "broke" Flagg in order to get his woman; then in Cuba, Flagg "broke" Quirt in revenge. This is why he is still only a sergeant, although a seasoned fighter. When Flagg departs for eight days' leave in Paris, Charmaine immediately switches her allegiance to Quirt, and the first scene ends with their kiss.

Once Flagg has returned from his leave, Charmaine's father, Cognac Pete, complains that his daughter has been ruined and demands restitution in the form of money for himself and a husband for the girl. Flagg assumes he is the man referred to and becomes more and more worried when Cognac Pete refuses to be bought off with money alone, insisting upon a marriage as well. Flagg is immensely relieved, and simultaneously angry, to learn that the Frenchman expects Quirt to marry his daughter. Flagg maliciously promises a wedding as soon as the mayor can be torn from his compost heap. In addition he commands that Quirt sign over a substantial portion of his pay to Charmaine. Obviously both Cognac Pete and Flagg view the proposed marriage in extremely cynical, instrumental terms. But it becomes apparent that Quirt does as well. Told that he faces court-martial if he does not marry Charmaine, Quirt is able to turn the tables on Flagg when he finds out that they are expected to leave for the front immediately. He points out that Flagg cannot possibly take a company largely composed of new recruits into the lines while his top sergeant is in jail. The pragmatic Flagg immediately bows to necessity and brushes off Cognac Pete's protestations.

Preceding the departure of the troops for the front, Charmaine explains to Flagg that she was not able to be "good" in his absence; he should have taken her to Paris if he did not want her to go with Quirt. He does not blame the girl and tells her that she is a "damn fine little animal" bent on having a good time. He comforts her, with only minimal irony, by saying that neither he nor Quirt is likely to return from the front, and that there will be many more sergeants moving through; she should find another and forget him. She tells him she will never forget him, and he is touched. As soon as he leaves, Charmaine starts to flirt with the mess sergeant, Ferguson, the sole military man left in town. She also explains why she likes soldiers (93): "They go into hell to die—and they are not old enough to die." She is clearly a sympathetic character, though without any trace of sexual fidelity. In fact, the plot depends crucially on her infidelity: it means that she is not an active participant in the contest between Quirt and Flagg for her favors. Since she will go with whoever is there, the resolution of the plot depends on how the men manipulate the military situation on the front lines, and each other, in order to get back first.[21]

The sexual rivalry between Flagg and Quirt continues throughout the scenes at the front in the second act. When Quirt is wounded in the leg, he exults at the opportunity this gives him to be the first to get back to Charmaine. Flagg, furious, realizes that his only hope in their contest is to capture an Alsatian "shavetail." His general has promised that if he can deliver an officer from one of the Alsatian regiments where deserters are filtering through, Flagg's company will get a month's rest and Flagg will get eight days leave. Flagg thereupon plans a highly risky military maneuver to capture such an Alsatian officer.

In the third act Quirt arrives first in Cognac Pete's tavern, but Flagg follows shortly after. When the men confront one another, they evince a semicomic camaraderie, despite their rivalry. The tone adopted here will influence the representation of male friendship in many subsequent films:

QUIRT: Flagg, you're out of this here detail. Your hands off my business after that dirty trick you put over on me. If I kill you there isn't a court can touch me for it in this man's army.

FLAGG: Quirt, you're drunk.

QUIRT: Both of us.

FLAGG: Yeah, both of us.

QUIRT: Well, then, Flagg, you're drunk. What are you going to do about it?

FLAGG: I'm gonna have a drink. [Turns to bar and takes bottle; pours two drinks.]

QUIRT: Both of us.

FLAGG: Yeah, both of us.

The men talk tough, each claiming he can out-drink, out-fight, and out-last the other in battle, and finally they get jealous enough to fight. They agree to play blackjack for Flagg's gun. The one who wins gets the gun, the loser gets a head start for the door. When Flagg wins, Quirt upsets the table and the light so that Flagg cannot get a clear shot. After Quirt's departure, Flagg announces to Charmaine that she is to spend the night with him, and he tells her that he has always loved her. In response to his question "You love me, Charmaine?" she responds, "Only you" (127). An aide reenters and tells Flagg that the whole battalion has been ordered to move up and that all leaves are revoked. Flagg complains bitterly about this but tells Charmaine goodbye, saying he will never see her again, advising her to put her money in real estate and to marry Quirt if she can. He exits. Quirt reenters from upstairs. He asks Charmaine if she loves him, and she assures him, *"Mais oui."* After a kiss he departs to follow the company.

Not only did the play *What Price Glory* abjure any moralizing with respect to Charmaine's promiscuity, but, just as difficult for the Hollywood filmmakers, it suspended the resolution of the romance plot. This lack of resolution is motivated, in part, by the sense that since the men are very likely to die, there is no point in Charmaine's making a definitive "choice." The sexual dynamic of the play thus dovetails with its pessimistic representation of the War. This element, too, proved difficult for the adapters.

Flagg is clearly presented as a rebel and a disaster as far as military discipline is concerned. Scene 2 of the play begins with Flagg returning drunk after eight days' leave. Reprimanded in Bar-le-Duc by an MP for having a swagger stick, a violation of the corps commander's regulations, Flagg had dared the man to take it away from him and was eventually arrested for attempted manslaughter. He and his aide spent the eight days of his leave in jail waiting to commit perjury to get him off; they never got to Paris.

Once Flagg returns to his headquarters, he is visited by a general with orders for the company. Their conversation exemplifies both Flagg's anti-authoritarian personality and Anderson's and Stallings's view of the absurdity of the military enterprise (87):

THE GENERAL [pointing to map, which he spreads out on table]: There she is, and here's the line. The corps wants it straightened out. It will take the steel, the cold steel. But they've got to have it straightened out. Give them the steel and you can do it. . . . You've got to run them down like rats. You give them the old cowering point. We've got to get them out. We want to go in there and run 'em out. We want to give 'em steel.

FLAGG: We? Staff going in there too, General?

THE GENERAL [disconsolately]: No—they won't risk us fellows, curse the luck.

FLAGG: That's too bad, General.

THE GENERAL: But we'll be behind you, Flagg.

FLAGG: How far, General?

The second act, a virtual catalogue of horrors, is relieved only by the banter between Flagg and Quirt and, later, by Flagg's interactions with two newcomers, young officers sent up for their first experience of battle. As the scene opens Flagg is offstage, tying down Lieutenant Aldrich, who has had his right arm blown off. A pharmacist's mate enters to set up operating tables, saying he was told to prepare for "two couples for bridge." Kiper, Flagg's aide, puns in response, "Low bridge around that lousy railroad station." Later in the act we are informed that Flagg regards the order to take the railway embankment as foolish, since it cannot be kept without a brigade, and they are vainly wasting men's lives as they drive the Germans out of the station, only to have them return later. Kiper demands to know "why the hell we want the Heinies out of that God damn railway station. Leave 'em there, I say. Let 'em sit where they damned well are. They ain't going anywhere." This establishes the futility of their enterprise.

Quirt enters, having brought back the weekly supplies for the troop and lost "only" four out of ten men. Flagg enters, helping Aldrich to a bunk and giving him morphine to take for his pain. Lieutenant Moore rushes in and, seeing Aldrich's wound, begins a tirade that became well known and is replicated in the film versions. He threatens to take his men out of the lines and shoot Flagg should he try to stop him, and in the course of his rant he enunciates the title of the play.

Lieutenant Moore's diatribe, which verges on the pathetic and quashes even Quirt's usual swagger, gives way to comedy with the entrance of the two "thirty-day-wonder" lieutenants sent up by the top brass for training. Flagg rags the young men mercilessly, asking what should be done with them, since he is down from four to two gunnery sergeants and therefore does not have anyone to spare to "teach little boys how to adjust their diapers." He facetiously suggests that they go after the German gunners in the railway station, since he cannot risk losing experienced men on the job. Later in the act, though, as Flagg prepares to assault the railway embankment himself in search of the Alsatian shavetail, a comic reversal occurs. Lieutenant Cunningham claims to be the tougher one (111–12): "I was a locomotive engineer on the Louisiana Midland. Three wrecks in my division last year. Christ, but this war shore is a great relief to me. . . . My brother's still driving an engine back home. Had a letter last month from him. He says, 'You dirty yellow sapsucker, quitting your job on the Louisiana Midland. I knew you always were a yellow dog, but I didn't think you'd go back on the road thataway.'" Thus a male camaraderie is established between Cunningham and Flagg based on the professional experience of danger but outside of the structures of military authority and training. It is only the experience of facing danger, and of continuing to work under its threat, that makes men adequate to the realities of battle. This is why the general, safe behind the lines and hoping to rearrange an abstract "line" on the map, is shown to be incompetent and out of touch. True to the pattern of alternating comic and horrific moments, the scene ends on a somber note, as a green recruit, Lewisohn, is brought in wounded, crying for Flagg to stop the blood. Flagg apologizes to him, saying he cannot, and holds him.

Anderson's and Stallings's satire on military dress and codes of conduct, as well as their biting criticism of the upper echelons of authority, deepen the pessimism of the play's stress on the inevitable suffering and death of the troops. No Hollywood film in the 1920s was fully able to mount this kind of representation of the War. The Marines and the army, as institutions, never come in for the same kind of satire or attack that is leveled against them in the play. And it is worth noting that *The Big Parade* was made with the cooperation of the Second Division of the United States Army and Air Service Units, stationed at Kelly Field. Nonetheless, some components of the play's representation of the War are taken up by the films and were much commented upon, and much appreciated, at the time of their release.

In its first review, immediately on the film's release, *Variety* (November 11, 1925: 36) compared *The Big Parade* to the play *What Price Glory*: "Instead of an officer and soldier fighting over a French girl as they do in 'What Price Glory,' Stallings worked this story out so that a buck private, after his corporal and another man were turned down, had a clear field with the French peasant girl." But King Vidor's film, although clearly inspired by *What Price Glory*, is not a straightforward adaptation of it. Shortly after the success of the play Irving Thalberg bought the rights to Stallings's short story "The Big Parade," which had been published in the *New Republic*.[22] According to King Vidor, Stallings then came to Hollywood with a treatment that became the basis for the film but did not manage to come up with a screenplay during his stay on the West Coast. Vidor, Stallings, and the screenwriter Harry Behn then rode the train to New York together, listening to Stallings's war stories. After spending more time with Stallings in New York, Vidor and Behn wrote the script upon their return to the West Coast.[23]

Unlike *What Price Glory, The Big Parade* focuses on the relationship between three, rather than two, soldiers: Jim (played by John Gilbert), Bull (Tom O'Brien), and Slim (Karl Dane). It allocates a romantic leading role to the star, while the comic rivalry that so dominates *What Price Glory* is confined to the supporting actors. It also very much alters the character of the woman, now called Mélisande (Renée Adorée). In addition, much attention is given to the hero's family in the United States and particularly to his relationship with his mother. All of this makes for a much more sentimental variant of the plot, a point I shall discuss in some detail, as it was not the general assessment at the time.

In *What Price Glory*, the only character who refers to his family is the new recruit Lewisohn. In act 1 the private nervously enters headquarters and announces to Flagg that he has lost his identification tag. Flagg rudely asks why he is bothering with this, and the private tells him that it would matter if he was hit, because then his folks could not be notified. Flagg dismisses Lewisohn with a barb but asks his aide to get the private a new tag, adding, "The God-forsaken fool's dying of grief away from his mother" (63). This is the only such reference in the play. By contrast, both the beginning and the end of *The Big Parade* stress Jim's special relationship with his mother. In the opening when his father is berating him for being lazy and self-indulgent, Jim is reluctant to counter that he has enlisted, out of concern for his mother, who is present. Near the end of the film Jim comes home on crutches, one leg amputated, and the camera tracks in on his mother, who has visions of him walking as a toddler. After his father says that they are proud of him, Jim goes into another room, alone with his mother, and leans back in her arms.[24] It is a scene, and a posture, that would have been unthinkable in *What Price Glory*, except in relation to boyish recruits. It is impossible to imagine Flagg or Quirt resting in a mother's lap.

From the start the characterization of Mélisande in *The Big Parade* is quite different from that of the heroine in the Anderson and Stallings play.

Jim first sees her in the company of her protective mother, next to their substantial farmhouse—she is clearly not a "drab" or a "tart" but a respectable girl. The next day Jim devises a makeshift shower beside a river that runs outside the town, and Mélisande laughs at seeing Bull's and Slim's backsides as they shower there naked. This incident moderates her respectability and establishes her as a hardy peasant type. *Exceptional Photoplays* commented upon this scene, which the reviewer found "illustrative of the kind of shrewd frankness that has given the characters of *The Big Parade* their human, earthy quality."[25] The film is careful to continue in this vein: Mélisande is sexual but not promiscuous. Upon first meeting the girl, all three of the men try to touch her and kiss her, but she fends them off. After she has chosen Jim, her exclusivity is stressed in a later scene; when Bull accosts her, she hauls off and belts him, then tells him off in pantomime, to Slim's great amusement.

The nonsentimental tone of *What Price Glory* is achieved at least in part through a debasement of the heroine and by a marked, and comic, misogyny. *The Big Parade* does not share this attitude in the least; here both the heroine and the love affair are highly idealized. This is most apparent in the well-known sequence in which, the company having been abruptly called to the front, Mélisande runs through the lines of departing soldiers desperately trying to find Jim to say goodbye. All of the commentators in the 1920s mentioned this scene. Robert Sherwood wrote, "Although the war scenes are naturally predominant in *The Big Parade*, the picture itself is essentially a love story—and a supremely stirring one at that."[26] The first *Variety* review described the love scene between Mélisande and Jim as he leaves for the front as "beautiful and heartrending" and asserted that Renée Adorée's performance in this scene alone entitled her "to a niche in the screen hall of fame." The reviewers for the *New York Times* (November 20, 1925: 18) and *Exceptional Photoplays* praised the final shot of this sequence, in which Mélisande, having clung as long as possible to a chain on the truck carrying her lover away, kneels alone on a now empty road, an abstract figure representing the women left behind in war. Iris Barry, writing for *The Spectator* in London, praised the sequence if not the sentiment: "It is new: it is better done than anything that has been done before: it is good."[27]

With the exception of Iris Barry, the reviewers did not find *The Big Parade* overly sentimental, although almost every review mentioned that the film moved spectators to both laughter and tears and commented upon the tender love story. I suspect that the film did not register as sentimental because most reviewers were comparing it not to the play *What Price*

Glory but rather to such earlier films about World War I as *The Little American* and *Hearts of the World*. *The Big Parade* at least acknowledges that soldiers in the AEF had love affairs with French women. It is clear that the reviewers considered the film much more realistic in its representation of the War than these previous films.

Robert Sherwood, one of the most cosmopolitan and advanced of critics, saw the film as antiheroic, a debunking portrait of the horrors of war. Mistakenly attributing the choice of director and the construction of the script to Stallings, he praised the film for having "not one error of taste or of authenticity—and it isn't as if I didn't watch for these defects, for I have seen too many movies which pictured the war in terms of Liberty Loan propaganda." *Photoplay* wrote, "War, not from the cushioned seat of a government job but the mud-splashed perspective of a cootie bitten private, has been brought to the screen by King Vidor's masterly direction of *The Big Parade*. . . . It is not make-believe. It is war as war actually is, with soldiers and women playing their parts bravely as plain human beings."[28] The first *Variety* review called the film "one of the greatest pieces of propaganda ever launched against war." In its second review *Variety* (December 2, 1925) dubbed it a "man's picture": "Coming in the same week as 'Stella Dallas,' the contrast was striking, the former being very much of a woman's film and 'Parade' having a strong masculine appeal." The reviewer for the *New York Times* praised the filming of the skirmish in the forest and the sequence in the shell hole: "There are incidents in this film which obviously came from experience, as they are totally different from the usual jumble of war scenes in films. It is because of the realism that the details ring true and it grips the spectator." The reviewer for *Exceptional Photoplays* wrote, "The scene in the shell-hole in which Jim and the mortally wounded German lad come to some dim understanding of the thing that has made puppets of them both and brought them together in a common catastrophe; the scenes of slowly advancing troops moving through the woods against the machine guns; the following scenes of hell-like aspect. . . . these have already been dwelt upon by many reviewers, and must be witnessed to be appreciated." Only Iris Barry demurred: "Mr. Bernard Shaw is being advertised widely as having said that he likes *The Big Parade* because he is a pacifist. This must be a joke. The War was not a great game ending in twenty-four hours of fighting: no film dare show what it resembled. But to say that a sentimental and romantic war-film like this does anything in the interests of peace is madness. It wreathes machine-guns in roses." I do not know what led Iris Barry to the conclusions she reached, although it may well have been the love story: the compendium of her reviews, which she published under the title *Let's Go to the Movies* in 1926, certainly takes a hard line against the romance plot.[29]

The film's representation of war is a more complicated question than any of the reviews suggest. *The Big Parade* showed the American forces in action in a way that I think was accurately perceived by the critics as new. It was, if not more "realistic," then certainly more pessimistic than the films actually made during the War. Nonetheless, *The Big Parade* does not match the cynicism about military authority in the play *What Price Glory,* nor does it insist to the same extent on the futility of the War.

In the second part of *The Big Parade* the troops, having marched out of Champillon, halt while their captain receives his orders. When informed that the woods ahead are alive with machine guns and snipers, he says simply, "We are ready for orders, sir." This is the only time that the higher military command has a presence in the film. Unlike in *What Price Glory,* the officers are shown in the field, not behind the lines, and they are shown to be decidedly aware of the risks they are asking the men to take. There is no suggestion that the goals set for the captain and his company are unimportant, merely "straightening out the line." Moreover, the captain does not appear to have the problem Flagg complains of, that of lacking men and military support for the job he has to do.

But one thing that the film can and does show is men dying in battle, which of course takes place off stage in *What Price Glory.* The sequence in Belleau Woods is a good example of the way Vidor constructs the battle scenes to evoke death and the fear of death from the perspective of the foot soldier. After the captain receives his orders, the troops, who have been traveling on a road, are called together and told to fix bayonets and assume attack formation. Jim looks bemused at the order, since the enemy is nowhere apparent. Several successive lines of troops are sent off into the wood that borders the road. They move in formation through neat lines of trees with no sign of the enemy but the fallen dead. As they march, soldiers in the line begin to fall, at first without any indication of where the shots are coming from. Finally Vidor cuts to a sniper in a tree. Slim shoots him while keeping pace with the forward movement of the line. A brief skirmish with a group of Germans concealed behind trees concludes with their surrender, but the troops in the line maintain their formation and march past them. Machine gun fire opens from a group hidden behind shrubbery. As the men continue to advance, the machine gun causes havoc in the line; many fall, until the Americans throw grenades that explode the shrubbery. There are more snipers, more grenades. A man who has been hit vainly struggles to keep up with the company, using his gun to support his upper body as he pulls himself along the ground. As the men near the edge of the wood, we see big guns firing and the line is exposed to shelling. They fall to the ground awaiting orders, and Jim again appears uncertain, hesitant:

> JIM: They're not going to send us out in that open field, are they?
>
> SLIM: Sure! We're gonna keep goin' till we can't go no farther!

Gas explodes in the field and all put on gas masks. Ordered forward, they advance through a barren landscape showing only a few remaining stumps of trees. The troop faces both machine gun fire and continuous shelling until it takes refuge in shell holes in a landscape now completely devoid of trees.

This sequence differs from the films that Sherwood referred to as "Liberty Loan propaganda" in that it allows the viewers to share the uncertainty and sense of vulnerability of the men in the field. This sense is increased in the next sequence, in the shell hole, which was much praised at the time and is justly famous today. The three friends are alone for much of the time, although once in a while another soldier crawls into their hole with orders from the captain.

It is clear that the soldiers are hemmed in. At night Jim is exposed to fire the instant he raises his head above the edge of the shell hole to pick a flower, and again when he peeks over the edge to thumb his nose at the Germans. The sense of constraint is treated humorously here. It becomes horrifying later, after Slim has crawled out after a sniper, been wounded himself, and lies crying for his friends within hearing but out of sight. Bull and Jim are ordered not to respond to their friend to avoid giving away their position. Like Lieutenant Moore in *What Price Glory*, Jim goes a bit crazy (successive dialogue titles are separated by slash marks):

> Orders! Orders! Who the hell is fighting this war—men or orders?/
> I came to fight—not to wait and rot in a lousy hole while they murder
>   my pal!/
> Waiting! Orders! Mud! Blood! Stinking stiffs! What the hell do we get
>   out of this war anyway!/
> —cheers when we left and when we get back! But who the hell cares . . .
>   after this?

Eventually Jim goes after his friend, who is dead by the time he crawls to him. Jim ends up in another shell hole with a German who has shot him and whom he has shot. He is about to finish off his enemy but cannot stick in his bayonet. In pantomime the German asks for a cigarette, and Jim gives it to him, then, after the boy dies, finishes smoking it himself.

There is no humor after Slim is shot; in this respect, too, the tone of the film is very different from *What Price Glory* where serious situations such as the disfigurement and death evoked in act 2 always alternate with cynical humor. When Lieutenant Aldrich's arm is shot off, for instance, the men speak of it as a "ticket home." The play is also much more cynical in its representation of the relationships among men. Flagg is loyal to his troops and almost tender with the young recruits that he simultaneously bullies. But the relationships between equals—between Flagg and Quirt, and, in the comic reversal already discussed, between Flagg and Cunningham at the end of act 2—is one of unfailing rivalry and one-upmanship. It is not until the end of the play that one gets a sense of the loyalty that joins the men, when Quirt unexpectedly leaves Charmaine with the great final line: "Hey, Flagg, wait for baby!"

The Big Parade places much less emphasis on male rivalry. Bull and Slim do jockey for power in the first half of the film. Initially Bull is corporal and pulls rank on Slim to get the best bunk, the first chance at girls, etc. Then, when Bull mistakenly kicks a superior officer in the behind and is deprived of his chevrons, their positions are reversed and Slim is made corporal. But this kind of rivalry evaporates in the second half. Under gunfire the three men are united. Ordered to take out a "Fritzie" sniper, Slim uses his superior position to set it up so that he goes out of the shell hole instead of his friends. Bull dies as he crawls alongside Jim in the attempt to rescue Slim.

The most enduring and important sign of male fellowship is the motif of the shared cigarette and light. Slim, who usually chews tobacco, takes Bull's cigarette and lighter at the beginning of the second half, while they rest after the march out of Champillon. Later Slim slaps a cigarette out of Jim's hand in the shell hole in fear that the light of a match will call attention to them, offering him a chaw of tobacco instead, an offer Bull takes up as well. And toward the end, Jim and the German he has shot share a cigarette.[30]

The battle scenes in *The Big Parade* resemble the scene in the cellar in the second act of *What Price Glory* in that both evoke the vulnerability of the men in the lines and even include similar outbursts against the War. But male comradeship is much more celebrated in the film, and there is commensurately little emphasis on competition or on the men exerting power over one another. The brutality of war is not mirrored in the men's treatment of one another, as it is in the case of Flagg and Quirt in the play.

Play and film have one other important feature in common: the use of the vernacular. The relatively uncouth language and behavior of the soldiers sets the film apart from the "high" tone of previous (and later) films. During the aerial battles in *Wings* the heroes frequently mouth cuss words, but the only slang that appears in the dialogue titles occurs when a sergeant chastises his men for being too interested in the pretty ambulance driver Mary and when the flier White (Gary Cooper) uses the word "chow" in an otherwise impeccable sentence. The demeanor of the characters in *The Big Parade* also differs from that in a film like Herbert Brenon's 1926 *Beau Geste* about the Foreign Legion, in which three brothers, upper-class Englishman played by Ronald Colman, Neil Hamilton and Ralph Forbes, unfailingly maintain their aristocratic bearing under pressure from a wicked Sergeant (Noah Beery) who is coarse and rude as well as cruel.

The Big Parade was obviously influenced by the linguistic experiments of the Anderson and Stallings play. Characters mouth profanities and, more important, the intertitles aim to replicate the play's use of slang, mixed English and French, and vivid and somewhat rough modes of expression. Intertitles replicate humorous military ditties:

> Eat your chow from tin mess-kits;
> Pick your teeth with bay-o-nits;
> Shine your shoes on hunks of pork;
> And the barber shaves you with a knife and fork!
> That's . . . the . . . life . . . in . . . the . . . arm-ee!

Bull's language to Melisande echoes Quirt's to Charmaine: "Come on, Bon Ami . . . slip Poppa a little kiss!" When Bull gets a letter from a French girl he asks Slim, "Can you readee-voo Francay?" and at another point he hails his friend, "AH! Monsewer Demi Tasse!" Even narrative titles drop into the vernacular: "After an hour of his best sign language, convincing the wine-shop keeper that he wanted a barrel, and not a fat girl, Jim started on his way back." Or: "That evening, Jim detailed himself to some more 'skirt duty.'"

However, the use of the vernacular is juxtaposed with a more self-consciously poetic tone adopted for the narrative titles once the troops set out for the front (the dialogue titles remain stylistically "low" in the film's second half). I have replicated the lines breaks and the punctuation of the original titles:

> Men! Men! Men!
> Moving up! Up! UP!
> MEN!

And later:

> IT HAD BEGUN
> THE BIG PARADE
> Men! Guns! Men!
> Men! Guns!

And finally:

> To the front!
> To the front!
> To the front . . .
> Front! . . . FRONT!

These experimental, almost Whitmanesque, titles comprise an interesting attempt to get away from the more typical, ponderous intertitles of the war film as, for example, this title from Griffith's *Hearts of the World:* "The Allies with fire and flame and souls of men win back inch by inch the sacred soil of France, righting her wrongs." However, subsequent films that show the influence of *What Price Glory* do not follow up on Vidor's experiments with narrative titles, although the use of the vernacular in dialogue titles, and eventually in spoken dialogue, becomes almost a hallmark of the form.

In addition to the language of the intertitles, Vidor found equivalents of the vernacular at the level of the actor's business: Jim thumbs his nose at the Germans, Bull kicks the ass of a superior officer. Many incidents in the film depend on a rough humor that approaches the style and tone of the play. When the three friends and several others arrive in the town of Champillon after a march of twenty miles, they are billeted in a barn and ordered to "police" the yard before turning in. Bull orders, "Hey you Bozoes! No sleep for you babies until you dress this manure pile!" The corporal, who had tried to stop the men from singing "You're in the army now" while they were marching, begins to sing for them:

> No use to raise a row;
> Shovel and chuck
> The goo and the muck,
> You're in the army now!

The scene ends with the corporal demanding that the men shovel faster and thereupon being pelted with cow manure.

The incident in which Bull and Slim get drunk in the farmhouse wine cellar while Jim politely sips wine upstairs with Mélisande's family and friends ends in an all-out comic brawl when Mélisande's mother calls the military police. Bull invites in the rest of the company—"Get in it, gang! This ain't a private fight!"—and, at its end, drunkenly shakes hands with Slim, both having acquired the uniforms of the MPs they were fighting. The incident is reminiscent of one recounted in *What Price Glory* where Flagg tangles with the military police over his swagger stick. A similar comic fight can be found in most of the films that bear the influence of the play, not to mention almost every film made by John Ford.

Two other incidents constituting memorable departures from decorum occur in scenes in which one would more likely expect noble or genteel behavior. While courting Mélisande with the aide of a dictionary, Jim presents her with a stick of gum, which she has never seen. He is chewing gum himself and, through gesture, explains how to use it. He also pulls on his gum, making a string of it between mouth and hand. Mélisande is unable to pull the gum into a string and swallows it by mistake. Jim pantomimes that one does not swallow gum, making a slight spitting gesture. Contrast this with any other love scene played by John Gilbert to get a sense of the originality of tone and conception.

Scenes of self-sacrifice are the bread and butter of the war film, but not, as we have seen, of the play *What Price Glory*. In *The Big Parade*, however, Slim's death is clearly meant to be deeply affecting. The November *Variety* review praised it for being "as realistic and touching as any death scene imaginable. It was heart-reaching, and had the majority of the audience in tears." But the scene begins with a tobacco-spitting contest between the three friends to decide who will be the one to go for the sniper. It is noble for Slim to set this up since, as a veteran tobacco chewer, he is sure to win. But the director goes out of his way to maintain a semicomic "low" tone. Slim draws a target on the dirt wall of the shell hole, and the men spit, whereupon a detail shot demonstrates where the three wads land. Such departures from decorum at moments usually reserved for grace or pomp are one of the great pleasures of the film. Perhaps this insistence on the vernacular is what prompted *Variety* to label it a "man's picture," even though it is unabashedly sentimental, indeed, has been taken by a present-day scholar to be a model of sentimental narrative construction.[31]

Fox's film version of *What Price Glory* follows the typical pattern of silent film adaptations of dramatic works: it shows us the backstory events that are simply recounted on stage. In the film we see two incidents, one in China and one in the Philippines, in which Quirt steals one of Flagg's girls. After America's entrance into the War, Flagg's company marches through France. Flagg is billeted at Cognac Pete's, where he flirts with, and is encouraged by, Charmaine, and then marches off to the front for battle. He returns to the village having lost over half his men, greets his new green recruits, and waits for his new top sergeant to arrive so that he can take leave. It is only at this point that the film takes up the action of the play.

Certainly the biggest change from the original is the characterization of the heroine. Whereas *The Big Parade* managed to avoid any hint of a promiscuous heroine, this was obviously not an option for Walsh, faced with the problem of adapting the Anderson and Stallings play. Walsh's film begins in China with the men in competition over a woman who is clearly a prostitute, Shanghai Mabel; the incident is then replayed over a Filipina, also apparently a prostitute. When Flagg first meets Charmaine, she seems to be the third in the series of "soldier's sluts" that the men have quarreled over. She makes herself sexually available to Flagg, encouraging his suggestion that he sleep upstairs at Cognac Pete's where she does. She openly kisses Flagg and accepts his gift of garters, as Shanghai Mabel had in the first scene. Although clearly Flagg's girl, the first time Charmaine sees Quirt, she looks him over and immediately begins to flirt, as the Filipina had in the second scene. As soon as Flagg has gone on leave, Quirt makes arrangements to move into Cognac Pete's and, in a sly reference to *The Big Parade,* pins his sharpshooter medal on her.[32]

From this point on, however, the film's depiction of Charmaine departs more and more markedly from the Anderson and Stallings play, and her character is progressively sentimentalized. The young recruit who loses his identification tag is called "Mother's Boy" in Walsh's film, in what appears to be a taunting reference to the hero of *The Big Parade.* When this soldier gets sick while Flagg is away on leave, Quirt and Charmaine go to comfort him. Charmaine gives the soldier wine and strokes his head until he falls asleep. Later, as he marches off to the front, he thanks her and asks her to watch out for letters from his mother. After she learns that the recruit was killed in battle, Charmaine goes to the muddy burial field and finds the boy's grave, marked, as are all the others, only with his rifle and helmet. She buries a letter from the boy's mother beside the body and sits with bowed head. Thus, while the film makes fun of the young man's attachment to his mother, it also places Charmaine in a maternal relation to him as part of the effort to make her a more sentimental character and, presumably, more acceptable to a popular audience.

Charmaine's relationships with both Flagg and Quirt are also altered significantly. As in the play, Flagg tries to force Quirt to marry Charmaine but in the film the reversal between the men is not brought about, as it is in the play, by Quirt's reminding Flagg that he needs his top sergeant to take his troops into battle. Instead, Charmaine is the one to stop the wedding. She rips up the allotment paper that would give her rights to Quirt's salary and yells at her father. "My heart—she ees my own. I don sell her." Thus she becomes the vehicle for enunciating, if not a romantic, then at least a noninstrumental view of marriage, a point of view that is entirely absent from the play.

When the men return after battle they quarrel over Charmaine and decide to play cards for the gun, as in the play. After Quirt loses and makes his escape, Charmaine tells Flagg that she is in love with the sergeant. When the company is called back to the front, Quirt limps in to tell her: "Goodbye, Charmaine. In all this dirt and muck I've found something to come back for—I guess it's—love." The film attempts, then, to create a love story around Quirt and Charmaine by having Charmaine make a definitive choice and by having Quirt, quite out of character, reciprocate her love.

The film's treatment of the heroine was given impetus by the theme song "Charmaine," a waltz written by Erno Rapee with lyrics by Lew Pollack. This was the first of three hits written by this team: it was followed by "Diane" for *7th Heaven* and "Angela Mia" for *Street Angel*, both directed by Frank Borzage. Sold as sheet music scored for piano, "Charmaine" became "the biggest-selling silent-movie theme song of the 1920s," according to music historian Russell Sanjek.[33] I defy anyone who has heard the recording of Gaylord Carter playing it on the Wurlitzer to keep a dry eye.[34] If worked properly into the musical accompaniment, "Charmaine" can be one of the most successful ways in which the film alters Anderson's and Stallings's original characterization.[35] For example, in the version available from Critics' Choice Video, taken from the Killiam Collection, the theme is played in the scene in which the wounded Quirt returns to Cognac Pete's and first greets Charmaine, a moment that anticipates his later declaration of love. Despite the cynical treatment of women and of sex with which the film opens, and which it inherits from the play, this shift into a romantic tone is almost rendered convincing by the music.

Although it retreats to a much more conventional love story than was present in the play, the film *What Price Glory* was not criticized for sentimentality in the 1920s, perhaps because reviewers tended to compare it with *The Big Parade* rather than with the play. It was seen to be more comic than its predecessor and to emphasize the relationship between the men, downplaying the War. *Moving Picture World* (November 29, 1926: 300–1) characterized it as "a story of soldiers rather than war." The review continues, "Cropping up continually through the humorous aspects is the deep set admiration of each for the other as a soldier and hatred because of their rivalry over women. So intense is this that every time Flagg and Quirt come together there is a regular electric thrill in the atmosphere and terrific suspense as to what is going to happen next, will it be drama or humor?" The reviewer for *Exceptional Photoplays* objected to what he considered Walsh's attenuation of the daring protest originally offered by the play and *The Big Parade:*

They were attempts to say that the War was not only glory and patri-
otism and high idealistic self-sacrifice. . . . In its original intent
Stallings' irony and bitterness, notably in *The Big Parade,* cut even
deeper than that. He was protesting against the hollow, smug literary
productions of the day which dressed up our soldiers as heroic puppets
because a willfully blind and sentimental public wanted to see them
that way. At that time it took courage to say that many of our soldiers
were mainly interested in wine and women, that their personal ani-
mosities concerned them more than the somewhat Messianic democracy for the sake of which we officially went into the war. *What Price
Glory* reaps all the benefit of this successful protest. Its makers knew
that the public today was sold so on the idea that soldiers were concerned only with wine and women and that they were at all times inex-
haustible humorists, that they could universalize the idea. They could
safely make a picture showing war to be a vast orgy into which actual
battle came only as an occasional nuisance and interruption.[36]

Although they evaluate the film differently, both the critic for *Moving Picture World* and the critic for *Exceptional Photoplays* agree that the relationship between Flagg and Quirt, "mighty in their cups, unquenchable in their
profanity, and irresistible in their rough and ready love making,"[37] has been
withdrawn from the context of the War and become an end in itself.

The battle scenes in *What Price Glory* are much more perfunctory than
those in *The Big Parade.* Because of the extended exposition there are two
episodes on the front line, but this repetition diminishes the impact of
the fighting there. In the first sequence at the front, shots are frequently
impersonal: feet marching through mud, or horses and guns dragging
through mud. There is a montage of guns, tanks, and bayonets. We see men
in trenches and men in shell holes, but there is no sense that they are
pinned down in them, the sense that is so vividly conveyed in *The Big
Parade.* After the battle is over and the men have returned to town, a soldier writes in his diary, "Back again after the first terrible experience under
fire. We lost all but eighty. The horror of it haunts me—the stench of the
dead—the blood—the maddening rumble of the guns." But this foot soldier's experience of war in the trenches is simply told to us, as opposed to
being shown in actual battle scenes. It would hardly have been necessary
for a character in *The Big Parade* to write such lines after the deaths of
Slim and Bull. Nor is the second battle at the front in *What Price Glory*
any more vivid. Flagg informs his men that they are going to push into a
town under cover of their own barrage. The barrage starts, represented by
explosions with superimposed long shots of troop movements. Flagg walks
along the line, encouraging his men before they are to leave the trenches.

They move out, and there are more shots of the barrage and of troop movements. The soldiers seem to move easily, sweeping the Germans before them, and the enemy quickly surrenders. There is no sense, as there is in the play, of the chaos and hopelessness of the military engagement. As far as one can tell, the higher command is capable; the barrage works for the Marines and enables them to capture the territory they are supposed to take. There is no corresponding barrage by the Germans and, despite the field of dead that Charmaine visits, no real sense of Americans being vulnerable during the battle.

The rather distanced evocation of battle, along with the pronounced comic tone in other scenes, makes for uneasy shifts into serious, somewhat pompous rhetoric about war, evident in narrative titles such as "Through the Scarlet Night—a dressing station beneath the earth—that earth to which so many men will return before the mocking guns of glory cease." The uncomfortable shift in tone is evident as well in Lieutenant Moore's crazed antiwar rant, necessary since it introduces the name of the play but not sufficiently motivated here.

Unlike either its dramatic or filmic predecessor, Walsh's film introduces pro-military elements. Left to himself for a moment in Shanghai Mabel's flat, Flagg pulls the cork out of a bottle with his teeth and drinks "to the Marines." After the second battle Flagg praises the young recruits who survive (subsequent titles are separated by a slash mark): "They sent me babies to baptize in blood and fire. You've gone through it and—" / "— from one old soldier to another, I'm as proud of you as America should be!" This speech is greeted with ironic applause from Quirt, but it is difficult to tell if this is because Quirt hates the rhetoric or hates Flagg. We do see stretchers carrying the dead being stacked into trucks immediately after Flagg's speech, which may be intended as a critique of it, but the film switches back into a personal mode at this shot, as Quirt informs Flagg of his injury and of his intention to return to Charmaine with the trucks carrying the war dead.

Ultimately the film does not have a coherent stance on the War; but it does have a coherent stance on the Marines. This institution, while it unfortunately sometimes kills off "Mother's boys," also makes men out of babies in a baptism of blood and fire, and provides the opportunities for the drinking, fighting, and gambling that make for male friendship. The ending of the film seems to reinforce the value of the Marines as an institution of male fraternity and is thus quite different in tone from Anderson's and Stallings's ending. In the play Flagg gets his orders to return to the front and, after swearing to disobey them, explains to Charmaine, "No, I'll go. I may be drunk, but I know I'll go. There's something rotten about this pro-fession of arms, some kind of damned religion connected with it that you can't shake. When they tell you to die, you have to do it, even if you're a better man than they are."

The return to battle is shown to be a matter of professional pride rather than loyalty to any military establishment—Flagg's antiauthoritarian atti-tude remains. In the film his lines are changed (subsequent dialogue titles are indicated by slash marks): "Charmaine girl, this war and glory racket is sorta like a religion." / "—th' bugle sounds an' we answer. We break every pledge but one. Somehow that call finds the old Marines—always faith-ful—" Charmaine salutes Flagg in tribute. Quirt's decision to follow Flagg bolsters his words. At the end of the film Flagg greets Quirt almost joy-ously, taking his crutch out of his hand so that he can support him with his shoulder as they march off together.

Walsh's film was important for subsequent filmmakers in that it solidi-fied the experiments with the vernacular found in *The Big Parade*. Pro-fanity is represented through the mouthing of cuss words, dialogue titles employ slang, broken or accented English spoken by the French, and Frenchified American. There is liberal use of "low" gestures and attitudes. Shanghai Mabel bends down to pick up something, then wiggles her back-side at a group of Marines watching her. Flagg's first sight of Charmaine also dwells on her behind as she attempts to roll a barrel to the bar. Kipper, Flagg's personal aide, gives his boss the "raspberry" without the captain's being able to identify the source of the sound.

Without a doubt, the biggest innovation made by the film along these lines lay in the casting of Victor McLaglen and his performance as Flagg. In *The Big Parade* John Gilbert had been consistently elegant and poised, even when chewing gum or pantomiming spitting it out. Karl Dane and Tom O'Brien were funny and indubitably "low" but too much like a vaudeville team to carry a serious film. In *What Price Glory* Victor McLaglen was predictably coarse, big, and ugly, quite a good comic, and also surprisingly able to act against type in serious moments. The scene in which he is touched but not surprised by the death of Mother's Boy, or the gracious way he bows out when Charmaine tells him she is really in love with Quirt, are superb for the way in which he maintains a rough exterior while suggesting a range of emotion underneath. Every critic praised the per-formance. *Variety* (December 1, 1926: 12) wrote, "Victor McLaglen stands out bigger than he ever has in any picture, and this production is going to 'make' him." *Moving Picture World* wrote, "We don't know which was intended to be the 'star of the show,' in another picture it would probably be Quirt for he wins out in the romance, but it is Flagg as portrayed by Victor McLaglen that dominates the picture. It is one of the most remarkable performances that the stage or screen has ever seen." *Exceptional Photoplays* agreed: "*What Price Glory* is lifted by one masterly performance. Far out ahead of Edmund Lowe's attempt to simulate Sergeant Quirt's smooth toughness by making faces and narrowing his eyes . . . the work of Victor McLaglen as Captain Flagg is a joy to see." Despite better titling than the Walsh film and the innovations in acting already discussed, *The Big Parade* nevertheless retained the distinction between a romantic lead and the comic men. McLaglen's performance stood out because he was able to be vulgar and comic while maintaining the panoply of emotion and expression called for in a serious male lead. It is a skill he perfected in the variants of *What Price Glory* that followed, and other actors, most notably George Bancroft, were to follow his lead.

The play and the two films discussed so far gave rise to many variants later in the 1920s. One of the earliest was *Behind the Front* (Paramount, released February 22, 1926) with Wallace Beery and Raymond Hatton as a pair of infantrymen fooled into volunteering for the AEF. Although its farcical representation of the War draws on earlier slapstick films such as *Shoulder Arms,* it is clearly, as Mordaunt Hall noted in the *New York Times* (February 10, 1926: 16), "a burlesque of *The Big Parade,*" in which Beery and Hatton corresponded to Slim and Buck but also, in comic transformations, parodied the more sentimental incidents associated with Jim. *Two Arabian Knights,* produced by Howard Hughes for United Artists and released in September of 1927, begins with a more tenuous burlesque of *What Price Glory.* The film opens with Sergeant McGaffney (Louis Wolheim) and Private Phelps (William Boyd) slugging it out in a shell hole while under enemy fire. The film rapidly departs from the World War I setting as the two, now friends, escape from a German prisoner of war camp and are mistakenly routed to Constantinople with a group of Muslim prisoners. They are briefly rivals for an Arab girl (Mary Astor). However, it soon becomes clear that she prefers the handsome Phelps, and McGaffney is reduced to the role of faithful comic sidekick. In her home town, the two men fight the emir, her father, as well as her Arab fiancé and his minions.

Following the conversion to sound, Walsh himself directed several sequels and adaptations of *What Price Glory.* The most important of these is probably the first, *The Cock-Eyed World,* released in October 1929. It renewed the pairing of Victor McLaglen as Flagg and Edmund Lowe as Quirt. Played simply for comedy, with songs, the plot begins with the Marines stationed in Russia and Quirt and Flagg in a contest over who will spend the night with Olga. Quirt wins but is then bested by Olga's Russian lover. The rivalry between Quirt and Flagg continues in New York, with Quirt, as usual, tricking Flagg out of his date and his dinner. When the Marines are shipped out to Nicaragua, the woman in contest is Mariana, and again both men lose out. The purely farcical *Women of All Nations,* a third film with McLaglen as Flagg and Lowe as Quirt, was released in May 1931 and was, by Walsh's recollection, the worst of the series.[38] The film owes more to *Two Arabian Knights* than to *What Price Glory* in its use of a harem setting and the strategy of pitting the heroes against Muslim men in their pursuit of women. The *American Film Institute Catalog of Feature Films* indicates that there was a fourth Flagg and Quirt film, *Hot Pepper,* directed by John Blystone in 1933.

Walsh also made *Hot for Paris,* a musical comedy variant released in December 1929, in which Victor McLaglen played a hard-drinking sailor on shore in Le Havre with his pal (El Grendel). In the same year MGM released *Marianne,* a musical remake of *The Big Parade,* directed by Robert Z. Leonard, about a love affair that develops between an American soldier and a French peasant girl when his company is temporarily bivouacked in her village after the Armistice.

Not all of the films deriving from *What Price Glory* were burlesques or purely comic variants of the plot. Walsh's emphasis on male fraternity was elaborated in two more important war films in the early sound period. Howard Hawks's *The Dawn Patrol* is usually related to *Journey's End,* a British-American coproduction released in 1930, based on a British play of 1929, about a group of fliers at the front. But in tone and theme both *Journey's End* and *The Dawn Patrol* are clearly indebted to the play *What Price Glory,* especially in the motifs of the constant turnover of personnel and the pathos of too-young recruits sent into battle. In *The Dawn Patrol* Dick Courtney (Richard Barthelmess) quarrels viciously with his commander, Major Brand (Neil Hamilton). It is said that they were rivals for the affection of a girl in Paris, but the real grounds for the friction between them is that the major, whose unit is short of personnel, must send inexperienced fliers into battle. Courtney needles his superior officer and accuses him of ruthlessly sending young men up to die. When the major is promoted, Courtney in turn becomes the commander. He quarrels for the same reasons with one of the men under him, Douglas Scott, formerly his best friend (Douglas Fairbanks, Jr.). Present-day *Variety* reporter and Hawks biographer Todd McCarthy shows that John Monk Saunders's original treatment for *The Dawn Patrol* gave much more prominence to the men's rivalry over women.[39] The decision to abandon this motivation suggests that Hawks quite deliberately set out to transform the *What Price Glory* plot and to place attention exclusively on the professional tensions developed within the military unit.

Auteur studies of the director give *The Dawn Patrol* a deservedly high reputation. McCarthy has characterized it as an outstanding early experiment in the use of sound, especially for its dialogue delivery, and as a work that contains what were to become many typically Hawksian narrative elements in embryo.[40] At the time of the film's release, however, it was seen as a potential problem at the box office. *Film Daily* (July 13, 1930: 10), which approved of the film's "punch," found it "a very courageous production, in that it entirely ignores the love angle, no female appearing in the cast, or being mentioned in a sentimental way." It characterized *The Dawn Patrol* as "a man's picture." The *Variety* review (July 16, 1930: 15) praised the film, especially the air sequences, but made reference to the fact that it was an all-male cast and called the film a "woman-less chronicle."

While distinctive in its focus on the all-male group, *The Dawn Patrol* was not the only film to try out this option. Ford's *Men Without Women*, released earlier the same year, begins following the antics of a group of sailors in a Shanghai bar, including what *Variety* (February 5, 1930: 24) called "flirting or fencing with the girls in various degrees of intimacy." But the bulk of the narrative, once the sailors are recalled to work, concerns the relationships between the officers and their men when their submarine is damaged and trapped on the sea floor.[41] *Variety* judged it to be "a picture that will get itself talked about and will contribute to the artistic prestige of the Fox product, but probably will be kept out of the high money group by women's adverse reaction to a story of heavy tragedy and brutal realism."[42]

I have argued that in the theatrical version of *What Price Glory* Charmaine is assigned a peripheral role in the resolution of the plot. Since she is perfectly willing to settle for either Flagg or Quirt, the play focuses on the struggle between the men and ends, appropriately enough, with them paired off. The adaptations by Vidor and Walsh retreat from this characterization of the heroine and give the romance plot much greater prominence. Outside of the genre of the war picture, however, one can find films seemingly influenced by *What Price Glory* that are structured primarily, or entirely, around male rivalry and friendship. This point may not seem remarkable to present-day readers, for whom the "buddy movie" has come to define a film with masculine appeal. But in the 1920s, as the reviews of *The Dawn Patrol* and *Men Without Women* suggest, such films were considered unusual and somewhat risky commercial bets. To understand the innovative nature of the examples that follow, it is worth emphasizing the importance accorded the romance plot in many films concerned with male adventure in the period. For example, although Mencken praised Conrad for "see[ing] clearly that the destiny and soul of man are not moulded by petty jousts of sex," the major Hollywood adaptations of Conrad in the 1920s did not hew to the original source material in this regard. Maurice Tourneur's *Victory* (1919) and Victor Fleming's *Lord Jim* (1925) amplify the love story present in each of the novels and, in the case of the Tourneur film, provide it with a happy ending. And in Herbert Brenon's adaptation *The Rescue* (1929) the romance plot becomes predominant, as will be discussed in chapter 6.

It is difficult to deal summarily with the Western, since this genre encompassed both a wide range of plots and films made in widely disparate budget categories, from super specials to low-budget product for the daily grind houses. But some comment is called for, since the idea of escaping the feminine and the domestic by "lighting out for the territory" has been important in American literature at least since Huckleberry Finn proposed it. It is certainly the case that the trade press assumed that most low-budget Westerns appealed largely to men or boys. Moreover, tough "he-men" Western stars such as Dustin Farnum, William Hart, and Tom Mix were prominent in the industry from the early 1910s. Nonetheless, female characters and some kind of courtship remain central to the most important narrative prototypes. For example, while Molly, the woman from the East, must learn to accept the codes of combat held by the man she loves, the eponymous Virginian, the struggle between these two, and their eventual reconciliation, is at the heart of Owen Wister's novel and its many silent film adaptations.[43] Jim Kitses's seminal study of the Western, which analyzes the structure of the genre in terms of a symbolic antinomy between East and West, helps to explain the importance of Molly and female characters like her: she embodies the best values of the East, those aspects of culture worth preserving in the wilderness.[44] The woman and the Western hero may not always marry at the story's close (although they do in *The Virginian*), they may not even entirely understand one another, but the woman represents everything that the Western hero fights for.

As late as 1957 Anthony Mann complained about the necessity of introducing women into the plots of Westerns: "In fact they always add a woman to the plot, because a Western without a woman wouldn't work. Although she isn't necessary, everyone seems to be convinced you can't do without her. And she always gets in your way when you get to the fight with the Indians or the chase scene, or the scene in which the hero meets the villain: you have to invent some device to get the woman somewhere

where she won't be around so you don't have to film her."[45] By this point in the history of the genre, and especially in the films of John Sturges and Samuel Peckinpah, female characters were becoming more or less periph-eral, although it could be argued that, despite Mann's complaint, women remain central to at least two of his Westerns, *The Naked Spur* and *The Far Country*. But I have not yet seen a Western from the 1910s or 1920s which entirely rejects the romance plot and denies the role traditionally ascribed to women in the genre.[46] To take just one example, in John Ford's recently restored *Bucking Broadway*, from 1917, the ranch hand Cheyenne Harry travels from Wyoming to New York City to rescue the girl he loves from a mustachioed Eastern dude who wants to seduce her.

The number of male adventure films from the 1920s that significantly downplayed the romance plot is thus quite small, and the first steps in this direction on the part of filmmakers were quite tentative. MGM's *Twelve Miles Out*, directed by Jack Conway, was released in July 1927, about six months after the first showings of *What Price Glory*. Two smugglers, Jerry (John Gilbert) and Red (Ernest Torrence), have a history of tricking each other, stealing each other's loot, and, in Jerry's case, stealing the ugly Red's women.[47] While smuggling bootleg liquor, Jerry tries his luck with Jane (Joan Crawford), whom he has temporarily taken hostage aboard his boat, along with her fiancé. The fiancé proves a coward, but Jane stands up to Jerry and rejects him. Red and his crew board Jerry's vessel, planning to rob him of his liquor. Once he discovers her presence on board, Red also makes attempts on Jane, and, in contrast with the worthless fiancé, Jerry defends her. Not sure that he can best Red in a fight, Jerry challenges his friend to a prolonged and comic drinking bout. The men finally do fight for possession of both the boat and the woman, while, on Jerry's orders, Jane steers toward a revenue cutter. He expects to go to jail and to lose his boat, but he feels he must do this to protect Jane, who has by this point indicated her interest in him. When the revenue officers board, Jerry and Red have resorted to guns, and both of them are wounded. The men, almost naked and exhausted from their beating, sink to the floor side by side as friends. Jerry says the boat is his, but Red, just before dying, claims the boat and the illegal liquor, thereby leaving his friend free to marry. Although adapted from a play by William Anthony McGuire that opened at the Playhouse Theater, New York, November 16, 1925, the film has many elements that seem to derive from *What Price Glory:* a friendship between men that is characterized by pro-fessional double dealing and sexual rivalry; a comic drinking bout that turns into a more serious fight as the centerpiece of the film; and a final reversal that unexpectedly stresses the loyalty between the men.[48] A relatively unknown film today, *Twelve Miles Out* was highly praised by *Variety* at the time of its release as a programmer that delivered both more humor and more suspense than expected. *Film Daily* (July 31, 1927: 9) wrote, "A real romance without any fancy boudoir trimmings. A story with guts. . . . They'll have to can the drawingroom stuff for Gilbert after this one." The film seems to me one of the most effective reworkings of *What Price Glory,* in part because of the performances of the male leads, and in part because the background of smuggling, and the plot of outlaw trickery and violence, are very effective substitutes for the role of the War in the original.

Victor Fleming's *Mantrap,* released prior to *What Price Glory* in the summer of 1926, was based upon the Sinclair Lewis novel published the same year. The film was seen as a modern comedy, enhanced by snappy titles and free use of the vernacular: *Film Daily* (July 25, 1926: 6) called the titling "smart" and *Variety* (July 14, 1926: 16) called it "corking." The plot also presages the emphasis on male fraternity that would come to the fore in *What Price Glory* and subsequent comic variants.

Mantrap's initial exposition is particularly interesting for the way it employs ellipsis. An attractive blonde flirts with Ralph Prescott (Percy Marmont), her lawyer, as she discusses her impending divorce. A narrative title informs us that "Ralph Prescott feels that even when a woman gives a man the best years of her life, he gets the worst of it." His client claims that her husband beat her, to which Prescott replies, "Good!" and then in a second title, "—er—good evidence!" As she continues to talk we see a shot of many superimposed images of her face, each one talking. Ralph finally manages to get rid of her, only to find that his waiting room is full of similarly dressed, attractive women, all eager for his attention. Slipping out the back door he meets a business acquaintance, Wesson Woodbury, who suggests that they go out into the Canadian backwoods for some camping and fishing. Although he knows nothing about the wilderness, Prescott agrees in order to escape from the women who are plaguing him at work.

Although the temporal relationships are not completely clear, it appears that the film then cuts back in time (a temporal manipulation that lays the groundwork for a later joke and allows for a more elegant exposition but was criticized in *Film Daily*). At the Mantrap river trading post in the Canadian outback, the storekeeper Joe Easter (Ernest Torrence) confesses to his friend Curly that he is "sick of this he-man country" and complains that "my last thrill was in 1906—when I seen a girl's ankle in Minneapolis." Curly tells him to go to Minneapolis again: "Ankles ain't the half of what they're showin' now." The sequence that follows seems to have influenced a similar representation of the movement of the central characters from country to city in *Sunrise*. *Film Daily* commended the series of shots that begins at the trading post and continues with town and then city views, all in tracking shots as if seen from a moving vehicle. The series concludes with a view of a street car on a busy city street, from which Joe appears, only to be almost run down by a car. Like the unfashionable protagonists of *Sunrise*, Joe also visits a barbershop, where he apologizes to the manicurist Alverna for his ugly hands, eventually getting up the courage to ask her out to dinner.

Mantrap burlesques the businessmen's pretensions to roughing it in a manner reminiscent of *Wild and Woolly* (Emerson, 1917), a Western parody starring Douglas Fairbanks that was shot by Fleming. Woodbury outfits Prescott with gear for their trip, and the men are shown sitting in front of a tent inside the shop, facing an elaborate mock camp that includes a stuffed deer hanging as if newly killed. Woodbury confidently predicts that a few weeks together in the outback will make them friends for life. The scene dissolves to a graphic match, the men sitting in front of a much rougher looking tent and camp, with the rain pouring down. The men exchange words and are soon fighting one another, to the amusement of their Indian guides. Without any motivation for his appearance, Joe Easter pulls up in his boat and gently teases them for scaring the fish. He decides to resolve matters by taking Prescott back to the trading post. The next day, headed for Mantrap in Joe's boat, Ralph is happily anticipating a vacation "twenty miles from Woodbury and a thousand miles from women" when he sees Alverna waiting for them on the dock. Only at this point is it revealed that Joe and Alverna have married.

It soon becomes clear that Alverna is at odds with the two people who make up the "respectable" society at the trading post: Mrs. McGavity, the fat and ugly wife of the owner of the only other store, and the Reverend Dillon. Alverna prefers to drink and flirt with the trappers who come to the post and with Curly, a handsome young forest ranger. She quickly begins to make advances to Ralph and twits him when he proves unresponsive. When two Indians try to break into Joe's store one night, Ralph scares them off by firing his gun. Anticipating the possible return of a marauding band, Ralph offers to stand guard until daybreak. Joe, who thinks this mock-heroic posture is amusing, goes back to bed. Pretending to be frightened, Alverna takes advantage of Ralph, as he sits, gun ready on the front porch. She manages to sit close to him and to rest her head on his shoulder. After a few weeks of trying to withstand Alverna's advances, Ralph concludes that he cannot trust himself with her and owes it to Joe to leave. Joe, aware of his wife's attempts at seduction, is relieved by this decision.

Traveling by canoe with an Indian guide, Ralph encounters Alverna alone in the woods with her things packed, eager to get back to the city. Ralph explains that his friendship with Joe and his honor forbid his taking her in his boat. Alverna pooh-poohs male honor as a "moth-eaten alibi" and threatens to walk back to Minneapolis, asserting that she has "walked home before." Ralph capitulates, and Alverna proves a boon companion, carrying camp supplies through the difficult portages. One evening Ralph breaks down, confesses his love, and proposes to ask Joe to divorce Alverna so that they can be married. The film makes it clear that they continue to sleep apart, however, and that only Alverna occupies the tent. Meanwhile, Joe has set out in his boat in pursuit of the couple with a loaded rifle. Ralph's Indian guide decamps with the boat and all of their food during the night, presumably afraid of trouble with Joe. The couple continue on foot until they are weary and weak from hunger. When a plane sees their signal and makes a water landing, Alverna immediately starts primping and flirting with the pilot. The pilot, a forest ranger, cannot take on passengers, but he leaves them some rations and promises to send help. After the plane takes off, Ralph, furious with Alverna for flirting, begins a quarrel.

When Joe arrives Ralph and Alverna are still quarreling. Ralph produces a gun, which Joe takes away from him, putting away his own shot gun as well. Joe announces that he did not come to kill Ralph but to save him from Alverna, who he is sure would drive his friend crazy with her flirtatious ways. A very funny scene follows, in which the men talk about what is to be done with Alverna, disregarding her protestations as best they can. Joe proposes to send Alverna to his aunt's in Minneapolis, while Ralph still hopes to marry her and take her to Europe for some continental polish. Alverna finally gets in Joe's boat and sails off, laughing and hurling insults at them, leaving the two men stranded, arm in arm on the shore.

In the epilogue Ralph returns to his New York office, pinches his secretary's cheek, and begins to flirt with his first client of the day. In *Mantrap*, Alverna returns to Joe, and they embrace, although, even as they do so, she cannot stop herself from making eyes at a handsome new ranger who wanders into the trading post.

The film version of *Mantrap* makes the heroine a more important and more sympathetic character than she is in the original novel. This is not least because of Clara Bow's performance, which was praised in both *Variety* and *Film Daily*. *Variety* thought her role as a "fast-working, slang-slinging manicurist" fit her persona well, comparing it to Colleen Moore's break-through role in *Flaming Youth*. The reviewer went on to comment, "Miss Bow just walks away with the picture from the moment she steps into camera range. Every minute that she is in it she steals it from such a couple of corking troupers as Ernest Torrence and Percy Marmont." But the prominence accorded to Alverna is not just a matter of Bow's performance. The filmmakers altered the plot of the novel, especially the ending, to build up the role of the heroine and correspondingly downplay those of the male leads. In Sinclair Lewis's novel, Alverna's incessant flirtations and interest in fashion, supposedly frivolous and out of place in the wilderness, irritate her husband deeply and lead to real dissension between them. And Ralph Prescott, after agreeing to take the girl with him on his trek out of the woods, agonizes more over his betrayal of his friend. There is also much greater suspense in the novel as to whether or not Joe will shoot Ralph, a threat doubled by a raging forest fire that dogs the couple in their flight. Novel and film both contain the rapprochement between the men and the girl's rebellion against the friends/rivals who wish to decide her future. But the novel differs from the film in that Alverna's departure for Minneapolis is followed by several chapters in which Ralph contemplates taking Joe to New York with him, Joe's store having been burnt down by Indians. In these chapters Joe's affection for Ralph is affirmed, as is his growing conviction that in the city he would be out of place and a burden to his friend. The book concludes with Joe's tricking Ralph into taking the train to New York without him and a hint that he intends to go to Minneapolis in search of Alverna. But she has no voice in this anticipated reunion of the couple, and at its close the novel emphasizes the separation between the men rather than either man's relation to the woman.

An examination of the original source material indicates how careful Fleming was to preserve the outline of a love story between Joe and Alverna and insure that the evocation of male friendship not overwhelm the role of the female lead. Nonetheless, *Mantrap* is remarkable for its pronounced, if cheerful, misogyny and for the comic reversal in which Joe puts away the guns and, instead of fighting over the woman, proposes to protect his friend from her. Given that Fleming was Hawks's mentor, *Mantrap* may well also have served as a model for the latter's *A Girl in Every Port*, released in February of 1928, which I regard as the definitive comic reformulation of the plot of *What Price Glory*.[49]

Writing in *Cahiers du cinéma* on the occasion of a screening of *A Girl in Every Port* at the Museum of Modern Art in 1962, Henri Langlois commented:

> For Paris *A Girl in Every Port* is not a recent event, but one which occurred in the 1928 season. It was the Paris of the Montparnassians

and Picasso, of the surrealists and the Seventh Art, of Diaghilev, of the "Soirées de Paris," of the "Six," of Gertrude Stein, of Brancusi's masterpieces. That is why Braise Cendrars confided a few years ago that he thought *A Girl in Every Port* definitely marked the first appearance of contemporary cinema. To the Paris of 1928, which was rejecting expressionism, *A Girl in Every Port* was a film conceived in the present, achieving an identity of its own by repudiating the past. To look at the film is to see yourself, to see the future which leads through *Scarface* to the cinema of our time.[50]

These claims for the modernity of the film are not overstated, and they must be considered at the level both of plot and of style. The narrative of *A Girl in Every Port* is distinctive in that it manages to avoid a sentimental treatment of the romance plot. Indeed, aside from the burlesques, it is the only film variant of *What Price Glory* that achieves this. Stylistically the film unites what I have described as two distinct trends: the interest in the vernacular emanating from *The Big Parade, What Price Glory*, and naturalist-inspired filmmaking generally, and the interest in understatement and economical narration emanating from *A Woman of Paris* and developed by Lubitsch and others in the realm of sophisticated comedy. The ellipses in *Mantrap*, such as the one that takes Joe Easter from country to city, or the one that takes the businessmen from their store-bought fantasy of a camp to the real thing in the woods, are clever, isolated "touches," although, of course they perform expositional functions with great efficiency. But in *A Girl in Every Port*, the economy of the narration, made possible by complex repetition structures, is apparent throughout. Perhaps it was the combination of a jaunty use of the vernacular and a simple but elegant mode of narration that in 1928 appealed to the Parisians, who were in the throes of rejecting "expressionism."

A Girl in Every Port begins with two failed seduction attempts separated in place and time, as in the film version of *What Price Glory*. Spike (Victor McLaglen) picks up a Dutch girl in Amsterdam and is doing well with her until he notices that she wears a bracelet adorned with a heart-and-anchor charm. He leaves her, saying that he is tired of finding an unknown rival's heart-and-anchor mark on "his" women. The same scenario is repeated in a Latin American locale.[51] Outwitting a barful of men to get to the dressing room of a dancer whose name appears in his little black book, Spike asks if she has been true to him, and she folds her hands as if in prayer: "Si señor—twice." But as love-making proceeds it becomes apparent that she too bears a heart-and-anchor, this time on her garter. By comparison with *What Price Glory* the narrative economy of the opening is apparent from the first incident in Holland, which makes it clear that the heart-and-anchor, if not the rival, have been met with before.

In a bar in Rio de Janeiro Spike meets Salami (Robert Armstrong), a name that was changed to Bill in some prints, apparently for censorship reasons, but that is given in the reviews in both *Variety* (February 22, 1928: 20) and the *New York Times* (February 20, 1928: 14).[52] A beautiful blonde comes into the bar, and Spike has hopes of making time with her, but she passes him by and sits with Bill, who smirks at his success. The two men begin to fight. When guards intervene, Spike and Bill join forces against them. The next morning they wake up in adjacent jail cells. At first the men are friendly. Bill says, "We were doing great, until they called out the army." Then Spike examines his jaw, where Bill had hit him the night before, and notices the heart-and-anchor mark on his own face. Bill asks Spike to pull his finger, which always goes out of joint when he hits someone. This allows Spike to confirm the presence of the ring that had made the imprint on his cheek and at the same time introduces the motif of rectifying the displaced finger with which Hawks marks the men's friendship.

Spike pays Bill's bail as well as his own so as to get another opportunity to fight with him, but they encounter guards everywhere they go and must move on. Finally they walk off the edge of a dock while arguing. Bill tries to fight with Spike in the water, but when he finds that Spike cannot swim, he rescues him instead. After pushing Spike's enormous bulk up a ladder to safety, Bill finds that his cigarettes are wet. Spike's are wrapped in plastic, and he gives Bill one and lights it before lighting his own. In the next scene they walk into a cantina, drunk and wearing the hats of two guards. This incident, like the sharing of cigarettes, is borrowed from *The Big Parade* but here presented much more elliptically. Spike tries to make time with a girl but is interrupted on three occasions when Bill repeatedly provokes fights and needs to be rescued. On the last occasion Spike excuses himself politely from the woman who is caressing his face, knocks out the sailor who is choking Bill, and then knocks out Bill so that he can have time for sex.

A narrative title, characteristically comic but brief, informs us of the lasting friendship that is formed between the two sailors:

> Spike and Bill—
> As time went on, sailors spoke of them together
> —like Tom and Jerry
> —like Rock and Rye.

But when their ship is loading in Marseilles "a toothache reduces the menace to France by one-half." Alone at a carnival, Spike meets Mam'selle

Godiva, also known as Marie (Louise Brooks), who does a high dive act. Marie's manager directs her attention to Spike's money roll. Meeting the girl later, Spike proposes to her, indicating by the calculations in his little black book how much money he has. When he asks, "Is there any chance for a big walrus like me, Baby . . . is there?" she replies, "Sure! There's always a chance." An ambiguity that is worthy of Charmaine, except that there is never any suggestion that Charmaine (as opposed to her father) sells her favors, or is out for anything but a good time.

Spike prepares to jump ship to be with Marie, despite Bill's warning that he is not really in love but just "broke out all over with monkey-bites." The two men quarrel. Later, alone in an apartment on shore, Spike wipes a tear away as he watches the ship, and presumably his friend, leave without him. Bill unexpectedly appears, and the friends are reunited.

That evening Spike introduces Bill to Marie and leaves them to get acquainted. The film signals the repetition of the opening incidents with the greatest economy, in two brief dialogue titles and two motifs. Bill speaks first:

> So you're Mam'selle Godiva, now? You used to be Tessie back in Coney Island.

Marie sits next to him and looks seductive. In a detail shot she touches his ring, then removes her arm band and shows her matching tattoo.

> What did you ditch me for? I thought I tattooed your mark on my arm for keeps—

Across this scene and the next Marie comes on to Bill, while Spike remains oblivious to their previous relationship and her essential duplicity. She finally corners Bill alone in bed in the apartment he shares with Spike. Modestly covering himself, he resists her advances and manages to get dressed and leave her, saying, "Nothin' doin', kid. That big ox means more to me than any woman." Spike enters and finds Marie strangely unresponsive. His attempt to grab her arm reveals her heart-and-anchor tattoo. Here again the turn in the plot has been reduced to a single visual motif, a character's view in a detail shot that alters everything. *Variety* thought Victor McLaglen overacted in his effort to punctuate this otherwise very understated reversal, but I find his change of expression spectacular: he puts back his head and laughs, then the laugh turns into a yell of pain and rage. Finally, he passes his hand down over his face, letting emotion drain from it, and pushes Marie out of the way to go after Bill.

In a bar Bill gets into a fight with two other sailors and calls for Spike to help, as he had earlier in the cantina in Rio de Janeiro. Spike finds him by this device so that what was previously an act of friendship and trust between them becomes the means of preparing his revenge. He quickly dispatches the two sailors, but when Bill holds out his hand for a shake, Spike knocks him out. He goes to the bar and, without thinking, orders two drinks (the two-drink motif in this film may derive from the scene in the play *What Price Glory* in which Flagg and Quirt confront one another and share drinks as well as insults with the repeated phrase "both of us"). When Spike realizes that he has automatically ordered for two, he pushes one off the bar and drinks the other. Then McLaglen gradually modulates his facial expression to show Spike calming down. He lifts Bill, who is coming to, into a sitting position on the floor. The men quickly come to an understanding, and Bill holds out his finger for Spike to pull back into place. Spike swears that nothing is going to come between them again and holds up two fingers for two drinks.

The vaunted classicism of this film is evident in comparison with the other variants of *What Price Glory*. In its carefully reiterated and varied motifs—the heart and anchor mark, the displaced finger, the brawls—the film achieves a kind of elegance that rivals Lubitsch, but it does so in a much less obtrusive way than the Lubitsch "touches" and without ever losing the flavor of a particularly American vernacular. Moreover, I would argue that Hawks's version of this plot goes the furthest in assimilating the cynical tone and the abjuration of pathos of the Anderson and Stallings play. By removing the male fraternity from the context of war, the film largely eliminates the kind of sentimentality found in *The Big Parade,* where male friendship is underscored with the threat of loss and death. Moreover, it avoids the need for the kind of patriotic boosterism intermittently found in Walsh's film. No need for the Marines to call for these buddies to get together. Most important, perhaps, by making the woman untrustworthy, *A Girl in Every Port* avoids the necessity of forming a romantic couple, a necessity that cripples the ending of Walsh's film.

Despite being more cynical than the other film versions, *A Girl in Every Port* is nonetheless ultimately more optimistic than the play, in which the relationship of Flagg and Quirt is defined by strategic maneuverings for advantage as well as vicious sparring, both verbal and physical. In eliminating the war theme, Hawks also dispenses with these Nietzschean undertones. The men fight as much because they enjoy it as for any other reason, and they are unfailingly loyal to one another not because they face death together but because they love one another. It is the film's one unabashedly sentimental note.

The film was not much commented upon at the time of its release. The *New York Times* briefly summarized the plot and concluded that it was funny and that McLaglen was good. *Variety* gave it a "moderate box office rating," concluding it was "okay for de luxe first runs anywhere," but criticized the film on the grounds that "the boys will find this picture to their liking, but what the dames may think is something else again. The plot deals with a Damon and Pythias friendship between two rough and tumble seamen. The pal stuff between two guys has never made any great hit with the ladies, and when the eulogy of male friendship includes several backhanded slaps at the feminine gender the reaction may be a matter of legitimate conjecture." Although *Variety* writes of the "pal stuff" as if it were old hat, I think the trade paper's worry about feminine reaction is indicative of the daring of Hawks's treatment of the romance plot.[53] All of the other variants of *What Price Glory* avoided, or backed away from, the play's treatment of Charmaine. I find it quite remarkable that the misogyny which was integral to Anderson's and Stallings's rejection of sentiment and, more generally, a pronounced tendency of literary modernism in the 1920s, proved to be one of the hardest elements for the classical Hollywood cinema to assimilate. Of course *A Girl in Every Port* does not strike us as particularly daring, nor vehemently antiwoman, today, but that is because, as Langlois noted, to see it is to see the future that leads through *Scarface* to the cinema of our time.

In 1929, after the release of *A Girl in Every Port*, Fox essayed a similar male buddy film starring Victor McLaglen, *Captain Lash*, which was directed by John Blystone and featured a music-and-effects track. Despite having a small budget and being by a much less important director than Hawks or even Fleming, the film merits mention because *Variety*'s response to it (February 6, 1929: 18) echoes its response to *A Girl in Every Port*. "Captain" Lash is actually a stoker on a large passenger ship (the set design and cinematography in the boiler room are indebted to Sternberg's *Docks of New York*), and Lash's comic sidekick, Cocky, has been charged by Babe, a girl waiting in Singapore, to keep Lash away from other women. Lash becomes attracted to Cora, who appears to be an upper-class passenger but is actually a member of a gang of jewel thieves. Cora uses her feminine wiles to steal the Kismet collection of jewels from another passenger, Condax, substituting fake gems in place of the real ones. In an effort to evade a police search, she gives Lash a sealed envelope containing the jewels and asks him, as a personal favor to her, to deliver them to her address in Singapore, a task he takes on with evident delight. When the ship docks in Singapore, Cocky examines the envelope with suspicion and tries to prevent Lash from going to Cora's. The two friends quarrel, Lash physically attacking his much slighter friend. At Cora's house Lash realizes her treachery when he is confronted by the gang. Upon opening the envelope, the thieves find that it contains only chips of coal, and they attack. Lash is managing to hold them off, when the authorities arrive, accompanied by Condax. The thieves are arrested, and Lash leads Condax to Cocky, who pocketed the jewels on board ship and proceeds to return them to their rightful owner. Condax thanks the two friends, who are now reconciled. Lash is about to walk off with his friend, swearing off women, when Cocky reminds him about Babe.

Variety liked the incidents in the plot, thought that the "roughneck" part fit McLaglen, and approved of the funny and idiomatic titles. However, the story and star were thought to present a potential problem: "Fighting or wooing McLaglen is a joy. This player is runner up to Wolheim for capitalizing a homely pan. The radiant smile that can break through that ugly map is a drama in itself. Women's reception of the picture is a gamble. This will mark the difference between moderate box office and exceptional business." The problem raised by *Variety* is that "femme fans" will not react well to "a gorilla hero who loves 'em and leaves 'em and gets away with it indefinitely." While the reviewer may be anticipating a moral objection to the character, the comment also points to the way in which the film minimizes the romance plot. Babe is largely marginal to the story even at the film's close, so that Cocky, Cora, and Lash form the triangle that motivates most of the action. But even Cora is not particularly important, since the men are not sexual rivals, and our knowledge of Cora's status as outlaw makes the reconciliation between the two sailors a foregone conclusion. In contrast, much time is taken up by Clyde Cook's (Cocky's) vaudevillian turns: he plays the concertina, often in a frantic effort to warn Lash when a woman is about to get him into trouble, he dances specialty numbers, and he plays the comic drunk. The film is so reliant on the performances of the two male leads that it approximates a men-without-women plot while having women in it.

The departures from sentimental narrative prototypes that one finds in *Mantrap, A Girl in Every Port,* and *Captain Lash* are moderated to some degree by the fact that all of the films are comedies. Other than the war film, it seems to me that the gangster film as it emerges in the late 1920s is one of the few genres that admits of a noncomic diminution of the romance plot and a concomitant escalation of the themes of male violence, power, and sexual rivalry. Gilbert Seldes, for example, wrote approvingly of the gangster cycle in 1935: "They brought a sense of actuality and a rude male vigor to an art given to prettiness and sentimentality, they shifted emphasis from women to men and created stars who were neither clothes models nor movie actors, but players in a new medium."[54] Similarly, writing in 1938 about a repertory screening of *Scarface* and *Hell's Angels,* a World War I film, Seldes found them both preferable to more recent films that gave undue emphasis to the love story.[55] Henri Langlois also pointed to the importance of the gangster film in his commentary on *A Girl in Every Port,* identifying *Scarface* as the next step toward a modern cinema. I shall therefore consider the genre briefly, as a coda to this discussion of *What Price Glory* and its avatars.

Some of the best-known early features about urban crime, Raoul Walsh's *Regeneration* (1915), Maurice Tourneur's *Alias Jimmy Valentine* (1915), and Chester and Sidney Franklin's *Going Straight* (1916), place emphasis on the moral reformation of the criminal or criminal pair, a process typically motivated by love.[56] In *Alias Jimmy Valentine,* for example, Jimmy, who is actually a notorious safecracker, pretends to a group of dignitaries visiting the prison in which he is incarcerated that he has no idea how to manipulate the lock on a safe, and he is released thanks to the good offices of one of them, Rose Lane. Falling in love with Rose, he tells his gang that he is through with crime and takes a position in her father's bank. A detective, Doyle, continues to investigate, determined to convict Jimmy of past crimes. Just as Jimmy finally convinces Doyle of his innocence, Rose's little sister is accidentally locked in the new bank vault, for which the combination is unknown. Jimmy cracks the safe in the detective's presence, saving the girl but thereby revealing the truth about his prior life of crime. Doyle, convinced that Valentine has in fact reformed, leaves him to his new life with Rose.[57]

Although less is known about what were called "crook melodramas" in the early to mid-1920s, a preliminary study by Bradley Schauer suggests that the story of an underworld denizen trying to go straight remained common. However, there were also many stories in which one or both of the apparently criminal protagonists turn out to be undercover agents for the law.[58]

In my view Josef von Sternberg's *Underworld,* released in August 1927, initiates a decided break with previous films about urban crime. However, some scholars have assimilated the film to other examples of the reformation plot. Thus Gerald Peary writes, "In gangster movies of the twenties— *Underworld,* for example—a gang leader who committed terrible deeds,

including murder, was allowed to absolve himself gracefully of his sins
through heroic sacrifice, often to save the sacred love of a young and innocent couple. By giving up his life for this moral cause, he would instantly
bring meaning to his existence, demonstrating knowledge of his sins and a
desire for reformation."[59] In my opinion this interpretation overmoralizes
the protagonist's motives and ignores the features of *Underworld* that
bring it closer to the subsequent, nonsentimental strain of the crime story.
Most importantly, the romance plot is not tied to the idea of regeneration,
as it is in films such as *Alias Jimmy Valentine*. Moreover, the plot turns on
the question of loyalty between men, a bond the heroine threatens to
break. It should also be noted that *Underworld* differs from *The Racket*,
another cynical crime melodrama released in June 1928, in that it is without any real sense of politics or urban sociology. Instead it focuses almost
entirely on male power struggles and sexual rivalries, elements that were
to become very important to the gangster cycle in the 1930s and that we
can also trace back to *What Price Glory*.

One reason that *Underworld* was so advantageous for von Sternberg's
career is that it made a star of George Bancroft, a large, ugly man in the
Victor McLaglen mold who had until then worked primarily in Westerns,
typically in bad man parts. *Variety* (August 24, 1927: 22) wrote of the
actor's performance in *Underworld*, "George Bancroft as 'Bull' Weed, a
sympathetic crook, explains why Paramount re-signed him by his performance in 'Underworld.' Bancroft will be heard from importantly from
now on if again given half the opportunities that are in this picture."
Exceptional Photoplays found that the film "stamps an American actor,
George Bancroft, with finality as of the elite among screen artists, a power
like Jannings and Krauss."[60] *Moving Picture World* (September 3, 1927:
48) noted, "Clive Brook is the first featured player, but George Bancroft
walks off with the honors by virtue of the more picturesque character."
Von Sternberg's career in the 1920s was enabled and largely defined by his
use of Bancroft, as it was to be enabled and defined by his use of Marlene
Dietrich in the 1930s.

In addition to jump-starting von Sternberg's career, *Underworld* provided Ben Hecht with one of his first jobs as a screenwriter.[61] Although von
Sternberg in later years minimized Hecht's contribution to the project, the
Paramount files make it clear that Hecht wrote the story on which *Underworld* is based and at least one version of the script.[62] A second and
presumably final script by Robert N. Lee builds upon Hecht's version,
although some further changes were made, particularly to the ending.[63] In
1927 both *Variety* and *Moving Picture World* attributed the realism of the

characters and setting in *Underworld* to Hecht's work reporting on the Cicero and South Side mob. But I consider the film's supposed realism less important than the narrative and stylistic innovations achieved through the combined efforts, however unwitting, of writer and director. And the intellectual milieu of the Chicago Literary Renaissance seems at least as important as the Chicago mob in inspiring those innovations. The film creates a proto-Nietzschean hero, what the reviewer for *Exceptional Photoplays* called a "Napoleon of crime," a man of great strength who accepts no social or moral limits. The style of the film, as reduced and elliptical as *A Woman of Paris* or *A Girl in Every Port*, achieves a cool, and sometimes ironic tone that accords well with its subject.

The film opens with two short scenes in which a great deal of action—a robbery, a police search, and the beginning of the friendship between the two protagonists—is suggested with very few cues. A narrative title and an elaborate process shot that combines a clock face and a skyscraper evoke the city, deserted, at night. A bum walks along a sidewalk beside a substantial building. An explosion is visible through its barred windows. The bum reels and then perceives Bull Weed coming out the door carrying a box. A single dialogue title informs us of the significance of the action and also puts the bum in danger of being rubbed out. He bows slightly and says: "The great Bull Weed—closing another bank account." Bull pulls the bum into his getaway car. Four shots schematically represent police discovery and pursuit. Later, dragged into the safety of a furnished room, the bum, drunk, but dignified, insists that he is no "squealer" but "a Rolls-Royce for silence." The gangster agrees to take a chance on him and gives him the nickname "Rolls-Royce."

At the Dreamland café, Buck Mulligan, a rival gang leader, indicates his interest in Bull's girl, Feathers. He also insults Rolls-Royce, who has taken a job there as janitor, offering him ten dollars and then throwing them into the spittoon.[64] When Rolls-Royce spurns the money, Mulligan tries to force him to reach for it, striking him down and threatening to kill him. Bull faces Mulligan down and tells Rolls-Royce to stick with his gang for protection.

Outside the Dreamland café, Feathers impatiently indicates that she wants to go. Bull points to a flashing advertising sign reading "The City Is Yours" and offers his girlfriend the city.[65] She gestures in annoyance at his grandiosity. Rolls-Royce poetically compares Bull to Attila the Hun at the gates of Rome. Bull does not understand but seems pleased, and he offers Rolls-Royce a bank roll, saying he plans to put him back on his feet. Rolls-Royce asks how he could possibly help Bull in return, and Bull explains that no one helps him; he helps other people. This sets the seal on the relationship between the men: despite Rolls-Royce's superior manners and intellect, Bull unquestionably has the upper hand.

The front for Buck Mulligan's gang is a flower shop, as was that of the real-life Chicago gangster Dion O'Banion.[66] We see miniature roses advertised as "Mulligan's Special," and, in a joke that also becomes something of a motif, Buck puts one in his buttonhole. In the back of the store is a man-sized cross, covered with flowers, and a banner reading, "Rest in Peace." Buck displays a banner he would like to add to the cross, which has Bull Weed's name printed on it. He tells his girl, "I'm going to bury that guy while these lilies are still fresh!"

Bull takes Feathers to their old hideout in a tenement, where Rolls-Royce, well-dressed and coiffed, now lives in a nicely furnished interior. Feathers is surprised at the change in his appearance, and Bull comments, "Look at him—cost me a thousand—looks like a million!" Hidden behind a substantial bookcase, filled with books that Bull explains Rolls-Royce actually likes to read, is a locked steel door. Bull gets the key from Rolls-Royce and shows them a secret passage leading to a neighboring warehouse that is owned by the gang. Bull brags that this allows for a perfect getaway.

Bull announces that he has to go out "on business." Feathers had earlier admired some jewelry in a shop window, and he undertakes a heist to bring her a surprise gift. Rolls-Royce puts a miniature rose in Bull's buttonhole, explaining, "The police all know Mulligan's Special. Plant the little flower where it will do the most good."

Left alone with Rolls-Royce, Feathers flirts with him. This scene, which is interrupted by the sequence of the jewelry heist, approaches the tone of *A Woman of Paris* in its wit and understatement. Feathers asks Rolls-Royce what he was before Bull Weed found him. He says he was sometimes a lawyer and always a drunkard. She asks if a woman was behind his drinking, and he says he is not interested in women. Piqued, she walks over to the couch where he sits and picks up his book. Returning to her chair, she pretends to read. Rolls-Royce walks over to her chair and, with elaborate politeness, turns her book right side up.

The incident of the jewelry heist is not, strictly speaking, necessary for the plot. Buck Mulligan is framed and, presumably, apprehended, but his arrest does not come to anything, since he attends the gangsters' ball that evening. Yet the sequence is a stylistic *tour de force*. Eleven detail shots, even more condensed than those of the opening bank robbery, evoke Bull Weed's criminal activities in a series of "touches" or motifs: a clock face pierced by a bullet, a hand grabbing jewelry out of a case, a miniature rose dropped on the floor.

At the hideout the flirtation becomes more serious. Rolls-Royce and Feathers pretend to read, staring at each other over the edges of their books. They finally begin to laugh. Rolls-Royce, approaching her, admires the feather trim on her coat. She explains that she wears them all over, inviting him to look at the trim on her lingerie. He asks, "What were *you* before Bull Weed—er—found you?" Feathers evades this question, an evasion that is suggestive in itself, by turning his earlier line against him: "I thought you weren't interested in women." She makes eyes at him as they exchange looks in a series of four extremely tight and compelling close-ups. They are about to kiss when Rolls-Royce gently pushes her away, saying that Bull Weed is their best friend. She replies that for the first time in a long while she feels ashamed.

Bull Weed enters and gives the jewels to Feathers. She jumps into his lap in delight. As Rolls-Royce looks on, pained, Feathers gives him a quick, apologetic glance. Before they leave, Bull orders Rolls-Royce to attend the gangsters' ball that night, despite his evident disinclination to do so.

At the gangster's ball Rolls-Royce and Feathers dance until Bull becomes jealous and recalls her to his side, rudely dismissing Rolls-Royce. Later that evening, sunk in a drunken stupor at his table, Bull is unaware of Buck Mulligan's machinations to get Feathers alone in a back room. Finally awakened by Mulligan's girlfriend, Bull finds them in time to save Feathers from assault and dives out of a window in pursuit of Buck. At the flower shop, in a final bit of black humor, Bull shoots Mulligan repeatedly until his rival falls in front of the flower-covered cross Mulligan had intended for Bull.

After Bull Weed's conviction for murder, Rolls-Royce explains his plan for a jail break to Feathers and another member of the gang. The men are to enter the prison inside the hearse meant to carry out Bull's body. Feathers is to wait in another car for Bull to join her. Rolls-Royce will act as a decoy, buying two tickets out of town at the railroad station, so that the cops will assume that Bull is leaving with him.

Later, Rolls-Royce bids Feathers good-bye. She declares her love for him, objecting, "We have a chance to lead a decent life. If we get Bull out— we're *his* again!" At first Rolls-Royce demurs, saying that they owe Bull everything, but eventually the two embrace, and he begins to pack so that they can leave together. As she is helping him her eye falls on the newspaper headline "'Bull' Weed to Hang Tomorrow, Killed Man Who Attacked

Sweetheart." She decides that they could not be happy if they betrayed Bull, and tells Rolls-Royce that he has taught her to be "decent."

At this point the film initiates a pattern of alternation that contrasts what we know about the loyalty of Rolls-Royce and Feathers with what Bull suspects about them and his mounting rage. The gang gets word to Bull to watch for the hearse at two o'clock. Bull, skeptical, tells his inform-ant that Rolls-Royce doesn't want him out of prison. Just prior to two o'clock, Feathers waits in her car. Bull asks the prison guard, Ed, if either Feathers or Rolls-Royce has tried to see him and is told no, "the whole town knows how they're carrying on." Rolls-Royce waits outside the train station. Bull engages Ed in a game of checkers, looking out the window of his cell from time to time. When the hearse pulls up outside the jail, the police find the gang inside it and capture them. None of this action is apparent to Bull. From his cell window he sees the hearse enter the inner courtyard and, when nothing happens, concludes that he has been double-crossed. Returning to his game of checkers, he waits for his chance: finally reaching through the bars, he chokes the guard.

Bull manages to escape from prison and make it to his hideout, where he finds a gun. He sneaks downstairs briefly to procure a newspaper. In addi-tion to announcing the jail break, the headlines assert that Feathers McCoy has proved fickle and has a new sweetheart. Alerted that the escape plan has gone wrong, and assuming that Bull has been hanged, Feathers drives to the hideout; she is followed, unbeknownst to her, by the police. She is delighted to find Bull still alive, but he grabs her by the neck and shakes her. When the police make their presence known, Bull assumes that she has set him up. He barricades the apartment and begins a gun battle with the cops. He tries to escape by way of the secret passage, planning to leave Feathers behind to take the punishment he supposes she planned for him. Finding that the door does not open, even in response to gun fire, he says of Rolls-Royce, "He sure cinched my finish—he's got those keys."

Upon learning that Bull is cornered at his old hangout, Rolls-Royce returns there. He joins the crowd of onlookers in the street, then breaks through the police lines and runs for the warehouse. He is wounded inad-vertently when Bull shoots out of the window. Holding onto his wounded arm, Rolls-Royce makes it through the secret passageway and falls at Bull's feet. The ending presents a rather abrupt and understated recogni-tion and reversal. Rolls-Royce's entrance convinces Bull of his loyalty. The gangster kneels beside him and helps him to his feet. Then, noticing how Feathers embraces Rolls-Royce, he has a change of heart and sends them out through the concealed door. Although Bull's remark "I've been all wrong, Feathers—I know it now—I've been wrong all the way—" can be read in isolation as an expression of remorse at his life of crime, within the context of the film it caps the recognition that motivates his sacrifice and thus stands as an apology for his suspicions. It is not a question of a moral regeneration; rather, he has regained his trust in his friend and is ready to reciprocate the help that Rolls-Royce has given him. He closes off the secret passage, surrenders to the police, and is led off to be hanged.

In an inversion of earlier crime films in which the gangster reforms for love of a woman, in *Underworld* the gangster inspires the reform of his male friend, rescuing Rolls-Royce from the gutter and saving his life. This does not involve reconciliation with the law; in fact, it takes place outside of it, as a function of Bull Weed's innate power and strength. The romance plot is also unconventional because the woman does not lead either man to accept traditional ideas of authority and law. Certainly a gold digger, perhaps a former prostitute, Feathers tests the bonds of male friendship before learning to be "decent," a decency she proves, ironically, by participating in the jail break. Moreover, although Feathers is certainly a more sympathetic character than Marie in *A Girl in Every Port*, *Underworld* resembles the Hawks film in that the crucial interactions are between men. The plot of *Underworld* is structured by contestations and alliances between the three male leads. Throughout the first half the jealous antagonism between Buck Mulligan and Bull predominates and is contrasted with the friendship between Bull and Rolls-Royce. Beginning with the gangsters' ball, however, the sexual rivalry that fuels the hatred between the two gang leaders also infects the relationship between Bull and his friend. Bull Weed is thinking of Rolls-Royce while he stews in the jail, and he longs to kill him as he already has Buck. The presence of Feathers in the hideout in the final scene is not enough to reassure and appease Bull; it is the appearance of Rolls-Royce, wounded and bearing the promise of escape, that engenders the final recognition.

The canonical gangster films of the early 1930s continue, indeed intensify, many of the trends that can be observed in *Underworld*. These films are preoccupied with exploring male violence and power rather than reconciling the protagonist with morality or law, a point that was, of course, to become an issue in the censorship of the crime film in the middle of the decade.[67] In addition, the romance plot becomes even less important than it was in von Sternberg's film. The male protagonist's relations with women are subsumed by his interactions with the men who determine his ascent within the hierarchy of the underworld. In *Scarface*, for example, Tony makes time with Lovo's girlfriend, Poppy, at the same time that he assumes Lovo's position as head of the gang. The death of Tom Powers in *Public Enemy* is brought on by his efforts to avenge the killing of Matt, his lifelong friend and partner in crime. The romance plot, if it can be called a romance—Tom's rejection of his girl Kitty in favor of the more glamorous Gwen Allen—has no bearing on the way he deals with his enemies. For example, informed of the emergency brought on by the death of the crime boss Nails Nathan, Tom simply walks out on Gwen Allen at the very moment when she indicates that she is finally willing and ready to sleep with him.

The diminution of the romance plot in the early gangster film went hand in hand with a far-reaching exploration of the vernacular. In *Underworld,* Bull Weed's crude and rough manner is contrasted with the urbanity of his intellectual friend. Although later films do not usually set up such a contrast, "ugly" stars such as James Cagney and Edward G. Robinson continued in the vein first established by Victor McLaglen and George Bancroft. Slang could now be rendered in spoken dialogue and became one of the staples of the genre, and actors played around with Italian or Irish accents, or pushed the speed of line delivery to the edge of incomprehensibility.[68] In addition, vulgar gestures and comportment became the norm for the male actors that played in these sorts of films. For example, in *The Public Enemy* the initial alliance between Paddy Ryan and Tom Powers is sealed by a matched pair of shots in which each actor turns to the side and spits off frame, a sound effect indicating that they have hit the spittoon. Both Cagney in *The Public Enemy* and Paul Muni in *Scarface,* perhaps following a strategy employed by George Bancroft in *Underworld,* make crude demeanor acceptable, even pleasurable, by employing stylized and highly repetitive gestures: Bancroft's signature laugh, the brief but prominent wave that Muni gives in greeting or parting, Cagney's affectionate poking at family and friends.

Taken as a group, the gangster films of the early 1930s are assuredly typical of the "tough stories in a tough manner" that we now hold to be characteristic of "masculine" genres. I have tried to show how such a confluence of narrative and style was produced across the course of the 1920s. The process involved quite disparate plot types: war films adapted from the play *What Price Glory;* comedies focusing on male friendship frequently indebted to Raoul Walsh's film *What Price Glory;* and films involving smuggling and urban crime. These films share a more or less tentative diminution of the romance plot, an emphasis on a male pair whose relationship is defined as much by rivalry as friendship, and an experimentation with the vernacular in both language and gesture. In the case of both *A Girl in Every Port* and *Underworld,* these elements were underscored by what was understood to be a modern, terse and elliptical mode of narration. It is important to note that the "tough manner" of these films is not simply a matter of the roughness of the characters and surroundings depicted but also of breathtakingly quick openings and expository passages, telling use of detail shots, and understated dramaturgy.

At the time of their release, most of the films discussed here were seen as distinctive—a departure from the typical war film or crook melodrama. Some, *The Big Parade, What Price Glory,* and, to a lesser extent, *Underworld,* were praised in the trade press for being realistic, hard-edged and nonsentimental. Others, *A Girl in Every Port, The Dawn Patrol,* and also *The Public Enemy* (see *Variety,* April 29, 1931: 12), were criticized for their masculine focus, which, it was thought, could alienate women viewers. The question arises, then, as to how films often held to appeal to women—films that highlighted the romance plot—were affected, if at all, by the decline in the taste for sentiment.

5　The Seduction Plot

It's not 'cause I wouldn't,
It's not 'cause I shouldn't,
And, lord knows, it's not 'cause I couldn't,
It's simply because I'm the laziest gal in town.
　　"The Laziest Gal in Town," words and
　　music by Cole Porter, 1927

The seduction plot was one of the cornerstones of eighteenth-century sentimental literature, the central motif of Richardson's novels, a possibility represented from the point of view of the sensitive man of feeling in Sterne's *A Sentimental Journey* and Oliver Goldsmith's *The Vicar of Wakefield*, and, by the nineteenth century, a common motif of stage melodrama and the three-decker novel.[1] Nonetheless, it held an ambiguous place in American nineteenth-century culture. Herbert Ross Brown has shown the enormous popularity in America of Richardson among other British writers of sentimental fiction.[2] Cathy Davidson has demonstrated how *Charlotte Temple*, one of the first American novels and a canonical example of the story of the woman seduced and abandoned, sold widely in all sectors of the American reading public.[3] But by the mid-nineteenth century, as Leslie Fiedler has remarked, quasi-pornographic descriptions of seduction attempts, such as are found in Richardson, were considered beyond the bounds of good taste. Fiedler discusses the changes in the seduction plot at the hands of what he calls "the lady purveyors of genteel, sentimental fiction," focusing not only on the expurgation of seduction scenes but also on the introduction of narrative substitutes for the struggle with the seducer.[4] Although she emphasizes somewhat different aspects of this trend, Nina Baym also argues that in the mid-nineteenth century the seduction plot became less prevalent in middle-class American fiction.[5] The American sentimental novel was frequently resolved more optimistically than were novels such as *Clarissa*, offering its readers pragmatic edification in the story of a young heroine finding a way to survive in the world rather than the pious spectacle of a slow and moving death.

　　Despite its attenuation in genteel fiction, there is consensus that the seduction plot continued to be a powerful convention throughout the nineteenth century in popular theater and in fiction ranging from the stories published in penny family newspapers to such critically acclaimed novels as George Eliot's *Adam Bede* and Charlotte Bronte's *Jane Eyre.* Sally Mitchell has argued that by the 1880s the working-class versions of the seduction plot in British family papers eschewed the exploration of the moral, social, or psychological aspects of the seduction found in more elite novels. They tended to concentrate upon the physical conflict between the heroine and her erstwhile seducer, often having the heroine withstand literal imprisonment or attack and sometimes stressing her physical prowess.[6] Popular theater also tended to represent the seduction as a physical assault upon the heroine, one from which she might or might not be saved either by her own actions or by those of others.[7] In discussing the importance of this plot in American working-class fiction, Michael Denning points to the role of Laura Jean Libbey, whose works appeared frequently in the weekly story papers *Fireside Companion,* the *New York Ledger,* and *Family Story Paper* in the 1880s and 1890s.[8] The *Dictionary of Literary Biography* provides a concise account of the plot formula found in almost all of her many serials: "Libbey used the setting of the workplace as the stage for stories of young women adrift in the world. Frequently orphaned, without the protection of family, her virtuous young working girls defend their status as 'only a working girl.'" Libbey's heroine retains her innocence in the face of trials that include multiple abductions, druggings, attempted suicides, fires, thefts, and caustic chemicals. In the end, despite the many dangers of living and working alone in the city, she usually marries an upper-class man.[9]

Thus by the early twentieth century the seduction plot existed in many forms, incorporating more or less physical violence and addressing quite different sectors of the reading public. The heroine could be an unmarried working girl facing an amorous and unscrupulous boss; she could be an innocent country girl lured or taken to the city; she could be a married woman of upper- or lower-class station, whose lover tempts her to leave her family. The plot could generate suspense about whether or not she would yield to the seduction attempt or, at the other extreme, it could touch on the seduction only briefly and concentrate instead upon the bitter aftermath, and/or find ways to justify the heroine's actions for the reader. Although the plot often concluded with the heroine's marriage, either to the reformed seducer or to the man who eventually saved her from his clutches, examples of unhappy endings can certainly still be found.

In their rejection of the seduction plot, intellectuals of the 1920s typically resorted to satire and other forms of humor rather than engaging in direct frontal attacks. Leslie Fiedler contrasts Oliver Goldsmith's song from *The Vicar of Wakefield,*

> When lovely woman stoops to folly,
> And finds too late that men betray,
> What charm can soothe her melancholy?
> What art can wash her tears away?
>
> The only art her guilt to cover,
> To hide her shame from ev'ry eye,
> To give repentance to her lover,
> And wring his bosom is—to die.

and Eliot's witty deflation in *The Waste Land:*

> When lovely woman stoops to folly and
> Paces about her room again, alone,
> She smooths her hair with automatic hand,
> And puts a record on the gramophone.[10]

The drama critics were more direct in voicing their disdain for this plot. In the early 1910s H. L. Mencken jeered at *La Dame aux Camélias* and the operas *La Traviata* and *Faust* in the pages of *The Smart Set.*[11] Robert Benchley frequently had fun with the plot in his *Life* column "The Drama." Writing of the Selwyns' production of *The Mirage,* with which they opened their new Times Square Theatre in 1920, Benchley teased:

> The little girl from Erie, Pa. (just why Erie should be picked as the seat of virtue and innocence is not clear. It was a man from Erie who once taught me how to stack a Canfield pack so that you can run out every time), comes to the Metropolis and, owing to the difference in the exchange rate between Erie and New York, falls victim to the lure of money. Then comes the Boy from the old home town. "What are you doing here?" . . . "What right have you to ask?" . . . "That woman has promised to be my wife!" . . . "I *nev*-er want to see you again! *Nev*-er, *nev*-er, *nev*-er!"[12]

In 1922 Alexander Woollcott complained about the ending of *The Awful Truth,* a farce in which a seemingly erring wife is shown to be "pure as the driveling snow" in the final scenes, arguing that there was no reason to inno-cent the rascally wife since it could scarcely be supposed that "a New York audience would swoon at the thought of an impure heroine."[13] The insou-ciant attitude to sex expressed in Cole Porter's "The Laziest Gal in Town," cited in the epigraph to this chapter, is of a piece with Woollcott's cynicism.

Attitudes toward the older, working-class variant of the seduction plot were, predictably, even more dismissive. Upon Laura Jean Libbey's death in

1924, the *New York Times* noted her efforts to ensure her immortality through the erection of a tombstone carved with her pen name, a site that, in a gesture worthy of Emmeline Grangerford in *Huckleberry Finn*, she liked to visit while still alive. But the *Times* opined that except among the large immigrant populations in the East and middle West, she was no longer popular, even with the stenographers and shop girls who had presumably been her principal audience.

Despite the deprecations of the intellectuals, one can find many versions of the seduction plot in the cinema of the 1920s: more or less optimistic, more or less sensational, high and low. Ince's *Anna Christie* and Sjöström's *Name the Man*, discussed in chapter 2, are exemplary of relatively high-brow naturalist variants. They are among the earliest of a group that might be said to include also Sjöstrom's *The Tower of Lies* and *The Scarlet Letter* (both 1926) and Raoul Walsh's *Sadie Thompson* (1928). But while these films were prestigious, and some of them profitable, they do not seem to have definitively shaped the more numerous and popular cinematic variants of this plot. I will show that the transformation of the seduction plot in film was much more heavily indebted to comic than to naturalist prototypes, both the ambiguously comic example of Chaplin's *A Woman of Paris* and the straight-up comedies that followed.

The reception of D. W. Griffith's *Way Down East*, one of his most popular films of the 1920s and still one of his best-respected of that decade, indicates the spectrum of early responses to dramatic variants of the seduction plot. *Way Down East* fits into two trends in Griffith's filmmaking of the period. Like *True Heart Susie* and *A Romance of Happy Valley*, it is a nostalgic story of pre-War rural life, "a simple story of plain folks." But unlike those bucolic romances, *Way Down East* was obviously planned as a big, expensive film from the start. It was one of two high-priced theatrical properties that Griffith acquired in 1920 (the other was the British success *Romance*).[14] *Way Down East* was particularly expensive, since Griffith had to pay the producer William Brady $175,000, as well as making payments to the original writer, Lottie Blair Parker.[15] While *Romance*, directed by Griffith's assistant Chet Withey, lost money, *Way Down East* was successful and seems to have motivated a third theatrical adaptation in 1921, *Orphans of the Storm*, based on the play *The Two Orphans*, by Adolphe d'Ennery and Eugène Cormon.

According to David Mayer the play *Way Down East* was an instance of "combination melodrama," a drama incorporating extended comic turns by well-known comedic actors (among them Harry Seamon playing Rube Whipple), songs, live animals on stage, and a climactic fist fight between the hero and his rival (William Brady had gotten his start in show business by organizing and promoting boxing matches).[16] Brady and his collaborator, Joseph Grismer, doctored the play severely, and in its final form it became a staple of the turn-of-the-century theater, with Florenz Ziegfeld staging the 1898 New York production, and two road companies making repeated tours to provincial theaters.

The film that Griffith derived from what Lillian Gish called a "horse and buggy melodrama," while differing in important respects from the ordering of events in the original and including considerably more "back story," is, like the play, indubitably an instance of the seduction plot in its more cheerful and liberal mode. Anna Moore is sent by her mother to rich relations in Boston to borrow money. The relations prove unsympathetic, but while Anna stays with them she meets the wealthy Lennox Sanderson, who tries to seduce her. When he is rebuffed, he tricks her with a sham marriage that he tells her she must keep secret because of difficulties likely to be posed by his family. After Anna returns home to her mother she discovers that she is pregnant and is abandoned by Sanderson. Following her mother's death, Anna retires to a boarding house in the town of Belden, where the baby is born and soon dies. She is turned out of the boarding house by the landlady, Mrs. Poole, who suspects that she is not married.

She is hired to work on the Bartlett farm, although Squire Bartlett harbors some suspicions about her character. That evening Anna discovers that Sanderson lives on a neighboring estate. Sanderson demands that she leave, afraid that her presence will prove a roadblock to his courtship of the Bartletts' niece, Kate. Anna contemplates going but is persuaded to stay by the squire's son, David, who, ignorant of her past, is falling in love with her. After some months David declares his love, and Anna sadly tells him that he must not speak of it again. That winter Martha Perkins, the town gossip, encounters Mrs. Poole and learns of Anna's past. After several delays Martha finally conveys her news to the squire at a neighbor's Christmas barn dance. Meanwhile, at the Bartlett home, David proposes to Anna and is told that she can "never be any man's wife."

The next day, the squire leaves for Belden and confirms Mrs. Poole's story. Upon arriving home he orders Anna out of the house. Before she goes she reveals that Sanderson, present as a guest at the squire's table, is the man who deceived her. Anna departs into a raging blizzard, followed shortly after by David, who is concerned for her safety. The squire orders Sanderson out of the house. The villain makes his way to a maple cabin, where he encounters David, who bests him in a tussle. Meanwhile, Anna has struggled through the storm to the river and faints on the ice at the river's edge. The ice begins to break up, and the ice floe that holds her drifts free, moving dangerously toward a waterfall. David discovers her and, leaping from floe to floe, manages to catch her just before she is tumbled over the falls. He carries her to the maple cabin, where the squire begs her forgiveness, she refuses Sanderson's belated offer of marriage, and she is accepted into the Bartlett family as David's wife.

Although Griffith's *Way Down East* was a popular hit and lauded in unusually glowing terms by critics, its reception, at least in the metropolitan press, was marked by a degree of condescension toward the source material.[17] This attitude is epitomized by playwright and director Winchell Smith's letter of congratulation to Griffith: "One of these days theatre people will wake up to what you've done. To make a big feature picture from the old plot of *Way Down East*—chuck it into a regular [i.e., legitimate] theatre—and get away with it! It's nothing less than wonderful!"[18] Most of the big New York papers wrote in a similar vein, with many critics at pains to distance the film from the original play, which is frequently dubbed a mere "melodrama." *Variety* (September 10, 1920: 36), which was extremely enthusiastic about the film ("it would be sacrilege to cut a single foot"), saw Griffith's role as that of transforming an old warhorse: "'D. W.' has taken a simple, elemental, old-fashioned, bucolic melodrama and 'milked' it for 12 reels of absorbing entertainment." *Wid's Daily* (September 12, 1920: 15), which thought the film "the biggest box office attraction of the times," was more respectful of the play as a big money-maker and a likely draw for audiences but nevertheless noted that the original "never reached the public finished off as artistically and as powerfully, as Griffith's picture." *Motion Picture Classic* also predicted commercial success for the film and called it Griffith's "greatest since his epic, 'The Birth of a Nation.'" While approving the morality of the original play, the reviewer notes however, "Not that we consider 'Way Down East' for a moment as a thing of literary or dramatic value. It was a melodrama of fearful dialogue and even more fearful construction. But a compelling message and a compelling background were there."[19]

The highbrow critics were even more vehement in their rejection of the play, although the film version usually came in for praise. In 1918 George Jean Nathan had compiled a list of popular plays he considered "pish and platitude." In addition to *Tosca, East Lynne, Camille,* and *The Old Homestead,* he included *The Two Orphans* and *Way Down East.*[20] For many, the story Griffith had chosen to tell simply overwhelmed his treatment of it: they could see the appeal of the film, especially of its last-minute rescue over the ice, but they still could not take it seriously.

Writing anonymously in the *New York Times* (September 4, 1920: 7) Alexander Woollcott quipped:

> Anna Moore, the wronged heroine of *Way Down East*, was turned out into the snowstorm again last evening, but it was such a blizzard as she had never been turned out into in all the days since Lottie Blair Parker first told her woes nearly twenty-five years ago. For this was the screen version of that prime old New England romance, and the audience that sat in rapture at the Forty-fourth Street Theatre to watch its first unfolding here realized finally why it was that D. W. Griffith has selected it for a picture. It was not for its fame. Nor for its heroine. Not for the wrong done her. It was for the snowstorm.[21]

Robert Benchley, in an often quoted joshing review of the film in the pages of *Life,* noted, "The whole picture, captions and all ('There stands the man who deceived me!'), might very well serve as a delightful burlesque just as it stands were it not for the fact that Nature, who is reputed to be even more prodigal than Mr. Griffith, has furnished some remarkably beautiful scenery and snow effects which make the whole picture worth sitting through."[22] In his film column in *Life* Robert Sherwood discussed *Way Down East* in a review of Hugo Ballin's production of *East Lynne*:

> "East Lynne" and "Way Down East" have been removed long since from the theatrical time-tables, and their revival in film form is only a means of reviving unpleasant memories. Westward the course of empire takes its way, and all the David Wark Griffiths and Hugo Ballins in the world can't controvert the force of that famous platitude. The town-hall-to-night melodramas should be relegated to the eternal graveyard, along with the gold brick, the shell game and the notion that Boston (Mass.) is the Hub of the Universe; and those ghoulish producers who seek to dig up that which is better buried are wasting their own talents and imposing on the public. Stay West, young men—stay West.[23]

Whereas Sherwood thought the adaptation of plays like *Way Down East* a bad strategy for the film industry, Ludwig Lewisohn, whose interest in psychoanalysis undergirded his attacks on what was then called "Puritanism," felt that the film reinforced backward and repressive sexual taboos. Granting the "magnificence" of the snow scenes, as well as the film's widespread appeal, he complained that Griffith had

> taken the tawdry old fable of "Way Down East"—the betrayal, the mock marriage, the villain's downfall, the happy ending—and left it, in all essentials, precisely what it was. The written legends on the screen that interpret the action in a style of inimitably stale sugariness serve but to intensify the coarse and blundering insufficiency of the moral

involved. These hectic appeals to the mob in favor of conventions as stiff as granite and as merciless as gangrene are powerfully calculated to tighten thongs that even now often cut to the very heart and to increase the already dreadful sum of social intolerance and festering pain.[24]

Despite the critical reception, the film did so well on Broadway that Griffith was eager to roadshow it on his own rather than make it available to United Artists, the distribution company he had just started with Pickford, Fairbanks, and Chaplin. According to Richard Schickel, the film's success enabled him temporarily to ease the enormous debt brought on by the considerable costs of making the film, as well as constructing a studio out of a mansion in Mamaroneck, Long Island, and borrowing from UA, which had helped underwrite the purchase price and production costs of *Romance*.[25] In part, the success of *Way Down East* may be explained by its reception outside the big cities, where critics and, presumably, audiences were prepared to take it "straight," as is indicated by this editorial from the *Evening World-Herald* of Omaha, Nebraska: "David Wark Griffith is not merely a keen business man exploiting 'the movies.' He is a man of culture and refinement and ideals—a true and a great artist. . . . And he has shown us, in this 'simple story of plain people,' how the screen can be used, with true art of a high order of excellence, not alone to entertain the people but to serve them. He has made the combination of beauty with truth. He has put art to its loftiest practical use as the hand-maiden of simple goodness."[26] Then as now, the film was also appreciated by sophisticated critics for the realism and/or spectacular nature of its conclusion. Richard Schickel has written, "It is the ability to show real sleigh rides and spacious barn dances, to place Gish and Barthelmess in a real blizzard, and on a real river as the winter ice breaks, that gives the film an insuperable advantage over the stage."[27] But it should be stressed that Griffith's success in this instance was hard to repeat; it depended upon having the resources to redo a well-known play in a new way. The novelty of the film depended not only on the cinematography of the scenes on the ice but also on the device of alternation used throughout the film's equivalent of the play's second act to heighten the suspense about Martha's impending revelation of the birth of Anna's illegitimate child. The critical attitudes that inspired the rejection of the original play were widespread, and one can see them influencing the way the film industry trade press evaluated other instances of the seduction plot that did not benefit from the ingenuity of Griffith's transformation of *Way Down East* and were, moreover, not as well crafted or expensively produced.

The 1922 version of *Tess of the Storm Country,* Mary Pickford's remake of the 1909 story first filmed with her in 1914, is an interesting attempt to rework the relatively more passive heroine played by Lillian Gish in *Way Down East.* Tess is a feisty and mischievous girl who lives in a squatter village of fishermen and their families. When the upper-class patriarch who owns the land tries to evict the squatters, she comically assaults the lawyer and game wardens who are attempting to displace her people. The patriarch Elias has two children: Frederick, who is well disposed to the squatters and eventually falls in love with Tess, and Teola, who is too frightened of her father to confess that the suitor of whom he disapproved, and who has been killed in a conflict with the squatters, has left her pregnant. Contemplating suicide, Teola falls in the lake, where Tess discovers her on the verge of drowning, saves her, and takes her to her shanty to bear the child. Tess cares for the child because Teola is too fearful to bring it home, and this ultimately endangers her own romance with Frederick, who thinks his girl has "sinned." The plot is resolved when Tess brings the sick baby to the church and demands, despite Elias's scorn, that the baby be baptized. She performs the act herself just before the baby expires, and Teola then claims her child just before dying herself (in the novel from which the film is adapted her death is motivated by consumption, but there is no such motivation in the film). The deaths of Teola and his grandson lead to a change of heart on the part of Elias, who eventually deeds the village to the squatters, and to a reconciliation between Tess and Fred.

Variety (November 17, 1922: 41) justly praised Mary Pickford's performance, holding the part of Tess uniquely suited to the star: "Miss Pickford acts with her head, hands and feet in this film." The reviewer particularly approved of the physical comedy: "It has everything in the sob line, offset by Tess' impetuosity that is just as natural with Tess as Mary Pickford is natural in her playing." *Variety*'s stance on this film is not dissimilar to the attitudes toward *Way Down East:* the work of a great artist, in this case Pickford rather than Griffith, helps to sell an otherwise outdated plot. The story is considered old fashioned, and not simply because it is a remake. Commenting on the opening title, which announces that the picture is being remade "under the conditions of modern photoplay reproduction," *Variety* offers a rebuff: "Speaking of remaking the story in modern picture style sounds like the bunk, as there isn't anything modern to be made out of 'Tess.'" The *New York Times* (November 13, 1922: 12) agrees, calling the story an "obvious, sentimental, unreal and artificially complicated melodrama," which it argues is saved by Pickford's acting skill: "She has several scenes, a number of intensely human moments, in which she becomes a real Tess in a real world of troubles, and, sometimes, joys."

Reactions to the cinematic adaptations of *Camille*, one in 1921 with Nazimova, and one in 1927 with Norma Talmadge, are quite similar to the discussions of *Way Down East* and *Tess of the Storm Country*. Both George Jean Nathan and H. L. Mencken had denounced this story in its theatrical and operatic variants. In the pages of *The New Yorker* in 1932, Alexander Woollcott evinced a somewhat more tolerant attitude to the play. He writes of it as an old warhorse: "There comes a time when one totters off to a fresh revival with the acquisitive eagerness of a maniacal philatelist in pursuit of a fugitive Nicaraguan. Thus I suspect it was chiefly as an irrational collector of theatrical memorabilia that I hied me to New Haven one day last week to see the tear-stained relic which the young man who wrote it called *The Camellia Lady*." While taking a superior attitude to the play, Woollcott nonetheless admits that a particular star's performance might be worthy of interest:

> Then, when one has said all that, how shall one find other words for certain moments of loveliness which, by sorcery, she does impart to this fond and foolish old play? All around her in the death scene there is a shining light which the puzzled electrician cannot account for. And when she retreats into the garden in Auteuil, there passes over her a shadow as delicate and fleeting as the reflection of a cloud in the mirror of a quiet lake. Or am I babbling? I really do not know how to translate into the print the tantalizing mystery of Lillian Gish. I do wish America had never been wired for sound.[28]

Variety's attitude to the cinematic versions is less condescending than Woollcott's. Assuming that the reader will be familiar with the plot *Variety* mentions only the ways in which the film diverges from its theatrical precedents. The 1921 version is criticized because Armand is not at Marguerite Gautier's bedside as she dies (September 16, 1921: 35), and the 1927 version for the beginning that shows Marguerite as a girl, being driven into the arms of her first lover by parental cruelty (April 27, 1927: 16).[29] The review of each version asserts that the film's success will rest on the star's performance, and both Nazimova and Norma Talmadge come in for praise. *Variety* suggests that the 1927 version will not hold up on Broadway as a two-dollar special, even though it will work as a "high-rate program release." Perhaps this is the commercial equivalent of Woollcott's judgment that the play is a "tear-stained relic"; there seems to be an assumption that it will not hold the most sophisticated urban audiences for long. Because both theatrical and cinematic renditions of *Camille* were largely rated in terms of performance, and because the story was taken as a given, the work seems to stand at least partly outside the changes in taste documented here. The attempts made to modernize the 1927 version are of interest, however, and I will discuss them in relation to the conventions of romantic drama in chapter 6.

Reviewers considered a film with a very similar plot to *Tess of the Storm Country,* Thomas Ince's *Hail the Woman,* to be a much more difficult sell than the Pickford film had been. Considered by *Variety* (January 20, 1922: 34) to be "rather feminist," the film puts blame on the male characters—both the overly stern father and the submissive son who deserts the girl he gets pregnant. The daughter of the family, falsely suspected by the father of being a "wanton" and thrown out of the house, finds the girl her brother abandoned and takes over the care of the baby at the mother's death. *Variety* finds the film theatrical and contrived, especially the final confrontation in the church which, as in the Pickford example, leads to a change of heart on the part both of the stern father and of the weak-willed son (although in this case the child in question does not die but is recognized as a member of the family). It notes that the film "is done with unmistakable sincerity and some of its moments of pathos brought a flutter of furtive handkerchiefs from women's wrist bags. Real tears from a theatre full of Broadway film fans ought to be sufficient testimony to the strength of the photoplay." However, *Variety* thinks the film is a risky proposition—"it would be a daring prophet who would attempt to forecast the probable fate of the offering"—and sees its only hope of a market among women. Clearly, the "feminist argument" of the piece was seen to be a problem, but so, I suspect, was its sincerity and pathos. The film lacks the kind of comedy that, in the estimation of the trade paper, provided Mary Pickford with such a good vehicle in *Tess of the Storm Country.*

Most of the films disparaged by *Variety* have a tendency to play the seduction straight as drama or, perhaps, melodrama. The J. Stuart Blackton version of *Passers-By,* distributed by Pathé, from a 1911 play by Charles Haddon Chambers, is associated with the work of Laura Jean Libbey. The *Variety* reviewer (June 25, 1920: 33) concludes:

> The "heart" matter is of the kind Laura Jean Libbey spilled over in books, and it may have looked, also sounded, better on the speaking stage than it screens for present-day audiences. The time when the lady who was wronged and wanders away, to be restored at the finale with her child to her sweetheart as his wife, could bring a gulp has passed away. Nevertheless, that does excite casual interest, for no one is quite so hardened that they may watch the lovelorn roam about in a fog

without hoping that in her wanderings she wanders into the home of the man she thinks has forgotten her. . . . *Passers-By* misses a punch, but where the shop or factory young lady abounds it will be certain of a draw from amongst them.

Although its heroine is a thief rather than a fallen woman, *In a Moment of Temptation*, adapted from a story by Laura Jean Libbey, is indicative of *Variety*'s evaluation of the audience for this type of fiction. Making reference to the "sugar-coated stories of the Horatio Alger sort of girls" that Laura Jean Libbey wrote of, the *Variety* reviewer (October 12, 1927: 20) concludes:

> This aged old story of a girl's rise to home and husband from a lowly position . . . will have appeal exactly to the masses of those workers who can appreciate her position of cash or wrapping girl in the large department store. There is too little intelligence in the story to appeal to anyone else, except those who may be dumber. There should be an audience for this. With its soft sentimentality, if given another and more likable scenario, it could have mildly attracted with all classes. . . . Now it's the neighborhoods mostly where there's shop or factory hands, and probably the small towns where they don't care or wherever they don't care.

It is significant that this film is described as appealing to working-class or small-town audiences. Although the reviewer does not say explicitly that the film will appeal to women, the reference to Laura Jean Libbey would have led most readers at the time to assume that the film was directed to lower-class women such as shop girls and factory hands, the same audience that was associated with *Passers-By*.

First National distributed two films in 1925 starring Dorothy MacKaill that were adapted from newspaper serials, *Chickie* and *Joanna*. Although the plots were considerably more spicy than those of the films discussed above, they were nonetheless disparaged by *Variety* reviewers. The *American Film Institute Catalog* gives the most coherent summary of the film *Chickie:*

> Chickie, a poor stenographer, is initiated by a high-stepping girl friend into the speedy circle of millionaire Jake Munson, at whose parties she submits to the advances of Barry Dunne, a young law clerk. Munson later invites her to dinner and takes her to his apartment, where they run into Barry and his companion, Ila, a rich young girl interested in winning Barry's affections. Barry misunderstands Chickie's presence in Munson's apartment and goes to London to work, followed closely by Ila. Munson finally proposes to Chickie, but when she tells him that she is no longer a virgin, he repulses her. Chickie later discovers that she is

pregnant and writes to Barry; Ila intercepts the letter and destroys it, falsely writing back that she and Barry are married. Chickie becomes a mother, and Barry, learning of her predicament, returns from London, assures her that he neither received her letter nor married Ila, and leads her to the altar.[30]

The *Variety* review (April 29, 1925: 34) explains that *"Chickie* was one of those circulation-making newspaper serials which come once in a genera-tion—one of those oh-so-true stories of the struggles within the heart of a poor girl who wants on one hand to go straight, and on the other luxuries and 'the life.'" The reviewer concludes that the story is a "cinch money-maker." *Film Daily* (May 3, 1925: 9) judges that "every little stenographer and every office girl, as well as all the flappers, are going to get a kick out of *Chickie,"* although this reviewer would have preferred it if they had "omitted making Chickie an unmarried mother."[31]

Joanna, based on a story by Henry Leyford Gates, concerns the epony-mous department store clerk who becomes an unsuspecting pawn in the million-dollar bet two society gentlemen make on her chastity.[32] Although she is led into a life of luxury and indulgence and tempted by the nephew of a bank president, she finally rejects his attentions, and the story ends with Joanna, her purity intact, happily marrying her original fiancé, a man of humble origins whom she has helped to renown as an architect. *Variety* (December 16, 1925: 39) notes that the film derived from a newspaper serial that "must have been eaten up in many a kitchen" and concludes:

> The story screens very much as it must have read, and will be thor-oughly snubbed by the clientele which likes the "worthwhile" things. Major city balcony trade should accept it as satisfying, and as and where illiteracy percentages mount so will the entertaining qualities of *Joanna. . . . Joanna* should and probably will draw that public which fol-lowed it in print. The costly looking production donated indicates that the author's readers will be appeased at this brain-child in celluloid form. But the money spent on it is out of all proportion to the actual worth of the lightweight theme.

Variety is, if anything, even more scornful of the seduction plot when it concerns a chorus girl or dancer. I assume this is because *Variety* was still largely a theatrical paper in the 1920s and hence an apologist for Broadway. It thus regarded the stereotypes of nefarious theatrical managers and showgirls of dubious virtue as libels on the theatrical profession. But reviewers also clearly found many plots old-fashioned. *Variety* complains of *After the Show* (October 7, 1921: 44) that it is "the mushy screen-old tale of a chorus girl being led to a flat instead of marriage." *At the Stage*

Door (December 16, 1921: 35) is called a "sob melodrama" and a "hokum story." The reviewer describes the incident that leads the rich young man to propose marriage as follows: "At a bazaar someone suggests to Philip that he's playing round a bit strong for a man with a fiancée in Europe and that all chorus girls are alike, anyway. He proposes to assure himself and so makes a suggestion that would break the heart of any girl truly good and pure. Mary's heart forthwith breaks and Miss Dove did this part as creditably and with as much reserve as the rest." Similarly, *Footlight Ranger* (April 5, 1923: 36) is disparaged as

> a tale that tries to prove Broadway is all bad and to succeed on the stage a girl must part with everything. In the end she goes back to the little rube town on the same train with the honest hard-working young feller who rescues her from the angel-villain's arms at the precise moment he wanted to collect in advance for backing a show that was to make her a Broadway star. It's the old, old, hoak, done again, and as it was good in the past it is just as good today as far as the smaller houses are concerned.

Variety estimates that the appeal of *Footlight Ranger* will be to the neighborhood theaters, it does not mention that this or the other Broadway stories above might appeal specifically to women. The magazine does assume that one film of this sort will appeal to rural audiences: *Plaything of Broadway* concerns a Broadway dancer "on intimate terms with all the 'Kings' of finance," who is reformed by love for a young doctor working in the tenements. *Variety* (March 18, 1921: 34) notes: "It ought to be profitable in the rural districts, where such ballads as 'There's a Broken Heart for Every Light on Broadway,' and 'You Made Me What I Am,' and that school of so-called lyric writing are popular." But the reviewer also compares this story to those of Laura Jean Libbey: "Laura Jean herself could go no further in mushy slobber." It is not clear whether this remark implies a feminine appeal. *Broadway Nights*, however, is less ambiguously reviewed. Calling the film "an old-fashioned story filmed under a modern title and both wasted," the reviewer (June 29, 1927: 22) judges it to be "about a one-dayer for the neighborhoods, where the women like sadness, a baby and weeps."[33]

Almost all of Frank Borzage's films, often celebrated as "romantic" by critics who wish to save his works from the epithet "sentimental," represent a kind of apotheosis of sentimental traditions, clearly running counter to the trends I am describing here. But despite his affiliations with these traditions, Borzage does not often employ the seduction plot. In 1919 he made a comedy, *Prudence on Broadway*, in which a girl (played by Olive Thomas) uses blackmail to outwit a would-be seducer. Three years later he essayed *Back Pay*, one of his last Cosmopolitan productions, based on a Fannie Hurst story, a drama about the redemption of a kept woman.

In its outlines *Back Pay* suggests a highly moralized version of the gold digger plot, "back pay" being not only the wages of sin enjoyed by the heroine but also the moral cost of her material success (at one point the heroine proclaims, "If sin has any wages, some of us are going to collect a lot of back pay!"). The film opens with Hester Bevins living in a boarding house in Demopolis, well outside New York City. She is courted by Jerry Newcombe but spends her time watching the trains leave for New York and dreaming of better things. She rejects Jerry's offer of marriage because he does not make enough money, telling him that she has a "crêpe-de-Chine soul," and leaves for the city. After five years she is the mistress of Wheeler of Wall Street and friends with Kitty, who is supported by Speed.

The four friends take a trip to Crystal Springs; on the way she tells Wheeler that Speed is about to buy a chinchilla coat for Kitty. By making him feel like a piker by comparison, she persuades him to let her wire New York immediately for the coat for herself. While at the resort, Hester motors over to Demopolis and meets Jerry. Assuming she has returned to him, he tells her that he has heard from a fellow who saw her in New York but that he does not care about the past; he still loves her and wants to marry her. She tells him that the $200 a month he earns would not pay for the tiny fur scarf she is wearing (a much smaller fur than the chinchilla coat). As she leaves she lies to him to save his feelings, claiming that she works as a fashion designer for a large salary and is not yet ready to settle down.

The film then intercuts Hester at a party and Jerry in the trenches in Europe during the War. He is injured. Upon his return, she visits him in a military hospital near New York, finding him blind and with his left lung injured by gas. Jerry believes that he will get well and even eventually get a job, despite his blindness, but the doctor tells Hester privately that Jerry has no more than three weeks to live. She gets Wheeler's permission to marry Jerry and take him back to her apartment, Wheeler promising to stay out of the way. When she takes Jerry home, she pretends to him that her luxurious apartment is a two-room flat with a kitchen. After several weeks he dies in her arms. Wheeler waits a decent interval of time and then returns to the apartment, expecting Hester to take up her old life. She attempts to do just that but finds herself bothered by nightmares in which she wakes and sees Jerry staring at her accusingly (these are rendered through superimpositions of his face). She finally leaves the flat, taking nothing but her wedding ring, the clothes she wore before she became Wheeler's mistress, and the twenty-five dollars she had last earned in wages. She goes back to her former employer to ask for a job. She visits the undertaker who arranged for Jerry's funeral and asks to pay off the bill on account, a little bit each week. She rents a bare attic room and pays the landlady out of her old salary money. That night she wakes up and sees Jerry smiling.

Reaction to the film was not unified. *Variety* (February 17, 1922: 40) described it as "that old-oaken bucket story about the country gal who goes to the big city and goes wrong along." The reviewer also complains: "There's [*sic*] never was any action. Much time is wasted planting the tale at the outset and much more along the way, in the mushy scenes between Hester and Jerry, their trysting place in the woods and their hospital meetings." This complaint echoes those *Variety* made about other dramatic variants of the seduction plot. But a contradiction in this argument soon becomes apparent. Hester Bevins is not a passive, suffering heroine; she anticipates the aggressive, gold digger heroines of the comic variants of the plot that became popular in the latter half of the 1920s. She knows exactly what she wants, tells Jerry she is going to get it, and then goes after it. The *Variety* reviewer disapproved of this aspect of the story: "Notwithstanding there is the usual sentimental appeal to the love interest, but even here it seems to be risking any picture when the leading figure in a romantic tale is given a totally unsympathetic role, such as Miss Owen has, making Hester Bevins a gold digger in the country before she knows what gold digging means, and finishing up her education along that line when she reaches the city. It's a bad story for young girls to see." In short, while the film is castigated for being mushy and clichéd, it is also considered overly "modern," or at least, to have potentially scandalous elements.

By comparison with *Variety, Film Daily* (February 19, 1922: 7) is more sympathetic to the film, which it sees as doing well in "the outlying districts" and "with everyone who is interested in the regeneration idea." For this reviewer, the tender scenes mitigate the rawness of the gold digger elements: "Miss Hurst has made her heroine of a very changeable frame of mind. She can't seem to decide just what sort of a life she wants to live. Even regardless of the fact that she loses your sympathy through her relations with Wheeler, played by Barney Sherry, her character is too inconsistent. Director Borzage has done very well with the story nevertheless, and through effective sentiment he lessens the more unpleasant phases to a considerable degree." The critic for the *New York Times* (February 13, 1922: 10) seems to prefer the hard-edged elements in the plot, describing it as "a sentimentalized story of a woman's reclamation which makes obvious efforts to shake off sentimentality and be real, and sometimes succeeds."

A comparison of the film with Fannie Hurst's original story may help clarify the sentimental aspects of Borzage's treatment, as well as its claims to realism. Hurst's text begins with the narrator contrasting the love story she started out to write with her pink pen, a "modish tale," and the more old-fashioned, but by implication also more realistic story of Hester Bevins that took over.[34] Hurst's story might be classified as realistic for its surprisingly unmoralized account of Hester's early career, as well as for its meticulous attention to money: for example, there is a discussion of the cost of cotton versus cheap silk stockings, an accounting of Hester's monthly expenditures for clothes once she has become Wheeler's mistress, and a most interesting comparison of the cost of maintaining Mrs. Wheeler with the three children on Long Island, and Hester in her apartment on Riverside Drive. Once the topic of the War is introduced about midway through the story, however, the prose becomes subjectivized, and the narration much more concerned with moral judgments and Hester's internalization of them. Initially it is the narrator who contrasts Hester's frivolous life style, made possible in the story by Wheeler's war contracts, and Jerry's suffering on the battlefield.[35] Later, though, Hester's reaction to Jerry's wounds, and her frightening night visions after Jerry's death, represent her growing awareness of the disparity between how she lives and how Jerry lived and died, a disparity that eventually forces change upon her.

Borzage's rendering of Hurst's story does not "shake off sentimentality" to quite the same extent. The film portrays the small town of Demopolis as closed and dull, and it is sympathetic to Hester's wish to escape. Hervé Dumont has pointed out the irony in the intertitle that introduces Jerry as "the most energetic clerk in The Big Store."[36] But whereas Hurst resorts to a highly emotional and subjective tone only after Hester encounters Jerry with his wounds, the film prepares for this change in tone from the start. The scene in which she rejects Jerry for the first time employs highly pastoral imagery of the countryside. As they speak, alone in a wooded glade at sunset, she sings the first two verses of "In the gloaming" for him. These motifs recur with greater emotional force: the pastoral imagery of the glade in the scene in which Heather rejects Jerry for the second time, and "In the gloaming" in the scene at Jerry's deathbed, when he asks his wife to finish singing it for him. *Variety* criticized the film's "slow" beginning and the "mushy" scenes in the woods, but in my view Borzage deliberately builds up these scenes to contrast with Hester's cold-hearted pursuit of material gain.

Yet I believe it would be inaccurate to classify Borzage simply as an old-fashioned director from the perspective of the 1920s, although, of course, he is highly inclined to pathetic scenes and situations. *Back Pay* contained elements that were new for 1922 and offensive to some. Even the more sympathetic *Film Daily* reviewer found some elements disturbing, notably the marriage that is underwritten by Wheeler's money: "This charitable act would have been really sincere and proven an even stronger conclusion for the story if the girl had denounced her old life upon her marriage. The following scenes drag anyway and since she renounces Wheeler finally it would have been much more effective if she had done it previously." This comment represents a more conservative moral stance than that in either the film or the Hurst story, for neither denounces Wheeler, indeed, both film and story emphasize Wheeler's delicacy toward Jerry: not only does he stay out of the way while Jerry is sick, he also sends an ambulance to France in Hester's name and expects to pay for the funeral. In both versions Hester thanks him for his thoughtfulness. Hester's redemption does not involve the denunciation of Wheeler but rather a recognition of her own moral failing in the light of Jerry's sacrifice. And precisely because she is active and did choose her own path, it is her failing and not Wheeler's that is at issue. It is not surprising that *Film Daily* would have liked a different treatment of Wheeler's relation to the marriage, since in canonical versions of this plot the man is always the tempter and the villain (unless the heroine is a vamp, in which case the gender roles are reversed). Imbricated in the novel treatment of the heroine, the characterization of Wheeler is one of the comparatively modern elements of *Back Pay*, one that anticipates the characterization of Pierre Revel. This would certainly support David Robinson's suggestion, reported by Dumont, that *Back Pay*, which was released ten months before production began on Chaplin's *A Woman of Paris*, served as a model for that film.[37]

The fact that comic variants of the seduction plot came to be preferred over dramatic ones may be placed in a larger context by one of the polemics of theater critic George Jean Nathan. In 1927 Nathan discussed a change in sexual mores that he asserted had already been already accomplished except in more "backward" rural districts: Americans were placing much less importance, if any, on female chastity. He attributed this change at least in part to "modern literature (both book and periodical), drama and even the cinema," as well as to increasing informality of address between the sexes. The result of these practices was a new attitude toward sexuality itself:

> It used to be thought pretty generally that sex was a grim, serious and ominous business, to be entered into only by those duly joined in holy wedlock or by those lost souls already in thrall to the devil. Sex was

synonymous with danger, tragedy, woe or, at best, with legalized baby carriages. This view of sex has gone out of style with such other contemporary delusions as French altruism, the making of the world safe for democracy and the evil of Bolshevist government. . . . Sex, once wearing the tragic mask, wears now the mask of comedy. And whenever one laughs at a thing, one is no longer afraid of it.[38]

Despite Nathan's claims, the comic treatment of the seduction plot was not an entirely new phenomenon in the 1920s. The plot has been subject to parody since its inception: Richardson's *Pamela* was immediately countered by Fielding's *Shamela*. And the American cinema of the 1910s certainly produced one- and two-reel burlesque versions.[39] But, given their parodic treatment and irreverent tone, such films do not present the seduction as a serious possibility, with actual or potential negative consequences for characters within the diegesis. Thus if the heroine jumps into the river trying to drown herself, this is given simply as a send-up of the typical suicide scene. Such burlesques can coexist with a taste for relatively straight dramatic versions in which the seduction is presented as a misfortune for the woman. Some of the early 1920s comic variants of the seduction plot seem novel, however, because they presented the seduction as a serious possibility but not necessarily as the ultimate misfortune: light-hearted treatments of the plot. These comic variants do not really proliferate until 1925 and 1927. At this point they become the norm against which the later dramatic versions, such as *Broadway Nights*, are judged unbearably corny.

Mack Sennett's *Molly O'*, released in December 1921, is an early example of a comic variant. *Variety*'s plot summary (November 25, 1921: 43) is both accurate and a worthy example of that journal's prose style:

> "Molly O" has the name role played by Mabel Normand, who is the daughter of a Tad family in a big town. Her dad is a day laborer, ma takes in washing to help along the cause, and Jim Smith has been picked to be Molly's hubby. He is a husky who works in the same ditch with dad. Molly, however, has other ideas, and she manages to capture the wealthiest young bachelor in town. He is a doctor, and they meet in a tenement where there is an infant ill. He takes her home in his car, and a few Sundays later they meet in church. He again takes her home and stays to Sunday dinner. Yes, a regular boiled one!
>
> After it is all over, dad tells the wealthy young doc that he has been trying to raise a respectable family and that he'll be just as well satisfied if doc will forget the address.
>
> But the church is giving a charity ball, and Molly steps in at the proper moment to lead the march with the young Prince (who is the doc) in place of the girl he is engaged to. The latter, who has been out

on the balcony spooning with her real love and has missed the cue for the march, breaks off the engagement then and there, and Molly steps right in. But when she gets home that night dad is waiting for her with a strap and turns her out. She then turns to the doc, who married her that night.

That logically should have been the finish of the picture, but the producer thought a few thrills were needed, and he padded out a few airship scenes and a couple of country club bits and little things like that. They weren't necessary at all, but they place the picture in the class of the big Drury Lane mellers and as such will help the box office angle in the factory and tenement neighborhoods.

The review gives an idea of the film's shifts in tone, the first part being what *Variety* calls "one of those sweet little Cinderella tales, somewhat of the 'Irene' type, that is ended when the hero marries the little heroine"[40] and the second part presenting the thrilling scenes on the airship, in which the kidnapped heroine must fight the villain for her honor while her husband attempts a daring rescue by hydroplane. *Variety* does not mention other shifts in tone between slapstick comedy and dramatic or sentimental scenes. The film commences in a decidedly slapstick vein: having left the barn where her mother does the laundry without turning off the stove, Molly accidentally starts a fire. She calls her father to warn him that the barn may catch fire while the family is already comically attempting to put out the flames. They fill washtubs that cannot contain enough water to do any good. A black worker with a blanket over her head is mistaken for the daughter and rescued, while her mother pleads, "Somebody save my poor child!" Molly rushes through traffic on her bicycle in a series of undercranked shots, nearly missing several vehicles and arriving at the scene in advance of the fire trucks. Her argument with her father about the fire escalates with her efforts to rescue his gold-plated watch, which she has inadvertently left in the barn, and then accidentally drops on the ground, smashing it to bits. The scene ends with the fire department spraying everyone with strong hoses. After this opening, the film intermittently drops back into slapstick. For example, Molly drops off the laundry at the home of the doctor's wealthy fiancée, Miriam, and steals some cookies, which she stashes in an umbrella. Later, after Molly and Miriam have exchanged insults, Molly makes an exit into the pouring rain, opening the umbrella and spilling the cookies in front of Miriam and her assembled guests.

In contrast with the slapstick gags, the backbone of the story, the conflict between Molly and her father concerning the doctor, is played in a serious vein. This is especially the case in the scenes toward the end, when Molly's father waits with a strap for her to come home from the ball and, later, finding her in a compromising position with the doctor, throws her out of the house and locks the door. The scene the next day, when Mr. and Mrs. O'Dair turn up at the doctor's house and find Molly in his pajamas, cavorting on his bed, carries equally grave consequences for the characters and is certainly not played for burlesque. When John assures the father that "after this blameless girl was turned out into the night, she found someone waiting who was honored by her trust in him," Molly must wipe the tears from her father's thankful eyes.

This film is interesting to me because, although it incorporates many slapstick elements, the portions devoted to the seduction plot—more precisely, what the father assumes is a threat of seduction—are not handled comically. Indeed, as in the expulsion scene or in the prose style of the dialogue title above, there are moments when this aspect of the plot becomes positively old-fashioned. The *New York Times* (sec. 20, November 21, 1921: 1) seems to have shared this assessment, calling the film a mixture of "good old-fashioned hokum and high jinks" and adding that "everything that may bear a broad label as funny, thrilling and sentimental has been poured into 'Molly O.'"

Two films released in 1923 were crucial in establishing a more thorough-going and consistent comic treatment of the seduction plot.[41] The first is Harry Beaumont's *The Gold Diggers*, released in September 1923 and an adaptation of David Belasco's 1919 production of the Avery Hopwood comedy of the same name. The second is *A Woman of Paris*.

I have not been able to locate a print of *The Gold Diggers*, but from plot summaries it appears that the film followed the general outlines of the play, the text of which is available.[42] Three chorus girls live in a New York City flat: Mabel, recently divorced, who is receiving alimony payments that will enable her to move into her own apartment; Violet, a young girl new to the chorus who is genuinely in love with Wally; and Jerry Lamar, who is more experienced than Violet and her protector. In the first act it becomes clear that Jerry is chaste; she gets her fabulous clothes free by working as a model and is good enough as a performer to have a solo song in the show. Nevertheless, she is adept at getting presents from men.

Violet's marriage to Wally is blocked by Wally's Uncle Steve, who threatens to withhold his nephew's inheritance if he marries a chorus girl. Steve's lawyer, Blake, is also suspicious of the match and defines the term "gold digger," which apparently was not in general usage at the time (indeed, the play is cited by the *Oxford English Dictionary* in its definition): "A gold digger is a woman, generally young, who extracts money and other valuables from the gentlemen of her acquaintance, usually without making them any adequate return."

The plot turns upon Jerry's pretending to Steve that she—not Violet—is the object of Wally's affection. Steve has mistaken Jerry for Violet and treated her with contempt, whereupon Jerry determines to act the part of Wally's fiancée and make Violet look good by comparison, adopting the manner of the most vulgar and mercenary chorus girl. Despite her best efforts, however, Steve becomes convinced that she is basically "good" and prepares to allow the engagement. Jerry, desperate, gets Steve drunk on champagne and "confesses" to a series of affairs. In his tipsy state Steve is so moved by this that he proposes on his own account. Jerry, chastened by his generosity, admits to the trick she has been playing. Steve eventually permits Wally to marry Violet and, forgiving Jerry her deception, repeats his proposal. Blake agrees to invest the price of a new motor car in stocks for Mabel.

Variety (September 13, 1923: 28) suggests that the play was altered for the screen because of fears of censorship: "Every chorus girl in this picture is a working girl as far as disclosed by the story and most become engaged to marry before the picture concludes." The play included many chorus girls who are shown to be living off men in one way or another, characters who were presumably eliminated from the film version. The reviewer judges that the film will make money without causing a scandal that would rebound to the discredit of the industry: "The picture opens with Hopwood's definition of a 'gold digger.' That definition is the spiciest thing in the entire picture without it being at all naughty—merely suggestively spicy, like the milk. Even the prudes will like the way the Warners have done this picture." The review's opening paragraph also contains an amusing aphorism, which may not have been intended seriously: "It [*The Gold Diggers*] sews up the women of the country immediately, the gold diggers and all of the others—one to see if it is done right and the other to see how it is done."

The critical success of *A Woman of Paris*, discussed in chapter 3, and that of *The Gold Diggers* confirm what the evidence in the trade press for the years 1921 and 1923 has already suggested: namely, that by this time it had become very difficult to sustain the seduction plot as drama. With a few exceptions, which I shall discuss later, most of the films that appear in 1925 and 1927 are closer in tone to *The Gold Diggers*. They are unambiguously comic, and they concern a heroine who, though she may be compromised, is not seduced and ultimately marries for love with a man who just happens to be rich. Although *Variety* jokingly ascribes a feminine appeal to *The Gold Diggers*, as the examples of Cinderella stories proliferate in 1925

and 1927, both the reviews and the emphasis on fashion in the films themselves suggest that women were understood to be an important part of the
audience for these films. However, unlike most of the purely dramatic variants of the plot, the comic films are not assumed to be limited to the nabes,
indeed quite the reverse: reviewers expected that these films would have
highly successful runs.

A case in point is *A Slave of Fashion* (1925), which concerns a country
girl on her way to New York City. As a result of a railroad crash, she is able
to assume the place of what the *Variety* reviewer (July 22, 1925: 31) calls a
"girl of pleasure" who had been lent the keys to the luxury apartment of a
former admirer while he was away on business. The reviewer enthuses,
"Just think of the transition of a small town girl from the wilds of Io-way
. . . to a Park avenue duplex with a maid and a man servant, a Rolls and a
charge account for everything from theatre tickets to clothes. Does she
step! And how!" The girl is placed in a compromising position when her
family comes to visit from Iowa, and even more so when the apartment's
owner returns home to find her posing as his wife. Needless to say, all is
made right when he decides to marry her. The *Variety* reviewer thinks the
film is so good that there is no need to market it specifically to women. He
notes that the display of clothes is "corking" and that the title suggests a
fashion show but that the exhibitor will not need to stage one since the
public is sure to come anyway.[43] *Film Daily* (August 9, 1925: 7) expressed
more excitement about the film's appeal to women, encapsulating the plot
in these terms: "A Cinderella from Iowa takes a frenzied fashion whirl in
New York. It will make clothes-hungry women cry for joy." According to
the reviewer, the women at the Capitol were oohing and aahing every time
Norma Shearer appeared in a new dress.

Alfred Santell's 1925 film *Classified*, from a story by Edna Ferber and
starring Corinne Griffith, provides an interesting contrast with *The Gold
Diggers*. While favorably reviewed for its mixture of comedy and romance
in *Film Daily* (October 11, 1925: 11), *Classified* was given a scathing review
in *Variety* (November 11, 1925: 39) for its immorality. The review is signed
"Sime," the pseudonym of the magazine's founding editor, Sime Silverman,
and the same reviewer who had praised *The Gold Diggers* in 1923 for its
restraint in handling a potentially scandalous theme. This would indicate
that *Classified* went farther than *The Gold Diggers* in portraying a heroine
who actively exploits her looks for material advantage and in detailing the
sexually compromising situations that result from her schemes.

Classified is about a working girl, Babs Comet, who lives with her family
in an immigrant neighborhood on West 66th Street in New York City. The

plot tracks Babs's encounters with a series of predatory males, encounters she tries, with moderate success, to shape to her own advantage. In one of the first scenes, for example, on the street outside her apartment, she avoids taking the subway by making eyes at the men traveling downtown in cars.

One Friday evening, on a date with a portly gentleman at the Aloha Club, when she makes it clear that she expects to return home after dinner, the man leaves, sticking her with the bill. A young man at the next table, one of the wealthy Spencer-Clarks, who had observed her kicking off her shoes under the table, returns one of them to her, addressing her as "Miss Cinderella," and pays her bill.

The next evening Babs has dinner with two men in the rag trade, Weinstein and Bernstein. At their urging she tries on a sequined dress, with a train and a tiara, as well as a fur coat. As she dresses in a separate room, the partners wrestle with each other, both trying to watch her through a keyhole. Later one of the partners makes a pass at her, and she belts him and runs away in her borrowed clothes. She takes a cab home, with Bernstein and Weinstein in pursuit. To escape them she asks Spencer-Clark, whom she finds waiting for her, to take her dancing. He takes her to the Charleston Night Club, where he checks her coat, which enables Weinstein and Bernstein, who have followed her there, to steal back their fur. They decide not to go after the dress, since "it would be embarrassing to get." At home the next morning Babs receives three gifts in the mail: a fur coat from the Charleston Night Club to replace the one the management assumes was lost in their cloak room, a second fur from Spencer-Clark, and, from Weinstein and Bernstein, her old cloth coat. When her mother asks suspiciously where she got the clothes, Babs assures her mother that she can take care of herself.

She begins to date a car mechanic who is a friend of her brother, but when this man is late one evening she goes out driving with Spencer-Clark instead. Out in the country Spencer-Clark's car breaks down conveniently close to an inn. Babs tells him to check out the inn and leaves the car while he is gone. She starts to walk back to the city and is offered a ride on a horse-drawn milk cart. The farmer driving the cart tells her that she is the fourth girl this week. When she arrives home at seven in the morning her family assumes the worst, but the mechanic, who has been waiting with them, tells her he likes her muddy shoes. The mechanic forces Spencer-Clark to come and verify her innocence to her family. Spencer-Clark then proposes, but Babs refuses him and chooses the mechanic instead.

The end of *Classified* shows the heroine technically chaste and married for love rather than money, but most of the film consists of her attempts to manipulate the men who are attracted to her. This is what apparently offended Sime. Without directly stating it, he suggests that the film will appeal to women and hypothesizes that the original Edna Ferber story was "probably in one of those true story magazines."[44] He approves of the humor, especially the "snappy titles," and estimates that the film will do well for a mass, if not a class, audience. But he complains that the film is "the worst kind of trash that can be put upon the screen for young girls and boys." He finds the scene with Weinstein and Bernstein "raw" and expresses surprise that it passed the censors. He takes particular exception to the scene of Babs's car ride with Spencer-Clark and "the pantomime that went with it," when the society man walked over to check out the inn. Sime characterizes the heroine as "wise" and "fresh" and the film as "too loose and too careless," in what sounds like yet another characterization of the heroine rather than the plot. It seems ironic that at the same time that several *Variety* reviewers are mocking films with passive and victimized heroines as sentimental, the editor complains about this one, where the heroine takes care of herself and tries to use her looks to her advantage. But despite Sime's objections the tone of films like *Classified* becomes the norm by 1927, judging by the films produced in that year.

It, starring Clara Bow, was adapted from Elinor Glyn's 1927 novel of the same name. This version of the cross-class romance is marked by an unusually aggressive heroine. A shopgirl in a department store, she is attracted to the son of the owner, Cyrus. Through another man, who is attracted to her, she engineers a meeting with Cyrus, and he becomes romantically interested in her. When, due to a misunderstanding, Cyrus tries later to avoid her, she stages a tantrum in his office, lying prone on his desk and kicking her feet. In the final scene she forces her way into a party on his yacht, saves Cyrus's fiancée, a helpless socialite who has fallen overboard, and convinces Cyrus that she is worth marrying. *Variety* (February 29, 1927: 14) mounts no objection to this film, which it expects will do well. Without explicitly saying that the film is for women, the reviewer does call it "one of those pretty little Cinderella stories where the poor shop girl marries the wealthy owner of the big department store in which she works."

Ankles Preferred stars Madge Bellamy as a model who works at the shop of McGuire and Goldberg and whose bosses enlist her aid in persuading a financier to invest funds with the partners. She ultimately rejects the financier, who has become presumptuous, in favor of her humble boy friend. *Variety* (April 20, 1927: 20) writes, "Miss Bellamy has 'it' for the boys and the women will like the costumes worn. . . . The younger element among picture goers should dote on the exaggerated depictions of their own troubles, while the sex tangent to the theme has yet to miss with the adults. . . . Little superfluous footage involved plus a couple of subtle touches that the wise mob will recognize. A box office title and a box office picture." The *New York Times* (April 18, 1927: 21) calls the film "a racy diversion" and notes that it "succeeded in arousing many a wave of laughter yesterday afternoon, and while the story is not one to make any deep impression upon a spectator, it at least holds the attention as it skips merrily along."

Variety (April 20, 1927: 21) compares *Orchids and Ermine*, starring Colleen Moore, with *Ankles Preferred*. In marked contrast to Sime's indignant review of *Classified*, the reviewer opines: "It's clean and light entertainment, again hoking up the pedestrianism of girls who take auto rides and the struggles of the working girl to marry for love and grab money at the same time." The only problem with this plot device is that by this time it has run its course: "An old subject refreshingly treated but basically too well worn to make it a smash." In line with its opinion of similar films, the *New York Times* (April 19, 1927: 24) considers the film a crowd pleaser of little importance.

Most of the post-1923 Broadway stories recapitulate the plots of these shop-girl films. Many follow the plot outline of *Rich but Honest* (*Variety*, May 11, 1927: 17), in which the humble boyfriend of an honest chorus girl proves unworthy, while her rich suitor turns out to be of honorable intent. *Rich but Honest* has what *Variety* terms the "familiar screen situation" where the heroine is taken for a ride in a roadster that just happens to break down far outside of town. The film is favorably compared to *Ankles Preferred*. Other titles in this vein are *Uneasy Payments* (reviewed in *Variety*, May 11, 1927: 21) and *Mirage* (reviewed in *Variety*, April 8, 1925: 40). Two late versions of the Broadway story, *Becky* (reviewed in *Variety*, October 26, 1927: 24) and *The Girl from Woolworth's* (reviewed in *Variety*, December 25, 1929: 26), deal with shop girls who get jobs in the chorus and ultimately reject their wealthy but unworthy suitors in favor of humble boyfriends.

Alongside the evolution of the seduction plot in a purely comic direction, one can find a few films that, like *A Woman of Paris*, could be considered dramas or at least bittersweet admixtures of drama and comedy. Several films with the chorus-girl plot feature multiple protagonists, following the prototype of *The Gold Diggers*, and accommodate both comic and dramatic subplots. Edmund Goulding's 1925 *Sally, Irene and Mary* has a comic subplot about the ingenue Mary and dramatic subplots about the other two eponymous heroines. Mary, an Irish girl from the East Side of New York, gets a job in the chorus of a Broadway show and there meets Sally, maintained in a luxurious flat by Marcus Morton, and Irene, like herself from a working-class Irish family. The courtship of Mary by her Irish plumber sweetheart, Jimmy, is complicated not only by his dislike of her revealing stage costume and his jealousy of the male attention she receives but also by the quarreling of their mothers, stock comical ethnic types.

Marcus Morton falls in love with Mary, to Sally's anger and dismay. He proposes to Mary and, prompted by one of Jimmy's jealous quarrels, she accepts. Irene, meanwhile, has been courted by two men: Nester, an experienced man of the world, and an untried college student of good family. Irene accompanies Nester to his apartment but when he discovers that she is a virgin he sends her packing, to her evident chagrin. In revenge she decides to run off with the college student, who proposes marriage. Their elopement ends with a car accident in which they both die. This news sends Mary back to her Irish sweetheart on Avenue B. Sally's story does not have a definitive resolution; the film ends as she half angrily and half pleadingly reminds Morton that she was once an innocent "good" girl like Mary.

Variety (December 9, 1925: 42) does not approve of the film, which it judges will never appeal to a major house. The reviewer complains that "the rurals are liable to take it verbatim, and it won't improve the general lay impression of chorus girls," concluding that the film is "not exactly what would be termed a wholesome tale." The reviewer also notes, accurately in my view, that the film is not very comic.[45] The *New York Times* (December 7, 1925: 19) was equally dismissive, calling the film "a species of melodrama packed with trite ideas and appallingly obvious situations. It is a tawdry preachment concerned with the night life of gold-digging chorus girls, at the close of which the old-fashioned moral holds good." However, while *Sally, Irene and Mary* is certainly not a comedy on the level of *The Gold Diggers*, it is far from being a didactic or old-fashioned rendering of the seduction plot. The departure from sentimental prototypes is apparent in the treatment of the secondary characters. Irene would have been better off seduced by Nester, since it is Nester's rejection that prompts her to run off with an irresponsible boy, an act which, though made "respectable" by a proposal of marriage, nonetheless leads to her death. And although Sally's position vis-à-vis Marcus is not a happy one, she is neither condemned nor punished for her role as mistress. What is perhaps most striking about this plot strand is the complete lack of resolution, moral or otherwise.

Like *Sally, Irene and Mary*, *After Midnight* (1927) is a Broadway story that departs from the predominantly comic trend of the late 1920s. Directed by Monta Bell, who had served as the assistant director of *A Woman of Paris* before going on to direct such sophisticated comedies as

Broadway After Dark and *The King on Main Street, After Midnight* shares the bittersweet quality of Chaplin's film. Although the *Variety* reviewer (August 17, 1927: 24) criticized the film's development "from light comedy into tragedy with a not-so-hot finish," it merits a sustained description for its original rendering of the seduction plot.

Two sisters, Mary, a cigarette girl in a nightclub, and Maisie, a chorus girl, live together in New York City. Mary carefully hoards her tips and makes sure there is money on hand to pay for groceries and the rent. She is also very careful to preserve her virtue, refusing overly large tips and outwitting the come-ons of the men in the club, in particular those of the persistent Gus. Maisie, like Mabel in *The Gold Diggers,* appears to be the typical comic sidekick. Slovenly and lazy, she spends her nights at parties and her money on clothes and cosmetic devices. She sometimes shows up at the nightclub where Mary works, in the company of the rich men she likes to date, wheedling tips for her sister.

Walking home after work one night, Mary is held up by a man, Joe, who offers to "sell" her a length of lead pipe for ten dollars. She hands over her tip money, and he gives her the pipe, saying he would not have hurt her. Angry, she follows and womps him over the head with the pipe. She then helps him up to her apartment to tend to his wounds. Joe returns to his low-class bar and friends, but the next evening he approaches Mary again. Although initially hostile, she finally encourages him in his efforts to look for a job.

Once he is gainfully employed in a gas station, Joe takes Mary out on a date. They dream of a future together. Joe wants to buy his own taxi, and they imagine eventually owning a fleet, the image of which is superimposed on the street through which they are walking. He proposes to her and suggests that they borrow money to set up house, but Mary does not want to start their life together in debt. She persuades him to wait to marry until he has saved enough to buy a taxi and she has saved one thousand dollars.

Sometime later Mary goes to the bank to buy a one-thousand-dollar Liberty bond with her accumulated savings. Meanwhile Maisie, who has been invited to a party, appropriates the forty dollars that her sister had put aside to pay for the rent, to buy a new dress. Along with all of the other chorus girls who attend the party, Maisie is given a one-thousand-dollar Liberty bond as a token.

Mary searches for Joe to show him her Liberty bond, but at the gas station she is told that he has quit his job. In his old hang-out Joe bargains with one of his cronies, Red, for a taxi costing four hundred dollars. A former lady friend comes over and convinces him to have a drink. As she walks by the bar Mary sees Joe drinking and apparently on intimate terms with another woman. In despair, she goes home, where she discovers that Maisie has taken the rent money. Her sister returns and shows off the Liberty Bond she received that evening. This incident precipitates Mary's decision to cash in her own bond and buy glamorous evening attire.

Working in her new finery, Mary finds her sister at a table with Gus and accepts his invitation to a party. Joe, waiting outside the club, sees Mary going off in the company of Gus and the other swells. Disillusioned, he returns with Red to the bar, where, plied with drinks by his former girlfriend, he proceeds to gamble away the four hundred dollars he had saved for the taxi.

Mary gets very drunk at the party and is in imminent danger of being seduced by Gus when Maisie decides she has to take her sister home. Physically fending off Gus's advances, Maisie gets Mary into a car, and the girls take off, pursued by Gus and others in another vehicle. A high-speed chase follows. While Maisie drives, Mary plays drunkenly with the lights and tries to grab the steering wheel. She causes an accident, in which Maisie is killed.

Returning to her apartment, Mary finds Joe there, drunk, broke, and angry. He tries to accost her but desists when she tells him about her sister's death. The next morning, as Mary arranges her sister's things, she finds Maisie's Liberty Bond. Joe apologizes for his behavior the previous evening and says he failed her. Mary replies: "We both failed. But she—she never failed me."

Perhaps most interesting is the reversal between the "good" and the "bad" sister, as well as the surprising way the film undercuts the moral position it had initially proposed. The reversal is articulated by means of a simple motif, akin to the pearls in *A Woman of Paris* or the flowers in *The Marriage Circle*. The very brief, ostensibly comic, incident of the party favor upsets the oppositions between spending and saving, between heedless play and earnest preparation for marriage, that had been set up in relation to the two sisters throughout the first two-thirds of the film. Maisie's Liberty bond makes clear, even to Mary, the futility of her sexual propriety and Protestant work ethic. Presumably it is this irony, as much as her suspicions about Joe, that leads Mary to abandon her previous self-control and self-denial. In the final plot twist, it is Maisie's frivolously obtained bond that enables the marriage and the film's resolution.

Variety assumes that Norma Shearer, who plays the "good" sister in *After Midnight*, will be a big draw and that her "usual transformation from moth to butterfly" will appeal to the star's following. But, as noted above, the reviewer did not appreciate the plot turn in which both Mary and Joe are led astray. The *New York Times* (December 16, 1927: 31) liked Monta Bell's direction and the work of the actors but complained that "quite a lot of talent is wasted on a childish yarn." The lukewarm reaction to *After Midnight*, like the reaction to *Sally, Irene and Mary*, indicates the difficulties that these films posed for reviewers. Both films invert or distort familiar situations and undermine clear-cut moral resolution. Although *Variety* complains that the plot of *Sally, Irene and Mary* cannot be dubbed "wholesome," the latter seems an unlikely adjective to apply to *Variety*-approved films such as *The Gold Diggers, Orchids and Ermine,* or *Ankles Preferred.* But it was easier to accept the comedies, with some hesitations over *Classified,* because they fit into an easily recognized, and highly successful, formula. Whereas Edmund Goulding and Monta Bell were trying something not as easily typed, even as late as 1927. It is as if these directors, taking advantage of the updating of the seduction plot accomplished largely in the comedic mode, were trying to devise new ways of reworking it in a dramatic mode as well.

Perhaps the strangest experiment in rendering a dramatic variant of the gold-digger plot is Edmund Goulding's *Women Love Diamonds.* The *Variety* reviewer (April 27, 1927: 17) had some difficulty establishing the film's market niche. He notes that it was playing in New York in "program houses," but that there was evidence of "more than average expenditure in the picture, in players and production." He commended both the sets and the cinematography, as well as the high caliber of the cast. The reason the film was relegated to the lower-priced theaters may have been its subject matter. *Variety* warns that the story is "based on a pretty delicate subject for the film trade," one that is weakened by the consequent "cautious handling" and may be vulnerable to further censorship in some states. Uncertainty about the title, given as *Women Want Diamonds* in the *Variety* review, and as *Women Love Diamonds* in the *Film Daily* review (April 17, 1927: 8) and elsewhere, may indicate that more than one version of the film was in circulation. The account here is based upon what seems to be a complete original print from the Turner/MGM studio vaults, which carries the title *Women Love Diamonds.* This print is congruent with the summary given in *Variety.* It differs significantly from that given in the *American Film Institute Catalog of Feature Films,* which probably derives from a review of a censored print.[46]

The heroine is introduced with the line "There is no better setting for diamonds than Mavis Ray." Mavis (Pauline Stark), who lives with a woman identified as her mother, is asked by Harlan (Lionel Barrymore), whom she calls "uncle," not to visit Jerry Croker-Kelley (Douglas Fairbanks, Jr.), a young man in high society who, the gossip columns speculate, intends to marry her. She refuses to heed Harlan's warning and accompanies Jerry to his family's estate for the first time. She obviously feels ill at ease with his upper-class mother; she is even more uncomfortable with his sisters, simply dressed, athletic types and a decided contrast to Mavis, who is wearing jewels and an elaborate hairstyle and hat. Once he is alone with Mavis, Jerry insists that they be married soon and informs her that he has invited her uncle to the estate with the goal of getting his permission. Mavis panics at hearing this and runs outside.

The scene between Jerry and the uncle is not explicit, but what Jerry learns as a result of their discussion is indicated through the actor's facial expression and use of gesture. Alone with Jerry in the library, Harlan walks over to the boy after he has threatened to elope with Mavis. The framing is over his shoulder, favoring Jerry's face. The film holds on this shot for a while, as Harlan talks. Finally Jerry speaks, smiling in disbelief, "What do you mean . . . you're not her uncle?" After a cut to Mavis speaking with Jerry's sisters, the film returns to the library. Jerry looks grim. He closes his eyes in pain and then opens them when Harlan taps him on the shoulder. He says, "And you dared to let her come here to meet my mother and sister?" Harlan replies, "When you grow up to be a man you'll realize that ladies and cyclones have their own way." Mavis enters. Jerry looks at her with scorn. She says to Harlan, "Will you please take me home?" Harlan bows. Mavis holds out her hand to Jerry and says, "Good-bye, Jerry. Thanks awfully for having me down." Jerry leans close to her, then withdraws his hand and puts it behind his back.

While Jerry's reaction is straight out of the older variants of the seduction plot, the treatment of both Harlan and Mavis strikes one as more unusual. Harlan makes clear that he loves Mavis "in his way" and is prepared to tell other men about their relationship to prevent her from leaving him for marriage. Mavis does not so much suffer remorse as chafe under his attempts to control her, responding first with tears and later becoming increasingly rebellious.

A narrative title informs us, "What was happening to Mavis Ray . . . that the glamour for which she had lived was losing its magic?" Wearing a dress of shiny gold material, a sequined arm band, a necklace of sparklers around her throat, and a headband of the same material as her dress, she sits next to Harlan, who is in a tuxedo. He lights a cigarette for her. She rips off the filter to smoke it straight. He is impressed and touches her foot with his under the table. She asks if they are going to the Follies or not. In what I

33   34

take to be a reference to her sexual rejection of him (but not an implication that their relationship is innocent), he replies: "Darling . . . sweetheart . . . angel . . . we aren't we." He puts a hand on her wrist; she takes it off. He says, "You're the only woman that has ever made a fool out of me!" She replies, "And you're the only man that will ever make one out of me!"

At this point Mavis runs into her room and has a temper tantrum at Harlan's capacity to dictate her actions. She tells her "mother" that if she has to stay at home she will call up a gang and have some fun, but when she picks up the phone she hears her chauffeur, Patrick (Owen Moore), being called to the hospital where his sister, seriously shocked by the news of an accident involving her husband, is about to have a baby. Mavis runs out to the hospital with the chauffeur, where her glamorous attire (she wears a cowl of the same material as her dress and a matching coat with a fur collar) gets wry glances from the nurses in uniform. The scene of Mavis and Patrick in the waiting room is beautifully photographed, showing the characters framed by double glass doors that separate them from the hospital corridor (figures 33 and 34). Mavis, who watches the nurses' reactions in the corridor, understands long before Patrick does that his sister is dead. Patrick's discovery of this fact ends the largely static framings of the scene: he runs down the hallway, Mavis following, in a tracking shot that ultimately moves in close on the weeping man and sympathetic woman.

This scene motivates a change in Mavis's character. She spends time with Patrick's sister's three children until Patrick's brother-in-law asks her to stop visiting and to fire Patrick as her chauffeur, since a "gear-crasher" may not be in love with a lady. She fires Patrick, explaining that love between them is impossible. When Harlan nevertheless threatens to tell Patrick the truth about their relationship, she does so herself, explaining in a dialogue title, "This man is not my uncle!" and mouthing the words "He is my lover." She also confesses, "—and that woman is not my mother! He employs her!" She runs out of the apartment.

There is a short epilogue, which occurs some months later. Patrick, now a cab driver, runs into Harlan's new mistress, Mavis's former chambermaid. She tells him that Mavis is working as a nurse. He drives to the hospital, where he is told that Mavis works in the children's ward. When she appears at the end of a long hallway, he runs to her and they kiss in extreme long shot. There is no dialogue between them.

The film displaces the moral judgments that usually surround the issue of female purity (i.e., the judgments made by Jerry) in favor of an examination of Mavis's status in terms of sexual and economic power. This is best revealed in the scene in which Harlan and Mavis argue instead of going to the Follies. He obviously wants her, which gives her the power of refusal, but he holds the purse strings, which makes her virtually his ward. *Women Love Diamonds* is as close as the Hollywood cinema of the 1920s came to making a Fassbinder melodrama. A scene from the middle of the film, just after Jerry rejects Mavis and before the death of Patrick's sister, is similarly interesting for the way it deals with sexual power and class status.

Patrick's sister, Mrs. Flaherty, having become aware that he is in love with his employer, decides to confront Mavis in an attempt to protect her brother. She encounters Mavis's gold-digger friend at the front door to Mavis's apartment. The well-dressed woman raises her arm to show off a bracelet and looks askance at Mrs. Flaherty's nice but simple attire (figure 35). As she enters, Mrs. Flaherty looks through a hallway and sees Mavis, standing immobilized in a dressing gown with a sheer train spread around her in a vast circle (figures 36 and 37). The maid takes Mrs. Flaherty to another room and then announces her presence to her mistress. Mavis, now smoking a cigarette in an exaggeratedly long holder, is crying, and the mascara runs down her cheeks. She says, "I shouldn't see anyone. . . . I'm too unhappy. Every time I make-up I cry and ruin it." In preparation for receiving her visitor, Mavis changes to a black, low-cut, sequined gown with a train, an outfit only slightly more practical than the outrageous dressing gown. She enters the room where Mrs. Flaherty is waiting and asks what she wants. Mrs. Flaherty, crying, can only say, "I'm sorry, Ma'am, I shouldn't have come." This is repeated three times as she makes her way out the door and escapes from the apartment. Mavis returns and says to her gold-digger friend, "I hate seeing women cry." The friend replies, "Is that what she was doing? It sounded like static on a radio." Mavis: "Why will women of her class neglect their figures?" She stands like a statue and lifts a glass of champagne while her friend looks on admiringly (figure 38).

35

36

37

38

With scenes like this one, it is not surprising that *Variety* should comment that the star "fails to draw sufficient sympathy" due to "too much affected posing." But surely the posing is part of a deliberate travesty of fashion and critique of the snobbishness of the gold diggers. Mavis's comment about lower-class women neglecting their figures seems especially cruel because the spectator (but not the heroine) knows that Mrs. Flaherty is pregnant and about to bear her fourth child. And, while Mavis and her gold digger friend revel in their own beauty and the trappings of wealth, Mrs. Flaherty, shown until this point to be a highly competent and lively woman, is rendered speechless in the face of them. She apparently assumes that it would be impossible for such a lofty creature as Mavis to concern herself with whether her chauffeur loves her or not. This scene replays dimensions of Mavis's rejection by the Croker-Kelleys, although now with the roles reversed. Among the "true" upper-class characters, the Croker-Kelleys, Mavis is out of place due not only to her deviant sexual status but also to her ostentatious mode of dress. In Mavis's relation to Mrs. Flaherty, on the other hand, this mode of dress defines her power.

The concern with class, and with clothes as the means of expression of class status, continues until the film's close. When her gold-digger friend warns her against slumming with "common people," Mavis rejects her. She also tells her "mother" that she is leaving to go to work. In their final confrontation Harlan makes fun of this idea, "What are you going to do . . . wrap packages at Macy's?" The film, somewhat improbably, gives Mavis the noble calling of nurse. This permits an echo and reformulation of the earlier scene in the hospital, which featured the striking contrast between Mavis in her gold lamé and the nurses in their professional uniforms. With adoption of working-class status also comes rejection of fashion.

Women Love Diamonds abandons the humor and cheerful materialism of the gold-digger films. It also rejects the convention by which a heroine remains a "good" girl, however suspicious her behavior or motives may appear to others. Working within the restrictions of censorship, the film goes as far as it can (and perhaps too far for many venues in the 1920s) to indicate that Mavis is Harlan's mistress and that she enjoys the material fruits of this relationship even while chafing under his control. Further, her redemption arises less from love than from her identification with the suffering of other women, and her initiation into the world of work. The film thereby manages an entirely dramatic rendering of the seduction plot, without recourse to the usual scenario involving predatory male and victimized heroine. And, while retaining some idea of the redemptive power of love, the film also suggests other, less typical, motivations for the resolution of the plot.

I have sought to indicate how the seduction plot was reworked over the course of the 1920s. Definitive of the eighteenth-century sentimental novel and prominent in nineteenth-century melodrama, the plot was already seen as old-fashioned and overly sentimental as early as 1921. This change in taste is suggested by the reception accorded *Way Down East*, which was praised but considered to be a miraculous transformation of an old "horse and buggy melodrama." It is even more clearly indicated by the scornful reception accorded films such as the 1920 *Passers-By*, which did not benefit from a high production budget or the participation of a well-known director or star. The low-budget films were often dismissed as appealing only to the neighborhoods or to rural districts, although trade press references to the work of Laura Jean Libbey indicate that they were also sometimes associated with feminine taste.

I have shown that the most important models for the updated versions of the seduction plot produced in the latter half of the decade were the 1923 releases *The Gold Diggers* and *A Woman of Paris*. In the years that followed, comic variants of the seduction plot became predominant. These were typically more expensively mounted than their dramatic counterparts and used such major stars as Norma Shearer, Colleen Moore, and Corinne Griffith. The trade press consistently judged the comic variants to have a feminine appeal, a point seconded by the fashion displays in the films themselves. Journalists also approved more of the comic variants than of the dramatic ones, considering them good commercial bets for the first-run, downtown theaters and amusing, if rather lightweight, fare. Films such as *Classified, Ankles Preferred,* and *Orchids and Ermine* defined a new narrative norm so incisively that it was possible for directors Edmund Goulding and Monta Bell further to manipulate and transform it, creating modernized dramatic variants in the late 1920s. I have suggested that their innovations were to some extent anticipated by Frank Borzage in *Back Pay*. But the form of that narrative, with its small-town romance, the fall from grace in the big city, and the heroine's whole-hearted repentance at her sweetheart's death bed, enabled reviewers to pigeonhole it as "the old-oaken bucket story," or, more sympathetically, as a film for the provinces. The evidence suggests that *Sally, Irene and Mary, After Midnight,* and *Women Love Diamonds* were much harder to typify. Journalists did not review these films extensively, dismissed them as both "unwholesome" and too serious, and seem to have had difficulty projecting a potential market for them. In addition, *Women Love Diamonds* was considered highly vulnerable to censorship. But despite their marginal status these films represent important new permutations of the seduction plot. While they contain some pathetic or affecting scenes—*Film Daily,* for example, referred to the "sobby scenes" of the chauffeur's reacting to his sister's death in childbirth in *Women Love Diamonds*—they seem to me to be the furthest removed from the old sentimental prototypes. They follow in the wake of *A Woman of Paris* in their cynicism, sly undercutting of conventionally "virtuous" postures, and displacement of chastity considered as a moral issue in favor of a more complex investigation of the effects of money and class on sexual dynamics.

6   The Romantic Drama

"Fazil" is primarily a woman's picture because it is devoted 100
per cent to the grand pash with little action or humor. The love
palpitations are unceasing from start to finish.

Variety, June 6, 1928

The "romantic drama" was recognized as a genre in the 1920s and considered to be preferred by women. It should be distinguished from the
"society drama," a term used in the trade press for love stories with a contemporary upper-class setting, and a genre also associated with feminine
viewing preferences. The terms "romance" and "romantic drama" were, by
contrast, applied to stories set in exotic locales or in the distant past. One of
the most important genres of the 1920s, it was associated with major stars
such as Rudolph Valentino, John Barrymore, John Gilbert and Greta
Garbo, Ronald Colman and Vilma Banky. But while the genre was quite
successful in financial terms, the trade press, especially *Variety*, was dubious about many of the films, frequently criticizing them for weak plots and
overblown love scenes. A review (November 2, 1927: 18) of a relatively
obscure film from 1927, William C. deMille's *Forbidden Woman*, exemplifies *Variety*'s view of the genre:

> Exotic drama, with the emotional stuff laid on thick. Has more the
> quality of Elinor Glyn than Elmer Harris and may pull with the
> women. Men will call it sloppy sentiment. Very artificial and theatrical,
> but has a certain screen effectiveness. The production is uncommonly
> beautiful and the acting graceful in spite of the stilted story. Good judg-
> ment to swing Jetta Goudal and Joseph Schildkraut into a romantic
> combination, a team that matches Colman-Banky, and since the enter-
> prise addresses itself deliberately to the femmes the selection is perfect.
> On this basis the picture has the marks of a moneymaker. But a little
> of this heavy Oriental romance goes a long way with men. This one
> overdoes everything from atmosphere to coincidence. The locale is the
> foreign legion in Algiers. . . . "The Sheik" started it and "Beau Geste"
> carried the vogue another step forward. It's beginning to lose its
> novelty.

Another example of the type is Howard Hawks's *Fazil,* categorized by *Variety* (June 6, 1928: 13) as "sheik stuff." According to Todd McCarthy, it was made prior to *A Girl in Every Port,* and perhaps the latter, more characteristically Hawksian, film was in part a reaction against the romantic drama as a genre.[1]

Beginning with the success of *The Sheik* in 1921, the Middle East was frequently employed as a setting for the romantic drama. But exoticism was more important in defining the genre than any specific locale. *Variety* (May 29, 1929: 26) called Tod Browning's *Where East Is East* a "romantic adventure yarn" and rather cynically called the film's setting in Indochina "as exotic as a diligent search of the Atlas can discover." Historical romances too were understood to be part of the trend. *Variety* (April 27, 1927: 16) compared *Camille,* starring Norma Talmadge, to two other love stories released in the same season, *Flesh and the Devil,* with Gilbert and Garbo, and *The Night of Love,* with Colman and Banky: "Romantic tales are evidently riding the crest, taking 'Flesh and the Devil' and 'A Night of Love' as examples. 'Camille' has a chance to follow up if released fast enough to be included on the incoming or maybe outgoing tide."

A brief consideration of the society drama is necessary here, since it has been more frequently discussed by scholars than the romantic drama and certainly helped define conceptions of feminine taste. The most important distinguishing characteristic of the society drama was setting: it was associated with elaborate mise en scène and great clothes. A *Variety* review of *Hush* (April 29, 1921: 41) noted that "the whole piece is done in the 'society play' style, which in the pictures seems to mean demonstrations of nouveau art furniture and the display of good breeding by being rude to servants. The interiors are so artistic and in such good taste that no one could possible live in them outside a film studio, and everybody's manners are polished beyond perfection. But the costuming is undeniably beautiful and the photography excellent." Six years later *Variety* made a similar point in relation to *Children of Divorce* (April 20, 1927: 21): "Rich settings, lots of clothes and all players adopting drawing room mannerisms. A parlor picture with everybody putting it on a bit, including Lloyd who directed." *Film Daily,* while inevitably not as caustic as *Variety,* seems to have shared this evaluation of the genre's settings, characterizing *Is Love Everything?* (November 2, 1924: 11) as "another case of a pretty weak story nicely dressed up with good looking settings, lavish display and society atmosphere."

The society drama encompassed many different plots. For example, despite its derivation from Wilde's play, Lubitsch's *Lady Windemere's Fan* was not considered a comedy but rather, in the words of *Moving Picture World,* "a society drama of the drawing room type" (December 12, 1925: 575) and, for *Variety,* an "English society drama." Presumably this assessment was a function not only of the upper-class setting but also of the central situation, involving an older woman who puts herself in a compromising position with a man in order to save the reputation of her daughter. The same situation can be found in many other films of the type, notably *The Sign on the Door,* with Norma Talmadge, and, in an updated variant with a flapper daughter and a new twist on the ending, *Dancing Mothers.*[2]

Two society drama plots became particularly prevalent during the 1920s. The first involved complicated permutations of infidelity and divorce. *Film Daily* (January 27, 1924: 10) wrote of *Let Not Man Put Asunder:* "So many divorces and marriages have seldom been crammed into one film. 'Let Not Man Put Asunder,' even outdoes Rupert Hughes' 'Reno,' another of this type. The story is a rambling one dealing with the loves of three couples chiefly, with a few minor affairs on the side. These three people swap husbands, divorce themselves at intervals, marry again, divorce again, and remarry their former husbands (or wives) without mercy for the spectator, that is if his patience will hold out that long." *Variety* similarly characterized *The Wild Goose* (May 13, 1921: 42) as "a society drama with the domestic triangle elaborated into a five-sided complication" and *Children of Divorce,* mentioned above, as "a society drama of the type of which the American picture patron has had more than a smattering. Cocktail parties, unhappy marriages and a dramatic ending."

Most such plots were assumed to appeal predominantly to women. In the independently produced *Souls for Sables,* a cad tempts two married women in succession with a gift of the eponymous fur. *Variety* (September 16, 1925: 40) called the film "one of those middle class society yarns that usually please the women and the shop girls." *Film Daily* (August 30, 1925: 8) dubbed it a "domestic drama in society life" and "the kind of picture a loving mother would almost leave a sick child to see." *Variety* found the five-sided complication of the triangle plot in *The Wild Goose* "pretty artificial fiction, although it may have a certain appeal to feminine sympathies." *Film Daily* (July 6, 1924: 8) similarly advised exhibitors that *Love of Women* "might appeal particularly to your women patrons. They are always more or less interested in marriage-divorce stories."

A second type of society drama plot, which overlapped to some degree with the first, focused specifically on the young, on "flaming youth," a generation the films self-consciously constructed as modern. Many of these stories concerned flappers and what both *Variety* and *Film Daily* called "the jazz life." Scholars often conflate the jazz life films with the comic variants of the seduction plot under the rubric of "flapper films," but there are distinctions to be made at the level of character and setting. In the comic variants of the seduction plot the heroine is usually a wisecracking working girl, a type characterized by *Variety* (October 26, 1927: 24) in the case of *Becky* as "the gum-chewing young freshie that knows how to slow up the sheiks and get them thinking about furniture and time payments." The flappers in the jazz life films, by contrast, are rich, and the films are set in an extravagant, upper-class milieu.

As early as its review of *Children of Jazz, Variety* (July 12, 1923: 29) referred to a formulaic plot concerned with "the exploitation of the supposed dissipations of the American rich, with a lot of racy sex stuff thinly disguised and absurdly elaborated 'society spectacle.'" The heroine of this film is described as "a half-naked young fool who goes from one affair to another with the sweethearts and husbands of her intimate friends and spends her time accumulating engagement rings and consuming synthetic gin." In the same year *His Children's Children* (reviewed in *Variety,* November 8, 1923: 26), set among the "socially elect," was said to feature "society flappers smoking and drinking, rolling their own and leaving their almost corsets in the retiring room." At the end of the decade this particular variant of the society drama was still being described in the same terms. *Variety* (September 11, 1929: 18) described the plot of *Our Modern Maidens* as the "jumbling" of a "loving quartet," and the film was held to have "plenty of extravagant settings, just one party after another, and lagoon affairs that would tax even the b.r. [bank roll] of a B. Bickering Brown. While each bridesmaid at the wedding received a diamond bracelet from the old boy. The flaps won't go for that—much." Cecil B. DeMille's *Dynamite,* which had "elaborate boudoir, bath, wild stew party, rakish Mercedes, fantastic spot carnival" and "enough people to fill one end of the Yale Bowl," was called a "society picture heavily seasoned with dramatic hoke" (*Variety,* January 1, 1930: 24).

Film Daily clearly shared *Variety*'s view of the flaming youth story as a subset of society drama. It dubbed *The House of Youth,* about a girl from a good family who gets caught up in a roadhouse raid alongside a married man, a "society drama" (November 30, 1924: 12). *Film Daily* advised exhibitors that *What Fools Men,* a cross-generation story about the misadventures of a flapper and her father, had "society and jazz angles" (October 11, 1925: 11). The same magazine called *The Marriage Whirl* (July 26, 1925: 8), about a young wife's efforts to wean her husband from "his love of jazz life and liquor," a "six-wheel whirl of society jazz life," and *Our*

Dancing Daughters, about "a rich set of jazzy youths," was called "the jazziest of the jazz pictures" (October 14, 1928: 4).

Following the success of *The Plastic Age* in 1925, a number of films appeared that feature a flapper heroine who becomes involved with a college athlete or, more unusually, in the case of Dorothy Arzner's *The Wild Party*, a professor.[3] Given that attendance at university was largely an upper-class prerogative in the 1920s, the settings in these films do not represent a radical departure from those typical of the society drama as a whole.

But, in a clear contrast with other types of society drama, it is much harder to generalize about the audience hypothesized for the flaming youth films. Certainly some films were said to be for women. Of *Black Oxen*, about an older woman's efforts to regain her youth, *Film Daily* (January 13, 1924: 5) reported that "flappers in raccoon coats and old women in sables jammed the Strand at six o'clock on Monday night." *The House of Youth* (*Film Daily*, November 30, 1924: 12) and *The Painted Flapper* (*Variety*, January 21, 1924: 36) were similarly thought to feature situations and fashions that appealed (or, in the latter case, failed to appeal) to feminine taste. But many jazz age films were thought to have wide audience appeal, irrespective of gender. The *Film Daily* review of *We Moderns* (December 13, 1925: 7) advised exhibitors that Colleen Moore, a star known for playing flapper parts, had "developed into one of the best box-office attractions on the screen." It went on to advise, "If you are not playing her up as you should, you might start in right here." There was no suggestion that Moore might appeal primarily to women. While the *Film Daily* review of *The Average Woman* (February 3, 1924: 5) proposed that exhibitors address some advertising slogans to women, along lines suggested by the title, the reviewer also noted, "This is another of the type of flapper stories that seem to be doing remarkably well at the box office and you can tell your people that it contains the usual elements of such stories." Reviews advising exhibitors about what to put in their trailers indicate what *Film Daily* considered to be the selling points of these films. Of *Wine of Youth* the magazine wrote (July 13, 1923: 11), "A trailer of some of the jazz scenes and you won't have to do another thing to bring them in. 'Snuff said. They'll tell the other fellow about the picture you're going to show and they'll all be on hand." Of *The Perfect Flapper*, "Good drawing points are the various parties and dancing sequences. Run trailers of these bits to get them interested" (June 29, 1924: 8); of *Passionate Youth*, "All you should have to do is show them a trailer including any of the gay parties attended by the jazz heroine" (July 12, 1925: 7). None of these reviews posited a feminine appeal for the films, a particularly telling point, since *Film Daily* almost always searched for ways to exploit films to women. *Variety* went so far as to posit a masculine appeal for the Joan Crawford movies; the likely audience for *The Taxi Dancer* was held to be "the flaps and their undergraduate or counter monarchs" while "older men won't find it hard to gaze on Miss Crawford and her array of nightgowns" (March 9, 1927: 16). The degree of Joan Crawford's undress is also commented upon in the *Variety* reviews of *Our Dancing Daughters* (October 10, 1928: 22) and *Our Modern Maidens*.

The factor most consistently mentioned in the trade press's estimations of the audience for flaming youth films was whether or not the films would be found offensive by censors or the family trade. *Variety* thought that *The Taxi Dancer* would be found objectionable by "the world-wide police force authorized by a ring." The *Variety* review of *Our Dancing Daughters* contained a comparison of the prints screened in New York, where the state censor board had not altered the film, with that screened in Pennsylvania, where some cuts had apparently been ordered. *Film Daily* judged that *Wine of Youth* could pose problems if the exhibitor catered to "small town, straight-laced patronage," and advanced similar cautions for *Prodigal Daughters* (April 22, 1923: 7). *Motion Picture News* (August 3, 1929: 477) wrote that *The Single Standard* "is highly sophisticated and in the main only suited for the big city houses; in the smaller towns it will appeal to the younger generation, but the elders will undoubtedly frown on its altogether too free an exposition of sex with the heroine maintaining the right that a single standard of conduct applies to women as well as men and proceeding to put her theory into effect." *Film Daily* reassured exhibitors that *Our Modern Maidens* had been "cleverly directed to steer clear of the coarseness and vulgarity of most of the flaming youth films, and is a picture you needn't be afraid to show to the family trade" (September 8, 1929: 9).

Although it is certainly not the case that young women were posited as the sole or main audience for flaming youth films, they were consistently associated with a taste for the more risqué ones. *Film Daily* (February 27, 1927: 8) noted that *Love's Greatest Mistake* offered "several snappy tete-a-tetes that are apt to shock the family circle but thrill the flapper." The *Variety* reviewer who was impressed with Joan Crawford *en déshabillé*, disagreed with *Film Daily*'s assessment of *Our Modern Maidens* as a discreet example of the type, writing that "its youth, hot stuff and abundant appeal for the flaps should sell it. Story is juvenile and silly, but the sort of silliness the more youthful fans gobble by the carload."

Given the assumptions about audiences found in the reviews for the romantic drama, the society drama, and the flaming youth story, one can better understand the logic of the 1931 *Variety* headline proclaiming "Dirt

Craze Due to Women." For all three plot types women, or sometimes "the flaps," were presumed to have a taste for sexually daring topics. The romantic drama provides the best avenue for further exploring this development in films and in the related assumptions about feminine taste. Although the jazz-age films have received much more attention from scholars, no doubt because they so explicitly referenced modern types and changing sexual mores, the romantic drama was more important in industrial terms. It encompassed a much greater number and variety of stars, as well as prominent directors ranging from the likes of Herbert Brenon, Clarence Brown, and Henry King to *auteurs* such as Maurice Tourneur and Monta Bell, and, at the most *outré* reaches of the plot type, Erich von Stroheim and Tod Browning. For the historian of taste, the reception of the romantic drama is also more instructive than that given the flaming youth story or the society drama. In the case of the jazz film, for example, one finds warnings in the trade press about state censorship or the family trade, as well as, early in the decade, complaints about gin-swilling heroines. But the romantic drama, generally made at much higher budget ranges and entertaining much greater aesthetic pretensions, provoked much more, and much more vitriolic, commentary. This distaste for the romantic drama constitutes a vital aspect of the decline of sentiment

The romantic drama changed decisively over the course of the 1920s. The examples cited above, *Forbidden Woman* and *Fazil*, are typical of the latter part of the decade but are quite different from the romances of the late 1910s and early 1920s. Maurice Tourneur's 1922 version of *Lorna Doone* may stand as a prime example of the old-fashioned, and respectable, variant of romantic drama. A best-selling romance in the Victorian period, R. D. Blackmore's 1869 novel had been adapted in 1911 by Thanhouser and in 1915 by Biograph. The story, set in seventeenth-century England, concerns an aristocrat, carried off by the robber Doone clan as a child, and, years later, saved from marriage to the brutal Carver Doone by John Ridd, a local yeoman. Lorna and John fall in love but she leaves him by order of the king to go to London to assume her title and position. After renouncing her title to become John's wife, Lorna is shot at the altar by Carver. John and his neighbors assume she is dead and mount a successful assault on the Doone stronghold. John comes home to find that Lorna has survived, and they are reunited.

The film is remarkable for Tourneur's signature *contre-jour* lighting effects and for extremely picturesque and soft exteriors, achieved in many shots by adding mist to the backgrounds and leaving the foreground figures in sharp focus, what *Variety* (December 8, 1922: 33) called "misted

39   40

photography." The reviews in *Film Daily, Variety,* and the *New York Times* all praised the film's pictorial values, the latter two singling out the scene of the Doone clan holding up the carriage that carries Lorna and her mother and absconding with the child (figures 39 and 40). The *New York Times* (December 4, 1922: 20) praised this sequence for its restraint, the compositions rather than the acting underscoring the severity of the situation:

> For Mr. Tourneur is a storyteller as well as a maker of motion pictures, and he knows the value of restraint as well as that of emphasis. He knows, rather, the part that restraint plays in emphasis, and so does not too heavily underscore any incident for the sake of the unrelated and independent effect he might obtain with it. For instance, the mother does not wallow on the sand in a prolonged closeup. She does not cry out, with the aid of a subtitle, "My Child! My Child!" or anything else. A flash of the figures on the sand, a gesture, the intensifying reflection—and that is all.

But despite approving of this restraint, and despite his praise for the film's pictorial effects, "pictures in soft tones and striking contrasts," the *New York Times* reviewer found the story old-fashioned. Confessing that he had not read the original novel himself, he characterized the plot of the film as "a romantic, sentimental old tale," which "for this reason, will have a special appeal for many and little or no attraction for others. It all depends upon your taste in entertainment." The *Variety* reviewer, who liked the film, in part because it was an old-fashioned romance, worried about its market appeal:

> If there is anywhere in the whole scale of literature an idyllic romance of young love, it is this simple, honest, unsophisticated tale. Done into screen form with a fairly adequate presentation, its fate takes on special

interest, for it puts to the test the argument of many commentators on the picture against sensational sex and problem plays. If the fans want poetic romance in the most colorful form, here it is in large proportions, in a work of fiction that has stood the test of time and supported by generations of romance lovers of all ages and varieties.

Pictorially, the film is a splendid effort. . . . Tourneur has managed to achieve a dignified and convincing atmosphere of romance in ancient times. The accoutrements strike one as authentic and the spirit of the production creates a satisfactory illusion, no mean feat in realizing for the eye a story that has lived until now only in the imagination. But the issue before the film public is more than production methods. The question is how will it respond to a poetic love story typical of the old fashioned school.

The opening title of *Lorna Doone* seems to anticipate (and perhaps to a degree have constructed) the terms in which the film was received:

FOREWORD

Tho this romance is of a time two and a half centuries gone, "Lorna Doone" triumphantly outlives more modern literature. Its story is never old, never new. By all tests, it stands today the best-liked and most widely read novel of great love and thrilling adventure. It has, in fact, become a literary heritage of Civilization.

The filmmakers seem to have felt the need to defend their source against the claims of "more modern" literature.

The reception of the 1922 version of *Smilin' Through* parallels that of *Lorna Doone*. Like *Lorna Doone*, *Smilin' Through* was an adaptation, in this case of Allan Langdon Martin's popular 1919 play.[4] Set in the Irish countryside, the plot is a love story spanning two generations. John Carteret is about to wed Moonyeen when his rival, Jeremiah Wayne, attempts to shoot him and kills the bride instead. Later, just prior to the outbreak of World War I, Kathleen, Moonyeen's niece and John's ward, falls in love with Jeremiah's son Kenneth. Her uncle, who nurses a grudge against all the Waynes, bitterly opposes the match. After Kenneth has gone to war and been wounded, John is persuaded to bring about a match between the young people. He dies, and his spirit is shown joining that of Moonyeen.

The play provided a juicy double role for the female lead and was acquired and produced by Joseph Schenck for his wife, Norma Talmadge, with director Sidney Franklin and the celebrated cinematographer Charles Rosher, already known for his work with Mary Pickford.[5] Talmadge's performance was largely seen as the selling point of the film. *Film Daily* (March 5, 1922: 2) deemed the film the best that the actress had made for

First National and added, "The crowd that loves Norma in anything will rave about her in this. And it should be a clean-up." The *New York Times* judged, "Chief among the other attractions of the photoplay, in addition to its photography and settings, which, on the whole, are exceptionally good, is Norma Talmadge. She is lovely as the Mid-Victorian Moonyeen and charming, too, as the more modern Kathleen. Also, her pantomime is often tellingly expressive." *Variety* (March 10, 1922: 41) noted that "Miss Talmadge ably handles the leading role and gives to the production a stamp of class in the acting division that places it well up on the list of program features."

Interestingly, in contrast with *Film Daily*'s enthusiastic endorsement, the *Variety* review classed the film, without further explanation, as a "program feature." Although the film was held to be technically competent, with a capable cast working up "the big points," and "all the necessary heart interest to warrant its success," *Variety* did not think it likely to attract much attention on Broadway, a point underscored by the perfunctory brevity of *Variety*'s review. The *New York Times* review (April 17, 1922: 22) fleshes out the context of reception: "The chances are that practically all those who inform themselves about 'Smilin' Through,' at the Strand this week, and then go to see it, will enjoy it. For it is entirely sentimental, and it is well done. Those who like photoplays deliberately sentimental will be attracted to it, therefore, and will find what they are looking for. Those who shy at such will not be attracted, and will stay away. So there'll be satisfaction all round. It's a happy division, isn't it?" As he did in the case of *Lorna Doone*, the reviewer distances himself from the subliterary source material by freely admitting that he is not familiar with it. While allowing the excellence of film technique and performance, he thinks that the feature will be attractive only to those whose tastes run to the sentimental. *Film Daily*, less concerned with sophisticated taste and urban audiences and more concerned with the mass audience outside the very largest urban centers, was more optimistic about the film's appeal.

The *Variety* review (December 2, 1921: 43) of *The Bonnie Brier Bush*, an obscure feature by Famous Players–Lasky British Producers,[6] provides a clear sense of the change in filmmaking practice that made films like *Lorna Doone* and *Smilin' Through* seem old-fashioned. The plot, set in the Scottish Highlands, concerns two romances that run counter to the dictates of class and tradition but are finally brought to successful conclusions. The film was adapted from an 1895 novel by Ian MacLaren, which had become the source of a play by James MacArthur produced on Broadway in 1901.[7] The reviewer endorsed the film for its location shooting and picturesque costumes but was nonetheless dubious about its chances for success:

Sunday evening, with weather conditions all against attendance, the theatre was less than half filled at the early show. Business in the other houses was off, but not to the same extent. The State, for example, with "The Sheik," drew sturdily. Here is a situation that seems to typify the artistic standards of film fans. "The Sheik," probably as trashy a screen story as has been screened by a representative producer in half a year, attracts them to the box office, and a screening of one of the tenderest and most beautiful idyllic tales in modern fiction goes neglected.

With the release of *The Sheik* in 1921 another sort of romance came to the fore. Thought to be less sentimental, in the sense of being less nostalgic or quaint, it was also criticized for being sensationalist and, somewhat paradoxically, overly genteel.

Much has been written on the significance of Valentino's star persona in the 1920s, but my concern here is with the effect his films had on the cultural status of the romantic drama and its perceived audience. It should be noted that *The Four Horsemen of the Apocalypse*, the film that secured Valentino's star status, is not indicative of more general cinematic trends. A war picture, released well before *The Big Parade* and *What Price Glory* and closer in tone to Griffith's *Hearts of the World*, it was accorded the highest prestige at the time of its release. *Variety* (February 18, 1921. 40), classing it with *Intolerance, Cabiria, Passion* (Lubitsch's *Madame du Barry*), *Hearts of the World*, and *The Birth of a Nation*, estimated that the film could run a year on Broadway as a road show and for three months in cities like Philadelphia, Boston, and Chicago. *Variety* praised the film for its cinematography, the expense and magnificence of the settings, and the acting of "a mighty cast of 32 principals." The review also gave much attention to the thematic treatment of the War. Other reviews praised Valentino, but always along with many others, including Wallace Beery, Alice Terry, and John Sainpolis. *Film Daily* (February 20, 1921: 3) singled out the scene in the tango palace, but more for the direction than for Valentino's performance. Both that review and the one in *Exceptional Photoplays* emphasized the work of the acting ensemble and interpreted the plot as working out an opposition between the French and German branches of Madariaga's Argentinian family rather than a love story focalized on Valentino's character.[8] Thus, while the film helped to establish a certain profile and persona for Valentino, it did not have a decisive impact on the romantic drama as such.

In contrast with the critical acclaim that greeted *The Four Horsemen of the Apocalypse, The Sheik,* Valentino's next major film, provoked a great deal of debate. The main point of controversy was the plot, although many commentators also objected to Valentino's performance, especially his habit of rolling his eyes. The *Variety* reviewer (November 11, 1921: 37) wrote that the "acting could not be worse than the story, but it is bad enough." But the primary objection to the film was that it was tame in comparison with the original novel. The *Variety* review is a fascinating document in the history of taste:

> Though by fear of censorship bled white of anything resembling human form, the popularity of Mrs. Edith M. Hull's novel on which this picture is based should carry it past the box office a winner. This same novel, preposterous and ridiculous as it was, won out because it dealt with every caged woman's desire to be caught up in a love clasp by some he-man who would take the responsibility and dispose of the consequences, but Monte M. Katterjohn's scenario hasn't even that to recommend it. He, in censoring, has safely deleted most of the punch. . . .
>
> Lady Diana has gone—disregarding all advice—alone into the desert with a native guide only to be captured by the young sheik, Ahmed Ben Hassan. But does this youth force his attentions upon her in the forward fashion of the unleashed Oriental? By your grandmother's halidom, he does not! When he kisses her hand and she shrinks, he detains her in his palace of a tent, and that is all. There comes to visit them a Frenchman whom Ahmed knew in Paris, where he was educated, and this doctor and novelist in one convinces the sheik he should not detain Lady Diana. Naughty, naughty—uncivilized. The mere thought of something so uncouth, properly presented to the Arabian mind, works its neat effect, and Ahmed decides to release her. So painful is the decision, so heroic the renunciation, a great light breaks on him. He loves her. Not only loves her, but loves her truly, nobly, as great souls love. Ooh, la, la!

The film is finally characterized as "an essay in film form on the sadistic urge, and a mealy, emasculated one at that." It thus fails on two counts: like the original novel, it is prurient, and, thanks to specific conditions of film censorship, it does not manage to indulge that prurience fully. *Variety* predicted that the film would be successful, a judgment confirmed by attendance reports in *Film Daily*, as well as by the *Variety* reviews of *The Bonnie Brier Bush* and *Forbidden Woman* cited above.[9] But even the prospect of this success could not contain the reviewer's scorn for the plot, a scorn that took the form of parody, unusual for a trade paper, which tended to treat the film industry's products with a minimum of respect. *The Sheik* became a kind of touchstone for *Variety;* one finds disparaging references to it throughout the first half of the 1920s, as can be seen in reviews for such Easterns as *The Man of Stone* (November 18, 1921: 43), *One Stolen Night* (February 1, 1923: 41), and *The Arab* (July 16, 1924: 22).

Most of the other reviews of *The Sheik* in 1921 were in agreement with *Variety*'s assessment, although milder in tone. *Film Daily* (November 13, 1921: 5) observed that "the daring of the novel hasn't been put into the film version" and that "Valentino isn't nearly as competent a lover as Miss Hull's Sheik." *Motion Picture Classic* characterized the novel as "a pretty cheap brand of fiction, i.e., a shocker designed to set the flappers blushing" and complained that Valentino failed to suggest the "self-centered, virile tribal leader he was even in Miss Hull's puerile novel."[10] The *New York Times* (November 7, 1921: 20) reviewer confessed (yet again) that he had not read the novel, but averred that the film did not seem to live up to the reports generally made of Hull's work: "These romantic Arabian movies, you know, never have the courage of their romantics."

By the time Valentino's next big film, *Blood and Sand*, was released *Film Daily* (August 13, 1922: 2), at least, had changed its assessment, calling the film "one of the year's big pictures not only from the box office angle but from an artistic standpoint." *Variety* and the *New York Times*, however, characterized *Blood and Sand* as flat and insipid, the latter writing (August 7, 1922: 14):

[I]n the beginning there is the plain promise that it [*Blood and Sand*] will show how the toreador loses his head when he becomes the idol of the crowds, how he is swept into amorous adventures in the boudoir as well as dangerous encounters in the bull ring, and how, at last, his dizzying world tumbles about him and leaves him where he began, with the one woman who loves him holding him in her arms. All this is clearly forecast, and it suggests a swiftly moving story, tense, tempestuous, true to life, and telling in its high climactic moments, without the retarding and dulling intrusion of conventional observations and moral exposition. But Gallardo does not lose his head. He remains remarkably steady and composed. And he is not swept into any adventures outside the bull ring. As designing a vampire as the screen has ever shown conducts a regular campaign for his attentions and the Puritan-born hero of a "down east," 100 per cent American melodrama could not resist her more austerely, nor yield, to the moderate extent that he does, with less abandon and greater repentance than this Spanish bullfighter shows. Even in the situation in which he is compromised before his wife the poor fellow is entirely innocent. No wonder the vampire leaves him. He isn't a bit of fun.

Also the photoplay takes great pains to reassure timidly and tyran- nically conventional folk as to its constant moral purpose. It is loaded with platitudinous subtitles, and among its characters is a tedious old fool who comes forward every now and then to utter some trite apho- rism or stale word of warning. All this is extremely annoying to the person who simply wants a good story.

Variety (August 11, 1922: 32) seconded this opinion, noting that the audience at the Rialto screening broke into laughter not intended by the filmmakers: "It was the struggles of the hero to resist the temptation of the siren widow that made them chuckle. The spectacle of the erstwhile sheik holding a beautiful woman at arm's length was too much." The reviewer went on to complain, "It's all deadly serious, even to the moral reflections of the philosophical old party who acts a sort of Greek chorus to the story and occasionally breaks out into sub-titles such [as], 'Passion is the devil's intention,' which evoked a guffaw during the vamping episode."

Whereas *The Sheik* and *Blood and Sand* were thought to be timid in sexual matters and, at least in the case of the latter, overly platitudinous, they were not said to be destined for the neighborhood theaters or primarily addressed to women (although Edith Hull's novel was sometimes assumed to have had a feminine appeal). The cheap knock-offs of *The Sheik* that appeared as early as 1921 were, however, unambiguously assigned to women and the lower rungs of the distribution hierarchy. *Variety* described *Man of Stone* as "a routine release for the neighborhood trade." The reviewer characterized it as being "entertaining in a Laura Jean Libbey sort of way," having fewer sexual situations than *The Sheik*, and destined to be popular with "the apparently large public that consumes this sort of literature." *One Stolen Night* was called a "woman-made melodrama." *Film Daily* (November 16, 1924: 6) described *White Man* as "for those who like romance and like it highly seasoned," adding that "it's the sort of thing that many men call 'silly love stuff.'" The same year *Film Daily* (June 1, 1924: 5) judged that *A Son of the Sahara* would appeal to "those strong on romance" but that it was a "pity that such excellent production values should be accorded a theme so threadbare and unoriginal. The sheik has lost his popularity." *Film Daily* (June 28, 1925: 8) assessed *The Spaniard*, Raoul Walsh's film of 1925 starring Ricardo Cortez and with a setting closer to that of *Blood and Sand* than that of *The Sheik*, as "a long drawn out and not particularly fascinating sheik affair with a famous matador pulling his caveman stunts on a haughty English girl." The exhibitor was advised that "women folks are your best bet." Two higher-budget films set in the East, Rex Ingram's *The Arab* (*Variety*, July 16, 1924: 22) and Maurice Tourneur's *Old Loves and New* (*Film Daily*, May 2, 1926: 7), were praised because they did not follow along the lines of the plot of the Valentino film. *Variety* contrasted the former favorably with *The Sheik*, deeming it "a compliment to the screen, a verification of the sterling repute of Rex Ingram, and, withal, a sure financial hit."

Gaylyn Studlar and Miriam Hansen have made it clear that Valentino was marketed to women as a great lover type and that such marketing resonated with a certain fan base.[11] However, trade press reviews of the films, as well as those published in the *New York Times,* indicate that even Valentino's biggest successes of the early 1920s were not considered daring but, rather, mealy-mouthed and verging on the homiletic. Returning to the sheik story in 1926, in what was to be Valentino's last film, *The Son of the Sheik,* the filmmakers showed the hero actually carrying through on his threat to rape the heroine, as if in response to the criticism of the earlier films.

An alternative model of the romantic drama in the early part of the decade is provided by the most elaborate of Erich von Stroheim's early productions for Universal, *Foolish Wives,* which premiered in January 1922. Unfortunately the surviving print is more than one hour shorter than the three-and-a-half-hour version screened at the premiere, thus we do not have access to what critics in the 1920s saw.[12] It is clear that the film generated much controversy.[13] Some critics thought that the amoral and dominating seducer played by von Stroheim went beyond the pale of good taste and of what most audiences would tolerate. And indeed, as Richard Kozsarksi has detailed, the film was subjected to censorship at multiple points in its production history.[14] If Valentino had not gone far enough, von Stroheim clearly went too far.

The reviewers were actually divided in their responses to *Foolish Wives.* Both *Film Daily* and the *New York Times* found the film acceptable for largely the same reasons that they had liked von Stroheim's earlier adultery story, *Blind Husbands*: the seducer character could be seen unproblematically as a villain. *Wid's* (October 19, 1919: 7) had dubbed *Blind Husbands* a successful twist on the old triangle story and assured exhibitors, "You are safe in billing this as clean wholesome entertainment"; the role of the other man, played by von Stroheim, was compared to the actor's previous performances as a wicked Hun, whom *Wid's* called a "willun" in a burlesque of the pronunciation of the term in old-time melodrama: "If you have played 'The Unbeliever,' 'Hearts of the World,' and especially 'The Heart of Humanity,' you may recall to your patrons that the willun of the above successes does what is probably the best work of his screen career in 'Blind Husbands.'" A similar reception was accorded *Foolish Wives* by this trade journal, now called *Film Daily* instead of *Wid's,* which promised exhibitors (January 15, 1922: 2) that von Stroheim "will convince them now, if never before, that he is the screen's greatest of villains." The *New York Times* (January 12, 1922: 15) characterized the central character of *Foolish Wives* as "a human beast of prey, an unbelievably contemptible animal whose vocation and avocation is preying on women—without scruple and indiscriminately. He takes their money and their honor, whether they are serving maids, half-witted girls or the wives of men in high station. And Mr. Von Stroheim makes this character most repellently realistic. All of the polish of such a villain, all of the cruelty, all of the cowardice, are portrayed in his finished, fiendish acting."

Because, however, *Foolish Wives* and, to a lesser extent, *Blind Husbands* were focalized around the point of view of the seducer, as opposed to that of the wife or her husband, it was difficult simply to dismiss this character as the "willun." Some critics thought that von Stroheim's films explored a new, franker, and more cynical view of sexuality through the supposedly evil character. *Variety* (December 12, 1919: 46) wrote of *Blind Husbands* that "this former Griffith heavy has written, directed and acted in a feature that makes others shown on Broadway seem like a novel by Chambers besides a masterpiece by Sudermann or Schnitzler." The flirtation scenes were said to have a "sex appeal that is at once charming and arousing." The reviewer mentioned the "pretty" scene in which the other man, in the absence of the husband, managed to insinuate himself into the wife's bedroom before she was fully dressed. The critic for *Motion Picture Classic* held that *Foolish Wives* proposed a more sophisticated and European view of sex, again comparing the film with the work of Schnitzler: "*Foolish Wives* has moments—indeed, whole stretches—of greatness. It is not for the provincial or the prude. Von Stroheim has taken the one real theme of life—sex—and played upon it with Continental discernment and, let us say, abandon. Where the Pollyanna American viewpoint dresses up sex in tinsel and spangles, von Stroheim looks upon it with the worldly and half cynical, half humorous Viennese viewpoint of a Schnitzler. Briefly, where we love to dress our sex illusions in Santa Claus whiskers, von Stroheim sees only the stocking at the fireplace."[15]

In contrast with *Motion Picture Classic*, many trade papers objected to the 1922 film's frank depictions of desire and sexual exploitation. While the *Variety* review of *Blind Husbands* had praised the innovative tone of von Stroheim's work, the trade paper found *Foolish Wives* (January 20, 1922: 35) harder to stomach and seems to have considered it a potential threat to the industry. Characterized as a "sensational sex melodrama," the film was said to be "frankly salacious. So disgustingly so at times that if the rawest 'turkey' burlesque show ever attempted anything like the scene where Erich von Stroheim, as Count Karamzin, sits beside the sleeping figure of Miss Dupont (Mrs. Hughes) and graphically depicts undisguised lust for the woman he has been pursuing, the reformers and vice suppression societies would descend on the show in jig time." The reviewer recommended that Will Hays, the then newly appointed head of the Motion Picture Producers and Distributors Association, take a look at the film. It was held to be not only overly graphic but also un-American: "With its two principal American characters conceived as unadulterated asses by the author and the foreigners by contrast shown as smart slickers who make monkeys out of the Americans at every turn, 'Foolish Wives' stands as a leering insult to Americans in general, and American womanhood in particular." This idea was echoed by the *Photoplay* review, which dubbed the film a "gruesome, morbid, unhealthy tale" and found it "unfit for the family to see," "an insult to American ideals and womanhood."[16] Much has been made about the reception of the film as un-American, but more important in this discussion is the fact that *Foolish Wives* is a romantic drama in which the Lothario had the courage of his convictions (or, rather, lack of them), and that the film was considered a bad bet for the industry, unsuitable for families, and an insult to women.[17]

As it evolved in the mid-1920s the romantic drama steered a course between the pusillanimity of *The Sheik* and *Blood and Sand* and the unabashed perversity of Erich von Stroheim's adultery stories. Two of the later Valentino films pointed the way. *Monsieur Beaucaire*, in 1924, was apparently a bid for the important first-run market. Despite a scene of Valentino posing nude to the waist, which *Variety* (August 13, 1924: 19) likened to a "strength act," the film had the marks of a prestige costume picture. Unlike *The Sheik*, it was adapted from a respected literary source, a turn-of-the-century novel, and subsequently a play, by Booth Tarkington. Both *Variety* and the *New York Times* (August 12, 1924: 12) commented favorably on the expensive sets, particularly the recreation of Versailles. It is difficult to generalize about how the trade press understood the audience for this film. *Variety* predicted that it would be a "money" picture, while noting that three-quarters of the audience at the Strand were women. The *Variety* review for *A Sainted Devil* (November 26, 1924: 24), the Valentino film that followed, noted that *Monsieur Beaucaire* was "said to have done a flop outside of the big towns," despite the fact that "it was the artistic type of production to draw good notices from the dailies." I think it is fair to say that the film was an attempt to retain Valentino's fan base—the shots of his musculature—while reaching out for metropolitan audiences and critical approbation.

The Eagle, in 1925, was well received by the trade press and the *New York Times*. *Variety* dubbed Valentino's role as more of a "he-man," a "Russian Robin Hood," and singled out the stunt riding done at the film's opening. Much praise was reserved for the film's central comedic situation—a Russian czarina aggressively pursuing the men in her own guard, exchanging sex for military favors—copied from Lubitsch's film of the previous year, *Forbidden Paradise* (the screenwriter Hans Kräly worked on both). *Variety* (November 11, 1925: 36) appreciated the racy scenes devoted to this situation in *The Eagle*, singling out Louise Dresser's performance as the czarina. The critic for the *New York Times* (November 9, 1925: 25) also liked the film but preferred Lubitsch's version. By borrowing this situation from the realm of sophisticated comedy, *The Eagle* managed to avoid the charges of over-seriousness and sexual timidity that had been leveled against Valentino's previous films, although it should be noted that it succeeded precisely because it engaged in a comic reversal of the great-lover part in at least certain of the scenes. Nonetheless, *The Eagle*, with its particular mixture of lavish historical settings and costumes and a plot that incorporated both stunts and farcical elements, provided a model for filmmakers. The film was thought to be inherently appealing to women but also gained access to the most lucrative first-run markets, as well as respectful treatment in the trade and popular press.

Even more than Valentino's historical romances, John Barrymore's *Don Juan*, released in August 1926, at the beginning of the 1926–27 season, epitomized this kind of filmmaking.[18] *Variety* had criticized George Melford, the director of *The Sheik*, for making the sheik's climactic rescue of the heroine after she was kidnapped by another Arab bandit, too easy: "So what was left of this picture, which could easily have been something by building up this photographic action-full possibility becomes nothing." Such criticism could not be directed at *Don Juan*, nor any of the later Barrymore vehicles, all of which were praised for their fight scenes and stirring last-minute rescues. *Don Juan* has little to do with the legend. It is set in Rome during the time of the Borgias, and the hero reforms after falling in love with the heroine (played by Mary Astor), whom he must then rescue from Lucrezia Borgia's clutches. *Variety* (August 11, 1926: 11) thought that the film aimed "directly at the women for pulling power." At the same time the film was commended as a special: "At $2 top it is quite apt to run at Warner's Broadway for six months and possibly a longer time." The film, with a music-and-effects soundtrack, famously premiered with the first program of Warners' Vitaphone shorts, and this surely influenced the way it was priced. But most of the reviews considered the film on its own terms (and, of course, they were writing for exhibitors who would not have been able to screen the feature with recorded sound). The riding stunts during the final chase were praised, as was the duel between Barrymore and Montague Love. *Variety* went so far as to compare Barrymore's acting to Garrick's. *Film Daily* (August 15, 1926: 6) also thought that the film was of "extended run calibre and destined to make plenty of money" and praised the lavish sets, the Fairbanks-like stunts, and Barrymore's "suavity and slight humorous twinkle." The *New York Times* (August 7, 1926: 6) succinctly noted, "Mr. Barrymore leaps through the scenes of this production in a captivating manner, and sometimes the principal character and the story remind one of a Fairbanks film, and in the amorous moments one is impelled to think of Valentino." The high-brow New York magazines were the only ones that did not follow suit; the *New Yorker,* for example, characterized Barrymore's performance as "a combination of every ham hero the screen has held."[19] But in general the film was released to great acclaim.

Warner followed the release of *Don Juan* with two more costume pictures starring Barrymore, both of which opened as specials on Broadway near the beginning of 1927, a confluence *Variety* considered unprecedented. *When a Man Loves* loosely followed the plot of *Manon Lescaut. Film Daily* (February 6, 1927: 12) praised the production values: "These costume stories of old France always run into heavy negative costs." Both the *New York Times* (February 4, 1927: 16) and *Variety* (February 9, 1927: 14) stressed the swashbuckling aspect—the sword fighting and the final mutiny that allows des Grieux and Manon to escape from the convict ship—although *Variety* did not find it as good as *Don Juan. Film Daily* stressed the film's appeal to women: "Barrymore a splendid romantic figure. Oh, how the women will fall for him in his resplendent costumes."

The Beloved Rogue, with Barrymore as François Villon, provided a role that *Variety* (March 16, 1927: 17) thought "just screamed for Fairbanks." Nonetheless, it is a mark of the presumed feminine appeal of the star and story that all of the trade industry reviews commented unfavorably on the star's grotesque make-up and low-comedy antics. *Film Daily* (March 20, 1927: 6) wrote, "The handsome Barrymore sacrifices considerable when he dons a clown's makeup. Jests and romps for the most part, but his admirers will find a generous share of romantic scenes as well." *Variety* commented, "As a purely romantic offering it has its defects. Much of the glamor is missing in the hero, who is for most of the time rather a disheveled sort of person—a picturesque enough rogue at all times, but not always the height of splendid romance." And *Photoplay* complained, "All the charm and romance in the life of the roguish Villon has been turned into regular slapstick comedy."[20]

During the same 1926–27 season that saw the three Barrymore specials, John Gilbert appeared in his own costume picture, *Bardelys, the Magnificent,* which also had a French setting. *Film Daily* (October 17, 1926: 8) characterized it as "a rip-roaring story, a Don Juan tale with a Fairbanks' finish plus John Gilbert and King Vidor's direction," presumably referring both to the Barrymore film released in August and *The Big Parade*, with the same director and star, which had been released the previous season. Gilbert's reputation as a romantic lead had been growing. He had already appeared under King Vidor's direction in such roles in *His Hour* (1924), *Wife of the Centaur* (1924), and *La Bohème* (1926), as well as in von Stroheim's much praised version of *The Merry Widow* (1925). Nonetheless, *Film Daily* asserted a general rather than feminine appeal for *Bardelys, the Magnificent*. The review was headlined: "Watch the money fill the coffers with this. One of those pictures that man, woman and child find equally entertaining." The review stressed the hero's sword fights, stunts, and last-minute escapes. *Variety* (October 13, 1926: 20) thought the film a good bet but stressed the feminine appeal more strongly: "John Gilbert shows that he is romantically inclined, that he has that necessary ingredient called 'It' by Mme. Glynn and that he is a carefree and all around hurdler and acrobat, as well as masterful salesman of his talents." The trade paper did not think that the film would stand up at a special admission price of $1.50 but did expect good grosses when it got to the regular first-run theaters.

Even when the popularity of the romantic swashbuckler was at its height, during the mid-1920s, *Variety* commented upon the lack of compelling roles for the female leads in such films. Of *Monsieur Beaucaire* the reviewer notes, "What may surprise is the wholesale relegating of practically the entire cast to the background, so that this feature amounts to nothing less than 100 minutes of Valentino. It's a 'pie' role for the star." In *Don Juan* "Miss Astor, featured in the billing, has but comparatively little action." In *When a Man Loves*, "That girl [Dolores Costello] is beautiful, she can act and does. Of course the picture is almost wholly Barrymore and every opportunity is given him to get all the footage possible." In *Bardelys the Magnificent:* "Miss Boardman, as Roxalanne, does her best to give a sincere interpretation, but does not seem to have 'It' which Gilbert has." Both female roles in Vidor's *La Bohème* were found wanting: "The girls are going to go crazy over Jack Gilbert as Rodolphe, the lover, and the boys will like Mimi as played by Lillian Gish, although she gives a rather watered mild characterization. . . . The women folk of the cast, other than Miss Gish, include Renée Adorée as Musette, which character has been emasculated to a tremendous degree and it is almost too bad that Miss Adorée was assigned to it."

The dominance of male stars in the romantic dramas thought to appeal to women is, of course, at variance with all of the descriptions of the woman's picture in the 1930s, said to be focalized on a female character and dependent upon a set of actresses—Bette Davis, Barbara Stanwyck, Joan Crawford, Irene Dunne—whose importance far outweighed that of the men with whom they usually played, among them George Brent, John Boles, Clive Brooks, and Paul Henried.[21] To be sure, the society dramas and flaming youth films of the 1920s had better parts for women and were associated with actresses like Corinne Griffith, Joan Crawford, and Clara Bow. But in the first half of the 1920s actresses in the romantic drama were not considered to be a major draw for women. I hypothesize that this is because it was difficult for the studios to create a plot formula that would allow a major actress to perform the kind of heavy lovemaking associated with these stories without offending audience sensibilities.

Consider, for example, Norma Talmadge, one of the most important stars of the decade. In 1923 First National released *The Song of Love,* a Talmadge vehicle directed by Chester Franklin and Frances Marion that obviously sought to play off the success of *The Sheik.* Talmadge played Noorma-hal, an Algerian dancing girl caught between an Arab chief intent on fomenting rebellion against the French colonial forces and a French spy with whom she eventually falls in love. Reviewers noted that the role was a departure for the star. The *New York Times* (February 25, 1924: 13) wrote: "In 'Ashes of Vengeance' she was cleverly effective, and she was charmingly sympathetic in 'Smilin' Through.' Now she is to be seen at the Rivoli this week in 'The Song of Love,' playing an utterly different type of damsel.... Imagine passing into the Rivoli with a vague impression of Miss Talmadge in poke bonnet and voluminous hoop skirts that jealously guard even her slender ankles from view, and suddenly beholding a startling vision of undeniable beauty, clad expensively, but not extensively."[22] *Film Daily* (January 13, 1924: 1) was more succinct: "Norma Talmadge in sheik story that is quite inferior to what she really requires.... Dancing girl garb appears to embarrass her." The film was seen as an unusual one for an actress who had made her reputation in more dignified and "old-fashioned" roles.

Talmadge seems to have retreated from the highly sexualized or exotic romantic drama after this point. In the mid-1920s she made *Graustark* and *Kiki,* largely comic films that were much better received, as well as the maternal melodrama *The Lady.* Although *Film Daily* (September 20, 1925: 4) implied that *Graustark* would please "romance lovers," that is, women, *Variety* (September 9, 1925: 35) saw it as an extremely well-made program release that was likely to please most audiences, "100 per cent suitable to any house." Both *Variety* and the *New York Times* (September 8, 1925: 29) described the understated comedy of the film's opening, in which hero and heroine first see each other at a train station while seated in trains headed in opposite directions. *Variety* characterized the plot as "the familiar tale of an American love for a royal princess. Because it is all romance with never a tinge of sexiness, 'Graustark' is in itself a great relief from the usual run of photoplays."[23] It was not until much later in the decade that Talmadge essayed more risqué parts, a point to which I shall return.

Like Talmadge, Lillian Gish stayed away from the racier forms of the romantic drama, even at the risk of giving the "rather watered mild characterization" of Mimi that *Variety* noted in *La Bohème*. After leaving Griffith's company following the production of *Orphans of the Storm*, Gish appeared in a series of high-budget historical dramas directed by the likes of Henry King *(The White Sister* and *Romola)*, Victor Sjöström *(The Scarlet Letter)*, and Vidor. While prestigious, her films were not usually thought to appeal to a feminine audience. The *New York Times* (September 6, 1923: 10) described the audience for the opening of *The White Sister* as "a most interesting assembly, which included persons prominent in society, distinguished politicians, well-known authors and writers, screen celebrities and heads of the motion picture industry. It seemed an occasion which revealed the standing of the films possibly more than any other photoplay presentation." One of the few suggestions that Gish might appeal to women was made by *Variety*, in an unfavorable review of *The White Sister*. The plot concerns an Italian heiress, Angela, left penniless by the machinations of her half sister, who enters a religious order after being informed that her fiancé has been killed in battle in Africa. The lover (Ronald Colman) returns unexpectedly and tries to convince her to abandon her vows. One night he tricks her into leaving the convent and holds her locked in a room against her will, but this is a rather chaste variant on the situation made popular by *The Sheik:* he does no more than plead with her to petition religious authorities for permission to marry. When Angela refuses, he threatens to keep her at his side by force, but the sight of her in prayer moves him to kiss her skirts and give her egress. An eruption of Vesuvius and ensuing flood, which resolve the plot by killing the lover, were obviously intended to provide a spectacular finish on the order of the breaking up of the ice floes in *Way Down East* or the French Revolution in *Orphans of the Storm. Variety* (September 13, 1923: 30) found the film "extremely tearful and depressing, with action that drags through endless reels of suffering" and likely to give "those of the women who enjoy a good cry a real chance."[24] This indicates that *Variety* considered *The White Sister* to have a feminine appeal, but it was of an entirely different order than that of the sheik films. Indeed, the problem for the reviewer presumably was that the hero appeared too timid and restrained in comparison with others of the period—although it would no doubt have been equally unacceptable for the filmmakers to essay a rape or almost-rape in a scene with Lillian Gish as a nun.

The *New York Times* (October 9, 1923: 17) teasingly claimed that Pola Negri's *The Spanish Dancer* was "originally intended for Rudolph Valentino and was to have been called 'The Spanish Cavalier.'" The reference to Valentino's *Blood and Sand* was not particularly apt; in fact, *The Spanish Dancer* was adapted from the same theatrical source as *Rosita,* the Mary Pickford vehicle directed by Ernst Lubitsch, and is much closer to the latter film. But the joke about Negri taking Valentino's place is telling; if any female star of the early 1920s could have filled Valentino's shoes, it would have been Negri. She was typed as an alluring siren in two German-made films, Lubitsch's *Madame Du Barry,* released in the United States as *Passion* in December 1920, and Dimitri Buchowetzki's *Sappho,* released in the United States as *Mad Love* in March 1923, and was, according to *Variety,* given a publicity push by gossip of an impending engagement between Negri and Charlie Chaplin.

One of Negri's first American films, *Bella Donna,* released in April 1923 and directed by George Fitzmaurice, was more justly compared to *The Sheik* by the *New York Times* (April 16, 1923: 20). In this film, based upon a novel by Robert Smythe Hichens, the eponymous heroine travels to Egypt in the company of her second husband, an English doctor, Nigel (Conrad Nagel). According to the summary of the plot in the *New York Times,* she attracts the attention of an Arab, Mahmoud Baroudi (Conway Tearle), who insists that the couple spend some time in his villa. One night, while her husband is off hunting jackal, Baroudi makes advances and kisses her. The *Times* reviewer noted, "In a spirit of deviltry she changes into a native costume, which is decidedly becoming to Pola Negri. Baroudi is entranced, fascinated and falls at her feet in admiration." When developments in England make it clear that Nigel will not inherit the title he had expected, Baroudi persuades Bella Donna to administer slow poison. When the murder plot is revealed and her husband saved, Bella tries to flee to Baroudi, but he is occupied with another woman and has no intention of interfering publicly in the affairs of an English couple. Bella Donna staggers out into the desert, where a panther lurks seeking prey.

Film Daily (April 22, 1923: 2) disapproved of the story as "unpleasant" and "unwholesome," but both the *New York Times* and *Variety* thought the vamp role made a good vehicle for the star. *Variety* (April 19, 1923: 35) thought that the film was well appointed and that Negri looked better than she had in her German films. This reviewer also predicted that Conway

Tearle would appeal to female viewers: "Tearle became the commanding figure with his Sheik role and manner but if that will make the women love him more than they do now, it won't be his fault." But, as in the case of *The Sheik, Variety* found the plot weak and made fun of such improbable elements as the panther in the desert, the filmmakers' feeble approximation of sand dunes in exteriors, and the sight of Pola Negri descending from a camel. It posited an audience in the sticks: "The story has been hashed up in a hundred ways but maybe in the woods it isn't the apple sauce it looks in Times square." It was finally judged to be "a simple tale for simple people but certain to fill the eye and mind of the usual picture house patrons."

The attempt to place Negri in an Eastern, and to pair the female seductress with the masterful sheik figure, does not seem to have been successful; at any rate, there are no further variants (although the early sound film *Wild Orchids*, discussed below, reprises the same plot with a "good" wife as the heroine). In 1924 Negri was featured in a more sophisticated romantic drama, *Lily of the Dust*, directed by Dimitri Buchowetzki (director of the German-made *Sappho*). This film was based on Sudermann's novel *Das hohe Lied*, and the subsequent play *The Song of Songs* by Edward Brewster Sheldon, which ran for over a year on Broadway in 1914. The plot of the film concerned a woman in a German garrison town who married a colonel (Noah Beery) because she was impressed with his social position, while continuing a flirtation with a lieutenant in the same regiment (Ben Lyon) and, after her divorce, becoming the mistress of a third man (Raymond Griffith). The *New York Times* (August 25, 1924: 16) praised the film as "intense and realistic, the atmospheric detail being splendid and true." Nonetheless, the film was subject to criticism both for going too far and for not going far enough. *Film Daily* (September 7, 1924: 8) complained that "Sudermann, one of the greatest authors of the day, knows his continental audience like a book and he has used a woman of a type that American people are not keen about as his basic figure. So if your people are not inclined to be finicky and don't mind the dusty lily type they may enjoy this. Squeamish mothers with adolescent daughters—there are such—may object, but otherwise this one will get by." In contrast, *Variety* (August 27, 1924: 25), in a forceful review, complained about the adulteration of the novel and play:

> The story itself, written by Sudermann and in its original, was the
> episodic history of a woman's downfall, with each step to the conclu
> sion definitely explained and logically presented. It wasn't a pleasant
> story—nor was it unpleasant—for Sudermann possessed enough
> sophistication to know that somewhere in the world there must be peo-

ple who didn't believe in the stork legend nor in the fallacy that a Republican administration is good for business.

Consequently, when he chose Lily as the protagonist of his theme, he wrote of her with a certain vigorous sympathy, making her path from that of an innocent girl to the mistress of an artist plain but plausible. One of the characters which he used but momentarily was a Lieutenant Prell, whose little love affair, according to Sudermann, taught Lily what lust meant. . . . But Paul Bern and Dimitri Buchowetski, in charge of this production for Paramount, have produced an abortive effort which has as its main theme the true love (never mentioned by Sudermann) of Lily and the lieutenant. . . . The principal fault is that a famous story has been maltreated beyond recognition to make a movie holiday, and the result is so mediocre than an audience will probably not break their necks to see it.

Paramount never seems to have hit upon a formula for Negri's dramatic films that would have permitted them to be both sexually daring and inoffensive. After *Lily of the Dust* was criticized for being both too "unpleasant" and too mild-mannered, Negri retreated from full-blown vamp roles. During 1924 and 1925 she appeared in Walsh's *East of Suez*, about a love affair between an orphan girl of Chinese descent and an Englishman, which was described by *Variety* (January 7, 1925: 37) as a "ripsnorting melodrama"; *Flower of Night*, a romance set in old California; and two sophisticated comedies: Lubitsch's *Forbidden Paradise* and Mal St. Clair's *A Woman of the World*. In 1927 she appeared in *The Woman on Trial*, a story of mother love that was described by *Variety* (September 28, 1927: 24) as "sentimental slush," and in two war stories, *Barbed Wire* and *Hotel Imperial*, in which she played a humble girl who falls in love with an enemy soldier. Both *Variety* (April 25, 1928: 28) and *Film Daily* (April 29, 1928: 5) considered *Three Sinners*, based on the play *Das zweite Leben* by Rudolf Bernauer and Rudolf Österreicher, to be a return to sophisticated fare, but the former deemed it "old fashioned in its artificial motivation" and without humor. While she remained typed as a Continental vamp, most of Negri's films of the mid- and late 1920s therefore actually represented a departure from that persona.

Although Norma Talmadge, Lillian Gish, and Pola Negri must certainly be counted among the most important female stars to be featured in romantic dramas or costume dramas in the mid-1920s, none of them was ever accorded the reception given charismatic male stars such as Valentino or Barrymore, nor were they held to attract a following among women. The actresses who came to predominate in the more risqué variants of the romantic drama in the same period, and who were thought to be favored by women, secured their reputations by means of a series of films that featured male/female acting teams.

Ronald Colman was paired with many actresses, including Lillian Gish in *The White Sister*. Before being teamed with Vilma Banky he gained praise working in tandem with Blanche Sweet in two features, *The Sporting Venus* in April 1925 and *His Supreme Moment* in May of the same year. The latter was released by Goldwyn with three color sequences. *Variety* (April 15, 1925: 36) called it "a well done tale with the sex element played up about as strongly as possible" and predicted that "the women are going to go wild over the love making Ronald Colman does on the screen." At the same time the review praised Blanche Sweet, especially the film's first scene: "Opening with a color sequence of a scene in a Moorish harem with Blanche Sweet a blonde dancer of the harem, the audience gets the impression it is going to see another of those sheik tales. When the switch arrives that gives them the realization they were viewing a stage spectacle and were just as much a part of the audience as the one that flashes on the screen there is an element of genuine surprise." The film is not a sheik tale—the heroine is, in fact, an actress. She finds herself in love with a mining engineer and, unsure whether or not to abandon the stage, accompanies him to Latin America and proposes that they live together on an experimental basis to see if she can adjust to her new surroundings. Apparently this created suspense over whether the hero could manage to refrain from sex with his roommate. *His Supreme Moment* was considered racy for 1925, and *Variety* expressed surprise that the opening had gotten past the censors. Without having seen a print, it is difficult to elucidate the force of the comparison with the Valentino films. But it seems clear that Sweet's character was supposed to be sexually exotic, and her performance was considered at least as important to the film's suspense and appeal as Colman's.

Two films already mentioned, *Flesh and the Devil* and *The Night of Love,* appeared in January 1927 and codified the male/female duo, as opposed to the charismatic male star, as the center of the romantic drama. *Flesh and the Devil*, adapted from Hermann Sudermann's novel *Es war,* was described by *Variety* (January 12, 1927: 14) as "sophisticated stuff" and by the reviewer for *Exceptional Photoplays* as a film "whose appeal will be most appreciated by adult audiences."[25] It was not understood to be a film specifically for women, although in my opinion it had a decisive influence on subsequent films that were typed as feminine.

The plot concerns Leo von Sellenthin and Ulrich von Kletzingk, two German aristocrats, who have been friends since boyhood. Ulrich's younger sister, Hertha, longs for Leo to take an interest in her, but Leo pursues a flirtation with a mysterious woman, Felicitas, whom he has met at a dance. Felicitas takes him to her rooms where, after sex, he discovers that she is married when her husband unexpectedly returns home. The men fight a duel, supposedly over a dispute at cards, and the husband is killed. Ordered to the African colonies for a period of time to allow the scandal to blow over, Leo asks Ulrich, who is unaware of his relationship with Felicitas, to watch over her.

While Felicitas is shown happily trying on widow's weeds after the death of her husband, the spectator gets the sense that she both regrets and is terrified by the idea of Leo's imminent departure in the scene in which they bid each other goodbye. She still appears to be grieving for Leo when Ulrich visits and asks if he can help her. When he mentions that he is wealthy and would be happy to offer financial support if she needs it, she shows only slightly more interest in her visitor.

After three years Leo is pardoned and returns to discover that Ulrich and Felicitas have married. Out of regard for Ulrich, Leo decides it is best to break off their friendship, a decision reinforced by his pastor, who knows the real reason for the duel. Our sense of Felicitas's duplicity, or, perhaps, weakness, gradually deepens. She convinces Leo to resume relations with Ulrich on the grounds that his friend is heartbroken and misses him. Later, when Ulrich is out of town, Felicitas visits Leo and declares her love, overwhelming his scruples when she proposes that they run away together. That night, while Felicitas is packing, Ulrich returns home bearing a gift of a jeweled bracelet. By the time Leo calls for her, she is reluctant to elope, since she wants to retain the comforts that the wealthy Ulrich can provide. She proposes continuing the affair while remaining in Ulrich's house. Leo, enraged by her perfidy, attempts to strangle her. When Ulrich rushes in and stops him, Felicitas tells her husband a half-truth: that she was attacked because she refused to run away with Leo. Leo does not explain, and Ulrich challenges him to a duel.

The duel takes place on the island where the men had sworn eternal fidelity as boys. As the men prepare to fight, Hertha confronts Felicitas and demands that she tell the truth and prevent the duel that would destroy both men. Hertha's prayers drive Felicitas into a guilty frenzy, and she finally agrees. As she runs across the ice-caked lake to get to the island, she falls through the ice and drowns. On the island, it is clear that Leo has no intention of firing upon his friend. When Ulrich lifts his pistol he is overtaken by memories of their past together and cannot fire. The two men are reconciled. Trade press reviews indicate that this scene was followed by what was considered a saccharine ending showing Leo and Hertha, and possibly Ulrich, together in springtime; this scene does not appear in the restored version prepared by Kevin Brownlow for Thames Television.[26]

Although the great friendship between the men is represented in the opening scenes at officer's training school and asserted throughout the film, it seems to me that *Flesh and the Devil* differs markedly from a male adventure film such as *A Girl in Every Port*. The friendship between the men, like the warnings of the grandfatherly pastor, functions largely as a foil against which the allure of what *Variety* elsewhere calls the "grand pash" can be brought to the fore. When, after Leo's return home, the pastor asks him not to see Felicitas again, Leo replies: "I promise—nothing," suggesting either that he fears his ability to resist temptation or, more strongly, a defiance of religious strictures against adultery. It seems to me that this idea of ungovernable passion works to excuse even the actions of Felicitas to a certain degree. It is instructive to contrast *Flesh and the Devil* with von Stroheim's *Blind Husbands* and *Foolish Wives*, as well as with Buchowetzki's *Lily of the Dust*, films which, as already noted, evoked Sudermann for contemporary reviewers, and which also dealt with adultery and seduction. *Variety* criticized *Lily of the Dust* for subscribing to an idea of romantic love that effectively whitewashed Sudermann's heroine. The same could not be said of Felicitas. In the scene in which she refuses to run away with Leo, proposes deceiving Ulrich in his own house, and then misrepresents Leo's actions to her husband, Felicitas is revealed as a villain without scruples and, in this sense, like the villains in whom von Stroheim specialized. But while von Stroheim's seducers are simply and inexplicably amoral, almost in the mode of the villains of early nineteenth-century theatrical melodrama, Felicitas's motivation is more ambiguous. This is partly a function of the fact that the full extent of her deviousness is not apparent to the spectator until the penultimate scene; prior to this, many of her actions, including very damning ones like happily experimenting with her widow's garb, could be put down to her overwhelming love for Leo. The ambiguity of Felicitas's motivations is also buttressed by scenes such as the one in which Leo takes leave of her to go to Africa, or the one in which she proposes that they run away, where she appears to be genuinely in love.

Trade press evaluation of *Flesh and the Devil* stressed the appeal of the couple as the main selling point, a great contrast with the reception of *Foolish Wives*, in which the von Stroheim character was discussed in isolation, and with that of *Lily of the Dust*, which focused almost solely on Negri's performance. *Variety* wrote of *Flesh and the Devil*, "Here is a picture that is the 'pay-off' when it comes to filming love scenes. There are three in this picture that will make anyone fidget in their seats and their hair rise on end." The reviewer forecast that the film was "certain to be a box office smash, no matter where they play it. It looks as though it should be big enough to smash the record at the Capital this week and possibly hold over next week for another record. After they get a load of this love making the audiences are going out and talk about it, and send others in."[27] *Photoplay* promised, "Here is the picture filmed when the romance of Jack Gilbert and Greta Garbo was at its height. Naturally, the love scenes (and there are several thousand feet of them) are smoulderingly fervent."[28]

In addition to finding the lovemaking a good business bet, reviewers were struck by the subtlety of Garbo's performance. At the time *Flesh and the Devil* was released John Gilbert was by far the more established. Garbo had only appeared in two previous American films, *Ibañez' Torrent* and *The Temptress.* Her performance nonetheless attracted more attention and comment than Gilbert's did. *Variety* concluded that "this film is a battle between John Gilbert, starred, and Greta Garbo, featured, for honors and if they don't star this girl after this picture Metro-Goldwyn doesn't know what it is missing. . . . This girl has everything. Gilbert has to keep moving to overshadow her, even though she has a most unsympathetic role." Garbo's performance was also discussed by the relatively more highbrow *Exceptional Photoplays:*

> The story is based upon Hermann Sudermann's novel, "The Undying Past." . . . Cut down to its essentials it is after all only another variation of the familiar vampire plot. Ordinarily that would in itself be enough to make the discriminating picture-goer sniff suspiciously. . . . The success of such a picture, in these days when audiences have become more sophisticated about ladies of vampirish repute, depends, as we have been at pains to point out, entirely upon the credibility of the lady in question. She must be "believable." And it must also be "believable" that men of standing should fall in love with her and not recognize her for what she is. . . . The leading contributor to the success of *Flesh and the Devil* is Greta Garbo. . . . A very good indication of the changing values and emphasis in the vampire picture is brought home to us if we compare Miss Garbo with the most famous screen vamp of yesteryear, Theda Bara. Miss Bara, with her robust voluptuousness, was the accepted prototype of the lady who has made men uneasy, from St. Anthony to Rudyard Kipling. Her appeal was nothing if not frank, and wise and sober men could be on their guard against her. Miss Garbo in her later day impersonation, shows a frail physique and a fragile, etherial [*sic*] air. She is infinitely more civilized and all the more subtle for not being so deliberate. When to these gifts of appearance and suggestion is added the real

histrionic power of Miss Garbo, the memorable impression which *Flesh and the Devil* is leaving upon contemporary audiences is already to a great extent explained.

There is a certain residual gentility at work here, the reviewer finding it implausible that "men of standing" could be carried away by a frankly sexual and aggressive woman. The gentility is admixed with a preference for understatement: Theda Bara's vamp roles are considered crude and overdone, while Garbo's frailty, "civilized" bearing, and decorum make her enactment of the seductress more believable and, presumably, more compelling.

Considered "adult," "subtle," and "sophisticated"—not to mention worthy of analysis in *Exceptional Photoplays*—*Flesh and the Devil* had a considerable cultural cachet. But it was ultimately classed with films that did not share this kind of prestige. *The Night of Love*, which played on Broadway at the same time as *Flesh and the Devil*, was the third film produced by Samuel Goldwyn starring Ronald Colman and Vilma Banky.[29] It was described by *Variety* (January 26, 1927: 20) as "a cross between the traditional vendetta attributed to Latin races and an out-and-out sequence made popular by Mrs. E. M. Hull in 'The Sheik.'" *Variety*'s summary made short work of the plot:

> Montero (Mr. Colman) has his Gypsy bride snatched from him on the bridal night by the dastardly duke (Montague Love). When the titled villain weds, the Gypsy leader reverses the former situation but on a more gentlemanly basis. Where the duke threatened Montero's bride so that she kills herself, the latter turns his fair-haired captive over to the care of tribeswomen after she has needlessly jumped from a castle window. As is expected each falls in love with the other. The duke, being the husband, stands in the way. . . .
>
> The picture starts out tempestuously enough with the reason for the strife between Montero and the duke, but when the love theme creeps in, there it is and it's a long while before the continuity gets back to the personal hostilities.

While the reviewer did not particularly like the film (comparing a film to *The Sheik* seems to have been one of the quickest ways to damn it in *Variety*), he was by no means certain that Broadway audiences would share his opinion: "Monday the Strand was confident 'The Night of Love' would do sufficient business to warrant holding over for a second week. A big Saturday and Sunday, the latter a miserable day as to weather, was the basis of that optimism. But this picture doesn't register as of holdover specifications." The acting duo, however, was thought to be a possible draw: "Yet with 'The Flesh and the Devil' [*sic*] at the Capitol with its Gilbert-Garbo team drawing into its third successive week, it may be the team rather than the picture will draw regardless." *Film Daily* (January 30, 1927: 6) was much more certain about the film's prospects: "Samuel Goldwyn is the sponsor of this very definite box office attraction, another of those passionate love affairs that are making a reputation for Colman and Banky as the screen's greatest pair of lovers. 'The Night of Love,' though not quite a worthy title, fully implies the type of story and tells the legion of romance lovers the world over that there are thrills galore in store for them in this picture." The film was thus assumed to be attractive to women ("romance lovers") on the basis of the acting team. The *New York Times* (January 25, 1927: 18) concurred with the opinions expressed in the trade papers, finding the plot slight but the actors attractive: "While there is nothing startlingly novel, so far as screen stories are concerned, in having a romance between a handsome gypsy chieftain and a lovely, flaxen-haired Princess, the idea is embellished when these characters are impersonated by Ronald Colman and Vilma Banky."

Following *Flesh and the Devil* and *The Night of Love*, First National released *Camille*, with Norma Talmadge and Gilbert Roland, in April 1927. Although *Variety* thought that there might be some market for the love story, given the trend in romances, it found the film less "vital" than its two predecessors: "In these times when hotsy-totsy film fare is splashed across the screen in unmistakable gestures, Camille's quick and well-nigh emotionless acceptance of the pater's demands [that she abandon Armand] is very apt to leave an audience cold." Nonetheless *Variety* commented, "Opposite Miss Talmadge is Gilbert Roland. Fandom in general is liable to tab these two as a 'cute' screen couple. That being so, it'll be enough." Similarly, *Film Daily* (May 1, 1927: 6) advised exhibitors, "Not the least important of the production's strong points are the long and delightful love sequences. The women will sigh and sigh over these." *Photoplay* called it "supersexy stuff."[30] Interestingly, this reception contrasts with that given the 1921 version of *Camille*, with Nazimova and Valentino (released prior to *The Sheik*). *Variety* (September 16, 1921: 35) discussed the 1921 film entirely in terms of its reworking of the theatrical tradition and Nazimova's performance. Valentino was mentioned only in passing, and there was no suggestion of feminine appeal. The *Film Daily* review of the Nazimova version (September 11, 1921: 2) informed exhibitors that women were typically attracted to the story of *Camille* on the grounds that they liked to cry: "They go to see it amply supplied with extra handkerchiefs." We see, then, that the assessment of both *Camille*'s plot and the nature of its appeal had shifted drastically between 1921 and 1927. *Variety* initially saw it simply as a part of the theatrical canon, and redefined it in 1927 as a romance. *Film Daily*'s explanation of women's interest in the story changed from an emphasis on its lachrymose qualities to its passionate love story.

A complete version of the Talmadge *Camille* is no longer extant. Less than one hour survives of the original ninety-six-minute running time.[31] Footage is missing throughout the film, rendering the continuity choppy and sometimes making it difficult to discern how scenes developed. The influence of *A Woman of Paris* on the 1927 version of *Camille* is apparent in the titles, as well as in the straightforward, sometimes humorous, exposition of Camille's rise to prominence in French society. The ellipsis between the film's opening, which shows Camille as an innocent and humble girl, and scenes of her life after she has been established as a wealthy courtesan derives directly from Chaplin's film. The film's frankness about Camille's status offended the critic for the *New York Times* (April 22, 1827: 19) who complained about a close-up that showed Camille passing Armand the key to her apartment, as well as intertitles that were considered "brazenly up to date and not infrequently colloquial." An example of the latter is a title in which a male onlooker describes Camille's place in Parisian society: "Camille is a climber. She went from the Count—to the Baron—to the Duke. God save the King!" The cinematography, by Oliver Marsh, is experimental for the period. *Variety* commented on the filmmakers' use of close-ups connected by dissolves in the scene in which Armand discovers that Camille has left their country haven to return to Paris. Beautifully lit and highly abstract close-ups are also apparent in the two big love scenes. One occurs after Armand is introduced to Camille, when he finds her alone in her room after a coughing fit obliges her to leave a party. Another follows a quarrel between the couple that leads to their decision to move to the country. These scenes are consonant with the emphasis on romantic leads that was emerging in the period.

By the time of Edmund Goulding's *Love,* an adaptation of *Anna Karenina* which opened in late November 1927, the Gilbert/Garbo team was the focus of all of the trade press commentary (although not the *New York Times,* November 30, 1927: 22, which discussed Garbo apart from Gilbert). *Variety* (December 7, 1927: 18) called them "the biggest box office mixed team this country has yet known. It's comparable to the following certain stock company dual leads have enjoyed, simply magnified by the field." While averring that *Love* was not as good as *Flesh and the Devil, Film Daily* (December 18, 1927: 6) had no doubt of its box office potential: "Garbo and Gilbert make a striking team. The vehicle gives them both opportunity to display their talents and indulge in some hectic love scenes." It is perhaps a mark of Tolstoy's cultural prestige that *Photoplay* was moved to irony:

> *Love* is right. The original title of *Anna Karenina* would have been wrong. It isn't Tolstoi, but it is John Gilbert and Greta Garbo which, after *Flesh and the Devil*, is what the "fans" are crying for. Tolstoi's devastating analysis of the tragedy of illicit love is almost completely made over into the recounting of a love affair between a desirable woman and a desiring man, beautifully presented and magnetically acted. . . . But if you think that the finer side of the book—the romance of Kitty and Kostia Levin—is even hinted at, you are nothing but a silly. The movie has separated the wheat of sex from the chaff of preachment.[32]

Unlike *Flesh and the Devil, Love* was unambiguously associated with women. Referring to the title, *Variety* predicted: " 'Love,' plus Gilbert, plus Garbo is a clarion call to shoppers. Shoppers mean women, and women mean matinees. Big ones. Try and keep the femmes away from this one." *Variety*'s assessment of the audience for *Love* also helps to clarify the film's place within the distribution hierarchy. *Variety* estimated that the film would not sell at two dollars as a road show and approved the studio's decision to open it in the 596 seat Embassy Theater, rather than at the Capitol, the largest of Loew's theaters on Broadway. The Embassy was thought to be the right setting, "about perfect in this house of intimate atmosphere, with no clamor of the mob coming and going. It doesn't start until 3 p.m., no intermission, and they're out by 4:30. Plenty of time for three shows daily on the week-ends. The feature should stay here at least 12 weeks, figuring that 'Flesh and the Devil' would have been good for 20 and without thinking twice about it." Projected without the prologues and intermissions typical of a road-show feature, the Embassy schedule presumably allowed the matinée crowd to get home in time to prepare dinner and the exhibitor to pack in more screenings than road-show presentation allowed. *Love* was clearly regarded as a highly desirable "program feature," a film that showed on Broadway as it would have done in the first- and second-run neighborhood theaters, playing to full houses with a minimum of expense for theater owners.

As is well known, Garbo's fame soon eclipsed that of Gilbert; by the time their next film together, *A Woman of Affairs,* was released in December 1928, all of the trade press reviews refer to what *Film Daily* (January 27, 1928: 4) called Gilbert's "secondary role."[33] Similar films confirmed the trend: by the late 1920s romantic dramas featuring steamy love scenes were consistently described by the trade press as appealing largely to women, and reviewers stressed the role of the female star as much as, if not more than, the male lead. *Variety* (April 3, 1929: 20) wrote of *Wild Orchids*, a 1929 release starring Greta Garbo as a married woman tempted to have an affair with a Javanese prince, played by Nils Asther, "'Wild Orchids' is fundamentally a woman's picture. It's a feminized plot all the way. Sex is the meat and marrow of its drama, the protagonist of its characters." *The Woman Disputed*, released in November 1928, again, like *Camille*, paired Norma Talmadge with Gilbert Roland. Here a prostitute is reformed by two friends, an Austrian officer and a Russian (played by Arnold Kent with a stiff military demeanor much indebted to von Stroheim). She falls in love with the Austrian and incurs the enmity of the Russian. When war is declared the Russian officer gains control of her city and demands that she sleep with him as the price of saving the lives of some prisoners, including a priest who is also an Austrian spy. The film is quite explicit about the heroine's profession in the opening scenes, as it is about the nature of the deal she strikes with the Russian lieutenant. *Variety* (November 14, 1928: 22) wrote, "The story opens and continues with a fallen woman as its major subject. The treatment is such as will practically insure matinee business." *Variety* (January 16, 1929: 14) described *The Rescue*, Herbert Brenon's adaptation of Conrad's novel, as "a story of mighty conflict between passion and honor. Passion, or box office, won." The hero, Tom Lingard (Ronald Colman), attempts to rescue the husband of Edith Travers (Lily Damita), who has been taken prisoner by natives on a Javanese island.[34] The selling point of the film, in *Variety*'s estimation, was the way in which Tom was brought to forget his obligations to Mr. Travers and, more important, to a Javanese prince whom he had pledged to restore to his throne: "She tries to make him forget his rigid resolutions but the boy is merely friendly though his eyes betray feelings which send shivers through every brassiere in the audience. What the woman looks like in these scenes, how her head droops, breast heaving, shoulders moving, and hands wandering, no typewriter can adequately convey." Even the male adventure story, indeed, a plot adapted from one of Mencken's favored authors, was thus transformed under the aegis of the romantic drama into a tale of *amour fou* dominated by an attractive *femme fatale*.

From the first commentary on *The Sheik* in 1921, the feminine appeal of the romantic drama was assumed to rest on the love story, and most frequently on sensationalistic scenarios of rape or seduction. It remains somewhat more difficult to situate the genre in relation to the more general decline in the taste for sentiment. The reviewers in the period identified the

early, relatively innocuous variants such as *Lorna Doone* and *Smilin'*
Through as sentimental and old-fashioned. By contrast, later films such as
Foolish Wives, Lily of the Dust, and *Flesh and the Devil* were held to be
sophisticated, "adult," and on the border of what popular taste would tolerate. It should be emphasized that neither the naïvely sentimental nor the
most sophisticated variants were specifically associated with feminine viewing preferences. The films most consistently associated with feminine
taste—the sheik stories and their derivatives, and most of the Garbo/Gilbert
and Colman/Banky vehicles—were more risqué than the "old-fashioned"
variants but, I would argue, remained out of step with what the trade press
deemed advanced or modern filmmaking. In contrast with the much praised
experimentation with highly economical and reduced modes of narration
initiated by *A Woman of Paris,* the romantic drama was usually considered
languid and slow paced. As already noted, *Variety* had complained about the
cessation of dramatic conflict in *The Night of Love:* "when the love theme
creeps in, there it is." *Film Daily* (April 19, 1925: 5) wrote similarly of *His
Supreme Moment:* "This almost seems like a story without an end so long
does it take the heroine to finally make up her mind that she really loves
hero . . . a love conflict holding forth with little action." In addition to its
slow pace, the romantic drama was at odds with other tendencies discussed
in relation to sophisticated comedy and the male adventure story: their
preference for downplaying or undercutting dramatic climaxes, and their
evocation of the vernacular at the level of gesture and the diction of intertitles. Emotional love scenes were one of the romantic drama's best selling
points. In addition, the historical or exoticized settings of the costume picture almost necessitated an attempt to evoke high-flown manners and
archaic or self-consciously "foreign" modes of speech. Both the attempt to
build up "big" love scenes, and the nature of the settings and characters
depicted contributed to a distinctively elevated performance style. The
romantic drama required elegant and attractive stars and attitudes to show
them off to the greatest advantage. It provided star acting turns for Rudolph
Valentino (although some reviewers thought he could not carry them off),
John Barrymore ("a combination of every ham hero the screen has held"),
and Greta Garbo (commended by *Exceptional Photoplays* for her frail
physique and fragile, ethereal air). Thus, despite its risqué subject matter,
the plots, the mode of narration, and the use of actors characteristic of the
genre were at odds with "antisentimental" trends. The dissatisfaction with
many of these dramas voiced in the trade press, and especially in *Variety,* is
an indication of the extent to which they came into conflict with newly
emerging tastes and criteria of judgment. A further indication of the disdain

for the romance may be seen in the films that sought to distort or deflate it, or to take it in new directions.

Deflations of the romantic drama did not appear until the type was well established: the earliest I have discovered is Vidor's *Proud Flesh*, released in April 1925. The film appeared after the most important Valentino vehicles, *The Sheik, Blood and Sand,* and *Monsieur Beaucaire.* It also followed Vidor's own essay into the form, *His Hour*, adapted from the novel of the same name by Elinor Glyn and one of the first romantic dramas to star John Gilbert.[35] It is worth noting the similarity of *His Hour* to the kind of stories in which Valentino was typically featured. *Variety* (October 8, 1924: 27) describes the plot:

> In the latest tome of gushing, passionate screen writing Elinor has worked a gentle-born Englishwoman against a stubborn and half-barbarian Russian prince. The prince wants the woman. The woman doesn't want the prince. He is persistent. In St. Petersburg he tricks her to his home. She faints. Upon awakening she finds her waist torn open (the prince had done that to see whether her heart was beating and also because it furnished the dirt punch of the film) and the woman assumed immediately that she had been violated. Thereupon she married the prince, only to find out later that he loved her and that when "his hour" arrived he had let it slide.

Variety particularly disliked this film but thought it would make money on the strength of its sensational subject matter in those regions where it was not too heavily censored. *Film Daily* (September 14, 1924: 4) concurred with the critical assessment: "King Vidor, capable of fine things, has allowed his better judgment to be influenced toward other directions . . . he's made a sexy, weak picture that will probably thrill great crowds and cheer many box offices but it is no artistic achievement."

It is tempting to see *Proud Flesh* as Vidor's reaction to the critical commentary on his previous work; it was certainly seen as a comic inversion of the type. *Variety* (April 15, 1925: 35) wrote that the film had "Harrison Ford satirically playing the Valentino type of screen lover" and *Film Daily* (April 19, 1925: 5) that, having paired Eleanor Boardman and Pat O'Malley, Vidor had "proceeded to surround them with humorous incident instead of straight, serious romance, which was a bit of very good judgment." Fernanda Borel (Eleanor Boardman) was born in San Francisco but reared in Spain, where she is courted by Don Jaime (Harrison Ford).[36] In an attempt to make her blasé lover jealous she leaves to visit relatives in San Francisco. In California a rivalry develops between Don Jaime, who surprises Fernanda by following her to the United States, and Pat O'Malley (Patrick O'Malley), a plumbing contractor who is a friend of her uncle. Fernanda finds Pat inappropriate as a romantic partner. At one point she tells him, "Mr. O'Malley, we have no plumbers in Spain. I should not be amused to receive attentions from one here." She is attracted to him, however, and one afternoon she is carried away and promises to marry him. Later she writes to break off the engagement, but Pat, angry at her snobbishness, takes her away to his hunting lodge. Don Jaime follows and brings her back home to her relatives. But Fernanda reverses herself once again and decides to marry the plumber after all, while Don Jaime comforts himself with one of many new women friends.

Both *Variety* and the *New York Times* (April 14, 1925: 26) described in some detail the sequence early in the film in which Don Jaime courts Fernanda. A title informs us that the Don "had worked out a leisurely system for taking care of his balcony trade." He arrives in a horse-drawn carriage, with servants running behind. After the carriage draws up he looks at himself in a mirror and brushes the cigar ash from his clothes. His men sing, and one plays the guitar while the Don sits in his carriage leaning on his cane. When Fernanda appears on the balcony he gets out of the carriage and throws his hat to the first singer, to his right. That hat is passed down the line of singers until it gets to a fat assistant at the end of the line, who carefully places it on a vine. Receiving Fernanda's permission to kiss her hand, he blows a whistle, and his men make a pyramid for him to climb up. To get high enough to kiss her hand properly, he needs to step from his men's shoulders to their heads. Shots of him speaking romantic lines such as "Just to be near you, fair Fernanda . . . is Paradise" are intercut with shots of his boots on the heads of the men beneath him. After telling Fernanda that she has "the most charming balcony in Barcelona," he kisses her hand multiple times and, blowing his whistle to alert his acrobatic crew, descends. His hat is returned to him once he reaches the ground, and he tips it to the lady as his carriage departs. His men run after it, many doing cartwheels as they go.

Several aspects of the great lover type are satirized here. His narcissism is indicated by his use of a mirror and care for his hat, a joke that is repeated later in the film when Pat abducts Fernanda from her uncle's house while Don Jaime remains oblivious upstairs in his room, carefully combing his hair, looking at his nails, and studying his appearance in the mirror. The idea of the grand passion is undermined by the elaborate and public nature of the courtship ritual, the clear sense of a practiced routine (Don Jaime working the balcony trade), and the laziness of the supposedly passionate aristocrat whose courtship occurs on the backs of his servants.

After the action moves to San Francisco the film makes much of the contrast between the aristocrat and the plumbing contractor. In an early scene Pat confronts Fernanda with her snobbishness: "You liked me well enough till you found out I was a plumber . . . and then you laughed at me!" He produces the predictable democratic rhetoric: "What did Washington fight for . . . and Lincoln, and Roosevelt, and Wilson? To make us *all* free and equal! That's why!" But this position is rather unexpectedly undercut when Don Jaime, who has overheard the tirade, applauds his rival and shakes his hand. He then invites O'Malley to stay for tea, also insisting that Rosita and Wong, servants in the home of Fernanda's relatives, be seated at the table. He wryly comments, "Now we are free and equal . . . and uncomfortable." The incident demonstrates that the Americans are not without their own class divisions. Indeed, the narrative is at pains to point out that O'Malley is not really a plumber but a plumbing contractor and a friend of her rich uncle Gus, who describes him as "the finest man in San Francisco. He's a K.C. . . . K.P. . . . B.P.O.E. . . . I.O.O.F. . . . W.O.W. . . . and O.K. . . . ." The difference between the rivals is not a matter of rich versus poor, but rather one of "class" in the sense of style or demeanor. Pat could pass for a plumber, and has been one, while Don Jaime comes from Spain, the land of romance, where "there are no plumbers." The contrast is evident in their respective manners of wooing. Pat is as sincere, vigorous, and direct as Don Jaime was pretentious and languid.

The contrast between Don Jaime and Pat, between European and American virtues, is perhaps somewhat less predictably summed up in the motif of the bathtub. This utilitarian and slightly ridiculous object (these are not DeMille's bathtubs) is consistently associated with America and with Fernanda's American boyfriend. In the opening of *Proud Flesh* a narrative title describes the heroine: "To the servants, Fernanda was insane. She wasted a tubful of water every day, just for bathing." We see her servants carry in a tub of water for her bath. When Fernanda threatens Don Jaime with her departure for America, she explains that she is going to visit her uncle who has "a house with seventeen bathtubs on a hill." This becomes a joke for Don Jaime, who first tells his servant to find out "the address of that hill with fifty-seven bathtubs" and later tells Fernanda that he came to America to "get acquainted with your uncle's eighty-seven bathtubs." Aware of the danger his rival poses, Don Jaime proposes a toast to O'Malley, "the amateur lover . . . the builder of ten thousand bathtubs!" To which Fernanda responds with a toast to her Spanish lover, "the climber of ten thousand balconies."

It may not have been very daring to make a film in which a rough-and-ready American beat out a Spanish aristocrat, but it was riskier, in my view, to associate the American with a motif so devoid of romance. This risk was exacerbated by the casting decision that put a handsome and well-known star, Harrison Ford, in the place of the Spaniard and a character actor, using his own name, Pat O'Malley, in the place of the American. O'Malley was by no means a star, a point brought home by the fact that his performance gained scant mention in the trade press.[37] For example, *Variety* praised the acting of Boardman and Ford extensively, but described O'Malley only as "very much in the spirit of the thing to nicely balance the triangle of the three featured players." Vidor's casting decisions here seem to me consistent with the aim of constructing the character of Don Jaime as a great lover type, a part associated with a charismatic male star within the romantic drama, and, in opposition to this, making the hero a character who evokes the American vernacular. Given that aim, it is logical that a Hollywood star should play the Spanish Don Juan and an unknown Irish mug play the Bathtub King.

Monta Bell's film *Ibañez' Torrent* appeared in February 1926, just a little less than a year after *Proud Flesh*. Unlike that film, *Ibañez' Torrent* was not a straightforward comedy, although it contained some comic elements. It was adapted from the novel *Entre Naranjos* by Vicente Blasco-Ibáñez, whose work had also provided the source for two historical war films by Rex Ingram, *The Four Horsemen of the Apocalypse* and *Mare Nostrum*, and two more straightforward romantic dramas, *Blood and Sand* and Alan Crosland's *The Enemies of Women;* another romantic drama drawn from Ibáñez, *The Temptress*, appeared in October 1926. Ibáñez's name figured prominently in the promotion of the film. Although the *AFI Catalog* lists the film simply as *The Torrent*, the name of the author is part of the title as it appears on the screen, a point stressed in the *New York Times* review (February 22, 1926: 14). *Ibáñez' Torrent* was also Greta Garbo's American debut, followed a few months later by her appearance in *The Temptress* (directed by Fred Niblo, taking over from Mauritz Stiller); both of these films helped to establish the Garbo persona solidified in *Flesh and the Devil*, her third American film, released in December 1926. Thus both the source and the star of *Ibáñez' Torrent* would seem to place it firmly within the tradition of the romantic drama. Indeed, it is not the least of Monta Bell's accomplishments that he managed to construct a diva role for Garbo while exploiting the more cynical components of the Blasco-Ibáñez novel to puncture the conventions of the romantic drama as a whole. He does this by juxtaposing the love affair with the bourgeois aspirations of the hero and, even more important, of the hero's mother.

The opening title hearkens back to the Latin American setting of the opening of *The Four Horseman of the Apocalypse* and the Spanish setting of *Blood and Sand:* "Spain—Springtime under the blue skies of Valencia—cobbled streets and hanging balconies—hot sunlight and orange blossoms—soft air drenched with sweetness." Leonora Moreno (Garbo), the daughter of a cash-poor farmer and his wife, possesses a beautiful singing voice. She is in love with Rafael Brull (Ricardo Cortez), whose mother, Doña Bernarda Brull (Martha Mattox), owns and manages much of the surrounding countryside in tandem with her lawyer, Don Andrès (Tully Marshall). Doña Bernarda forecloses on the Moreno farm but allows Doña Moreno, Leonora's aging mother, to remain in the house as scrubwoman. Unaware of his mother's actions, Rafael meets Leonora at the back of the garden, accepts her token of a spray of orange blossoms, and promises to marry her when he can obtain his mother's consent.

Now without a home, Leonora's father proposes to take his daughter to Paris to pursue her singing career. She sends a message to Rafael informing him of her impending departure and imploring him to remember his vow to marry her. Rafael's receipt of the letter provokes a quarrel with his mother that reveals that Doña Bernarda has foreclosed on the Moreno farm in order to break off the romance between Leonora and her son, fearing that such a disadvantageous match would interfere with her plans to have him elected deputy. She nags and taxes her son with lack of respect for all that she has sacrificed for him, and he reluctantly accedes to her wishes.

When Rafael does not arrive, Leonora says goodbye to her mother. An ellipsis follows, similar to the one in *A Woman of Paris.* Leonora is shown in Paris as the opera star La Brunna, singing a duet on stage with the tenor Salvatti. A woman in the audience comments to her male companion, "They say that after her father died, Salvatti trained her voice for nothing." The man replies, "Tenors never do anything for nothing." Later the denizens of a café regard her and remark on the number of affairs she has had.

In the village Rafael has been running for deputy and courting Remedios (Gertrude Olmsted), his mother's choice of a bride. Leonora arrives, accompanied by a retinue that includes pets, servants, and many trunks, and she overwhelms her mother with gifts. She is visiting her old singing master, Cupido, when a parade celebrating Rafael's election passes by. The new deputy stops to make a speech, and she joins the crowd, laughing when he promises to conduct himself honorably.

Seeking to capitalize upon her son's success, Doña Brull dines with Remedios's father (Mack Swain), the "pork king," and demands that an extra hundred head of hogs be added to the girl's dowry. As they negotiate, he asserts the virtues of his hogs by picking up a roasted suckling pig that sits on the table before him and demonstrating its fine points, including its curly tail.

Rafael returns to Cupido's in search of Leonora. He is initially condescending, saying that Leonora "did not look prosperous" and asking Cupido whether she knows that he was elected deputy. Leonora appears singing an aria from *Carmen* and reveals herself to be La Brunna. Then, having punctured his self-importance, she mocks him and throws away the dried spray of orange blossoms that she finds in his pocket. She is even more scornful when he approaches her on the following day, whereupon he flees to Remedios, begging her to marry him as soon as possible. As they kiss it begins to rain, and a narrative title follows: "Then a torrent—as furious and relentless as the passion that surged in the hearts of the lovers."

The town streets are flooded as the river overflows its banks. Informed that the dam is leaking, posing a potential threat to the Morenos' farmhouse, Rafael and Cupido embark upon a rescue effort. They are making their way down river in a rowboat when the dam bursts, the boat is swamped, and they must swim for their lives. Wet and muddy, they burst into the farmhouse to find Leonora calmly reading in bed. She makes light of the storm, saying that the farmhouse has stood for a hundred years. She gives Cupido and Rafael dry clothes that make both men look ludicrous: Cupido in a fur-trimmed dressing gown and Rafael in a voluminous fur-trimmed coat. Talking alone with Rafael, Leonora thanks him for his effort to protect her but continues to tease him, asking if his mother knows that he has come to her and showing off the jewels given to her by former lovers. He castigates her for being a loose woman and flees from her presence once again.

Escaping from the party thrown to celebrate his betrothal to Remedios and the sight of his future father-in-law consuming vast quantities of food, Rafael goes to the Morenos' farm. A narrative title evokes the romantic setting: "Twilight and memories—the overpowering scent of orange-blossoms. An irresistible force drew him to the old garden." There he is joined by Leonora, who abruptly reverses herself, declares her love, and receives his embraces.

The next day Doña Bernarda visits Doña Moreno and informs her that her family has been disgraced. She tells the old woman about Leonora's affair with Rafael and reveals the source of her daughter's wealth. Shocked, Leonora's pious mother orders her daughter to leave the farm.

Leonora departs for Madrid, where many men, including a prince, pay her homage. Just as she is about to leave on a tour of America, Rafael arrives, insisting that they must find a way to be together. Delighted, she sends him out to buy orange blossoms so that she can feel "like a bride." After he leaves she asks the prince who has been paying court to her to further Rafael's career. Meanwhile Don Andrès catches Rafael in the act of buying the flowers. He cautions that they will be for Rafael's mother's grave if he continues with his plan and predicts that La Brunna, a woman whose affairs are the talk of all Madrid, will "drag him down." Rafael finally agrees to return to the village and sends a note of apology to his beloved.

Many years later La Brunna, still in partnership with Salvatti, is singing *Carmen* in Madrid. Rafael sends a gift of orange blossoms that please her greatly, but she is shocked when he enters her dressing room. He has gained weight, his shoulders are rounded, his hair has grayed, and he wears wire-rimmed spectacles. Learning that he has married the bride his mother selected and has many children, she spurns him. She goes onstage to sing the last act and accepts the applause of the crowd, including that of the prince seen earlier. Rafael goes home, where his wife shows him their sleeping children and settles him comfortably by the fire. Leonora then appears outside the opera house wearing a coat that, even by the standards of this film, is luxuriously trimmed in fur.[38] She gets into a cab, alone. A woman in the crowd says, "She must be happy. She has everything she wants."

The film undermines the idea of romantic love in many ways, two of which provoked criticism in the trade press at the time of the film's release. *Film Daily* (March 7, 1926: 9) praised Monta Bell's direction but complained about the resolution of the plot: "Its direct appeal to the public in general, however, is hardly universal. They still want the heroine to marry the hero and the disillusion brought about by the complete change in the hero, for the worst, will probably not be to their liking." *Variety* (February 24, 1926: 42) was somewhat less critical. Much of the short review was devoted to congratulating Louis Mayer on the discovery of Greta Garbo. The review refers to the closing scenes more neutrally than did *Film Daily*, in the context of a discussion of the male star: "Ricardo Cortez, in the earlier scenes, looks as handsome as ever, but also shows that he has possibilities as a character man in the closing action." However, *Variety* also judged that: "while 'Torrent' is well played and capably directed there is nothing about the picture that is going to make the public crazy about it." The two trade papers agreed that the film was unlikely to do well at the box office, and the *Film Daily* reviewer explicitly tied its lack of appeal to the fact that the love story fizzled out in disillusionment.

Second, the reviewers found fault with the handling of the storm. *Variety* noted that "it is evident that the great scene of the rush of waters was counted on to carry the picture, but at this late date a bursting dam doesn't mean anything in a picture except as an incident." The *New York Times* objected to the title that introduced the storm: "Quite a number of the sub-titles are a trifle too verbose, especially one concerned with the torrent, which is alluded to as 'a torrent as furious and relentless as the passion in the hearts of the lovers.'" It also criticized the staging of the storm itself: "It is singularly well done, but part of the action that goes on in Leonora's abode in the small Spanish town causes one to think that the breaking of the dam and the deluge of water have been grossly exaggerated by the camera. At any rate all is soon serene." In my opinion, stressing the danger posed by the torrent very deliberately builds up to the anticlimax that shows Leonora in no need of rescue. This undercutting of Rafael's heroism is capped by the absurd picture he makes trying to romance the heroine while dressed in her clothes. The storm scenes also form part of the larger narrative pattern in which Rafael fails to live up to his avowed passion. The unnecessary "rescue" of Leonora is both preceded and followed by an episode in which she really does need him and he does not come: first when she is about to leave the village for Paris and then later when she is about to leave Madrid for America.

In *Ibañez' Torrent* the formation of the couple is not blocked, as it is in Barrymore's *Don Juan*, through the intervention of a scheming villainess on the order of Lucrezia Borgia, but, much more prosaically and perhaps also more disturbingly, through a manipulative mother allied with a tricky lawyer. The nature of their demands on Don Rafael is indicated by their conversational clichés: he is repeatedly warned that his career will suffer (although, in the sequence in Madrid, the intercutting makes it clear that Leonora would, in fact, be able to further his career), and he is threatened with hastening the death of his mother. Although Doña Bernarda rises to real villainy, especially in the brilliant scene in which she turns Doña Moreno's piety against her daughter, she most frequently asserts the ordinary claims of career, family, and middle-class respectability over and against the promise of the orange-blossom-scented garden. The virtues for which she stands are consistently burlesqued throughout the film, especially in the form of Mack Swain's pork king, but they attain an ominous resonance in the film's final scenes. When the dispirited Rafael returns home and is led to view his cherubic sleeping children, they rest beneath a large portrait of his mother, now dead but finally triumphant.

Unlike *Proud Flesh,* which was welcomed by the trade press for its comic inversions of the romantic drama, *Ibañez' Torrent* was rather coolly received. Reviewers in the 1920s saw the ridiculing of heroic postures and use of anticlimax as failed realizations of genre conventions. In my view, however, these elements were far from inadvertent. The film evokes sun-drenched Spain, proposes an attractive hero and heroine, and promises a certain idea of passion only to dash that promise on the rocks of filial piety and bourgeois avarice.

Loves of Carmen, released in September 1927, departed more markedly from genre conventions than either *Proud Flesh* or *Ibañez' Torrent* and can only marginally be considered a romantic drama, despite its source. But it provides a good indication of what *Variety* (September 28, 1927: 25) considered preferable to the usual run of the genre: "Plenty of hell, sex and box office in this latest film biography of a well known Spanish damsel. The male population is going to eat it up, the censors in a couple of the states are going to find something to do, and meanwhile it's going to make dough besides increasing the prestige for Winnie Sheehan's idea of a pulsating maiden." Directed by Raoul Walsh, *Loves of Carmen* paired Victor McLaglen and Dolores Del Rio, fresh from the success of *What Price Glory. Variety* commented that McLaglen was "so reminiscent at times that you can still see his 'Glory' uniform draped on him," and the *New York Times* (September 27, 1927: 31) similarly noted the actors' previous work with Walsh.

In contrast with the opera and earlier American film versions (Cecil B. DeMille had directed one in 1915 with the diva Geraldine Ferrar, Walsh another in the same year with Theda Bara), *Loves of Carmen* substantially increased the role of the toreador Escamillo, played by McLaglen. In the opera Escamillo does not appear until he enters the tavern in act 2, where he first lays eyes on Carmen and sings his one substantial aria ("Votre toast, je peux vous le rendre"). In act 3 at the gypsy camp, which is largely devoted to Don José's jealous bickering with Carmen, Escamillo appears in search of her, fights with her lover, and exits, inviting all to watch him at the bullfight. Act 4, which begins after Carmen has taken up with Escamillo, shows the couple only briefly in the procession that leads to the ring. They declare their mutual love and part, Escamillo to kill the bull offstage, Carmen to meet her death at the hands of Don José. In Walsh's 1927 film Escamillo appears in the opening scenes in the town square; in addition, prior to the action that constitutes the opera's final act, a sequence shows Carmen's pursuit of the bullfighter.

The film differs from other adaptations of *Carmen,* and from most instances of the romantic drama, in its insistence on the crude demeanor of the principal characters and in its introduction of low comedy. The *New York Times* reviewer disapproved: "Mr. McLaglen as Escamillo is a Toreador who guzzles wine and eats like a hog. . . . Mr. McLaglen is splendid as the Toreador, but it does seem that his manners might have been toned down a trifle, for the sight of a man talking with his mouth full of bread is not necessarily humorous." *Variety*, however, approved: "And with all the emphasis on the sex thing, still a light vein runs through prominently enough to make it almost seem as if cast and director were well nigh winking at the original script. Which makes it appear all in good fun." *Film Daily* (October 2, 1927: 6) seems to have agreed with *Variety*, dubbing the film, which it considered "excellent entertainment," a "comedy drama."

Near the film's opening, Escamillo, escorted by an attendant, arrives in town. The attendant tells him that all of the women are interested in him. This is borne out by the droves of upper-class women from the town and lower-class women from the nearby cigar factory who gather in the central piazza trying to attract his attention. He turns away, indicating his lack of interest, and sits at an outdoor café demanding drink. When a little boy and his small donkey get stuck in a pool of mud in the square, Escamillo carries them out of it. The gypsy Carmen too demands his help to get through the mud. He picks her up, slinging her over his shoulder like a sack of potatoes. When she flirtatiously asks whether he would like to carry her often, Escamillo unceremoniously dumps her in the mud. She rubs her bottom and curses him rudely.

Later Escamillo decides to take a bath in the public fountain. When he takes his shirt off, upper-class women appear on a balcony to watch him, and the factory girls go outside for the same purpose. When he gets to his pants all of the women retreat inside (we see their reactions, not his actions). The only two left watching are Carmen and the forewoman from the factory, who tries to block Carmen's view.

Carmen and her gypsy compatriots are as crude as the bullfighter. When Carmen and Emilia depart for work, for example, the women who live next door berate and insult them. In return, the gypsies pelt them with food taken from a neighborhood peddler. The fight inside the cigar factory that provokes Carmen's arrest is both sexy and played for laughs. As they fight, the women make their way into the bathroom. Don José and two soldiers, who have been summoned to restore order, are reluctant to enter this female preserve. The forewoman goes in, tries to separate them, and comes out defeated, with her hair in disarray. The other woman runs out bloodied and hides behind the soldiers. Carmen appears, her hair down and her blouse torn. She is ready to fight further, until the soldiers restrain her.

The sequence in which Carmen succeeds in seducing Escamillo is played entirely in the same rough-and-ready comic tone (this is obviously the scene that offended the *New York Times* reviewer). Having selected bulls for the fight, Escamillo orders his coachman to take him to an inn famous for its food and drink. Despite Escamillo's efforts to get rid of her, Carmen manages to hitch a ride outside his carriage. While he orders a large meal at the inn, Carmen enters the kitchen posing as his maid. She urges the innkeeper to give him much wine and spices the bird he is being served with hot pepper. Escamillo is not pleased to see her when she brings him the food, but he quickly settles down to eat. He ignores the knife she hands him and rips a leg off the bird. As he chows it down, the hot pepper heats him up. She fans him, an attention he accepts because of his heated condition. She keeps filling his wine glass. Directing the musicians at the inn to play, she begins to dance on the table in front of Escamillo, bare-footed and bare-legged. He reaches for her, but she eludes him. She runs outside, where he chases her through a field and around a haystack. When he catches her, he carries her out of our view. When the innkeeper follows, presumably looking for his money, Escamillo appears from behind the haystack, pulling up his pants, and orders him away.

The only character who escapes the low comic treatment is Don José (Don Alvarado). Unlike Escamillo, he is from the first passionately in love with Carmen and chivalrous in his treatment of her, bringing her flowers and tenderly binding her wounds in jail. But in the context of the film he appears as a wimp. When he complains to Emilia that Carmen does not take his declarations of love seriously, she tells him that Carmen needs a man who can tame her. He remains a secondary character in this version, easily manipulated by the gypsy until the final moment of his desperate revenge. By departing from the plot's usual focalization on Don José, Raoul Walsh turned a romantic tale of a man who sacrificed all for passion into quite another story. The *Loves of Carmen* is reminiscent of *What Price Glory* in its carnal and humorous depiction of sex, as well as in the resolutely uncouth demeanor of its leading couple. Perhaps this may account for *Variety*'s assumption that the film would appeal to men. Not only was the display of Dolores Del Rio's legs insistent and impressive but also the film was entirely at odds with the elevated treatment of love found in the most influential romantic dramas such as the Barrymore or the Gilbert and Garbo vehicles.

Like Vidor, Bell, and Walsh, Frank Borzage must be counted among the important auteurs who manipulated the conventions of the romantic drama during the 1920s. He differs from the others in that, far from seeking to undercut or debase the romance plot, he created what is surely the most exalted variant of it in *7th Heaven*. And his efforts were greeted with great acclaim at the time. It is necessary to explain this apparent anomaly within the matrix of 1920s plot formulae and within the paradigms of contemporary taste. A reading of Austin Strong's play *7th Heaven,* in which the religious themes are developed in a rather didactic vein, might lead one to expect that Borzage's adaptation would have been given the kind of reception accorded the adaptation of Channing Pollock's equally popular and religiose play *The Fool,* which *Variety* (see chapter 3) had estimated would only do well outside of metropolitan districts.[39] Moreover, the plot of *7th Heaven,* which deals with the mutual redemption of a prostitute and an atheist, can be considered an even more old-fashioned variant of the seduction plot than Borzage's *Back Pay,* which *Variety* in 1922 characterized as "the old-oaken bucket story." Yet *7th Heaven* received the highest kudos in the trade press. *Variety* (May 11, 1927: 14) wrote, "It is a great big romantic, gripping and red-blooded story told in a straight to the shoulder way and when the last foot of some 11,000 or so feet is unwound, if there is a dry eyelash on either man, woman or child, they just have no red blood. This Frank Borzage production is an out-and-out hit and one on the $2 order." *Film Daily* (May 29, 1927: 6) concurred, "There are so many things to be said in favor of and in praise of 'Seventh Heaven' that in limited space it would be impossible to do everyone justice. . . . The story blends romance, pathos, humor of a delightful order, all in a very smooth fashion. It reaches great dramatic heights, it sinks to sorrowful depths but in the end joy is triumphant and happiness reigns. It embodies a beautiful love story." It was, then, a romantic drama not just for women but for "man, woman and child"; a "beautiful love story" but "red-blooded." Even the way in which it was praised suggests that *7th Heaven* did not fit readily into the categories current in the critical discourse of the period.

Given Borzage's present-day reputation as an arch-romanticist, it is important to stress the quasi-naturalist elements in his oeuvre, elements that long predated *7th Heaven* and formed an important context for the reception of that film. His first big hit, *Humoresque,* released in September 1920, dealt with poor Jewish immigrants in New York City and depended upon dialect and the exploration of "low" working-class gestures and demeanor. Hervé Dumont has pointed to the use of Yiddish words such as *nebich* and *ganef* in the titles.[40] The mangled English of the immigrants includes, for example, a complaint made by Leon's father, "A four dollar feedle he wants! So, we shall have another feedler in the family for some thirty-cent lessons out of my pants while I sleep!" In addition, at the time of the film's release *Variety* (June 4, 1920: 27) praised the acting of Vera Gordon, a veteran of the Yiddish theater, for her performance as a Jewish mother defending her son's ambition to become a musician: "For the most part she is the picture. She lends a warmth, a pathos, a natural humanity to those early well shot, excellently conceived and competently directed scenes in the Ghetto." According to *Variety,* Alma Rubens, who played Leon's love interest and was therefore the "featured" female lead, threatened to leave the production when she realized that all the acting honors would accrue to Vera Gordon (Rubens played Gina Ginsberg, a childhood friend from the ghetto whom Leon meets again later in life after her father has made his fortune; in the film she thus appeared elegantly dressed and coiffed and more in the mold of a Hollywood star).

Following the release of *Humoresque,* Borzage seems to have committed himself to the production of films about ordinary people and everyday life. In an interview in *Motion Picture Classic* headlined "The Photoplay of the Proletariat," he is quoted as saying, "I intend to do stories of the people. . . . I know the folk who go to motion pictures are interested most of all in the problems, the joys and the sorrows of their own daily life, and I hope to bring to the films a reflection of all this. Of one thing I am sure—the photoplay has been too far from the realities of life. Screen people haven't breathed with life. Their film experiences have been false and artificial adventures."[41] Two years later, speaking with Peter Milne, he noted, "But just stop and see where the plain, average character when elevated to the position of importance in a film or a play, has captured the hearts of thousands, millions. I refer to the plays *Lightnin'* and *The First Year* and to *Humoresque,* the picture. Here were plain, everyday people, just like all of us and just because they were so like all of us we like them better than we like swashbuckling heroes in modern adventure pictures and entirely too wide-eyed and pretty heroines in pictures supposed to be representing life."[42]

Many of Borzage's subsequent film projects reflect the aims he expressed in interviews in the early 1920s. During his tenure at Cosmopolitan he made, in addition to *Humoresque* and *Back Pay,* two more films derived from stories by Fannie Hurst. *The Good Provider,* released in April 1922, reprised *Humoresque* in its concern with a Jewish immigrant family; this time, though, the plot was focalized on the character of the father. *The Nth Commandment,* released in March 1923, dealt with the trials and tribulations of a young married couple of modest means. When Borzage moved to Fox in 1925 he was able to engineer a deal with the theatrical producer John Golden, whereby the studio acquired the rights to the plays mentioned in Borzage's 1922 interview: *Lightnin'* (the adaptation was directed by John Ford and released in 1925) and *The First Year* (the adaptation was directed by Borzage and released in 1926).[43] *The First Year,* taken from a play by Frank Craven, is much more consistently comedic than *The Nth Com-*

mandment, but the films resemble one another in their concern with the everyday domestic squabbles and financial difficulties experienced by a young couple.

Fox acquired the rights to *7th Heaven* along with those to Golden's other theatrical productions. The play shared the comedic tone and emphasis on homely virtues characteristic of these other works. The *New York Times* (October 31, 1922: 20) wrote of the original play, "Nothing is more admirable in this phantasy than the humor and sympathy with which it catches the naïve intimacy and familiarity which simple folk in France bestow upon their Creator." Clearly the play matched Borzage's own interest in "proletarian drama."

Several factors contributed to the reception accorded Borzage's *7th Heaven.* Made after Murnau's *Sunrise* but released prior to it, the film benefited from the experimentation with camerawork and set design that Murnau's presence on the Fox lot inspired.[44] Ernest Palmer's camerawork when the couple ascends the stairs to Chico's flat was specifically mentioned both in the *Variety* review and in the *New York Times* (May 26, 1927: 22), and the filmmakers were praised more generally for their level of technical accomplishment. In addition to Murnau's influence, it is important to recognize Borzage's debt to *What Price Glory* and, even more important, *The Big Parade. Variety* noted this in the first paragraph of its review: "Abundance of war pictures that have hit the clear and been placed in the road show or $2 class. With anything now coming along with a tinge of war in it, there is a bit of skepticism as to its success. However, no fear in any direction as to the success of 'Seventh Heaven.' . . . It is going to click as big if not bigger than any of its predecessors. Though 'The Big Parade' got a big start on it, there is no reason why this one will not turn in the shekels just as fast and as consistent as the M-G-M product." Yet, as *Variety* noted, the War was not prominently featured in *7th Heaven:* "There were not more than 2,500 feet of actual warfare in the film. Balance of the story is romance." I would argue that what Borzage took from the example of *The Big Parade* was not so much its treatment of World War I as the handling of the romance plot, in particular the introduction of "low" comedic elements and the emphasis on everyday speech and gesture.

The film famously begins in the sewers of Paris, where Chico (Charles Farrell) is working in tandem with Sewer Rat. They look up a manhole at the light. Gobin, the street cleaner, tosses dirty water down into the sewer, inadvertently soaking them. We discover that Chico has aspirations to become a street cleaner himself and to wield a hose in the sunshine. He is confident of achieving his goals, telling Sewer Rat that he is "a very remarkable fellow." Chico's cheerful self-regard is contrasted with the situation of the brow-beaten Diane (Janet Gaynor). Abused by her older sister Nana, Diane is forced to sell stolen goods to sustain Nana's addiction to absinthe. Further humiliation follows when a long-lost aunt and uncle materialize and Diane's conscience leads her to confess to her uncle that she and her sister are "bad," that is, streetwalkers.

Chico rescues Diane from her situation in an offhand and casual way. The initial scenes between them are marked as much by his contempt for her weakness and her profession as by his unthinking chivalry. In a rage at Diane's having confessed to their relatives, Nana pursues her into the street and proceeds to choke her as she lies prostrate in front of a manhole cover. Chico emerges from below ground, manhandles the older girl, and frightens her away. He then joins his friends, Sewer Rat and Papa Boul, a taxicab driver, for an impromptu curbside lunch. Annoyed by the sight of the senseless Diane, Chico commands Sewer Rat, "Give me that violet" and proceeds to waft half an onion beneath her nose to revive her. Later, when he walks off, Diane attempts suicide, and he roughly intervenes, "With MY knife! I like that!" But he inadvertently confesses to feeling sorry for her. Finally Nana, under arrest for solicitation, maliciously identifies her sister as a prostitute to the police. Chico again intercedes and prevents Diane's arrest by claiming her as his wife. He is immediately dismayed to find that the police intend to check on his story; he takes Diane home with him to pose as his wife only until they do so.

Interpolated within the events leading to Diane's "rescue" is a frequently discussed scene between Chico and his friends in which he voices doubts about the existence of God (Diane is there but remains silent, leaning against the wheel of Papa Boul's taxicab). He has paid to light candles and prayed twice: once asking to be made a street sweeper and once asking for a pretty blonde wife. God did not come through, and, if He exists, He owes Chico 10 francs. Overhearing this conversation, Père Chevillon genially remonstrates by unexpectedly producing the coveted promotion. It is important to see that Chico's much vaunted atheism in this scene is linked with a number of other character traits with important consequences for the romance plot: above all his almost Nietzschean celebration of strength and disdain for weakness, and his narcissism, summed up in his trademark phrase "I am a remarkable fellow!" He may have prayed for a wife, but love is the last thing on his mind. Moreover, Chico's language and gesture—the informal curbside lunch, the use of the "violet," the concern to retrieve his knife at the moment of the suicide—stand in sharp contrast to the demeanor usually ascribed to a romantic lead.

Chico's posture is brilliantly reversed, of course, in the scenes in his seventh-floor flat. The quotidian space is itself endowed with special qualities: by the famous camera movement that follows the couple up the stairs; by the painted views of Paris rooftops seen outside his window; by the charming bridge, two planks stretched high above the street, that connects Chico's apartment to that of the street sweeper Gobin in the building across the way; and, most explicitly, by Chico's bragging, "I work in the sewer—but I live near the stars!" At first he keeps his distance from Diane. Much to her relief, he does not attempt to sleep with her. The next morning, gobbling down the breakfast she has prepared for him, he complains, "Women are all alike—they try to reach a man through his stomach—" and he warns her, "After the police come, you go!" On the day the police detective arrives, Chico is busy admiring himself in a hand mirror while Diane gives him a haircut. He prevents her from leaving but remains noncommittal: "If you want to stay—you're not in my way," but he seems more absorbed in the cut of his hair than the invitation he has just extended. The marriage proposal is done in an equally desultory manner. He comes home from work with a gift box but says nothing. Diane observes on her own that the dress inside looks like a wedding dress. When she regrets that he has never said "I love you," he demurs because it is "too silly." He produces a half-humorous substitute in its place, "Chico—Diane—Heaven," which Diane forces him to repeat, continuing the joke.

The sequence of the departure for the front marks a shift into a more pathetic register. The influence of the Vidor film is particularly evident here. In *The Big Parade* the mobilization of the troop is juxtaposed with Mélisande's movement through and against the tide of marching soldiers as she looks for Jim. The couple then desperately try to cling to one another as the truck carrying Jim's unit moves out. Borzage similarly juxtaposes the movement of troops with the couple's private realm, but he does so by crosscutting. The sequence moves across three spaces: the apartment in which Chico finally declares his love, the apartment next door, where Gobin feeds his pregnant wife soup as he bids her good-bye, and the street below where soldiers mass amidst the onlooking crowd. The music track echoes the discordances of tone, mixing the sentimental waltz "Diane" with the sound of drums and martial band music. The pathos generated in this sequence allows the film to move from Chico's initially antiromantic stance to one that exalts love (and, parenthetically, God). The call to arms precludes a formal marriage ceremony. Although Chico had made clear that, being an atheist, he would not marry in church, he "gives God one more chance," and the couple improvise a private ceremony that involves the exchange of religious medals bestowed upon Chico by Père Chevillon.

Following the departure of the men for the front, the film cuts between battle footage and Diane's activities at home. She fights off Nana when her sister tries to resume her former dominant role, fends off the attentions of an admirer, and goes to work in a munitions factory. As agreed upon, Chico and Diane "meet" every day at eleven o'clock, when each stops to reiterate "Chico—Diane—Heaven." Due to her experience of spiritual communion, Diane initially refuses to believe the news of Chico's death. The priest brings seemingly irrefutable proof in the form of Chico's religious medallion, as a crowd in the street begins to celebrate the signing of the Armistice. Diane challenges Père Chevillon, echoing Chico's atheism:

> For four years I have called this Heaven— I prayed—I believed in God—
> —I believed He would bring Chico back to me—
> —And Chico is dead!

At this point the film cuts to Chico, now blind, making his way through the crowd. Borzage does not plausibly motivate the last-minute reversal. For example, there is no scene in a hospital showing the injured soldier's recovery and return to Paris. Chico is simply there on the city streets. He repeats the couple's previous action of climbing the stairs and comes through the door at eleven o'clock. It is, of course, possible to interpret this ending as a providential intervention, but the important point is that the surprise of Chico's reappearance renders the reunion of the couple itself as a miracle.

On the face of it, it is hard to imagine a less "realistic" film than *7th Heaven*, with its Paris setting entirely a construct of designer Harry Oliver on the Fox lot, its highly stylized lighting and camera movement, and its plot, structured to produce maximal tonal contrast and resolved by an entirely unmotivated peripeteia. Yet, within the context of the 1920s, the film can be seen as hewing to the aspirations that Borzage had himself enunciated after the release of *Humoresque*. It turned away from the usual realm of the romantic drama—a world peopled by Arabian sheiks and European aristocrats—to the realm of the proletariat, a world where sewer rats aspired to clean the streets and taxicab drivers gave their all for France. The mundane setting permitted Borzage to create an extravagant love story that was completely invested in the "grand pash" and nonetheless avoided the bombastic love scenes and elevated tone more typical of the period. Contemporary reviewers seem to have been struck by the film's lack of pretension. Thus the *Variety* critic who called it a "red-blooded story told in a straight to the shoulder way" or the reaction of Welford

Beaton writing in *The Film Spectator:* "It is a beautiful picture because the souls of unimportant people are important."

Borzage followed the success of *7th Heaven* with another romantic drama set in Europe, the 1928 *Street Angel,* a virtual reprise of the earlier film with the same stars. In his subsequent career in the sound period, Borzage did not frequently return to the historical romance, despite his interest in love stories (although his 1941 version of *Smilin' Through* represents a return to a somewhat older set of conventions). His brief engagement with the genre is instructive, however, because it reveals by contrast the romantic drama's typical exoticism and its repudiation of the vernacular. With the coming of sound, these aspects of the genre were rendered increasingly problematic.

I have tried to show that *Variety,* and less consistently *Film Daily* and the *New York Times,* generally disapproved of the highly risqué and overblown variants of the romantic drama. This judgment softened somewhat after the great financial success of films such as *Don Juan* and *Flesh and the Devil* but was never entirely effaced, even in the later part of the silent period. Films such as *Proud Flesh, Ibañez' Torrent,* and *Loves of Carmen* echoed this dissatisfaction with the form. The coming of sound helped further to discredit the genre, or at least the variant of it focalized on a charismatic male star. An apocryphal account of this development may be found in "The Dueling Cavaliers," the hilarious parody of the early sound costume picture found in the 1952 musical *Singin' in the Rain.* But the historical record bears out some aspects of Stanley Donen's version of events. *Variety* (October 9, 1929: 41) wrote of *His Glorious Night:* "A few more talker productions like this and John Gilbert will be able to change places with Harry Langdon. His prowess at love making, which has held the stenoes breathless, takes on a comedy aspect in 'His Glorious Night' that gets the gum chewers tittering at first and then laughing outright at the very false ring of the couple of dozen 'I love you' phrases designed to climax, ante and post, the thrill in the Gilbert lines."

The scene to which *Variety* refers occurs near the opening of the film, when the calvary officer Kovacs (Gilbert) secretly meets the Princess Orsolini (Catherine Dale Owen). The dialogue runs as follows:

KOVACS: Princess, my princess, I love you, love you, love you.

ORSOLINI: Please, please. Don't you realize the risk I'm taking.

KOVACS: Sweet, tell me just once more that you love me.

ORSOLINI: I've never told you that I loved you.

KOVACS: You didn't have to, your eyes did. Why didn't you smile at me a little when I rode up to the booth this afternoon?

ORSOLINI: Because I was trying to control myself. All during and before the race my aunt and uncle talked of nothing but Kovacs. I was trying not to look at you.

KOVACS: Trying not to look at me when I rode for you.

ORSOLINI: I was afraid you might fall.

KOVACS: I couldn't fall because I knew you were watching me. I love you. I've never known anyone in my life like you. I suppose you know that you are driving me insane.

That this was not just an isolated example of unfortunate writing is indicated by *Variety*'s review (November 6, 1929: 19) of Ronald Colman's performance in *Condemned* in the same year:

> They can't and won't stomach overly sweet love scenes in dialog. The same thing can, has and will be accomplished by less obvious and awkward means. For it's quite evident that sympathizers become embarrassed for their screen favorites during these sequences in the face of the resultant laughter and the knowledge, or instinct, that these scenes simply don't belong. And that "Condemned" is going to draw snickers as it approaches its conclusion is as certain as that the cutter is going to stay up nights trying to find a way out. But Colman plays well. . . . If ever given a chance he will probably scintillate in a light comedy theme.

The hope for Colman, in *Variety*'s prescient view, was to lend his talents to another kind of plot.

The romantic drama did not vanish completely with the coming of sound. Such films continued to be made, often as echoes of 1920s successes and generally emphasizing a female star. Rouben Mamoulian's 1934 *Queen Christina,* one of John Gilbert's last featured roles in a production that was entirely structured around Greta Garbo's star persona, is a case in point. As the genre waned, Josef von Sternberg and Marlene Dietrich made it their own, although often in highly ironic and even parodic variants. *The Scarlet Empress,* for example, replays the situation presented in *Forbidden Paradise* and *The Eagle* of a czarina who makes sexual advances to her military attendants. Von Sternberg's version, from the point of view of a young noblewoman being initiated into the ways of the Russian court, is rendered no less comically, but much more perversely, than either of its two antecedents. Despite the persistence of such instances of the form, it seems that, by the end of the silent period, discomfort with the elevated tone of romantic drama had spread well beyond the wiseacres writing for *Variety*. But it is important to realize that sound was not the sole cause of the genre's disrepute. The negative responses to the early sound costume picture followed logically from criticisms made much earlier in the decade, indeed, from the first reactions to *The Sheik*.

The romantic drama was almost completely identified with women. Scorned as overheated and bombastic, the films were out of step with anti-sentimental trends evident in the genres of sophisticated comedy and the male adventure film, and evident as well in the reworkings of the romantic drama directed by the likes of Vidor, Bell, Walsh, and even Borzage. Nonetheless, one needs to be wary of too ready and easy an equation between femininity and sentimentality. For example, the developments in the seduction plot discussed in chapter 5 seem to have occurred largely under the aegis of films thought to be preferred by women. Although "old-fashioned" variants of the plot were associated with rural and working-class audiences of both sexes, as well as with shop girls, the updated comic variants, with their emphasis on clothes and active female characters, were much more exclusively identified with feminine tastes.

In addition, much of the evidence presented here, the trade press discourse, as well as the taxonomy of 1920s film genres, suggests that the films most frequently criticized for being old-fashioned and cloyingly sentimental were identified with rural and suburban audiences. Naïve taste, at least as the trade press understood it, was certainly not restricted to women's genres. It favored stories about firemen and policemen as well as stories about dying babies. It included a predilection for "hoke" slapstick and "hoke" pathos, delivered, to quote *Variety*, "with more force than grace." Indeed, the scandalous or potentially scandalous scenarios of rape or seduction, which predominated in the romantic drama, stand in clear contrast to the more conservative and moralizing films that the trade press usually judged best-suited to small towns and neighborhood theaters. Thus with regard to the long-standing opposition between "hoke" and "sophisticated" films I think it fair to say that region and class were held to be much more important than gender as determinants of taste.

Furthermore, although there certainly were isolated comments in the trade press to the effect that women enjoy movies that make them cry, the cinematic genres consistently associated with feminine taste in the 1920s were not especially lachrymose. Neither the comic inversions of the seduction plot nor the sexually daring romantic dramas and society dramas were notably pathetic; an obvious exception such as Borzage's *Back Pay* was specifically criticized for being old-fashioned.

My observations about women's genres in the 1920s clash with descriptions of the woman's picture of the 1930s and 1940s, which were often characterized as "weepies" both by the trade press and, subsequently, by scholars trying to explain the appeal of the films. In one of the first scholarly treatments of the subject Molly Haskell writes, "At the lowest level, as soap opera, the 'woman's film' fills a masturbatory need, it is soft-core emotional porn for the frustrated housewife. The weepies are founded on a mock-Aristotelian and politically conservative aesthetic whereby women spectators are moved, not by pity and fear but by self-pity and tears to accept, rather then reject, their lot."[45] One way to resolve the disparity between this view of the woman's picture and the one that emerges from an examination of the industry trade discourse in the 1920s is to refine our sense of the plot types associated with feminine taste and to consider how these types might vary over time. Haskell's description of prototypical plots for the woman's picture includes stories of medical affliction, rivalry in love, mothers separated from their children, and women who suspect that their husbands may be criminal or potentially murderous. But clearly, prior to the advent of sound, other sorts of films were associated with feminine viewing preferences, among them the adventure serials of the 1910s described by Ben Singer and Shelley Stamp, and the Orientalist excesses of the romantic drama in the 1920s.[46] In short, I would argue that the "woman's picture" cannot be considered as a single, coherent, and historically stable entity.

I would emphasize that the identification of any given plot with women within the trade press discourse is open to change and can be more or less tenuous. For example, one of Haskell's plot types, stories of maternal suffering and self-sacrifice, while very numerous in the 1920s, was typically assumed to have had wide popular appeal, especially in the neighborhood and small-town theaters. A good example is Fox's 1920 hit *Over the Hill to the Poorhouse,* described by *Variety* (September 24, 1929: 44) as a "hymn to mother love." *Moving Picture World*'s weekly "Straight from the Shoulder Reports" columns indicate that this film was a mainstay of small-town exhibitors as late as 1922. Even the cynical Robert Sherwood, writing in the pages of *Life,* called *Over the Hill to the Poorhouse* an "interesting and well-acted sob drama of old age and poverty" and "the sort of rural sob drama that warms the cockles of your heart, provided you have such outlandish features."[47] Although considered extremely sentimental, then, the film was not presumed to play largely to the matinée crowd. The assumption in the 1920s that stories of mother love would appeal across gender is confirmed by a number of films in the latter half of the decade that were devoted to stories of paternal suffering and self-sacrifice, including *Lazybones, Sorrell and Son,* and *The Music Master.* Indeed, this trend continued into the early sound period with Vidor's *The Champ.* This is to suggest not that stories of maternal love and self-sacrifice were never identified with feminine viewing preferences but, rather, that this kind of plot was significantly less gendered in the 1920s. Because assumptions about gender preferences can change over time, it is crucial for the historian to attend to the discourses that structured the reception context. One cannot assume that any plot is eternally feminine. For example, while no reviewer in the 1930s would have considered von Sternberg's *The Scarlet Empress* a "woman's picture," an examination of the 1920s trade press discourse reveals that this 1934 film was referencing a tradition that was indubitably considered feminine in an earlier phase of its history.

As discussed in chapter 1, the attack on sentimentality and genteel culture by literary intellectuals just prior to and after World War I contained an unmistakably misogynist component. A similarly misogynist strain can be observed in the antisentimental trends associated with the male adventure film. Nonetheless, I do not think one can explain the converse of this—the *persistence* of sentiment within the cinema—as a function of an attempt to appeal to women or to an underlying feminization of popular culture. It is only when we acknowledge the wide and deep appeal of sentimental narrative prototypes in the Hollywood cinema as a whole that we can begin to understand the transformations wrought by a relatively small number of films and filmmakers over the course of the 1920s. A new note was struck in *Greed* and the naturalist-inspired films that followed in its wake, in *A Woman of Paris* and the sophisticated comedies that followed in its wake. Directors assimilated the stylistic and narrative innovations of these films sporadically, across a range of genres, both "masculine" and "feminine," in war films, gangster films, and gold digger stories. They initiated a sea change as great as the coming of sound, although harder to date and trace, providing the modernist underpinnings of a contemporary cinema.

Afterword

It is hard for me to believe, at this moment in 1957, in the full
current of rock'n'roll and Elvis Presley, that the jazz represented
by Paul Whiteman and Vincent Lopez should have been so
desperately feared, so violently attacked, as the enemy of
music. . . . It is hard to believe that the appearance of George
Gershwin, playing his own songs, at Aeolian Hall and of Paul
Whiteman in the same hall, to introduce *The Rhapsody in Blue*,
were considered desecrations of those sacred premises. I can, with
some effort, make allowances for critics who seriously discussed
the art (they really did) of Hergesheimer and James Branch Cabell,
but their failure to recognize, at that time, that Ring Lardner was
more than a baseball reporter who wrote stories in slang, still goes
beyond my retrospective power to forgive. The battle for jazz, for
Lardner, for Chaplin and the Keystone cops was won long ago, by
them and by the swift movement of events more than by the
critics who saw their true worth. But the critics helped and I am
glad I was one of them.

> GILBERT SELDES, "A Personal Preface," *The Seven Lively Arts*

Seldes's modest and moving recollection of the battles of his youth points to
the ways in which the young intellectuals of the 1920s, and those working
in the "lively arts" in the same period, participated in a decisive transformation of taste.[1] One cannot help but be struck by the prescience of Seldes and
his colleagues in the 1920s when considered from a later historical vantage
point: the appreciation of Ring Lardner's vernacular, the insistence on the
legitimacy of jazz and its centrality to American music (if only Fletcher
Henderson's band, with Louis Armstrong, had been elevated in the place of
Paul Whiteman's!), and the wholesale rehabilitation of what had been one
of the American cinema's most maligned genres. Yet the qualified approval
of the cinema and the judgments made about particular filmmakers were
skewed by the very terms of the 1920s debates: away from the drama
understood as *le côté Puccini*, and toward slapstick, understood as the spon-
taneous and joyful destruction of gentility and decorum. *The Seven Lively
Arts* specifically excludes the middle, valorizing the unmistakably low and
vulgar aspects of popular culture, and the avant-garde of Picasso and Joyce,
while rejecting the rest as pretentious or sloppily sentimental "bogus" art.

Seldes's position became even more powerfully consecrated in Dwight Macdonald's well-known essay "Masscult and Midcult," in which most Hollywood cinema—with the familiar exceptions of D. W. Griffith, von Stroheim, Chaplin, Keaton, and Welles—was assumed to participate in the leveling effects of mass culture.[2] Although such distinctions between high, low, and middle have gradually been eroded, beginning with 1950s pop art and, later, the embrace of popular culture by New Left intellectuals, it still seems necessary to rethink the consequences of Seldes's celebration of the vulgate and attack on more polite forms of cinema for our understanding of the history of American film in the 1920s.[3]

Seldes and his confrères recognized Chaplin as a master of slapstick, but they were aware neither of the importance accorded to *A Woman of Paris* within the organs of film culture nor of the works by Lubitsch, Monta Bell, and others that took up the techniques essayed in Chaplin's film. It may be that the very refinement of the sophisticated comedies, their visual elegance, their wit, their largely upper-class settings and characters, proved a barrier to critics who conceived of the cinema at its best as rough and naïve. In any case, the literary intellectuals failed to address themselves to what, in my view, is the crucial development in Hollywood filmmaking in the 1920s: the emergence of a preference for a laconic and understated style.

I would emphasize that the trade and popular press deemed the style associated with sophisticated comedy radical and new. There can be no doubt that, as Kristin Thompson has recently argued, the American phase of Lubitsch's career is characterized by a mastery of the rules for scene dissection such as glance/object and shot-reverse-shot editing, rules that were first devised in the 1910s.[4] Nonetheless, the import of his films resides not merely in the elaboration of devices that were in any case already available to filmmakers but, more important, in the innovation of strategies of narration that were experienced in the 1920s as a qualitative break with the past. *A Woman of Paris, The Marriage Circle,* and the many films that followed their lead were valued for the economy of their mode of representation: for the eschewal of big climaxes, succinct repetitions of objects and situations, and the narrative weight thereby assigned to seemingly insignificant details—a flower, a heart-and-anchor tattoo, a Liberty bond. But although the films using the new techniques were praised, they were also considered potentially risky and possibly too subtle for the average filmgoer. In 1927 *Variety* seems to have agreed with Seldes's conception of American vernacular taste when it despaired of the commercial potential of sophisticated comedy and contrasted the fastidious discrimination of the French, "sipping their pastimes like old wine," with the American habit of gulping "their screen and stage sensations like straight redeye." It seems that this is one of the few occasions when *Variety* failed to do justice to an important film industry trend.

A growing distaste for "bunk" or "hokum" is one of the predominant tendencies of the 1920s, evident in both reviews and in the films themselves. One can see it in the reception of the sentimental and religiose films discussed in chapter 3, which were considered best fit for rural theaters and the nabes. One can see it in the travesties of the romantic drama and its persistent disrepute despite the sexy subject matter and the important stars and directors so frequently involved with the genre. One can even see it in the response to naturalist-inspired filmmaking: in the criticism of *Greed* and *The Wind* for overemphatic symbolism, and in the criticism of von Stroheim's direction of actors as "squeezing the lemon a little too hard." Throughout the spectrum of genres considered here, the reviewers reiterated their preferences for a reduced and straightforward style, for simple plots. Like continuity editing and three-point lighting, these criteria of judgment became crucial and enduring norms of the classical Hollywood cinema.

In itself, this account does not necessarily overturn Seldes's characterization of the emerging feature cinema as under the sway of "bogus" bourgeois art. The norms embraced by film reviewers in the 1920s can be and have been assimilated to a conservative aesthetic. For example, Noël Burch analyzes, and anathematizes, the valorization of an unobtrusive style and the corresponding predominance of narrative within what he calls the Institutional Mode of Representation.[5] But my sense of how canons of taste evolved in the course of the 1920s leads me to suggest that these norms carried a somewhat different aesthetic charge. The emphasis on simplicity and economy was perceived as distinctive, efficient, and streamlined, a departure from more old-fashioned ways of making movies. Moreover, the films considered up to date were congruent with a number of the transformations of literary culture adduced in chapter 1. Filmmakers abandoned high-flown rhetoric and violated decorum as they experimented with the vernacular in their use of titles and deployment of actors. Highly didactic or moralized stories were often treated with sarcasm or scorn. In some cases the romance plot was reworked to favor a more cynical, or a more carnal and humorous, view of sexuality. If Hollywood filmmaking became more refined than the rough and naïve vulgate that is nostalgically evoked in Seldes's writing on Sennett, it nonetheless frequently acquired the edge and the force of the rejection of sentiment. To extend *Variety*'s metaphor, the style that evolved was akin not to "straight redeye" but rather to that quintessential Prohibition-era cocktail—the dry martini.

Notes

1. TOWARD A HISTORY OF TASTE

1. See, for example, Sumiko Higashi, *Virgins, Vamps and Flappers: The American Silent Movie Heroine* (Montreal, Quebec: Eden Press, 1978); Janet Staiger, *Bad Women: Regulating Sexuality in Early American Cinema* (Minneapolis: University of Minnesota Press, 1995); Sara Ross, "Banking the Flames of Youth: The Hollywood Flapper, 1920–1930," PhD diss., University of Wisconsin–Madison, 2000; for a discussion of male stars in the 1920s, see Gaylyn Studlar, *This Mad Masquerade: Stardom and Masculinity in the Jazz Age* (New York: Columbia University Press, 1996).

2. Lary May, *Screening Out the Past: The Birth of Mass Culture and the Motion Picture Industry* (New York: Oxford University Press, 1980); Sumiko Higashi, *Cecil B. DeMille and American Culture: The Silent Era* (Berkeley: University of California Press, 1994).

3. To forestall misunderstandings I should perhaps emphasize that this book is concerned with sentiment and sentimentality, not with melodrama. The two things are not the same, despite the fact that many melodramas are sentimental. The literature of sentiment predates melodrama, and there are melodramatic traditions that are not sentimental—indeed, as Steve Neale has pointed out, 1920s commentators associated melodrama more with sensationalism than with sentiment. See Steve Neale, "Melo Talk: On the Meaning and Use of the Term 'Melodrama' in the American Trade Press," *Velvet Light Trap* 32: 66–89. There is a considerable literature on melodrama in both theater and cinema, to which I have contributed myself, but it is beyond the scope of the historically localized changes in taste under consideration here.

4. Richard Crawford, *America's Musical Life: A History* (New York: Norton, 2001); Allen Forte, *The American Popular Ballad of the Golden Era, 1924–1950* (Princeton, NJ: Princeton University Press, 1995); Charles Hamm, *Yesterdays: Popular Song in America* (New York: W. W. Norton, 1979); and Charles Hamm, *Irving Berlin: Songs from the Melting Pot: The Formative*

Years, 1907–1914 (New York: Oxford University Press, 1997). Among the many contemporary accounts of jazz and popular song, see those of Gilbert Seldes, "Toujours Jazz" and "Say It with Music," in *The 7 Lively Arts* (New York: Harper & Brothers, 1924), 83–108 and 57–66. *The 7 Lively Arts* was reprinted in 1957 in a heavily revised version. Unless otherwise stated, quotations and page numbers in this book refer to the 1924 edition.

5. Roland Marchand, *Advertising the American Dream: Making Way for Modernity 1920–1940* (Berkeley: University of California Press, 1985), 140–48; Adrian Forty, *Objects of Desire: Design and Society from Wedgwood to IBM* (New York: Pantheon Books, 1986); Bevis Hillier, *The World of Art Deco, an Exhibition Organized by the Minneapolis Institute of Arts, July–September 1971* (New York: E. P. Dutton & Company, 1971); and Theodore Menten, *The Art Deco Style in Household Objects, Architecture, Sculpture, Graphics, Jewelry* (New York: Dover Publications, 1972).

6. Henry May, *The End of American Innocence: The First Years of Our Own Time, 1912–1917* (Oxford: Oxford University Press, 1959); Robert Cantwell, "Journalism—the Magazines," in *In America Now: An Inquiry into Civilization in the United States*, ed. Harold E. Stearns (New York: Charles Scribner's Sons, 1938), 345–55; and Frederick Hoffman, Charles Allen, and Carolyn Ulrich, *The Little Magazine: A History and a Bibliography* (Princeton, NJ: Princeton University Press, 1946).

7. Christine Stansell, *American Moderns: Bohemian New York and the Creation of a New Century* (New York: Henry Holt, 2000); and Henry May, *The End of American Innocence*, 283–85, 251–55.

8. The most detailed study of changes in the canon of American prose fiction is Kermit Vanderbilt, *American Literature and the Academy: The Roots, Growth, and Maturity of a Profession* (Philadelphia: University of Pennsylvania Press, 1986); on the 1920s, see 185–252. Henry May gives a more schematic but nonetheless instructive account of the literary tastes of the more conservative critics in *The End of American Innocence*, 45–50; on Whitman's importance, see 269–70, 306, 324–25.

9. Henry May, *The End of American Innocence*, 185–86.

10. Ibid., 187.

11. Vanderbilt, *American Literature and the Academy*, 198.

12. Ibid., 1–14, 185–201.

13. "Zola," *Smart Set* (August 1912): 154, cited in William H. Nolte, "Editor's Introduction," *H. L. Mencken's Smart Set Criticism* (Ithaca, NY: Cornell University Press, 1968), xxxii–xxxiii.

14. Janet Todd, *Sensibility: An Introduction* (London: Methuen, 1986), 6–9, 129–46.

15. Randolph Bourne, "Paul Elmer More," *Seven Arts* 1 (April 1917), reprinted in his *War and the Intellectuals: Collected Essays, 1915–1919*, ed. Carl Resek (New York: Harper & Row, 1964), 168. H. L. Mencken's distrust of progressive political rhetoric is evident in "The Style of Woodrow," originally published January 1921 and reprinted in *H. L. Mencken's Smart Set Criticism,*

119–21. For his disapproval of moral didacticism in the novel, see Mencken, "Joseph Conrad," *A Book of Prefaces,* 26–27. On Babbitt's dislike of sentimentality, see Henry May, *The End of American Innocence,* 60; on Babbitt's and More's views of naturalism, see Vanderbilt, *American Literature and the Academy,* 355–56.

16. H. L. Mencken, "Mush for the Multitude" and "Lacrymose Love," in *H. L. Mencken's Smart Set Criticism,* 166–70 and 170–74; also his "The Last of the Victorians," *Smart Set* (October 1909): 153–55. In "The Heart of the People," *New Republic* (July 3, 1915), reprinted in Bourne, *War and the Intellectuals,* 173–74, Randolph Bourne, although more regretful than the unapologetically elitist Mencken, rejected the movies as overly sentimental and called them a form of culture as "worthy of resistance" as that of the universities and museums. In a 1916 editorial in *Seven Arts,* James Oppenheim categorized popular art in similar terms: "We say it lacks greatness; we say it is flabby and sentimental; we say that it discovers no depth and no height in the human being"; cited in Paul R. Gorman, *Left Intellectuals and Popular Culture in Twentieth-Century America* (Chapel Hill: University of North Carolina Press, 1996), 59. The New Humanists did not write extensively on popular culture, and I take their rejection of it as a matter of course: they understood the role of the public intellectual as one of upholding standards in a period of moral and aesthetic decline; see Joan Shelley Rubin, *The Making of Middlebrow Culture* (Chapel Hill: University of North Carolina Press, 1992), 44–47.

17. H. L. Mencken, "Theodore Dreiser," *A Book of Prefaces,* 88–89; see also 70, 94; Mencken quotes from Hugh Walpole, *Joseph Conrad* (New York: Henry Holt, 1916), 97–98.

18. Mencken, *A Book of Prefaces,* 92–93.

19. William Winter, "Ibsenites and Ibsenism," *The Wallet of Time: Containing Personal, Biographical and Critical Reminiscence of the American Theatre* (New York: Moffat, Yard & Company, 1913), vol. 2, 592, reprinted in *The American Theater as Seen by Its Critics, 1752–1934,* ed. Montrose J. Moses and John Mason Brown (New York: Cooper Square Publishers, 1967; first published 1934), 94–101. Despite his acceptance by what Henry May called "the most tolerant of the arbiters of American taste," professional performances of Ibsen were rare in American as late as the 1910s. James Gibbon Huneker, *Egoists: A Book of Supermen* (New York: Scribner's Sons, 1909), 319, noted that "adverse criticism, especially in America, was vitiated by the fact that Ibsen the dramatist was hardly known here. Ibsen was eagerly read, but seldom played." The Internet Broadway Database (www.ibdb.com) provides a guide to the relative frequency of professional productions of Ibsen on Broadway; it reveals that between 1889, when the first productions are recorded, and the end of World War I there were nine productions (some of these revivals from previous seasons) of *A Doll's House* and eight of *Hedda Gabler.* These two, the most frequently produced, provided starring roles for the popular actresses Mrs. Fiske, Nance O'Neill, Ethel Barrymore, and Alla Nazimova. Other Ibsen works played much less frequently: *Rosmersholm* only twice, in

1904 and 1907 (the revival starring Mrs. Fiske), and *The Wild Duck* only once, and that not until 1918. *Ghosts*, one of the most controversial of Ibsen's plays, was staged in 1894 and 1903, revived for four performances in 1912 and two performances in 1915, and then had a relatively long run of a month in 1916 with the Washington Square Players.

20. Mencken, *A Book of Prefaces*, 138–39; Vanderbilt's account of this often described debate is the one most sympathetic to Sherman, *American Literature and the Academy*, 208–13.

21. Bourne, "Traps for the Unwary," *Dial* (March 28, 1918), reprinted in his *War and the Intellectuals*, 179–80.

22. *Mrs. Warren's Profession*, written in 1894, was first publicly performed in 1902 in London by the Stage Society, a private club exempt from the ban that the Lord Chamberlain, who exercised censorship over the British stage, had imposed on the work. When Arnold Daly produced the play in New York in 1905 he was subject to legal proceedings for indecency; see Shaw's preface to *Mrs. Warren's Profession* in *The Complete Prefaces of Bernard Shaw* (London: Paul Hamlyn, 1965), 219, 233.

23. "The Limit of Stage Indecency," from the *New York Herald*, October 31, 1905, reprinted in *The American Theater as Seen by Its Critics*, 163–67.

24. Mencken, "Puritanism as a Literary Force," *A Book of Prefaces*, 253–76; later protests in the same vein include Heywood Broun and Margaret Leech, *Anthony Comstock, Roundsman of the Lord* (New York: A. & C. Boni, 1927); and Morris L. Ernst and William Seagle, *To the Pure . . . A Study of Obscenity and the Censor* (New York: Viking Press, 1928). For an account of Dreiser's struggles with censorship, both literary and filmic, see my article "*An American Tragedy:* A Comparison of Film and Literary Censorship," *Quarterly Review of Film and Video* 15, no. 4 (1995): 87–98.

25. Richard Aldington, "The Influence of Mr. James Joyce," *English Review* xxxii (April 1921): 333–41; extracts reprinted in *James Joyce: The Critical Heritage*, ed. Robert H. Deming (New York: Barnes & Noble, 1970), vol. 1, 186–89.

26. Richard Ellmann, *James Joyce*, rev. ed. (Oxford: Oxford University Press, 1982), 497–504.

27. Patrick Parrinder, "The Strange Necessity: James Joyce's Rejection in England (1914–1930)," in *James Joyce: New Perspectives*, ed. Colin MacCabe (Bloomington: Indiana University Press, 1982), 151–67.

28. While some critics, particularly Mencken, rejected anything that smacked of Progressivism in the realm of culture, others, notably Randolph Bourne, were more sympathetic; see his "Sociologic Fiction," *New Republic* 12 (October 27, 1917): 339–60, reprinted in his *War and the Intellectuals*, 175–78. Richard Hofstadter, *The Age of Reform* (New York: Random House, 1955), 197–98, makes the affiliations between muckraking journalists and naturalist novelists apparent when he cites Cantwell, "Journalism—the Magazines," 347:

> It was not because the muckrakers exposed the corruption of Minneapolis, for example, that they were widely read, but because they

wrote about Minneapolis at a time when it had not been written about, without patronizing or boosting it, and with an attempt to explore its life realistically and intelligently. They wrote, in short, an intimate, anecdotal, behind-the-scenes history of their own times. . . . In doing this they drew a new cast of characters for the drama of American society: bosses, professional politicians, reformers, racketeers, captains of industry. . . . At the same time, the muckrakers pictured stage settings that every everybody recognized but that nobody had written about—oil refineries, slums, the red-light districts, the hotel rooms where political deals were made—the familiar, unadorned, homely stages where the teeming day-to-day dramas of American life were enacted.

29. Bourne, "Traps for the Unwary," in his *War and the Intellectuals*, 182.

30. Mencken, *A Book of Prefaces*, 79–88.

31. Richard Bridgman, *The Colloquial Style in America* (New York: Oxford University Press, 1966), 130.

32. William Veeder, *Henry James—the Lessons of the Master: Popular Fiction and Personal Style in the Nineteenth Century* (Chicago: University of Chicago Press, 1975).

33. Veeder, *Henry James*, 10, 146–47. Jonathan Freedman, *Professions of Taste: Henry James, British Aestheticism, and Commodity Culture* (Stanford, CA: Stanford University Press, 1990), xiii–xv, argues that variants of the Brooks-Parrington thesis continue to have an effect on James studies, making it difficult for scholars to assess his relationship to British aestheticism.

34. According to Bridgman, *The Colloquial Style in America*, 100, Ezra Pound was an exception, finding James's style both exquisite and colloquial.

35. Van Wyck Brooks, *The Pilgrimage of Henry James* (New York: E. P. Dutton & Company, 1925), 166. Vanderbilt, *American Literature and the Academy*, 399, notes that there were only three studies of James published in the period between 1918 and 1925 (including Brooks's monograph) and only two more in the early 1930s, an astonishing fact considering the importance later accorded James.

36. Brooks, *The Pilgrimage of Henry James*, 131.

37. Mencken, "Puritanism as a Literary Force," *A Book of Prefaces*, 223, and "Final Estimate," originally published in October 1919 and reprinted in *H. L. Mencken's Smart Set Criticism*, 187; Sherman's evaluation of Twain's late works is cited in Vanderbilt, *American Literature and the Academy*, 224.

38. "Twain and Howells," in *H. L. Mencken's Smart Set Criticism*, 178–79.

39. Van Wyck Brooks, *The Ordeal of Mark Twain* (New York: E. P. Dutton & Company, 1920), 122.

40. Brooks, *The Ordeal of Mark Twain*, 122–23.

41. Edmund Wilson, "Mr. Lardner's American Characters," *Dial* (July 1924): 69–72, reprinted in Wilson's *The Shores of Light: A Literary Chronicle of the Twenties and Thirties* (New York: Farrar, Straus & Giroux, 1952), 94–98;

see also Wilson's rendition of a Sherwood Anderson anecdote, "A New Orlean-
ian," and his 1957 commentary on the use of dialect by that author, in his *The
American Earthquake: A Documentary of the Twenties and Thirties* (New
York: Doubleday, 1958), 126–28; on the correspondence between Van Wyck
Brooks and Sherwood Anderson concerning Mark Twain's language, see Bridg-
man, *The Colloquial Style in America*, 152–53.

42. Ernest Hemingway, *Green Hills of Africa* (New York: Charles Scribner's Sons, 1935), 22, cited in Henry Nash Smith, *Democracy and the Novel:
Popular Resistance to Classic American Writers* (New York: Oxford University Press, 1978), 107; Bridgman's compelling account of how writers solved
the problem of using the vernacular in modern prose fiction begins with Twain
and James and ends with Hemingway; see *The Colloquial Style in America*,
152, 195–230.

43. This was first published as *The American Language: A Preliminary
Inquiry into the Development of English in the United States* in 1919; under
the new title *The American Language: An Inquiry into the Development of
English in the United States*, it was substantially revised and enlarged for the
1921 and 1923 editions, with further revisions and supplements appearing
intermittently until 1963. I cite from the third edition, published by Alfred
Knopf, 1923.

44. Mencken, *The American Language*, 3.

45. Ibid., 33–34.

46. Wilson, "The Lexicon of Prohibition," *New Republic* (March 9, 1927):
71–72, reprinted in *The American Earthquake*, 89–91.

47. H. L. Mencken, "The American: His Language," *Smart Set* (August
1913): 89–96.

48. Wilson, "The Doom of Lulu," *New Republic* (May 27, 1925): 20–21,
reprinted as "Can New York Stage a Serious Play?" in *The American Earthquake*, 64–66. Wilson refers to Gilbert Seldes's appreciation for "musical
shows," a taste that can be documented in Seldes's "Plan for a Lyric Theatre in
America," in *The 7 Lively Arts*, 161–73, and in "Torch Songs," *New Republic*
(November 19, 1930): 19–20, where he writes:

> In the old musical shows the moment always occurred when the
> juvenile lead and the soprano met under the spotlight and sang to
> each other, usually in three-four time, a song of lifelong devotion to
> the tune of which they afterwards waltzed. The masterly composi-
> tions of the Viennese about twenty years ago made these songs
> attractive, but after a time something too rigid in the mechanism
> was found distasteful, and when Mr. Jerome Kern began his magnifi-
> cent collaboration with P. G. Wodehouse, the song of sentiment (in
> fox-trot time) was more likely to be dainty and gay than heavily
> emotional.

See also Lee Davis, *Bolton and Wodehouse and Kern: The Men Who Made
Musical Comedy* (New York: James H. Heineman, 1993).

49. Wilson, "Broadway," *New Republic* (March 2, 1927): 45, reprinted in *The American Earthquake*, 86–88. In "Eugene O'Neill as Prose-Writer," *Vanity Fair* (November 1922): 24, reprinted in *The Shores of Light*, 99–101, he argues similarly that O'Neill's middle-class characters speak in dull and uninspired prose, but that his working-class characters employ a vernacular that has "a rhythmical eloquence very rare in naturalistic drama."

50. Wilson, "The Seven Low-Brow Arts," *Dial* (September 1924): 244–50, rewritten and published as "Gilbert Seldes and the Popular Arts (1924)," in *The Shores of Light*, 156–64; I quote from the original.

51. Seldes, "The Keystone the Builders Rejected," *7 Lively Arts*, 4.

52. Ibid., 16.

53. Ibid., 19–20.

54. Ibid., 21–22.

55. For canonical examples of this argument as applied to Sennett, see James Agee, "Comedy's Greatest Era," *Life* (September 3, 1949), reprinted in *The Silent Comedians*, ed. Richard Dyer MacCann (Metuchen, NJ: Scarecrow Press, 1993), 22–26; and Gerald Mast, *The Comic Mind: Comedy and the Movies* (Chicago: University of Chicago Press, 1973), 47–54. For a celebration of the anarchic qualities of sound comedy, indebted to Seldes's analyses of both slapstick and vaudeville, see Henry Jenkins III, *What Made Pistachio Nuts? Early Sound Comedy and the Vaudeville Aesthetic* (New York: Columbia University Press, 1992).

56. Theodore Dreiser, "The Best Motion Picture Interview Ever Written," *Photoplay* 34, no. 3 (August 1928): 32–35, 124–29; this and subsequent references are to the version reprinted in George C. Pratt, *Spellbound in Darkness: A History of the Silent Film* (Greenwich, CT: New York Graphic Society, 1973; first published 1966), 182–83.

57. Ibid., 184. I agree with Walter Kerr, *The Silent Clowns* (New York: Alfred Knopf, 1975), 68–69, who argues that Sennett's films were in fact quite indebted both to Griffith and to melodrama: "It is difficult to tell, especially when watching one of his so-called 'parody' films, just when comedy is intended and just when the presumably parodied melodrama is actually being played straight."

58. Ibid., 191.

59. The first appellation comes from Seldes, "The Keystone the Builders Rejected," *The 7 Lively Arts*, 7; the second from Seldes, "Before a Picture by Picasso," *The 7 Lively Arts*, 345.

60. Seldes, "An Open Letter to the Movie Magnates," *The 7 Lively Arts*, 332–33.

61. Ibid., 327, 338.

62. Ben Brewster and Lea Jacobs, *Theatre to Cinema: Stage Pictorialism and the Early Feature Film* (Oxford: Oxford University Press, 1997), 48.

63. Noël Burch, *Life to Those Shadows*, trans. Ben Brewster (London: BFI Publishing, 1990).

64. Tom Gunning, "The Cinema of Attractions: Early Film, Its Spectator and the Avant-Garde," in *Early Cinema: Space, Frame, Narrative*, ed. Thomas

Elsaesser (London: BFI Publishing, 1990), 56–62; Tom Gunning, "An Aesthetic of Astonishment: Early Film and the (In)Credulous Spectator," in *Viewing Positions: Ways of Seeing Film*, ed. Linda Williams (New Brunswick, NJ: Rutgers University Press, 1995), 114–33; and Ben Singer, *Melodrama and Modernity: Early Sensational Cinema and Its Contexts* (New York: Columbia University Press, 2001).

65. Francis Haskell, *Rediscoveries in Art: Some Aspects of Taste, Fashion and Collecting in England and France* (Ithaca, NY: Cornell University Press, 1976), 17.

66. Ibid., 7. Among the many sociological studies of taste, Pierre Bourdieu's *Distinction: A Social Critique of the Judgment of Taste*, trans. Richard Nice (Cambridge, MA: Harvard University Press, 1984), is one of the most frequently cited, but, as with many such studies, it depends upon survey data not available to the historian.

67. Douglas Gomery, *Shared Pleasures: A History of Movie Presentation in the United States* (Madison: University of Wisconsin Press, 1992); Gregory A. Waller, *Main Street Amusements: Movies and Commercial Entertainment in a Southern City, 1896–1930* (Washington, DC: Smithsonian Institution Press, 1995); Gregory Waller, ed., *Moviegoing in America* (Oxford: Blackwell Publishers, 2002); Kathryn H. Fuller, *At the Picture Show: Small-Town Audiences and the Creation of Movie Fan Culture* (Charlottesville: University Press of Virginia, 2001); and George Peter Potamianos, "Hollywood in the Hinterlands: Mass Culture in Two California Communities, 1896–1936," PhD diss., University of Southern California, 1998.

68. For an extended discussion of how film genres are institutionally defined and elaborated, see Rick Altman, *Film/Genre* (London: BFI Publishing, 1999), 30–68.

69. Richard Maltby, "Sticks, Hicks and Flaps: Classical Hollywood's Generic Conception of Its Audiences," in *Identifying Hollywood's Audiences: Cultural Identity and the Movies*, ed. Melvyn Stokes and Richard Maltby (London: BFI Publishing, 1999), 23–41.

70. See, for example, the *Variety* reviews of *Man Crazy* (December 21, 1927: 22) and *Souls for Sables* (September 16, 1925: 40).

71. A similar claim is made earlier in the decade; see *Variety*'s review of *The Little Grey Mouse* (December 24, 1920: 28): "The story is of the Mrs. Southworth–Laura Jean type, with its direct obvious appeal to the woman fans" and recommended for "neighborhood establishments where the feminine clientele is in the vast majority."

72. On the location of suburban movie theaters in the case of Chicago, see Douglas Gomery, "U.S. Film Exhibition: The Formation of a Big Business," in *The American Film Industry*, ed. Tino Balio, rev. ed. (Madison: University of Wisconsin Press, 1985), 220–21.

73. A market differentiation not discussed in this book is that of race, because the trade press does not provide sufficient information on the matter. There were theaters and circuits of theaters dedicated to African Americans, but they do not figure in the habitual calculations about where a film will play

in the distribution hierarchy, except in the special case of movies such as King Vidor's *Hallelujah* (1929), which had an all-black cast.

74. Robert J. Landry, "'Variety's' Four-Letter Signatures, the Dog-Tags of Its Critics," *Variety* (January 9, 1974): 26. I am indebted to Madeleine Matz for this reference.

75. H. L. Mencken, *The American Language*, 4th ed., 560; Walter Winchell, "Your Broadway and Mine," New York *Graphic* (October 4, 1928), and "A Primer of Broadway Slang," *Vanity Fair* (November 1927), 66, 132, 134; Jack Conway, "Why I Write Slang," *Variety* (December 29, 1926): 5, 7.

76. Ira Carmen, *Movies, Censorship, and the Law* (Ann Arbor: University of Michigan Press, 1967), 129.

77. H. H. Hedberg, "Straight from the Shoulder Reports," *Moving Picture World* (November 13, 1926): 106.

78. Richard Maltby, "'To Prevent the Prevalent Type of Book': Censorship and Adaptation in Hollywood, 1924–1934," *American Quarterly*, vol. 44, no. 4 (December 1992): 554–82.

79. Other examples include the low-budget *The Manicure Girl*, criticized by *Variety* (June 17, 1925: 35) as "melodramatic fodder" rather than good "comedy-drama," and *Speed* (June 22, 1925: 35) and *Naughty Baby* (February 6, 1929: 18), both praised for being brief, light, and pleasant program pictures.

80. Richard Koszarski, *An Evening's Entertainment: The Age of the Silent Feature Picture, 1915–1928* (New York: Charles Scribner's Sons, 1990), 30, cites two newspaper articles dating from the 1920s, one in the *New York Times* and one in *Moving Picture World*, both of which asserted that women made up the majority of motion picture audiences (although they differed in the proportion of the audience said to be female). Some scholars have taken these articles at face value, although they are not based on scientific surveys and seem to me highly unreliable sources. However, as Roland Marchand, in *Advertising the American Dream*, 34, 66–69, has made clear, most advertising firms in the 1920s conceived of the consumer as feminine. This was given added impetus in the case of the film industry by the fact that, during the nickelodeon period, exhibitors sought to attract middle-class women to their theaters in an attempt to guarantee the respectability of their establishments. It seems to have become industry wisdom by the 1920s that women were crucial to a film's success; whether or not this was really the case is another matter.

2. HOLLYWOOD NATURALISM

1. Kristin Thompson, "The Limits of Experimentation in Hollywood," in *Lovers of Cinema: The First American Film Avant-Garde, 1919–1925*, ed. Jan-Christopher Horak (Madison: University of Wisconsin Press, 1995), 70–77. I am also indebted to James Naremore for his comments about the importance of aestheticism in American film.

2. Tom Gunning, *D. W. Griffith and the Origins of American Narrative Film: The Early Years at Biograph* (Urbana: University of Illinois Press, 1991), 214–18.

3. Steven J. Ross, *Working-Class Hollywood* (Princeton, NJ: Princeton University Press, 1998), 70–72.

4. Very little is known about this film, and no print seems to have survived, although a still from the film is reproduced in Jean Mitry, *Histoire du cinéma, 1895–1914*, vol. 1 (Paris: Éditions universitaires, 1967).

5. Sumiko Higashi, *Cecil B. DeMille and American Culture: The Silent Era* (Berkeley: University of California Press, 1994), 71–78.

6. For more on the social problem film, see Kay Sloane, *The Loud Silents: Origins of the Social Problem Film* (Urbana: University of Illinois Press, 1988); and Kevin Brownlow, *Behind the Mask of Innocence: Sex, Violence, Prejudice, Crime: Films of Social Conscience in the Silent Era* (New York: Alfred Knopf, 1990).

7. How to sustain a plot for the length of a feature film was a prominent problem in the 1910s; see Ben Brewster, "*Traffic in Souls:* An Experiment in Feature-Length Narrative Construction," *Cinema Journal* 31, no. 1 (Fall 1991): 37–56.

8. Ben Brewster, "*A Romance of Happy Valley,*" in *The Griffith Project*, vol. 9, *Films Produced in 1916–18*, ed. Paolo Cherchi Usai (Pordenone: Le Giornate del Cinema Muto/London: BFI Publishing, 2005), 176–91.

9. See the reviews of *A Romance of Happy Valley* in *Wid's* and *Moving Picture World* above.

10. Vance Kepley, "Griffith's *Broken Blossoms* and the Problems of Historical Specificity," *Quarterly Review of Film Studies* 3, no. 1 (1978): 37–47.

11. Pickford certainly played rural types, most prominently in *Rebecca of Sunnybrook Farm* (1917), *Pollyanna* (1920), and the Western *M'liss* (1918), but some of her most successful comedic roles were in an urban setting, as in the films *Amarilly of Clothes-Line Alley* (1918), *The Hoodlum* (1919), and *Suds* (1920).

12. Burns Mantle, *Photoplay* (May 1921): 51, reprinted in Anthony Slide, *Selected Film Criticism*, vol. 3, *1921–1930* (Metuchen, NJ: Scarecrow Press, 1982).

13. After writing this I read Tom Gunning's elegant analysis of Griffith's use of intertitles in his entry on *True Heart Susie* in *The Griffith Project*, vol. 10, *Films Produced in 1919–46*, ed. Paolo Cherchi Usai (Pordenone: Le Giornate del Cinema Muto/London: BFI Publishing, 2006), 18–27.

14. Gale's original novel was published in 1920; the play that she adapted from it was produced on Broadway by Brock Pemberton in 1921. Zona Gale was the first woman to win the Pulitzer Prize for drama; see Leslie Goddard, "Zona Gale as Dramatist," in *Dictionary of Literary Biography*, vol. 228, *Twentieth-Century American Dramatists*, 2nd Series, ed. Christopher J. Wheatley (Detroit, MI: Gale Group, 2000), 73–80 (now available online at http://galenet.galegroup.com).

15. Scott O'Dell, *Representative Photoplays Analyzed* (Hollywood: Palmer Institute of Authorship, 1924), 86–87.

16. Constance Mayfield Rourke, "Transitions," *New Republic* (August 11, 1920): 315–16.

17. Anonymous, "The Literary Spotlight," *Bookman* 57 (April 1923): 168–72.

18. For a similar assessment, see Carl Van Doren, *Contemporary American Novelists, 1900–1920* (New York: Macmillan, 1922), 164–66.

19. On the lack of dramatic structure, see the reviews by Alexander Woollcott in the *New York Times* (December 28, 1920: 9, and January 9, 1921: 6); for criticism of the revised ending, see Ludwig Lewisohn, "Drama," *Nation* (February 2, 1921): 189; and for a defense of Gale's ending, see Heywood Broun, "As We Were Saying," *New York Tribune* (sec. 3, February 6, 1921): 1.

20. Lewisohn, *Nation* (February 2, 1921), 189, and F. H., "After the Play," *New Republic* (January 12, 1921): 204–5.

21. *Literary Digest* 68 (February 12, 1921): 26.

22. Heywood Broun, "Books," *New York Tribune* (January 7, 1921): 8.

23. This is the ending that appears in the published version of the play: Zona Gale, *Miss Lulu Bett: An American Comedy of Manners* (New York: Appleton, 1921).

24. Lewisohn, *Nation* (February 2, 1921): 189.

25. *New Republic* (January 12, 1921): 204–5; see also the review in *Literary Digest* (February 12, 1921): 26, which takes a similar view of the character of Dwight Deacon.

26. Heywood Broun, "How They Found Miss Lulu Bett," *Collier's Weekly* 67 (January 29, 1921): 13.

27. Robert Benchley, "Books and Other Things," *The World* (July 10, 1920): 8.

28. "Babbitt," adapted by Dorothy Farnum, Copyright Deposit Scripts, Motion Picture, Broadcasting and Recorded Sound Division, Library of Congress.

29. A second and perhaps better-known version was made in 1930 with Greta Garbo.

30. Christine Dymkowski, "Introduction," *Anna Christie and Emperor Jones*, by Eugene O'Neill (London: Royal National Theatre and Nick Hern Books, 1991), x, xviii.

31. Burns Mantle, *The Best Plays of 1921–1922* (New York: Small, Maynard & Company, 1922; rpt. Dodd, Mead & Company, 1943), 22. All page references to this series are to the reprinted editions.

32. O'Neill, *New York Times* (December 18, 1921), cited in Dymkowski, xvii.

33. George C. Pratt, *Spellbound in Darkness: A History of the Silent Film* (Greenwich, CT: New York Graphic Society, 1973; first published 1966), 174.

34. Review of *Anna Christie*, *Exceptional Photoplays* (October–November 1923): 1–2, reprinted in Slide, *Selected Film Criticism*, vol. 3, 15–17.

35. Vitagraph made sixty-seven adaptations of O. Henry stories that were released by the General Film Company under the O. Henry/Broadway Star Features label between March 1917 and October 1918—roughly one a week. Five released between August and November 1917 were four-reelers; most,

including *The Cop and the Anthem*, released in May 1917 and directed by Thomas R. Mills, were two-reelers.

36. Richard Koszarski, *The Man You Loved to Hate: Erich von Stroheim and Hollywood* (New York: Oxford University Press, 1983), 141–44.

37. The original script has been published in Erich von Stroheim, *Greed*, ed. Joel Finler (London: Lorrimer Publishing, 1972). Joel Finler, in *Stroheim* (Berkeley: University of California Press, 1968), compares Norris's novel, the script, and the film.

38. Von Stroheim, *Greed.*

39. Koszarski, *The Man You Loved to Hate*, 124, describes the reconstruction of a turn-of-the-century mining camp at the site of the Big Dipper Mine for the opening scenes.

40. Koszarski, *The Man You Loved to Hate*, 124, notes that the filmmakers chose the corner of Hayes and Laguna in San Francisco to reproduce the streets originally described by Norris, which had been destroyed by earthquake and fire in 1906.

41. The copy of *Anna Christie* to which I had access, a videotape released by Grapevine Video, does not have the original title cards; possibly the titles were worded differently in the release print, but they strike me as plausible for the period.

42. *Exceptional Photoplays* (December 1924–January 1925), reprinted in *From Quasimodo to Scarlett O'Hara: A National Board of Review Anthology, 1920–1940*, ed. Stanley Hochman (New York: F. Ungar, 1982), 37–38.

43. Iris Barry, "'Greed'—A Film of Realism," *Spectator* (March 14, 1925): 402.

44. Robert Sherwood, *Life* (January 1, 1925): 24. In the 1920s *Life* was a New York humor magazine very different from the photojournalism showcase edited by Henry Luce that succeeded it in 1936.

45. *Chicago Daily News* (February 23, 1925), reprinted in Carl Sandburg, *Carl Sandburg at the Movies: A Poet in the Silent Era, 1920–1927*, ed. Dale Fetherling and Doug Fetherling (Metuchen, NJ: Scarecrow Press, 1985), 121–24. See also the positive review in the New York *Herald Tribune* (December 14, 1924), cited in Koszarski, *The Man You Loved to Hate*, 147.

46. Koszarski, *The Man You Loved to Hate*, 129.

47. Ibid., 117.

48. The contract between Griffith and Moss is dated June 20, 1924, and an unidentified clipping dated July 4, 1924, reports the departure of Griffith and his company to Germany to make a film at that point entitled "Dawn"; microfilm reel 12, *The Papers of D. W. Griffith, 1897–1954* (Sanford, NC: Microfilming Corporation of America, 1982).

49. See, for example, Paul Rotha, *The Film Till Now: A Survey of World Cinema*, with an additional section by Richard Griffith (London: Hamlyn House, 1967; original version published 1930), 159. Thompson, "The Limits of Experimentation in Hollywood," also stresses the continuity between the films.

50. Paul Spehr, *The Movies Begin: Making Movies in New Jersey, 1887–1920* (Newark: Newark Museum, 1977), 87–88; Josef von Sternberg, *Fun in a Chinese Laundry* (New York: Macmillan, 1965), 28, 41–42.

51. Spehr, *The Movies Begin*, 106; Richard Koszarski, *Fort Lee: The Film Town* (Rome, Italy: John Libbey Publishing, 2004), 242–46.

52. Von Sternberg, *Fun in a Chinese Laundry*, 201–3.

53. Ibid., 200; these scenes were shot on a dredge making a channel in San Pedro harbor.

54. Ibid., 200; the street exteriors were shot in front of some brick hovels in Chinatown in Los Angeles.

55. Ibid., 200; these scenes were shot in the San Fernando Valley, and the sign was already there.

56. *Chicago Daily News* (February 14, 1925), reprinted in Carl Sandburg, *Carl Sandburg at the Movies*, 121.

57. *Exceptional Photoplays* (December 1924–January 1925), reprinted in *From Quasimodo to Scarlett O'Hara*, ed. Hochman, 39–40.

58. This film is discussed in greater detail in chapter 4.

59. *Film Mercury* (October 26, 1928): 6, reprinted in Slide, *Selected Film Criticism*, vol. 3, 79–81.

60. King Vidor, *A Tree Is a Tree* (New York: Harcourt, Brace & Company, 1952), 152–53.

61. The Turner/MGM Scripts, Academy of Motion Picture Arts and Sciences, Margaret Herrick Library, Special Collections, Beverly Hills, California (hereafter AMPAS), contain the text of what appears to be the alternate ending. It is given in a set of loose pages marked in pencil "old pgs out of 1–20–28," contained within a bound copy of the Cutting Continuity, dated January 21, 1928, with changes dated February 20, 1928. The bound copy adheres to the ending of the film as we know it today.

62. *Film Spectator* (April 14, 1928): 6–7, reprinted in Slide, *Selected Film Criticism*, vol. 3, 73–75.

63. *The New Republic* (March 7, 1928), reprinted in Pratt, *Spellbound in Darkness*, 469–71.

64. *Exceptional Photoplays* (March 1928), reprinted in *From Quasimodo to Scarlett O'Hara*, ed. Hochman, 102–3.

65. *Variety* (January 17, 1924: 26) noted: "The Hall Caine story is well known. It has been run as a serial in a popular fiction magazine and published in book form."

66. See Bengt Forslund, *Victor Sjöström: His Life and Work* (New York: Zoetrope, 1988), 183–90, and, on the relationship between *Name the Man* and *Greed*, 202.

67. I have not included Murnau's *Sunrise* in this chapter. Although it focuses on a rural couple and has been classed as a naturalist work by present-day critics (see Thompson, "The Limits of Experimentation in Hollywood," 84), at the time of its release it was celebrated largely for its technical virtuosity and stylistic artifice, as, for example, in the review by Louis Bogan, *The New*

Republic (October 16, 1927): 263–64, reprinted in Pratt, *Spellbound in Darkness*, 461–63. While the film's visual style influenced many Hollywood directors in the late silent period, *Sunrise* does not seem to me to have contributed substantially to models of the naturalist plot.

68. *The Wind*, Philip Siff, Scenario Record, October 31, 1925, Turner/MGM Scripts, AMPAS.

69. See the scenario by Frances Marion, October 30, 1926, and the Fourth Temporary Script, February 3, 1927; by the script dated February 24, 1927 (Turner/MGM Scripts, AMPAS), Roddy is really dead.

70. *Exceptional Photoplays* (December 1928), reprinted in Pratt, *Spellbound in Darkness*, 473.

71. Victor Seastrom was the Americanized form of Sjöström's name used in the credits of all his American films.

72. *Photoplay* (November 1927), reprinted in Slide, *Selected Film Criticism*, vol. 3, 315.

73. The release print does not survive, but according to Janet Bergstrom the silent version found in the Twentieth-Century Fox studio vaults in 1969 is complete and reasonably close to the film as Murnau had shot and planned it; Janet Bergstrom, "Murnau in America: Chronicle of Lost Films," *Film History* 14, nos. 3–4 (2002): 430–60.

3. SOPHISTICATED COMEDY

1. Alan Dale, "Eugene Walter's 'The Easiest Way,'" *New York American* (January 20, 1909), reprinted in Montrose J. Moses and John Mason Brown, eds., *The American Theater as Seen by Its Critics* (New York: Cooper Square Publishers, 1967), 184–87.

2. With the help of Rebecca Fischler, I reviewed all of the "Straight from the Shoulder Reports" in *Moving Picture World* for the 1926–27 season. The reports, which came from independent exhibitors in small towns, are not systematic; only some exhibitors chose to send information to the trade journal. The majority of films shown in these small-town theaters were Westerns, and there is ample evidence of a preference for lachrymose tales such as *Over the Hill to the Poorhouse*, a story about a suffering mother that was a big hit in 1920 and was still being played in small towns in 1926–27. However, some sophisticated comedies seem to have been appreciated, particularly Sidney Franklin's *Her Sister from Paris*. All reports on the film *Variety* were positive, among them the entries from Placerville, California, and Montpelier, Idaho (October 23, 1926: 505); Indianapolis, Indiana, and Robinson, Illinois (*Moving Picture World*, November 13, 1926: 108); and Arvada, Colorado (November 29, 1926: 304).

3. Jennifer Chung, "Too Sophisticated for the Sticks? Small Town Reception of Sophisticated Comedies, 1924–1928," unpublished paper (2005), gives examples of these trends. In Lincoln, Nebraska, the *Lincoln Star*'s coverage (February 3, 1926) of *Lady Windemere's Fan* included quotes from the *New*

York American, New York Evening World, New York Herald Tribune, and *New York Sun.* Reviews of *The Fast Set* in the Bridgeport, Connecticut, *Bridgeport Telegram* (October 25, 1924) and the Oshkosh, Wisconsin, *Daily Northwestern* (November 29, 1924) use the same phrases, which were apparently taken from a press kit; the language of the Wisconsin reviews of *Her Sister from Paris* in the *Appleton Post-Crescent* (October 21, 1925) and of *Exchange of Wives* in the *Wisconsin Rapids Daily Tribune* (December 12, 1925) also seem to derive from publicity material.

4. See chapter 1, note 67.

5. I am indebted for this reference to Sara Ross, "Banking the Flames of Youth: The Hollywood Flapper, 1920–1930," PhD diss., University of Wisconsin, Madison, 2000, 60–61.

6. *Variety* refers to Harold Bell Wright, one of America's best-selling novelists prior to World War I. A minister himself, his novels frequently had ministers as their protagonists. According to Edward Ifkovic, Wright, although attacked for his sentimentality and sermonizing, was revered by a large public as a religious writer, and his works were distributed by mail order to rural areas and small towns. See Ifkovic, "Harold Bell Wright," in *Dictionary of Literary Biography,* vol. 9, *American Novelists, 1910–1945,* ed. James J. Martine (Detroit, MI: Gale Research Co., 1981), 188–93 (available online at http://galenet.galegroup.com).

7. Matthew Bernstein, *Walter Wanger, Hollywood Independent* (Berkeley: University of California Press, 1994), 65–68, discusses the opposition between "sophisticated" and "hokum" pictures in relation to Wanger's career in the early sound period.

8. Percy W. White, "Stage Terms," *American Speech* 1, no. 8 (May 1926): 437.

9. Walter Winchell, "A Primer of Broadway Slang: An Initiate Reveals Some of the Mysteries of the Much Quoted Theatrical Idiom," *Vanity Fair* (November 1927): 67, 132, 134. See also Don Marquis, "Origin of 'Hokum' and Other Slang," *Billboard* (August 27, 1927): 42; for a discussion of the term when applied to jazz musicians, see Anonymous, "Hokum Wanted," *Billboard* (October 15, 1927): 46.

10. *Film Daily,* too, often used the term in this way, as when it described *The Little Church Around the Corner* (April 1, 1923: 3) as "sob-provoking hokum" that "will do where they like this kind of melodrama."

11. In addition to the reviews cited in the text, see those of *For You, My Boy* (April 26, 1923: 25) and *A Wife's Awakening* (September 9, 1921: 45).

12. *Variety* refers to the eastern circuit of theaters established by E. D. Stair and John H. Havlin in 1900; the circuit was devoted to 10–20–30 melodrama until 1910, when the owners shifted to small-time vaudeville; see Ben Singer, *Melodrama and Modernity: Early Sensational Cinema and Its Contexts* (New York: Columbia University Press, 2001), 161–65.

13. Richard Koszarski, *An Evening's Entertainment: The Age of the Silent Feature Picture, 1915–1928,* vol. 3 of *History of the American Cinema,* ed. Charles Harpole (New York: Scribner's, 1990), 225.

14. Pearl Latteier, "Griffith, Weber and the Decline of Progressive Film-making," unpublished paper (2005). The comparison of Weber and Griffith that follows is indebted to this paper.

15. "'Anne Boleyn' Rated in Class of 'Passion," *Variety* (January 21, 1921): 45.

16. For other examples, see the reviews of *Don't Tell the Wife* (February 23, 1927: 16) and *No Place to Go* (December 14, 1927: 23). From quite early in the decade, *Film Daily* also praised snappy intertitles; see, for example, *Home Stuff* (June 19, 1921: 8) and *Woman's Place* (October 23, 1921: 5).

17. Lary May, *Screening Out the Past: The Birth of Mass Culture and the Motion Picture Industry* (New York: Oxford University Press, 1980), 209–11. Sumiko Higashi, *Cecil B. DeMille and American Culture: The Silent Era* (Berkeley: University of California Press, 1994), 30, sees much more of a continuity between Griffith and DeMille in terms of the way in which they were recognized as directors in the 1910s and in the cultural aspirations of their early features. Nonetheless, she, too, thinks that consumption was crucial to motivating the sexual dynamic of the society comedies.

18. Sumiko Higashi, "The New Woman and Consumer Culture: Cecil B. DeMille's Sex Comedies," in *A Feminist Reader in Early Cinema*, ed. Jennifer M. Bean and Diane Negra (Durham, NC: Duke University Press, 2002), 298–332; Charles Musser, "Divorce, DeMille, and the Comedy of Remarriage," in *Classical Hollywood Comedy*, ed. Kristine Brunovska Karnick and Henry Jenkins (New York: Routledge, 1995), 282–313 and 392–98; and Musser, "Letter to the Editor," *Film History* 15, no. 1 (2003): 110–15. Koszarski, *An Evening's Entertainment*, 250, seems to agree that DeMille is an important influence on Lubitsch and thus on the elaboration of sophisticated comedy as a narrative type.

19. *Photoplay* 14, no. 3 (August 1918): 102, reprinted in Anthony Slide, *Selected Film Criticism*, vol. 2, *1912–1920* (Metuchen, NJ: Scarecrow Press, 1982), 184.

20. In contrast to the reviews cited above, *Variety* (May 24, 1918: 40) reviewed *Old Wives for New* in its "Among the Women" column, a review entirely devoted to the fashions displayed in the film.

21. An advertisement for the film using this language may be found in *Moving Picture World* (June 8, 1918: 1366–67).

22. The subtitle of the *Motion Picture News* review (February 8, 1918: 921) is "Points a Moral to Married Folk, or Those to be Married," and the story is deemed "clean and interesting."

23. Burns Mantle, "The Shadow Stage," *Photoplay* 17, no. 6 (May 1920): 64–65, reprinted in George C. Pratt, *Spellbound in Darkness: A History of the Silent Film* (Greenwich, CT: New York Graphic Society, 1973; first published 1966), 241–42.

24. See also *Variety*'s back-handed compliment on the intertitles in *Forbidden Fruit* (January 28, 1921: 39), "generally well written despite a leaning toward the obvious and a play on words," and the complaint about the "philosophic subtitles" in *The Golden Bed* (January 21, 1925: 34).

25. In its review of *The Golden Bed, Film Daily* (January 25, 1925: 6) also commented upon "the customary lavish display."

26. *Motion Picture News* (March 6, 1920: 2389) seems to have found the latter scene in bad taste: "The fight scenes between the two women might be toned down a bit."

27. On the derivation of sophisticated comedy plots from theatrical farce, see Billy Budd Vermillion, "The Remarriage Plot in the 1910s," *Film History* 13, no. 4 (2001): 359–71, and Ben Brewster, "The Circle: Lubitsch and the Theatrical Farce Tradition," *Film History* 13, no. 4 (2001): 372–89.

28. The influence of *A Woman of Paris* on Lubitsch is discussed by Kristin Thompson, *Herr Lubitsch Goes to Hollywood: German and American Film after World War I* (Amsterdam: Amsterdam University Press, 2005), 100–1; and the influence of *A Woman of Paris* on Ozu is discussed by David Bordwell, *Ozu and the Poetics of Cinema* (Princeton, NJ: Princeton University Press, 1988), 152, 156. For Eisenstein, see S. M. Eisenstein, "The New Language of Cinematography," *Close Up* 4, no. 5 (May 1929): 10–13.

29. Harry Carr, "Chaplin Explains Chaplin," *Motion Picture Magazine* 30 (November 1925): 31, 88.

30. Ted Le Berthon, "Absolutely, Mr. Chaplin! Positively, Mr. Freud!: Psychoanalysis Comes to the Movies," *Motion Picture Classic* 17 (August 1923): 37, 88.

31. Douglas Z. Doty, "Charles Chaplin and 'A Woman of Paris': A New Era for the Screen Is Marked by This Production, Written and Directed by Charles Chaplin Himself," *The Storyworld and Photodramatist* (September 1923): 16–20.

32. *Photoplay* (December 1923): 73, reprinted in Slide, *Selected Film Criticism*, vol. 3, 318.

33. *Exceptional Photoplays* (October–November 1923): 3.

34. Charles W. Wood, "With the Bunk Left Out," *Collier's* (November 17, 1923): 31.

35. Harry Carr, "Will Charlie Kick Off His Old Shoes?" *Motion Picture Magazine* 26 (December 1923): 28–29, 86.

36. Wood, "With the Bunk Left Out," 31.

37. Ibid., 31, and Scott O'Dell, *Representative Photoplays Analyzed* (Hollywood: Palmer Institute of Authorship, 1924), 258.

38. O'Dell, *Representative Photoplays Analyzed*, 260.

39. The *New York Times* (February 4, 1924: 23) also compared Lubitsch's film to Chaplin's on the basis of the "hitherto unknown rapidity of the action" and its simplicity and subtlety.

40. *Exceptional Photoplays* (December 1923–January 1924); reprinted in Stanley Hochman, ed., *From Quasimodo to Scarlett O'Hara: A National Board of Review Anthology, 1920–1940* (New York: F. Ungar, 1982), 33.

41. *Photoplay* 25, no. 5 (April 1924): 61; reprinted in Slide, *Selected Film Criticism*, vol. 3, 185–60.

42. Robert Sherwood, "Revivals," *Life* (January 7, 1926): 26. Although Sherwood's judgment that *Broken Blossoms* lacks "pictorial expressiveness" is

clearly unwarranted, the example confirms that, in comparison with the films of Chaplin and Lubitsch, among others, Griffith's use of intertitles was considered both too copious and redundant with the images.

43. Iris Barry, "The Cinema: Hope Fulfilled," *The Spectator* (May 17, 1924): 788; reprinted in Pratt, *Spellbound in Darkness*, 316–17.

44. Iris Barry, *Let's Go to the Movies* (1926, rpt. New York: Arno Press, 1972), 82–83.

45. For a comparison of play and film, see Brewster, "The Circle," 381–82.

46. My analysis is indebted to Raymond Bellour, "L'évidence et le code" and "Segmenter/Analyser," both in *L'analyse du Film* (Paris: Éditions Albatros, 1979), 123–30 and 247–70; translated by Diana Matias as "The Obvious and the Code" and "To Segment/To Analyze," in Bellour, *The Analysis of Film* (Bloomington: Indiana University Press, 2000), 69–76, 103–215.

47. Lewis Jacobs, *The Rise of the American Film: A Critical History* (New York: Teacher's College Press, 1975; first published 1939), 356–57.

48. In the *Film Daily* review of *Don't Call Me Little Girl* (June 26, 1921: 13), starring Mary Miles Minter, the reviewer notes that she "virtually steals a part away from Constance Talmadge, inasmuch as it requires a strenuous series of vampings in which the heroine steals her aunt's fiance—a part usually associated with the bob-haired comedienne."

49. Thompson, *Herr Lubitsch Goes to Hollywood*, 84–89.

50. The reviewer added:

Henley's raciness in direction creeps out in handling Miss Adoree, for she is a woman with much sex appeal, and he photos it all. In the interests of family audiences and the houses playing Sunday films in the territories where there is sentiment against such a practice she should have worn a brassier constantly, and Henley shouldn't have been so anxious to show off the outlines of the lady's breasts. Maybe it's good stuff for big city crowds, but, notwithstanding, it is T.N.T. for the church elements, which are working for censorship. However that is a phase concerned purely with the producers and if they wanted to take the chance it's their business, insomuch as the reflection will be on them. It's likely to get some of the smaller exhibitors in bad with his clientele, however.

51. In 1941 MGM released another version of this plot, *Two-Faced Woman*, directed by George Cukor, which had to be much attenuated due to the protests of the Catholic Legion of Decency; the dispute is detailed in the entry on this film in the *American Film Institute Catalog of Feature Films*.

52. Jennifer Chung confirms this; see "At Last: 'Her Sister from Paris' at Sigma," *Lima News* (September 6, 1925), cited in Chung, "Too Sophisticated for the Sticks? Small Town Reception of Sophisticated Comedies, 1924–1928," unpublished paper (2005), 11. Apparently the film was also censored in Chicago; Chung, 11, cites another Ohio newspaper article, "Chicago Coppers Censor Feature," *Zanesville Signal* (October 1, 1925).

53. Vermillion, "The Remarriage Plot in the 1910s," discusses the long history of this farce on the American stage, as well as the many cinematic adaptations of it in the 1910s.

54. *Photoplay* (January 1926): 26, reprinted in Slide, *Selected Film Criticism*, vol. 3, 159.

55. *Photoplay* (April 1926): 54, reprinted in Slide, *Selected Film Criticism*, vol. 3, 117.

56. *Photoplay* (February 1926): 50, reprinted in Slide, *Selected Film Criticism*, vol. 3, 162.

57. Edmund Wilson, "Mürger and Wilde on the Screen," *New Republic* 46 (March 24, 1926): 144, reprinted as "A German Director in Hollywood" in Wilson, *The American Earthquake: A Documentary of the Twenties and Thirties* (New York: Doubleday, 1958), 78–79.

58. Gilbert Seldes, "American Humor," in *America as Americans See It*, ed. Fred J. Ringel (New York: Literary Guild, 1932), 347–60.

59. Bellour, "The Obvious and the Code" and "To Segment/To Analyze"; on Lubitsch's classicism, see Thompson, *Herr Lubitsch Goes to Hollywood;* on classical Hollywood narration, see David Bordwell, Janet Staiger, and Kristin Thompson, *The Classical Hollywood Cinema: Film Style and Mode of Production to 1960* (London: Routledge & Kegan Paul, 1985), 1–84.

60. Ezra Pound, Letter to Iris Barry, July 1916, *The Letters of Ezra Pound, 1907–1941*, ed. D. D. Paige (New York: Harcourt Brace, 1950), 90, cited in Richard Bridgman, *The Colloquial Style in America* (New York: Oxford University Press, 1966), 202.

4. THE MALE ADVENTURE STORY

1. Mencken, *A Book of Prefaces* (New York: Alfred Knopf, 1917), 35.

2. Leslie Fiedler, *Love and Death in the American Novel* (Normal, IL: Dalkey Archive Press, 1997; first published 1960); and Jane Tompkins, *West of Everything: The Inner Life of Westerns* (New York: Oxford University Press, 1992).

3. Ned Buntline [Edward Z. C. Judson], *The Black Avenger of the Spanish Main: or, The Fiend of Blood, A Thrilling Story of the Buccaneer Times* (Boston: F. Gleason, 1847), is discussed by Henry Nash Smith, *Democracy and the Novel: Popular Resistance to Classic American Writers* (New York: Oxford University Press, 1978), 8.

4. In *Entretiens sur Le Fils naturel*, Diderot advocated the creation of a new, emotionally touching genre based upon the ordinary circumstances and situations of bourgeois life. This genre is given different names in his dramatic criticism, but the best known are *drame bourgeois, genre sérieux*, and *comédie larmoyante*. While *The Black Avenger of the Spanish Main* proposes a rather contrived and fantastic plot, the final scenes of domestic reconciliation are done in the manner proposed by Diderot as a series of wordless tableaux, or stage pictures, which the spectators within the story find supremely touching. See *Le*

Fils naturel and *Entretiens sur Le Fils naturel,* in *Œuvres complètes de Diderot,* vol. 10: *Le Drame bourgeois,* ed. Jacques Chouillet and Anne-Marie Chouillet (Paris: Hermann, 1980), 83–162.

5. Franco Moretti, "Kindergarten," in *Signs Taken for Wonders: Essays in the Sociology of Literary Forms,* trans. Susan Fischer, David Forgacs, and David Miller (London: NLB, 1983). This article is cited by Steve Neale, "Melodrama and Tears," *Screen* 27, no. 6 (November–December 1986): 6–22, and Mary Anne Doane, *The Desire to Desire: The Woman's Film of the 1940s* (Bloomington: Indiana University Press, 1987), 90–91.

6. See also *Variety*'s review of *The Man from Nevada* (September 18, 1929: 55).

7. The *Variety* review of *Speakeasy* (March 13, 1929: 28) describes the film as a boxing film disguised by its title and claims that boxing films in general are "poison to women."

8. For the influence of Nietzsche on American fiction, see Melvin Drimmer, "Nietzsche in American Thought 1895–1925," PhD diss., University of Rochester, 1965; for a discussion of Jack London, see Charles Child Walcutt, *American Literary Naturalism, A Divided Stream* (Minneapolis: University of Minnesota Press, 1956), chapter 5.

9. John Driscoll, "Laurence Stallings," in *Dictionary of Literary Biography,* vol. 44, *American Screenwriters,* 2nd series, ed. Randall Clark (Detroit, MI: Gale Research Co., 1986), 357–63 (available online at http://galenet.galegroup .com).

10. There were two reviews of the film in *Variety.* One reported on the print screened at Grauman's Egyptian Theater in Hollywood on November 9 (November 11, 1925: 36); the other, on the print at the Astor in New York City on November 19 (December 2, 1925: 40). The latter review notes some censorship cuts made between the Los Angeles and New York screenings, but both prints ran 130 minutes.

11. Kenneth MacGowan, "Introduction," *Famous American Plays of the 1920s* (New York: Dell Publishing, 1959), 21. MacGowan recalls that he preferred formal experimentation to realist works, and, sharing the overvaluation of Eugene O'Neill characteristic of the period, he writes: "In the first half of the twenties, I applauded the realism of *Anna Christie, What Price Glory?* and *They Knew What They Wanted,* but cheered louder for the freer form of *The Emperor Jones, The Hairy Ape, The Great God Brown,* and *Strange Interlude.*"

12. Ibid., 13.

13. Burns Mantle, *Best Plays of 1921–1922 and the Year Book of the Drama in America* (New York: Dodd, Mead & Company, 1943; first published 1922), 22.

14. Burns Mantle, *The Best Plays of 1924–1925 and the Year Book of the Drama in America* (New York: Dodd, Mead and Company, 1942; first published 1925), viii, 8.

15. MacGowan, "Introduction," *Famous American Plays of the 1920s,* 19.

16. Mantle, *Best Plays of 1924–1925,* 30.

17. *New York Times* (September 6, 1924): 14.

18. MacGowan, "Introduction," *Famous American Plays of the 1920s*, 19.

19. One of the anomalies of this example is that the film versions were not subject to censorship. I would expect that, at least in the case of Walsh's film, the Motion Picture Producers and Distributors of America would have attempted to intervene under the terms of the Formula, a policy governing the purchase and adaptation of literary works that the industry adopted in 1924. Letters in the *What Price Glory* file, Fox Legal Files, Arts Special Collections, UCLA, Los Angeles, indicate that the studio acquired the silent film rights to the play in August 1925. Technically, it could have been subjected to review by MPPDA officials under the Formula, and this would seem likely, given that the play had already aroused protests and been targeted for legal censorship as noted above. However, there is no evidence of any negotiations between Fox and the MPPDA in either the Fox Legal Files, the Fox Produced Script Files held at UCLA, or the Production Code Administration Files, Special Collections, Margaret Herrick Library, Douglas Fairbanks Study Center, Academy of Motion Picture Arts and Sciences, Beverly Hills.

20. All references in this book to the text of the play *What Price Glory* by Maxwell Anderson and Laurence Stallings are to the version in *Famous American Plays of the 1920s*, ed. MacGowan, 53–129; the stage direction quoted here appears on 61 and the dialogue on 57. MacGowan's edition is a reprint of that included in Maxwell Anderson and Laurence Stallings, *Three American Plays* (New York: Harcourt Brace and Company, 1926), 5–89 (except that Mac-Gowan adds a query to the title). While obviously preferable to the frankly bowdlerized version that appears in Mantle, *Best Plays of 1924–1925*, 30–55, this edition may still reflect the tampering of the New York district attorney referred to above. To my knowledge, no one has established a definitive edition of the play.

21. Hecht's and MacArthur's *The Front Page* seems to have been inspired by this way of structuring a plot but employs one rather than two scheming men: given a deadline, the departure of Hildy's train for New York, Walter Burns does everything he can to manipulate events to prevent Hildy's leaving.

22. Stallings, "The Big Parade," *New Republic* (September 17, 1924): 66–69. The story of the film differs significantly from this brief sketch, about a lieutenant who has only nine men left of his original company of ninety. He is told to bring eight of them to Paris to represent the regiment in a Fourth of July parade. The men draw straws, and the runner, Gianonni, purposefully shortens his straw so that he will be left behind. Hot and bored, the lieutenant thinks of Gianonni while he and his men are marching, worried that Gianonni will be dead by the time they get back. In a final twist, as he takes the train to return to the trenches with his men, the lieutenant sees Gianonni in a stolen major's uniform leaving for Deauville in the company of a blonde.

23. Vidor, in *A Tree Is a Tree* (New York: Harcourt Brace and Company, 1952), 111–14, says that Stallings provided one five-page treatment; in an interview with Nancy Dowd and David Shepard in *King Vidor*, ed. Edward

Schilling, A Directors Guild of America Oral History (New Jersey: Directors Guild of American and Scarecrow Press, 1988), 73, Vidor says that Stallings wrote four or five treatments that became the basis of the film. In *The Big Parade* script file in the MGM Collection, Doheny Library, University of Southern California, Los Angeles, there is one undated five-page memo from Laurence Stallings to Irving Thalberg that is identified as "First draft— Original Story" and titled "The Big Parade." This story is different from the one published in *The New Republic* and from what was finally filmed. But Stallings's treatment does contain elements that were incorporated into the film's plot: the device of scenes set in the United States at the beginning and end, the epilogue in France, and the characters of the spoiled and wealthy Jim, the enlisted man Bull, Mélisande, and the girlfriend back home, Justyn, who eventually prefers Jim's brother. Although presented much differently, the battlefield episode of Jim first wounding and being wounded by a German soldier and then befriending him is also included. I am grateful to Ned Comstock of the Doheny Library for his help in clarifying the complicated textual history of *The Big Parade*.

24. After the film was completed, the beginning and ending scenes in the United States were recast and reshot. In *King Vidor*, ed. Edward Schilling, 91, the director recalls, "After we completed the picture, we thought we'd better recast the people in the American home life, the family. After the studio saw the cut, they said, 'My God, this is such a terrific picture, it should have the best actors you can get.' Part of that sentimentality is due to Mr. Mayer wanting more material with the mother. They thought that the last scene didn't live up to the rest of the picture. So, I reshot the beginning and end, changed the casting for the family, and that was that." Kevin Brownlow, *The War, the West, and the Wilderness* (London: Secker & Warburg, 1978), 192–93, also refers to Vidor's finding the reshot ending sentimental.

25. *Exceptional Photoplays* (November–December 1925), reprinted in Stanley Hochman, ed., *From Quasimodo to Scarlett O'Hara: A National Board of Review Anthology, 1920–1940* (New York: F. Ungar, 1982), 47–50.

26. Robert E. Sherwood, review of "The Big Parade," *Life* (December 10, 1925): 24–25.

27. Iris Barry, *The Spectator* (June 5, 1926): 946–47.

28. *Photoplay* (January 1926): 46, reprinted in Anthony Slide, *Selected Film Criticism* (Metuchen, NJ: Scarecrow Press, 1982–85), vol. 3, 36–37.

29. See Barry, *Let's Go to the Movies* (New York: Arno Press, 1972; first published 1926), 48, 59–60, 68–69.

30. This motif also pervades the adventure films of Howard Hawks, reaching as far as the Western *Rio Bravo*, where Dude, who has shaking hands after recovering from a three-year alcoholic binge, fails while trying to roll his own cigarettes and takes them from his friend Chance without any words passing between them.

31. Neale, "Melodrama and Tears," 7.

32. In *The Big Parade* Bull receives a letter at mail call. It is from a woman and written in French. He takes it to the intellectual of the company to read to him. Instead of reading it out loud, the soldier becomes fascinated and reads it to himself, mouthing "Oh, boy" at one point and taking out his handkerchief to wipe his forehead at another. When he finishes reading the letter he shakes Bull's hand, saying, "My boy, you certainly know your onions!" He then pins a sharpshooter medal to Bull's chest.

33. Russell Sanjek, *Pennies from Heaven: The American Popular Music Business in the Twentieth Century*, updated by David Sanjek (New York: Da Capo Press, 1996), 553. Lyrics and music may be found in *Songs of the 20's: Piano, Vocal, Guitar* (Milwaukee: H. Leonard Corp., 1989). The lyrics follow:

> *First verse:* You went away one dreary day
> I knew you had to go
> 'mid tears and cheers I heard you say
> "Charmaine, I love you so
> Tho' old tears turn to new
> My heart keeps calling you.
> *Refrain:* I wonder why you keep me waiting,
> Charmaine cries in vain,
> I wonder when bluebirds are mating,
> will you come back again
> I wonder if I keep on praying
> will our dreams be the same?
> I wonder if you ever think of me, too,
> Charmaine's waiting, just waiting for you.
> *Second verse:* I can't forget that night we met,
> how bright were skies above.
> That precious mem'ry lingers yet,
> when you declared your love.
> And then you went away,
> and now each night and day (repeat *Refrain*).

34. "The Mighty Wurlitzer: Music for Movie Palace Organs" (New World Records, Recorded Anthology of American Music, Inc., 1977).

35. Donald Crafton, *The Talkies: American Cinema's Transition to Sound 1926–1931*, vol. 4, *History of the American Cinema* (New York, Charles Scribner's Sons, 1997), 93–94, writes that in the summer of 1927 *What Price Glory* was reissued with a nonsynchronized music-and-effects track, among the first Fox feature films to be endowed with sound. I have not been able to determine if the Rapee/Pollack song was prepared for, or recorded on, this track, but since most theaters were not wired for sound in 1927, it seems unlikely that large numbers of people would have heard it in this way. I am inclined to think that most audiences heard the song "Charmaine" as part of the live musical accompaniment for the film and that this is what propelled the large sheet music sales.

36. *Exceptional Photoplays* (December 1926), reprinted in Hochman, ed., *From Quasimodo to Scarlett O'Hara,* 72–74.

37. Hochman, ed., *From Quasimodo to Scarlett O'Hara,* 73.

38. Olivier Eyquem, Michael Henry, and Jacques Saada, "Interview with Raoul Walsh," in *Raoul Walsh,* ed. Phil Hardy (Colchester, England: Vineyard Press Ltd., for the Edinburgh Film Festival, 1974), 46.

39. Todd McCarthy, *Howard Hawks: The Grey Fox of Hollywood* (New York: Grove Press, 1997), 105.

40. Ibid., 115–17.

41. The plot of *Men without Women* is built around a sentimental stereotype, the gentleman who assumes a new, déclassé identity to protect the reputation of the woman he loves; this stereotype also underpins such blatantly sentimental plays and films as *The Squaw Man* and *Beau Geste.* But the visual absence (except in the pages of an illustrated magazine) of the woman in question and the emphasis on the conflict between the hero, Chief Torpedoman Burke, and his nemesis, Commander Weymouth, R.N., justify the title and the inclusion of the film as an example in this context.

42. *What Price Glory* resurfaces later in John Ford's career. He directed both a theatrical version with Ward Bond and Pat O'Brien in 1949 and a film remake with James Cagney and Dan Dailey in 1952. The casting of the stage version given here is taken from the filmography in Tag Gallagher's *John Ford: The Man and His Films* (Berkeley: University of California Press, 1986), 532. In the text, however (275), Gallagher says that Flagg was played by John Wayne (Wayne was Ford's choice for the part in the 1952 film, but the director was overruled by Fox). According to Andrew Sinclair, in *John Ford: A Biography* (London: Lorrimer, 1979), 160, the 1949 production, a benefit for the charity the Military Order of the Purple Heart, toured California towns with different Hollywood stars in the lead parts in each venue, and Wayne played Flagg in one or more of these.

43. Three versions were produced before 1930: one in 1914 by Cecil B. DeMille for Famous Players Lasky; one in 1923 by Tom Forman for B. P. Schulberg's Preferred Pictures; and one in 1929 by Victor Fleming for Paramount.

44. Jim Kitses, *Horizons West* (London: Thames & Hudson, 1969).

45. Charles Bitsch and Claude Chabrol, "Entretien avec Anthony Mann," *Cahiers du cinéma* 12, no. 69 (March 1957): 6.

46. There are early Westerns in which the symbolic structure described by Kitses does not apply. In a film like Selig's *Ranch Life in the Great South-West,* from 1910, the Wild West show elements—rope tricks, riding stunts, and fancy shooting—predominate without being completely integrated within the narrative. *Variety* (September 18, 1929: 55) similarly assesses a much later, low-budget Western produced by J. P. McGowan, *The Man from Nevada:* "There's a girl, Natalie Joyce, in the motherless big sister role. Not much love stuff. J. P. is all for the men. Plenty of hard riding, with the audience not so often forgetting what it is all about."

47. My sense of the backstory comes from the *Variety* review (July 27, 1927: 18); the version I saw on the Grapevine Video release, deriving from a

9.5mm French-language print, begins at the moment when Jerry is chased by the Coast Guard and breaks in on Jane and her fiancé.

48. Burns Mantle's brief summary of *Twelve Miles Out,* in his *The Best Plays of 1925–1926 and the Year Book of the Drama in America* (New York: 1945; first published 1927), 497, and reviews in the *New York Times* of the New York production (November 17, 1925: 29) and the London production (February 20, 1927: 1) indicate that the play was less like *What Price Glory* than the film. Although references to comic writing suggest that there may have been elements of a Quirt-Flagg relationship in the repartee between McCue and Jerry, the action makes the former a more simply villainous character. Jerry defeats him in the fight over Jane (who is married to Burton, and is not, as in the film, his fiancée, an obvious censorship change) and then renounces her; the next day he gives himself up to the revenue men and agrees to reform, whereupon she decides to divorce Burton and marry him. As the only schooner involved is McCue's, he cannot exculpate Jerry by falsely claiming ownership of the boat and its cargo.

49. McCarthy, *Howard Hawks,* 40–42.

50. Henri Langlois, "The Modernity of Howard Hawks," in *Howard Hawks American Artist,* ed. Jim Hillier and Peter Wollen (London: BFI Publishing, 1996), 72; originally published in *Cahiers du cinéma,* no. 139 (January 1963) and originally translated in *Focus on Howard Hawks,* ed. Joseph McBride (New Jersey: Prentice-Hall, 1972). In the same volume, 13–14, see Jean-George Auriol, "*A Girl in Every Port,*" trans. John Moore, originally published in *La Revue du cinéma* (December 1928).

51. In the print I viewed the title introducing this sequence ran: "Rio de Janeiro. Still trying to overhaul a heart and anchor"; a later one that introduces the sequence in which Spike and Bill actually meet runs: "Central America. Just a port behind the Branding Romeo." As the two men are in the same port in this second sequence, the second title makes no sense here. I assume that the titles were misplaced and should be swapped and that the meeting takes place in Rio.

52. McCarthy, *Howard Hawks,* 91, explains that the New York censor board insisted on the name change.

53. *The Air Circus* (September 1928), a lost film, bears comparison with both *A Girl in Every Port* and *The Dawn Patrol* in that Hawks seems to have tried to introduce sympathetic female characters into a story about an all-male group, perhaps in response to the criticism of *A Girl in Every Port.* The bulk of the plot is concerned with the adventures and mishaps of a group of student pilots, and particularly the professional competition between two friends, but a couple of important female characters have been included: Sue, herself an accomplished aviator who spurs on the hero, and the boy's mother. It is not clear how much Hawks had to do with the Movietone sequence added to the film after it was completed, but the script pages by Sidney Lazarus, dated July 7, 1928, Fox Produced Scripts, Arts Special Collections, UCLA, suggests that in them the mother becomes an important and somewhat ambiguous figure. The

sound sequence occurred after the boy panics in the air during his first solo flight and the mother, who has already lost one son in an air battle during World War I, makes a sentimental appeal to her only surviving child to give way to his fear of flying and return home with her.

54. Gilbert Seldes, "The Movies in Peril," *Scribner's* (February 1935): 82.

55. Gilbert Seldes, "The Best Pictures of Last Tuesday," *Esquire* (August 1938): 72, 90.

56. Larry Langman and Daniel Finn, *A Guide to American Silent Crime Films* (Westport, CT: Greenwood Press, 1994), xvii.

57. For more on the film and the play on which it was based, see Ben Brewster, "*Alias Jimmy Valentine* and Situational Dramaturgy," *Film History* 9, no. 4 (1997): 388–409.

58. Bradley Schauer, "Justice and Redemption in the Underworld: The Crook Melodrama of the 1920s," unpublished paper (2005); William Everson, *American Silent Film* (New York: Oxford University Press, 1978), 227–28, also mentions the masquerade plot in connection with *The Gangsters and the Girl* (Thomas Ince, 1914). One amusing variant of this plot concludes with the heroine disappointed to find out that the man she has fallen in love with is not, in fact, a gangster, as in *The Exciters* (*Variety*, June 7, 1923: 24) and *Come Across* (*Variety*, July 17, 1929: 57). *Variety* comments on the prevalence of the masquerade plot in the review of *Dressed to Kill* (March 14, 1928: 23): "This version has several angles to vary the stereotyped crook story. Heroine instead of turning out to be a detective is a girl seeking to recover bonds for the theft of which her lover, bank official, is in prison."

59. Gerald Peary, "Introduction, *Little Caesar* Takes Over the Screen," in *Little Caesar* (Madison: University of Wisconsin Press, 1981), 20; Steve Neale, *Genre and Hollywood* (London: Routledge, 2000), 80; and Lee Grieveson, "Gangsters and Governance in the Silent Era," in *Mob Culture: Hidden Histories of the American Gangster Film*, ed. Lee Grieveson, Esther Sonnet, and Peter Stanfield (New Brunswick, NJ: Rutgers University Press, 2005), 32, seem to share this view of *Underworld* as a typical reformation plot.

60. "Underworld," *Exceptional Photoplays* (August 1927), reprinted in Hochman, ed., *From Quasimodo to Scarlett O'Hara*, 92; Bancroft's performance is also praised in the review of *Underworld* in *Photoplay* (September 1927): 52, reprinted in Slide, *Selected Film Criticism*, vol. 3, 299–300, and the *New York Times* (August 22, 1927: 21).

61. According to William MacAdams, *Ben Hecht: The Man Behind the Legend* (New York: Charles Scribner's Sons, 1990), 95, *Underworld* was Hecht's second film assignment; his first experience was polishing the script for *The New Klondike* (1926). I agree with Todd McCarthy, *Howard Hawks*, 76, that MacAdams's account of the production history of *Underworld* is otherwise highly implausible.

62. Von Sternberg, *Fun in a Chinese Laundry* (New York: Macmillan, 1965), 214–15. Ben Hecht, "*Underworld*, '(an original story of Chicago),'" typescript in blue folder, n.d., Paramount Script Collection, Special Collections, Margaret Her-

rick Library, AMPAS. This story contains the final situation of the film: a gangster about to be hanged has broken out of jail suspecting a loyal member of his gang of being after his girlfriend. All three main characters die in the end as the police close in on the house in which the criminal is sequestered. Ben Hecht, "Underworld," complete script, n.d., Paramount Script Collection, Special Collections, Margaret Herrick Library, AMPAS, contains the meeting between Bull Weed and the character eventually played by Clive Brook, called "Weasel" in this version, and the scene in the Dreamland café. In this version of the ending Bull Weed dies, but Weasel and Feathers do not. The *Underworld* Production File, Paramount Production Files, Special Collections, Margaret Herrick Library, AMPAS, shows a reimbursement dated December 3, 1926, for Hecht's transportation from New York to Los Angeles as well as six payments made to Hecht and stenographers from December 11, 1926 to January 22, 1927.

63. Robert N. Lee, "Underworld," complete script, March 28, 1927, introduces the secret passageway in Bull's hideout, which helps to motivate Weasel's return to the barricaded apartment more logically, since he has the only key to the hidden door. In the film the ending is modified still further in that the Weasel character, now called Rolls-Royce, uses the passageway to gain entrance to the apartment during the shoot-out with the police, and, at Bull's urging, it becomes the means by which the couple make their final getaway.

64. Charles Furthman is credited with the adaptation of *Underworld*, although I have not been able to determine his contribution to the project precisely. Both the name "Feathers" and the idea of throwing money into a spittoon to humiliate a drunk were reprised in his brother Jules Furthman's script for *Rio Bravo* (1959).

65. This use of a flashing sign to indicate the gangster's ambition and self-regard is of course reprised in *Scarface*.

66. Brownlow, *Behind the Mask of Innocence: Sex, Violence, Prejudice, Crime: Films of Social Conscience in the Silent Era* (New York: Alfred Knopf, 1990), 205.

67. On the censorship of the gangster film in the 1930s, see Richard Maltby, "'Grief in the Limelight': Al Capone, Howard Hughes, the Hays Code and the Politics of the Unstable Text," in *Movies and Politics: The Dynamic Relationship*, ed. James Combs (New York: Garland Publishing, 1993), 133–82.

68. I discuss the tempo of the line delivery in *Scarface* in "Keeping Up with Hawks," *Style* 32, no. 3 (Fall 1998): 402–26. The speed and deftness of Cagney's line delivery seem to me to become a veritable trademark for the actor; Robert Sklar, *City Boys: Cagney, Bogart, Garfield* (Princeton, NJ: Princeton University Press, 1992), 33–34, discusses Cagney's performance style and diction in *The Public Enemy*.

5. THE SEDUCTION PLOT

1. Janet Todd, *Sensibility: An Introduction* (London: Methuen, 1986), 147–49, discusses the movement of sentimental motifs from the eighteenth-century

novel of sensibility to such popular forms as Victorian melodrama and the popular novel. See also Sally Mitchell, *The Fallen Angel: Chastity, Class and Women's Reading, 1835–1880* (Bowling Green, OH: Bowling Green University Popular Press, 1981).

2. See the chapter on Richardson in Herbert Ross Brown, *The Sentimental Novel in America, 1789–1860* (Durham, NC: Duke University Press, 1940).

3. Cathy N. Davidson, Introduction, *Charlotte Temple*, by Susan Haswell Rowson (New York: Oxford University Press, 1986).

4. Fiedler, *Love and Death in the American Novel* (Normal, IL: Dalkey Archive Press, 1997; first published 1960), 82–93.

5. Nina Baym, *Women's Fiction: A Guide to Novels By and About Women in America, 1820–1870* (Ithaca, NY: Cornell University Press, 1978), 25–26.

6. Mitchell, *The Fallen Angel*, 151–52.

7. See, for example, James Smith, *Melodrama* (London: Methuen, 1973); Michael Booth, *English Melodrama* (London: Herbert Jenkins, 1965), chapter 5; and Ben Singer, *Melodrama and Modernity: Early Sensational Cinema and Its Contexts* (New York: Columbia University Press, 2001), chapter 8.

8. Michael Denning, *Mechanic Accents: Dime Novels and Working-Class Culture in America* (London: Verso, 1987), 94–97, 185–200.

9. Jean Carwile Masteller, Heidi L. M. Jacobs, and Jennifer Putzi, "Laura Jean Libbey," in *Dictionary of Literary Biography*, vol. 221, *American Prose Writers, 1870–1920*, ed. Sharon M. Harris (Detroit, MI: Gale Research Co., 2000), 253–64 (now available at http://galenet.galegroup.com).

10. Fiedler, *Love and Death in the American Novel*, 70. Oliver Goldsmith's song appears in chapter 24 of *The Vicar of Wakefield*.

11. H. L. Mencken, "The Taste for Romance" (May 1911) and "Lachrymose Love" (February 1915), both reprinted in *H. L. Mencken's Smart Set Criticism*, ed. William H. Nolte (Ithaca, NY: Cornell University Press, 1968), 132–33, 170–74. For a more extended, but also later, humorous reworking of a fallen woman plot, see his "A Girl from Red Lion, P.A.," first printed in *The New Yorker* (February 15, 1941) and reprinted in *Newspaper Days, 1899–1906* (New York: Knopf, 1941), 227–380.

12. Robert Benchley, "The Drama," review of "The Mirage," *Life* (October 21, 1920): 724–25; for a similar joshing of the seduction plot, see Benchley's "The Drama," review of "Respect for Riches," *Life* (May 27, 1920): 992–93.

13. *New York Times* (sec. 6, September 24, 1922: 1), cited by Jane Greene, "The Road to Reno: *The Awful Truth* and the Hollywood Comedy of Remarriage," *Film History* 13, no. 4 (2001): 357, n. 10.

14. *Romance* was written by the American Edward Sheldon and first produced in 1913. The play became a big success only in England, where Doris Keane and Basil Sydney played the title roles. Griffith's contract with Keane called for an advance of $150,000 as well as a percentage of the profits, a deal that Richard Schickel calls "unprecedented for its day." Schickel, *D. W. Griffith and the Birth of Film* (London: Pavilion Books, 1984), 427.

15. Schickel, *D. W. Griffith and the Birth of Film*, 429.

16. David Mayer, *"Way Down East:* Theatrical Sources," in *The Griffith Project,* vol. 10, *Films Produced in 1919–46,* ed. Paolo Cherchi Usai (Pordenone: Le Giornate del Cinema Muto/London: BFI Publishing, 2006), 95–103. See also William Brady, *Showman* (New York: E. P. Dutton & Company, 1937), 77–109.

17. This discussion of the reception of Griffith's film is drawn from my entry on *Way Down East* in *The Griffith Project,* vol. 10, *Films Produced in 1919–46,* ed. Paolo Cherchi Usai, 81–95, and is reprinted with kind permission of Le Giornate del Cinema Muto.

18. Winchell Smith, Letter to D. W. Griffith, 5 September 1920, *The Papers of D. W. Griffith 1897–1954* (Sanford, NC: Microfilming Corporation of America, 1982).

19. Frederick James Smith, "The Celluloid Critic," *Motion Picture Classic* (November 1920): 43, 86, 98, 100.

20. George Jean Nathan, *The Popular Theatre* (New York: Knopf, 1918), 19.

21. For some reason this review does not appear in the anthology *The New York Times Film Reviews, 1913–1931;* it is reprinted in George C. Pratt, *Spellbound in Darkness: A History of the Silent Film* (Greenwich, CT: New York Graphic Society, 1973; first published 1966), 252.

22. Robert Benchley, "The Drama," review of "Way Down East," *Life* (September 23, 1920): 542–43.

23. Robert Sherwood, "The Silent Drama," review of "East Lynne," *Life* (March 31, 1921): 468.

24. Ludwig Lewisohn, "Drama: An Evening at the Movies," *Nation* (September 18, 1920): 332.

25. Schickel, *D. W. Griffith and the Birth of Film,* 428–29, 443–49.

26. Clipping dated February 9, 1921, microfilm reel 7, *The Papers of D. W. Griffith 1897–1954.*

27. Schickel, *D. W. Griffith and the Birth of Film,* 431. See also one of the best-known celebrations of this sequence and this film, although tied to notions of character expressivity rather than realism, Vsevolod I. Pudovkin's *Film Technique and Film Acting* (New York: Lear Publishers, 1949), 100–1.

28. Alexander Woollcott, "Lillian Gish's *Camille,*" *The New Yorker* (October 22, 1932), reprinted in Montrose J. Moses and John Mason Brown, eds., *The American Theater as Seen by Its Critics, 1752–1934* (New York: Cooper Square Publishers, 1967; first published 1934), 250–52.

29. A similar point is made in the review in *Photoplay,* vol. 32, no. 1 (June 1927): 54, reprinted in Anthony Slide, *Selected Film Criticism* (Metuchen, NJ: Scarecrow Press, 1982–85), vol. 3, 59.

30. The serial was published in book form: Elenore Meherin, *"Chickie," a Hidden, Tragic Chapter from the Life of a Girl of This Strange "Today"* (New York: Grosset & Dunlap, 1925).

31. The *New York Times* reviewer, on the other hand (April 27, 1925: 15), finds the story awful and concludes that the producers underestimated the intelligence of shop girls.

32. This story, too, was published in book form; see Henry Leyford Gates, *Joanna, of the Skirts Too Short and the Lips Too Red and the Tongue Too Pert* (New York: Grosset & Dunlap, 1926).

33. The *New York Times* (June 28, 1927: 29), by contrast, likes the film for its many "human touches and competent acting." There is no mention of the film's being old-fashioned or intended for women. As might be expected, Mordaunt Hall, writing for the *Times*, is more conservative in his tastes than the trade press.

34. Fannie Hurst, "Back Pay," in *The Vertical City* (New York: P. F. Collier & Son, Broadway edition, 1922), 57–105.

35. Ibid., 87:

> This is not a war story except that it has to do with profiteering, par-
> lor patriots, and the return of Gerald Fishback. While Hester was
> living this tale, and the chinchilla coat was enveloping her like an
> ineffably tender caress, three hundred thousand of her country's
> youths were at strangle hold across three thousand miles of sea, and
> on a notorious night when Hester walked, fully dressed in a green
> gown of iridescent fish scales, into the electric fountain of a seaside
> cabaret, and Wheeler had to carry her to her car wrapped in a sable
> rug, Gerald Fishback was lying with his face in Flanders mud, and
> his eye sockets blackly deep and full of shrapnel, and a lung-eating
> gas cloud rolling at him across the vast bombarded dawn.

36. Hervé Dumont, *Frank Borzage: Sarastro à Hollywood* (Milan: Edizioni Gabriele Mazzotta, 1993), 82.

37. Ibid., 83.

38. George Jean Nathan, *Land of the Pilgrim's Pride* (New York: Knopf, 1927), 19, 23–24.

39. I am grateful to Tom Gunning for the example of the three-reel Vitagraph film *Goodness Gracious or Movies as They Shouldn't Be* (1914).

40. The reference here is to the stage musical comedy *Irene*, first produced in November 1919, about a poor Irish girl who ends up marrying a wealthy man. It was made into a feature film starring Colleen Moore by First National in 1926.

41. *Rouged Lips* (*Variety*, August 30, 1923: 27) appears in August, just prior to *The Gold Diggers*. In this film the rich boyfriend suspects the chorus girl of having a sugar daddy but then is assured of her innocence and marries her. The film is listed as a "melodrama" in the *American Film Institute Catalog*, but the *Variety* review suggests it is a comedy; the snappy titles particularly come in for praise as noted in chapter 3.

42. The title page of the playscript reads *The Gold Diggers: A Comedy in Three Acts*, by Avery Hopwood, Nixon's Apollo Theatre, Atlantic City, 23 June 1919; New York Lyceum Theatre, 30 September 1919, David Belasco presents Ina Claire. Filed under *Gold Diggers of 1933*, Box 158, United Artists Collection, Wisconsin Center for Film and Theatre Research, Madison, Wisconsin.

43. The *New York Times* review (July 21, 1925: 26) agrees; it finds the light comic acting in the film likely to appeal to the "intelligent viewer" and much more important than the clothes. Unfortunately, I could not locate a print of this film; it does not survive in any of the major film archives, nor, as far as I can tell, in the MGM vaults. But it seems incredible to me that a film that starred Norma Shearer and Lew Cody has completely disappeared. I have hopes that a print may yet be discovered.

44. "Classified" was originally published in *Cosmopolitan* (November 1924) and subsequently reprinted in the British periodical *Nash's & Pall Mall Magazine* (February 1925) before it appeared in the short story collection *Mother Knows Best* (Garden City, NY: Doubleday, Doran & Co., 1927), 69–98. While the advertising in *Cosmopolitan* was directed at women, it was not a "true story magazine"; it published middlebrow fiction as well as nonfiction articles on politics and the arts. The British periodical *Nash's & Pall Mall Magazine* was a general interest magazine.

45. A later example of this type of multiple chorus girl plot, *Husband Hunters* is better received in *Variety* (February 23, 1927: 19), perhaps because the three main heroines are comic types—an innocent ingenue and two gold diggers who carry a copy of Bradstreet's stock market ratings to look up the holdings of the men they meet at parties. A fourth girl, in love with the wealthy married man who is courting the ingenue, eventually runs off with him and comes to a bad end.

46. The 35mm print I viewed was about 6,149 feet; according to *Film Daily* (April 17, 1927: 8), the original was 6,373 feet, and the *American Film Institute Catalog of Feature Films* gives a similar figure of 6,365 feet. According to records held in the Library of Congress, two sources were consulted for the *AFI Catalog*, *Variety* (April 27, 1927:17), and the one it relied upon, the *Motion Picture News Booking Guide* (April 1927). The latter summarized the plot as follows: "Society drama of young girl who, supported by wealthy uncle, discovers unholy secret of her parentage. As a consequence she leaves home and separates herself from lover chauffeur, who eventually finds her ill in hospital. A reconciliation follows." I do not believe this is simply a misreading of the film; it is too obviously bowdlerized. The *Motion Picture News Booking Guide* was directed to exhibitors at the end of the distribution hierarchy—according to the April 1922 issue, those who "can not and do not book pictures on a first run basis," and sometimes had to wait up to two years to book films. These small-town exhibitors were more likely to have a relatively conservative audience in matters of taste, and also to receive older prints that had been censored by state censor boards at some point in their circulation.

6. THE ROMANTIC DRAMA

1. Todd McCarthy, *Howard Hawks: The Grey Fox of Hollywood* (New York: Grove Press, 1997), 84–86.

2. The *Film Daily* review of *The Sign on the Door* (April 24, 1921: 8) notes that the "main situation is not entirely new, because some time ago the same thing was used—the wife who sacrificed her own happiness to save her husband's child." The title of the previous film is not given. The *Variety* review of *Dancing Mothers* (February 17, 1926: 40) explains: "In plot this is the old one about the mother who put on her vamping clothes to get the man with whom her daughter was in love—to get him and throw him over, as a protective measure for the kid. But the mother, who had patiently sat by the fireside for years while her husband and daughter went the wild pace of the day, fell for the man who 'threatened' her daughter."

3. In addition to *The Plastic Age*, films about flappers and college life include *The College Widow, The Fair Co-Ed, Rolled Stockings,* and *Swim, Girl, Swim.*

4. The Internet Broadway Database (www.ibdb.com) indicates that the play was produced by the Selwyns at the Broadhurst Theatre and ran for 175 performances from December 1919 through May 1920. Jane Cowl played the double roles of Kathleen and Moonyeen. According to *Film Daily* (March 5, 1922: 2), the play was acquired by producer Joseph Schenck for $75,000. It was adapted twice in the sound period, in 1932 by Sidney Franklin with Norma Shearer, and as a musical in 1941 by Frank Borzage with Jeanette MacDonald.

5. The *Film Daily* review specifically praises Rosher's cinematography and notes his connection with Pickford.

6. Strictly speaking, *The Bonnie Brier Bush* (original title *Beside the Bonnie Brier Bush*) is a British film, and in general I have avoided discussing foreign-produced films screened in the U.S. in the 1920s. However, it was produced by an overseas outpost of an American company, Famous Players–Lasky, and directed by an American director, Donald Crisp, who also played the male lead, and thus legitimately belongs in the feedback circuit of reviewing and film production I am considering in this book.

7. The Internet Broadway Database (www.ibdb.com) indicates that it was produced by Kirke La Shelle at the Theatre Republic, September 23, 1901.

8. *Exceptional Photoplays* (March 1921), reprinted in Stanley Hochman, ed., *From Quasimodo to Scarlett O'Hara: A National Board of Review Anthology, 1920–1940* (New York: F. Ungar, 1982), 15–16.

9. "53,629 See 'The Sheik,'" *Film Daily* (November 10, 1921: 1), reported on attendance at the Rivoli and the Rialto for the first three days of release—Sunday, Monday, and Tuesday—and predicted that by the following Saturday night attendance at the two theaters would be 120,000, "a new record in Broadway entertainment history."

10. "The Celluloid Critic," *Motion Picture Classic* (January 1922): 66.

11. Miriam Hansen, *Babel and Babylon: Spectatorship in American Silent Film* (Cambridge, MA: Harvard University Press, 1991), 245–94; Gaylyn Studlar, *This Mad Masquerade: Stardom and Masculinity in the Jazz Age* (New York: Columbia University Press, 1996), 150–98.

12. On the history of the print, see Richard Koszarski, *The Man You Loved to Hate: Erich von Stroheim and Hollywood* (New York: Oxford University Press, 1983), 80–81.

13. See Koszarski, *The Man You Loved to Hate*, 87–88; and Janet Staiger, *Interpreting Films: Studies in the Historical Reception of American Cinema* (Princeton, NJ: Princeton University Press, 1992), 124–38.

14. Koszarski, *The Man You Loved to Hate*, 79–80.

15. Frederick James Smith, *Motion Picture Classic* (April 1922): 48–49, 57, reprinted in Anthony Slide, *Selected Film Criticism* (Metuchen, NJ: Scarecrow Press, 1982–85), vol. 3, 99–101. For a similar defense of the film, see Willis Goldbeck, "Von Stroheim, Man and Superman," *Motion Picture Classic* (September 1922): 18–19, 82–83.

16. *Photoplay* (March 1922): 70, cited in Slide, *Selected Film Criticism*, vol. 3, 101–2. For a similar denunciation of the film, see the opinion piece by Arthur James, editor in chief of *Moving Picture World*, "A Million! A Million!" (January 21, 1922: 267). A review in the same issue (316) objects primarily to the film's length.

17. A similar opposition between too little and too much may be found in the cases of two Elinor Glyn adaptations. *Three Weeks*, adapted from the novel of the same name, was described by *Variety* (April 2, 1924: 22) as "a mild, almost milksop 'Three Weeks,' toned down in its sex kick by both [director] Crosland and Miss [Aileen] Pringle. She plays the queen more royal than romantic. While the story carries out the well-known plot without dodging its responsibilities, it never rises at any time to a single moment of supreme passion." *Film Daily* (April 6, 1924: 9) similarly thought the film would disappoint "sensation seekers." By contrast, *His Hour* was considered a bit risky. *Film Daily* (September 14, 1924: 4), noting that "the very vigorous love making of John Gilbert far outdoes the mild-in-comparison efforts of Conrad Nagel in 'Three Weeks,'" cautioned: "Strong sex appeal spoils it for family trade but it will likely stand a good show at the box office." *Variety* (October 8, 1924: 27) thought that the film would do well in the big cities on the strength of its "paper-back sensationalism" but expected that it would lose its kick through censorship "down in Maryland, out in Ohio, over in Pennsylvania and a few other centers where Democrats, Republicans and Methodists control the censor board."

18. In my view *Don Juan* is the first of the Barrymore costume pictures to show the influence of Valentino's films and to be associated with feminine tastes. Although Gaylyn Studlar, *This Mad Masquerade*, 90–149, argues that *Beau Brummel*, a historical film starring Barrymore released in March 1924, was seen as a woman's film, I have found no evidence to support this claim. The *Variety* review (April 2, 1924: 22) stresses the prestige of Barrymore's theatrical reputation and the fact that the part of Beau Brummel was played on the stage by Richard Mansfield, "the role most celebrated of the repertoire of the greatest and most famous actor of America in the last score of years." The problem was that the genre was thought unlikely to draw: "It is simply a question of whether the costume play is a thing of the past and if there is sufficient

interest in this stage star in the smaller towns to attract sufficient to make it worth while." While *Film Daily* (April 13, 1924: 6) made one of its characteristic judgments about exploiting films to women—"delightful love story should appeal to women patrons"—the review largely stressed Barrymore's theatrical reputation as the film's selling point. Like *Variety, Film Daily* was concerned about the film's ability to draw outside of New York: "Unfortunately John Barrymore doesn't make enough pictures to insure a great fan clientele." The *New York Times* (March 31, 1924: 20) called the film "one of those artistic celluloid efforts that come along none too frequently" and concluded that "this is a stirring picture, not merely for the 'upper ten,' but also for O. Henry's four million and several other millions."

19. Reviews of *Don Juan*, by Oliver Claxton, *The New Yorker* (August 14, 1926): 33–34, and by Robert Sherwood, *Life* (August 26, 1926): 26, both reprinted in Slide, *Selected Film Criticism*, vol. 3, 33–34 and 26, respectively.

20. *Photoplay* (June 1927): 139, reprinted in Slide, *Selected Film Criticism*, vol. 3, 33. The *New York Times* (March 14, 1927: 16) also noted the transformation of the handsome Barrymore but was less censorious, perhaps because the reviewer was less concerned about the film's feminine appeal.

21. Jeanine Basinger, *A Woman's View: How Hollywood Spoke to Women, 1930–1960* (New York: Knopf, 1993), 13–17; and Molly Haskell, *From Reverence to Rape: The Treatment of Women in the Movies*, 2nd ed. (Chicago: University of Chicago Press, 1987), 155–56.

22. In addition to *Smilin' Through*, the reviewer refers to *Ashes of Vengeance*, released in August 1923. The story concerned familial and political rivalries among aristocratic families in sixteenth-century France. It involved sword play, scenes of torture, and a last-minute rescue of the heroine, and seems to have resembled the later *Don Juan* and its imitations. There was apparently less stress on lovemaking. *Film Daily* (August 19, 1923: 3) described the plot as "not without dramatic moments whose occasional climaxes provide thrills of a more or less hair-raising variety; the romance is uppermost, however, and always charmingly portrayed against a backdrop of unusual beauty." Nonetheless, the reviewer cautioned that it might not "fulfill box office expectations, that is to the extent that it should in lieu of the money expended upon it." The film was recommended to exhibitors whose clientele "take to costume dramas." There was no mention of a potential appeal to women. *Variety* (August 30, 1923: 26) similarly noted the high production values, but obviously found it lacklustre: "always pleasing to the eye and in a drowsy manner that would be perfect to watch were one installed in a loge chair at the Capital."

23. The *Variety* review of *Kiki* (April 7, 1926: 36) similarly stressed the comedic elements, describing it as "so filled with situations, slapstick and laughs that in its present excellent scenario form, there's not a chance of its flopping before a real audience." It also offered a tribute to an actress who has been largely forgotten by present-day audiences: "If any other screen actress has held up so good a record in recent years as Miss Talmadge, it might be well

to recall no other actress on the stage or screen has played such varied roles with unmistakable skill and ability."

24. All the reviews praised the exteriors, shot in Italy, and the performance of the star. *Film Daily* (September 8, 1923: 3) called it a "magnificent production" but thought that the sad ending would hurt it at the box office. The *New York Times* (September 6, 1923: 10) described the film as "notable" and "artistic." *Variety*'s negative review of the film may have been influenced by a review of the 1909 play upon which it was based; the stage production of *The White Sister* was among a number of plays criticized by Alan Dale for being sentimental, dismal, and likely to appeal only to women; see Alan Dale, "The Tear-Drenched Drama," *The Cosmopolitan Magazine* 48, no. 2 (January 1910): 199–204.

25. Review of *Flesh and the Devil* in *Exceptional Photoplays* (February 1927), reprinted in Stanley Hochman, ed., *From Quasimodo to Scarlett O'Hara*, 82–85.

26. *Film Daily* (January 16, 1927: 6) called it "a fairly unconvincing, sugar-coated ending." The *New York Times* (January 10, 1927: 20) described the film as "a compelling piece of work in which there are but few conventional movie notes. There is, it is true, a flood of sunshine and a wealth of flowers for the final sequence, but in the previous chapter tragedy had stalked into the picture." *Variety* noted "the happy ending when the spring comes and the blossoms bloom"—not an overt criticism but a suggestion that the ending was highly stereotyped.

27. *Film Daily* (January 16, 1927: 6), ever mindful of the needs of the smaller exhibitor, cautioned, "The story has strong sex appeal and may cause a little trouble from that angle," but it also predicted success for the film, calling it "the first of the new year's big pictures."

28. *Photoplay* (February 1927): 52, reprinted in Slide, *Selected Film Criticism*, vol. 3, 97.

29. The first film made with this team, *Dark Angel*, released in September 1925, concerned a couple separated during World War I. Their second film, *The Winning of Barbara Worth*, which opened in October 1926, was a historical epic about bringing water to the Imperial Valley taken from a best-selling novel by Harold Bell Wright. Although it contained a romance plot, it was not really in the mold of the romantic drama. *The Night of Love* adhered more closely to the generic prototype.

30. *Photoplay* (June 1927): 54, reprinted in Slide, *Selected Film Criticism*, vol. 3, 59.

31. The running time of ninety-six minutes is given in the *Variety* review; both that review and the one in *Moving Picture World* (May 2, 1927: 848) indicate that the film had a frame story that does not appear in the surviving print, which *Moving Picture World* describes as follows: "The auction sale of the personal effects of Camille, the famous Parisian courtesan, is in progress. Armand buys her diary and picture and as he reads her story it is pictured."

32. *Photoplay* (November 1927): 62, reprinted in Slide, *Selected Film Criticism*, vol. 3, 177–78.

33. *Variety* (January 1, 1923: 18) complained that Gilbert had "an utterly blah role." Welford Beaton in the *Film Spectator* (November 24, 1924: 7–8; reprinted in Slide, *Selected Film Criticism*, vol. 3, 316–18) wrote that "Jack sat back and allowed Greta to earn all the bows."

34. The print I viewed at George Eastman House was about one reel (869 feet) short. Most of what is missing seems to be from reel 7, although the print also suffered from garbled exposition, which may be the result of footage missing from earlier sections. Nonetheless, the cinematography by George Barnes and Gregg Toland makes the film of great interest. Particularly striking is the set of the wreck, with an open central cabin covered in mosquito netting, which permits beautiful shots from interior to exterior and vice versa, as well as allowing for nice diffusion and lighting effects.

35. Previous films along similar lines starring Gilbert include *Arabian Love*, directed by Jerome Storm for Fox and released in September 1922, and *A Man's Mate*, directed by Edmund Mortimer for Fox and released in March 1924.

36. The character is called Don Jaime in all of the contemporary reviews, but the titles in the print I viewed call him Don Diego.

37. A review of Pat O'Malley's credits for the years 1923 through 1928 in the *American Film Institute Catalogue of Feature Films* reveals that most of his major roles were in low-budget films produced by Universal and Tiffany-Stahl. During the years 1924 and 1925, however, he appeared in two films directed by Paul Bern for Paramount, *Worldly Goods* and *Tomorrow's Love*, and three Metro-Goldwyn films in addition to *Proud Flesh: Happiness*, directed by King Vidor; *The Beauty Prize*, directed by Lloyd Ingraham; and *White Desert*, directed by Reginald Barker.

38. The *New York Times* reviewer describes the use of furs with a precision that is beyond me: "She arrays herself for suppers in ermine and moleskin, and on other occasions in plain ermine streaked with sealskin."

39. Austin Strong, *Seventh Heaven: A Play in Three Acts* (New York: Samuel French, 1922). According to the Internet Broadway Database (www.ibdb .com), Strong's play opened at the Booth Theater and ran from October 1922 to July 1924 for a total of 704 performances. In comparison with other stage successes chosen for adaptation by Hollywood, plays such as *Anna Christie* or *What Price Glory*, Strong's work seems highly conservative. John Corbin, in the *New York Times* (October 31, 1922: 20), described the opening scene in John Golden's production: "In the centre of the stage is a sewer manhole, out of which our hero Chico emerges, proclaiming himself an atheist. Behind it is a church with lighted window and murmuring organ, the church of Pére Chevillon, ambassador of le bon Dieu to derelict humanity."

40. Hervé Dumont, *Frank Borzage, Sarastro à Hollywood* (Milan: Edizioni Gabriele Mazzotta, 1993), 78.

41. Harrison Haskins, "The Photoplay of the Proletariat," *Motion Picture Classic* (September 1920): 18, 88; reprinted in *Griffithiana* 46 (December 1992), 127–28.

42. Peter Milne, *Motion Picture Directing* (New York: Falk Publishing Company, 1922), 113–14; reprinted in *Griffithiana* 46 (December 1992), 131–32.

43. Dumont, *Frank Borzage*, 108. *Lightnin'*, by Winchell Smith and Frank Bacon, ran for three years on Broadway between 1918 and 1921. It is a rural melodrama set in Nevada; the eponymous central character is lazy, frequently inebriated, a teller of tall tales. When his exasperated wife threatens divorce over a financial matter, his real worth is finally revealed to his family. Although Borzage did not direct the film version of *Lightnin'*, his first film for Fox, *Lazybones*, released in November 1925, was a rural melodrama adapted from a play by Owen Davis that was clearly indebted to Winchell Smith's well-known hit. The hero is shiftless, the village ne'er-do-well, but he sacrifices his own chance for marriage when he adopts the abandoned baby of a respectable girl.

44. Dumont, *Frank Borzage*, 118–19, 126; Richard Koszarski, "Ernest Palmer on Frank Borzage and F. W. Murnau," *Griffithiana* 46 (December 1992): 115–20.

45. Molly Haskell, *From Reverence to Rape*, 155.

46. Ben Singer, *Melodrama and Modernity: Early Sensational Cinema and Its Contexts* (New York: Columbia University Press, 2001), 221–62; Shelley Stamp, *Movie-Struck Girls: Women and Motion Picture Culture after the Nickelodeon* (Princeton, NJ: Princeton University Press, 2000).

47. The quotes are from Sherwood's encapsulated reviews in the "Recent Developments" section of his column, the first from *Life* (February 10, 1921): 214, the second from *Life* (March 17, 1921): 396.

AFTERWORD

1. Gilbert Seldes, "A Personal Preface," *The Seven Lively Arts*, rev. ed. (New York: Sagamore Press, 1957), 5–6.

2. Dwight Macdonald "Masscult and Midcult," in *Against the American Grain* (New York: Random House, 1962), 38; first published in *Partisan Review* (Spring 1960).

3. For Macdonald's puzzled reaction to New Left attitudes to popular culture, see asterisked note in his "Masscult and Midcult," 64.

4. Thompson, *Herr Lubitsch Goes to Hollywood: German and American Film after World War I* (Amsterdam: Amsterdam University Press, 2005).

5. Noël Burch, *Life to Those Shadows* (London: BFI Publishing, 1990); see also Noël Burch and Jorge Dana, "Propositions," *Afterimage* 5 (Spring 1974): 40–67.

Bibliography

Aldington, Richard. "The Influence of Mr. James Joyce." *English Review* 32 (April 1921): 333–41.

Allen, Robert C., and Douglas Gomery. *Film History: Theory and Practice*. New York: Alfred Knopf, 1985.

Altman, Rick. *Film/Genre*. London: BFI Publishing, 1999.

Anderson, Maxwell, and Laurence Stallings. *What Price Glory?* In *Famous American Plays of the 1920s*, ed. Kenneth MacGowan. New York: Dell Publishing, 1959, 53–129. First published in *Three American Plays*, by Maxwell Anderson and Laurence Stallings. New York: Harcourt Brace & Company, 1926, 5–89.

Anonymous. "Hokum Wanted." *Billboard* (October 15, 1927): 46.

———. "The Literary Spotlight." *Bookman* 57 (April 1923): 168–72.

———. *Songs of the 20's: Piano, Vocal, Guitar*. Milwaukee: H. Leonard Corp., 1989.

Auriol, Jean-George. "*A Girl in Every Port*." Trans. John Moore. In *Howard Hawks: American Artist*, ed. Jim Hillier and Peter Wollen. London: BFI Publishing, 1996, 13–14.

Barry, Iris. "The Cinema: Hope Fulfilled." *The Spectator* (May 17, 1924): 788.

———. "'Greed'—A Film of Realism." *The Spectator* (March 14, 1925): 402.

———. *Let's Go to the Movies*. New York: Arno Press, 1972. First published 1926.

———. Review of "The Big Parade." *The Spectator* (June 5, 1926): 946–47.

Basinger, Jeanine. *A Woman's View: How Hollywood Spoke to Women, 1930–1960*. New York: Knopf, 1993.

Baym, Nina. *Women's Fiction: A Guide to Novels By and About Women in America, 1820–1870*. Ithaca, NY: Cornell University Press, 1978.

Bellour, Raymond. *L'analyse du Film*. Paris: Éditions Albatros, 1979.

———. *The Analysis of Film*. Edited by Constance Penley. Bloomington: Indiana University Press, 2000.

Benchley, Robert. "Books and Other Things." *The World* (July 10, 1920): 8.

———. "The Drama." Review of "The Mirage." *Life* (October 21, 1920): 724–25.

———. "The Drama." Review of "Respect for Riches." *Life* (May 27, 1920): 992–93.

———. "The Drama." Review of "Way Down East." *Life* (September 23, 1920): 542–43.

Bergstrom, Janet. "Murnau in America: Chronicle of Lost Films." *Film History* 14, nos. 3/4 (2002): 430–60.

Bernstein, Matthew. *Walter Wanger, Hollywood Independent.* Berkeley: University of California Press, 1994.

Booth, Michael. *English Melodrama.* London: Herbert Jenkins, 1965.

Bordwell, David. *Ozu and the Poetics of Cinema.* Princeton, NJ: Princeton University Press, 1988.

Bordwell, David, Janet Staiger, and Kristin Thompson. *The Classical Hollywood Cinema: Film Style and Mode of Production to 1960.* London: Routledge & Kegan Paul, 1985.

Bourdieu, Pierre. *Distinction: A Social Critique of the Judgment of Taste.* Trans. Richard Nice. Cambridge, MA: Harvard University Press, 1984.

Bourne, Randolph. *War and the Intellectuals: Collected Essays, 1915–1919,* ed. Carl Resek. New York: Harper & Row, 1964.

Brady, William. *Showman.* New York: E. P. Dutton & Company, 1937.

Brewster, Ben. "*Alias Jimmy Valentine* and Situational Dramaturgy." *Film History* 9, no. 4 (1997): 388–409.

———. "The Circle: Lubitsch and the Theatrical Farce Tradition." *Film History* 13, no. 4 (2001): 372–89.

———. "*A Romance of Happy Valley.*" In *The Griffith Project.* Vol. 9, *Films Produced in 1916–18,* ed. Paolo Cherchi Usai. Pordenone: Le Giornate del Cinema Muto/London: BFI Publishing, 2005, 176–91.

———. "*Traffic in Souls:* An Experiment in Feature-Length Narrative Construction." *Cinema Journal* 31, no. 1 (Fall 1991): 37–56.

Brewster, Ben, and Lea Jacobs. *Theatre to Cinema: Stage Pictorialism and the Early Feature Film.* Oxford: Oxford University Press, 1997.

Bridgman, Richard. *The Colloquial Style in America.* New York: Oxford University Press, 1966.

Brooks, Van Wyck. *The Ordeal of Mark Twain.* New York: E. P. Dutton & Company, 1920.

———. *The Pilgrimage of Henry James.* New York: E. P. Dutton & Company, 1925.

Broun, Heywood. "As We Were Saying." *New York Tribune* (February 6, 1921): sec. 3, 1.

———. "Books." *New York Tribune* (January 7, 1921): 8.

———. "How They Found Miss Lulu Bett." *Collier's Weekly* 67 (January 29, 1921): 13.

Broun, Heywood, and Margaret Leech. *Anthony Comstock, Roundsman of the Lord.* New York: A. & C. Boni, 1927.

Brown, Herbert Ross. *The Sentimental Novel in America, 1789–1860.* Durham, NC: Duke University Press, 1940.

Brownlow, Kevin. *Behind the Mask of Innocence: Sex, Violence, Prejudice, Crime: Films of Social Conscience in the Silent Era.* New York: Alfred Knopf, 1990.

———. *The War, the West, and the Wilderness*. London: Secker & Warburg, 1978.

Buntline, Ned [pseud. of Edward Z. C. Judson]. *The Black Avenger of the Spanish Main: or, The Fiend of Blood, A Thrilling Story of the Buccaneer Times*. Boston: F. Gleason, 1847.

Burch, Noël. *Life to Those Shadows*. Trans. Ben Brewster. London: BFI Publishing, 1990.

Burch, Noël, and Jorge Dana. "Propositions." *Afterimage* 5 (Spring 1974): 40–67.

Cantwell, Robert. "Journalism—the Magazines." In *In America Now: An Inquiry into Civilization in the United States*, ed. Harold E. Stearns. New York: Charles Scribner's Sons, 1938, 345–55.

Carmen, Ira. *Movies, Censorship, and the Law*. Ann Arbor: University of Michigan Press, 1967.

Carr, Harry. "Will Charlie Kick Off His Old Shoes?" *Motion Picture Magazine* 26 (December 1923): 28–29, 86.

———. "Chaplin Explains Chaplin." *Motion Picture Magazine* 30 (November 1925): 31, 88.

Chung, Jennifer. "Too Sophisticated for the Sticks? Small Town Reception of Sophisticated Comedies, 1924–1928." Unpublished paper, 2005.

Conway, Jack. "Why I Write Slang." *Variety* (December 29, 1926): 5, 7.

Cowley, Malcolm, ed. *After the Genteel Tradition: American Writers since 1910*. New York: W. W. Norton, 1937.

Crafton, Donald. *The Talkies: American Cinema's Transition to Sound 1926–1931*. Vol. 4 of *History of the American Cinema*. New York, Charles Scribner's Sons, 1997.

Crawford, Richard. *America's Musical Life: A History*. New York: Norton, 2001.

Dale, Alan. "Eugene Walter's 'The Easiest Way.'" *New York American* (January 20, 1909).

———. "The Tear-Drenched Drama." *The Cosmopolitan Magazine* (January 1910): 199–204.

Davidson, Cathy N. Introduction, *Charlotte Temple*, by Susan Haswell Rowson. New York: Oxford University Press, 1986, xi–xxxiii.

Davis, Lee. *Bolton and Wodehouse and Kern: The Men Who Made Musical Comedy*. New York: James H. Heineman, 1993.

Deming, Robert H., ed. *James Joyce: The Critical Heritage*. New York: Barnes & Noble, 1970.

Denning, Michael. *Mechanic Accents: Dime Novels and Working-Class Culture in America*. London: Verso, 1987.

Diderot, Denis. *Le Fils naturel* and *Entretiens sur Le Fils naturel*. In *Le Drame bourgeois*. Vol. 10 of *Œuvres complètes de Diderot*, ed. Jacques Chouillet and Anne-Marie Chouillet. Paris: Hermann, 1980.

Doane, Mary Anne. *The Desire to Desire: The Woman's Film of the 1940s*. Bloomington: Indiana University Press, 1987.

Doty, Douglas Z. "Charles Chaplin and 'A Woman of Paris': A New Era for the Screen Is Marked by This Production, Written and Directed by Charles

Chaplin Himself." *The Storyworld and Photodramatist* (September 1923): 16–20.

Dreiser, Theodore. "The Best Motion Picture Interview Ever Written." *Photoplay* 34, no. 3 (August 1928): 32–35, 124–29.

Drimmer, Melvin. "Nietzsche in American Thought 1895–1925." PhD diss., University of Rochester, 1965.

Driscoll, John. "Laurence Stallings." In *Dictionary of Literary Biography*. Vol. 44, *American Screenwriters*, 2nd series, ed. Randall Clark. Detroit, MI: Gale Research Co., 1986, 357–63. Now available online at http://galenet.galegroup.com.

Dumont, Hervé. *Frank Borzage: Sarastro à Hollywood*. Milan: Edizioni Gabriele Mazzotta, 1993.

Dymkowski, Christine. "Introduction." *Anna Christie and Emperor Jones*, by Eugene O'Neill. London: Royal National Theatre/Nick Hern Books, 1991.

Eisenstein, S. M. "The New Language of Cinematography." *Close Up* 4, no. 5 (May 1929): 10–13.

Ellmann, Richard. *James Joyce*. Rev. ed. Oxford: Oxford University Press, 1982.

Ernst, Morris L., and William Seagle. *To the Pure . . . A Study of Obscenity and the Censor*. New York: Viking Press, 1928.

Everson, William K. *American Silent Film*. New York: Oxford University Press, 1978.

Ferber, Edna. "Classified." *Cosmopolitan* (November, 1924). Reprinted in *Mother Knows Best*. Garden City, NY: Doubleday, Doran & Co., 1927.

Fiedler, Leslie. *Love and Death in the American Novel*. Normal, IL: Dalkey Archive Press, 1997. First published 1960.

Finler, Joel. *Stroheim*. Berkeley: University of California Press, 1968.

Forslund, Bengt. *Victor Sjöström: His Life and Work*. New York: Zoetrope, 1988.

Forte, Allen. *The American Popular Ballad of the Golden Era, 1924–1950*. Princeton, NJ: Princeton University Press, 1995.

Forty, Adrian. *Objects of Desire: Design and Society from Wedgwood to IBM*. New York: Pantheon Books, 1986.

Freedman, Jonathan. *Professions of Taste: Henry James, British Aestheticism, and Commodity Culture*. Stanford, CA: Stanford University Press, 1990.

Fuller, Kathryn H. *At the Picture Show: Small-Town Audiences and the Creation of Movie Fan Culture*. Charlottesville: University Press of Virginia, 2001.

Gale, Zona. *Miss Lulu Bett: An American Comedy of Manners*. New York: Appleton, 1921.

Gallagher, Tag. *John Ford: The Man and His Films*. Berkeley: University of California Press, 1986.

Gates, Henry Leyford. *Joanna, of the Skirts Too Short and the Lips Too Red and the Tongue Too Pert*. New York: Grosset & Dunlap, 1926.

Goddard, Leslie. "Zona Gale as Dramatist." In *Dictionary of Literary Biography*. Vol. 228, *Twentieth-Century American Dramatists*, 2nd series, ed. Christopher J. Wheatley. Detroit, MI: Gale Research Co., 2000, 73–80. Now available online at http://galenet.galegroup.com.

Goldbeck, Willis. "Von Stroheim, Man and Superman." *Motion Picture Classic* 10, no. 1 (September 1922): 18–19, 82–83.

Gomery, Douglas. *Shared Pleasures: A History of Movie Presentation in the United States.* Madison: University of Wisconsin Press, 1992.

———. "U.S. Film Exhibition: The Formation of a Big Business." In *The American Film Industry,* ed. Tino Balio. Rev. ed. Madison: University of Wisconsin Press, 1985, 218–28.

Gorman, Paul R. *Left Intellectuals and Popular Culture in Twentieth-Century America.* Chapel Hill: University of North Carolina Press, 1996.

Greene, Jane. "The Road to Reno: *The Awful Truth* and the Hollywood Comedy of Remarriage." *Film History* 13, no. 4 (2001): 337–58.

Grieveson, Lee. "Gangsters and Governance in the Silent Era." In *Mob Culture: Hidden Histories of the American Gangster Film,* ed. Lee Grieveson, Esther Sonnet, and Peter Stanfield. New Brunswick, NJ: Rutgers University Press, 2005, 13–40.

Griffith, David Wark. *The Papers of D. W. Griffith, 1897–1954.* 36 microfilm reels. Sanford, NC: Microfilming Corporation of America, 1982.

Gunning, Tom. "An Aesthetic of Astonishment: Early Film and the (In)Credulous Spectator." In *Viewing Positions: Ways of Seeing Film,* ed. Linda Williams. New Jersey: Rutgers University Press, 1995, 114–33.

———. "The Cinema of Attractions: Early Film, Its Spectator and the Avant-Garde." In *Early Cinema: Space, Frame, Narrative,* ed. Thomas Elsaesser. London: BFI Publishing, 1990, 56–62.

———. *D. W. Griffith and the Origins of American Narrative Film: The Early Years at Biograph.* Urbana: University of Illinois Press, 1991.

———. "*True Heart Susie.*" In *The Griffith Project.* Vol. 10, *Films Produced in 1919–46,* ed. Paolo Cherchi Usai. Pordenone: Le Giornate del Cinema Muto/London: BFI Publishing, 2006, 18–27.

F. H. "After the Play." *New Republic* (January 12, 1921): 204–5.

Hamm, Charles. *Irving Berlin: Songs from the Melting Pot: The Formative Years, 1907–1914.* New York: Oxford University Press, 1997.

———. *Yesterdays: Popular Song in America.* New York: Norton, 1979.

Hansen, Miriam. *Babel and Babylon: Spectatorship in American Silent Film.* Cambridge, MA: Harvard University Press, 1991.

Haskell, Francis. *Rediscoveries in Art: Some Aspects of Taste, Fashion and Collecting in England and France.* Ithaca, NY: Cornell University Press, 1976.

Haskell, Molly. *From Reverence to Rape: The Treatment of Women in the Movies.* 2nd ed. Chicago: University of Chicago Press, 1987.

Haskins, Harrison. "The Photoplay of the Proletariat." *Motion Picture Classic* (September 1920): 18, 88; reprinted in *Griffithiana* 46 (December 1992): 127–28.

Hemingway, Ernest. *Green Hills of Africa.* New York: Charles Scribner's Sons, 1935.

Higashi, Sumiko. *Cecil B. DeMille and American Culture: The Silent Era.* Berkeley: University of California Press, 1994.

———. "The New Woman and Consumer Culture: Cecil B. DeMille's Sex Comedies." In *A Feminist Reader in Early Cinema*, ed. Jennifer M. Bean and Diane Negra. Durham, NC: Duke University Press, 2002, 298–332.

———. *Virgins, Vamps and Flappers: The American Silent Movie Heroine*. Montreal, Quebec: Eden Press, 1978.

Hillier, Bevis. *The World of Art Deco, an Exhibition Organized by the Minneapolis Institute of Arts, July–September 1971*. New York: E. P. Dutton & Company, 1971.

Hochman, Stanley, ed. *From Quasimodo to Scarlett O'Hara: A National Board of Review Anthology, 1920–1940*. New York: F. Ungar, 1982.

Hoffman, Frederick, Charles Allen, and Carolyn Ulrich. *The Little Magazine: A History and a Bibliography*. Princeton, NJ: Princeton University Press, 1946.

Hofstadter, Richard. *The Age of Reform*. New York: Random House, 1955.

Huneker, James Gibbon. *Egoists: A Book of Supermen*. New York: Scribner's Sons, 1909.

Hurst, Fannie. "Back Pay." In *The Vertical City*. New York: P. F. Collier & Son, Broadway edition, 1922.

Ifkovic, Edward. "Harold Bell Wright." In *Dictionary of Literary Biography*. Vol. 9, *American Novelists, 1910–1945*, ed. James J. Martine. Detroit, MI: Gale Research Co., 1981, 188–93. Now available online at http://galenet.galegroup.com.

Jacobs, Lea. "*An American Tragedy:* A Comparison of Film and Literary Censorship." *Quarterly Review of Film and Video* 15, no. 4 (1995): 87–98.

———. "Keeping Up with Hawks." *Style* 32, no. 3 (Fall 1998): 402–26.

———. "Men without Women: The Avatars of *What Price Glory*." *Film History* 17, nos. 2–3 (2005): 307–33.

———. "The Seduction Plot: Comic and Dramatic Variants." *Film History* 13, no. 4 (2001): 424–42.

———. "Way Down East." In *The Griffith Project*. Vol. 10, *Films Produced in 1919–46*, ed. Paolo Cherchi Usai. Pordenone: Le Giornate del Cinema Muto/London: BFI Publishing, 2006, 81–95.

Jacobs, Lewis. *The Rise of the American Film: A Critical History*. New York, 1939. Reprint, New York: Teacher's College Press, 1975.

James, Arthur. "A Million! A Million!" *Moving Picture World* (January 21, 1922): 267.

Jenkins, Henry, III. *What Made Pistachio Nuts? Early Sound Comedy and the Vaudeville Aesthetic*. New York: Columbia University Press, 1992.

Kepley, Vance. "Griffith's *Broken Blossoms* and the Problems of Historical Specificity." *Quarterly Review of Film Studies* 3, no. 1 (1978): 37–47.

Kerr, Walter. *The Silent Clowns*. New York: Alfred Knopf, 1975.

Kitses, Jim. *Horizons West*. London: Thames & Hudson, 1969.

Koszarski, Richard. "Ernest Palmer on Frank Borzage and F. W. Murnau." *Griffithiana* 46 (December 1992): 115–20.

———. *An Evening's Entertainment: The Age of the Silent Feature Picture, 1915–1928*. Vol. 3 of *History of the American Cinema*, ed. Charles Harpole. New York: Scribner's, 1990.

———. *Fort Lee: The Film Town.* Rome, Italy: John Libbey Publishing, 2004.
———. *The Man You Loved to Hate: Erich von Stroheim and Hollywood.*
New York: Oxford University Press, 1983.
Landry, Robert J. "'Variety's Four-Letter Signatures, the Dog-Tags of Its
Critics." *Variety* (January 9, 1974): 26.
Langlois, Henri. "The Modernity of Howard Hawks." In *Howard Hawks:
American Artist,* ed. Jim Hillier and Peter Wollen. London: BFI Publish-
ing, 1996, 72–75.
Langman, Larry, and Daniel Finn. *A Guide to American Silent Crime Films.*
Westport, CT: Greenwood Press, 1994.
Latteier, Pearl. "Griffith, Weber and the Decline of Progressive Filmmaking."
Unpublished paper, 2005.
Le Berthon, Ted. "Absolutely, Mr. Chaplin! Positively, Mr. Freud! Psycho-
analysis Comes to the Movies." *Motion Picture Classic* 17 (August 1923):
37, 88.
Lewisohn, Ludwig. "Drama: An Evening at the Movies." *Nation* (September
18, 1920): 332.
———. "Drama." *Nation* (February 2, 1921): 189.
MacAdams, William. *Ben Hecht: The Man Behind the Legend.* New York:
Charles Scribner's Sons, 1990.
McBride, Joseph, ed. *Focus on Howard Hawks.* New Jersey, Prentice-Hall,
1972.
MacCann, Richard Dyer, ed. *The Silent Comedians.* Metuchen, NJ: Scarecrow
Press, 1993.
McCarthy, Todd. *Howard Hawks: The Grey Fox of Hollywood.* New York:
Grove Press, 1997.
Macdonald, Dwight. "Masscult and Midcult." In *Against the American
Grain.* New York: Random House, 1962, 3–75. First published in *Partisan
Review* (Spring 1960).
MacGowan, Kenneth. "Introduction." *Famous American Plays of the 1920s.*
New York: Dell Publishing, 1959.
Maltby, Richard. "'Grief in the Limelight': Al Capone, Howard Hughes, the
Hays Code and the Politics of the Unstable Text." In *Movies and Politics:
The Dynamic Relationship,* ed. James Combs. New York: Garland Publish-
ing, 1993, 133–82.
———. "Sticks, Hicks and Flaps: Classical Hollywood's Generic Conception
of Its Audiences." In *Identifying Hollywood's Audiences: Cultural Identity
and the Movies,* ed. Melvyn Stokes and Richard Maltby. London: BFI Publishing, 1999, 23–41.
———. "'To Prevent the Prevalent Type of Book': Censorship and Adaptation
in Hollywood, 1924–1934." *American Quarterly* 44, no. 4 (December
1992): 554–82.
Mann, Anthony. "Entretien," by Charles Bitsch and Claude Chabrol. *Cahiers
du cinéma* 12, no. 69 (March 1957): 6.
Mantle, Burns. *The Best Plays of 1921–1922 and the Year Book of the Drama
in America.* New York: Dodd, Mead & Company, 1943. First published
1922.

————. *The Best Plays of 1924–1925 and the Year Book of the Drama in America*. New York: Dodd, Mead & Company, 1942. First published 1925.

————. *The Best Plays of 1925–1926 and the Year Book of the Drama in America*. New York: Dodd, Mead & Company, 1945. First published 1927.

Marchand, Roland. *Advertising the American Dream: Making Way for Modernity 1920–1940*. Berkeley: University of California Press, 1985.

Marquis, Don. "Origin of 'Hokum' and Other Slang." *Billboard* (August 27, 1927): 42.

Mast, Gerald. *The Comic Mind: Comedy and the Movies*. Chicago: University of Chicago Press, 1973.

Masteller, Jean Carwile, Heidi L. M. Jacobs, and Jennifer Putzi. "Laura Jean Libbey." In *Dictionary of Literary Biography*. Vol. 221, *American Prose Writers, 1870–1920*, ed. Sharon M. Harris. Detroit, MI: Gale Group, 2000, 253–64. Now available online at http://galenet.galegroup.com.

May, Henry. *The End of American Innocence: The First Years of Our Own Time, 1912–1917*. Oxford: Oxford University Press, 1959.

May, Lary. *Screening Out the Past: The Birth of Mass Culture and the Motion Picture Industry*. New York: Oxford University Press, 1980.

Mayer, David. "*Way Down East:* Theatrical Sources." In *The Griffith Project*. Vol. 10, *Films Produced in 1916–18*, ed. Paolo Cherchi Usai. Pordenone: Le Giornate del Cinema Muto/London: BFI Publishing, 2006, 95–103.

Meherin, Elenore. *"Chickie" a Hidden, Tragic Chapter from the Life of a Girl of This Strange "Today."* New York: Grosset & Dunlap, 1925.

Mencken, Henry L. "The American: His Language." *Smart Set* (August 1913): 89–96.

————. *The American Language: An Inquiry into the Development of English in the United States*. New York: Alfred Knopf, 1921. Rev. ed., Knopf, 1923. 4th ed., Knopf, 1943.

————. *The American Language: A Preliminary Inquiry into the Development of English in the United States*. New York: Alfred Knopf, 1919.

————. *A Book of Prefaces*. New York: Alfred Knopf, 1917.

————. *H. L. Mencken's Smart Set Criticism*. Ed. William H. Nolte. Ithaca, NY: Cornell University Press, 1968.

————. "The Last of the Victorians." *Smart Set* (October 1909): 153–55.

————. *Newspaper Days, 1899–1906*. New York: Knopf, 1941.

Menten, Theodore. *The Art Deco Style in Household Objects, Architecture, Sculpture, Graphics, Jewelry*. New York: Dover Publications, 1972.

Milne, Peter. *Motion Picture Directing*. New York: Falk Publishing Company, 1922.

Mitchell, Sally. *The Fallen Angel: Chastity, Class and Women's Reading, 1835–1880*. Bowling Green, OH: Bowling Green University Popular Press, 1981.

Mitry, Jean. *Histoire du cinéma, 1895–1914*. Vol 1. Paris: Éditions universitaires, 1967.

Moretti, Franco. "Kindergarten." In *Signs Taken for Wonders: Essays in the Sociology of Literary Forms*. Trans. Susan Fischer, David Forgacs, and David Miller. London: NLB, 1983.

Moses, Montrose J., and John Mason Brown, eds. *The American Theater as Seen by Its Critics, 1752–1934*. New York: Cooper Square Publishers, 1967. First published 1934.

Musser, Charles. "Divorce, DeMille, and the Comedy of Remarriage." In *Classical Hollywood Comedy*, ed. Kristine Brunovska Karnick and Henry Jenkins. New York: Routledge, 1995, 282–313, 392–98.

———. "Letter to the Editor." *Film History* 15, no 1 (2003): 110–15.

Nathan, George Jean. *Land of the Pilgrim's Pride*. New York: Knopf, 1927.

———. *The Popular Theatre*. New York: Knopf, 1918.

Neale, Steve. *Genre and Hollywood*. London: Routledge, 2000.

———. "Melo Talk: On the Meaning and Use of the Term 'Melodrama' in the American Trade Press." *Velvet Light Trap* 32: 66–89.

———. "Melodrama and Tears." *Screen* 27, no. 6 (November–December 1986): 6–22.

Nolte, William H. "Editor's Introduction." In *H. L. Mencken's Smart Set Criticism*. Ithaca, NY: Cornell University Press, 1968, xi–xxxvii.

O'Dell, Scott. *Representative Photoplays Analyzed*. Hollywood: Palmer Institute of Authorship, 1924.

Parrinder, Patrick. "The Strange Necessity: James Joyce's Rejection in England (1914–1930)." In *James Joyce: New Perspectives*, ed. Colin MacCabe. Bloomington: Indiana University Press, 1982, 151–67.

Peary, Gerald. "Introduction: *Little Caesar* Takes Over the Screen." In *Little Caesar*. Madison: University of Wisconsin Press, 1981, 9–28.

Potamianos, George Peter. "Hollywood in the Hinterlands: Mass Culture in Two California Communities, 1896–1936." PhD diss., University of Southern California, 1998.

Pound, Ezra. *The Letters of Ezra Pound, 1907–1941*. Ed. D. D. Paige. New York: Harcourt Brace, 1950.

Pratt, George C. *Spellbound in Darkness: A History of the Silent Film*. Greenwich, CT: New York Graphic Society, 1973. First published Rochester, NY: Rochester University Press, 1966.

Pudovkin, Vsevolod I. *Film Technique and Film Acting*. New York: Lear Publishers, 1949.

Ross, Sara. "Banking the Flames of Youth: The Hollywood Flapper, 1920–1930." PhD diss., University of Wisconsin, Madison, 2000.

Ross, Steven J. *Working-Class Hollywood*. Princeton, NJ: Princeton University Press, 1998.

Rotha, Paul. *The Film Till Now: A Survey of World Cinema*. With an additional section by Richard Griffith. London: Hamlyn House, 1967. Original version first published 1930.

Rourke, Constance Mayfield. "Transitions." *New Republic* (August 11, 1920): 315–16.

Rubin, Joan Shelley. *The Making of Middlebrow Culture*. Chapel Hill: University of North Carolina Press, 1992.

Sandburg, Carl. *Carl Sandburg at the Movies: A Poet in the Silent Era, 1920–1927*, ed. Dale Fetherling and Doug Fetherling. Metuchen, NJ: Scarecrow Press, 1985.

Sanjek, Russell. *Pennies from Heaven: The American Popular Music Business in the Twentieth Century,* updated by David Sanjek. New York: Da Capo Press, 1996.

Schauer, Bradley. "Justice and Redemption in the Underworld: The Crook Melodrama of the 1920s." Unpublished paper, 2004.

Schickel, Richard. *D. W. Griffith and the Birth of Film.* London: Pavilion Books, 1984.

Seldes, Gilbert. "American Humor." In *America as Americans See It,* ed. Fred J. Ringel. New York: Literary Guild, 1932, 347–60.

———. "The Best Pictures of Last Tuesday." *Esquire* 10 (August 1938): 72, 90.

———. "The Movies in Peril." *Scribner's* (February 1935): 82.

———. *The 7 Lively Arts.* New York: Harper & Brothers, 1924. Rev. ed., New York: Sagamore Press, 1957.

———. "Torch Songs." *New Republic* (November 19, 1930): 19–20.

Shaw, George Bernard. "Preface" to *Mrs. Warren's Profession.* In *The Complete Prefaces of Bernard Shaw.* London: Paul Hamlyn, 1965, 219–36.

Sherwood, Robert. Review of "The Big Parade." *Life* (December 10, 1925): 24–25.

———. Review of "Greed." *Life* (January 1, 1925): 24.

———. "Revivals." *Life* (January 7, 1926): 24–25.

———. "The Silent Drama: Recent Developments." *Life* (February 10, 1921): 214.

———. "The Silent Drama: Recent Developments." *Life* (March 17, 1921): 396.

———. "The Silent Drama." Review of "East Lynne." *Life* (March 31, 1921): 468.

———. "The Wronged Heroine." *Life* (October 13, 1921): 21.

Sinclair, Andrew. *John Ford: A Biography.* London: Lorrimer, 1979.

Singer, Ben. *Melodrama and Modernity: Early Sensational Cinema and Its Contexts.* New York: Columbia University Press, 2001.

Sklar, Robert. *City Boys: Cagney, Bogart, Garfield.* Princeton, NJ: Princeton University Press, 1992.

Slide, Anthony. *Selected Film Criticism.* Vol. 2, *1912–1920.* Vol. 3, *1921–1930.* Metuchen, NJ: Scarecrow Press, 1982–1985.

Sloane, Kay. *The Loud Silents: Origins of the Social Problem Film.* Urbana: University of Illinois Press, 1988.

Smith, Frederick James. "The Celluloid Critic." *Motion Picture Classic* (November 1920): 43, 86, 98, 100.

———. Review of *Foolish Wives, Motion Picture Classic* (April 1922): 48–49, 57.

Smith, Henry Nash. *Democracy and the Novel: Popular Resistance to Classic American Writers.* New York: Oxford University Press, 1978.

Smith, James. *Melodrama.* London: Methuen, 1973.

Spehr, Paul. *The Movies Begin: Making Movies in New Jersey, 1887–1920.* Newark, NJ: Newark Museum, 1977.

Staiger, Janet. *Bad Women: Regulating Sexuality in Early American Cinema.* Minneapolis: University of Minnesota Press, 1995.

———. *Interpreting Films: Studies in the Historical Reception of American Cinema*. Princeton, NJ: Princeton University Press, 1992.

Stallings, Laurence. "The Big Parade." *New Republic* (September 17, 1924): 66–69.

Stamp, Shelley. *Movie-Struck Girls: Women and Motion Picture Culture after the Nickelodeon*. Princeton, NJ: Princeton University Press, 2000.

Stansell, Christine. *American Moderns: Bohemian New York and the Creation of a New Century*. New York: Henry Holt, 2000.

Sternberg, Josef von. *Fun in a Chinese Laundry*. New York: Macmillan, 1965.

Stroheim, Erich von. *Greed*. Ed. Joel Finler. London: Lorrimer Publishing, 1972.

Strong, Austin. *Seventh Heaven: A Play in Three Acts*. New York: Samuel French, 1922.

Studlar, Gaylyn. *This Mad Masquerade: Stardom and Masculinity in the Jazz Age*. New York: Columbia University Press, 1996.

Thompson, Kristin. *Herr Lubitsch Goes to Hollywood: German and American Film After World War I*. Amsterdam: Amsterdam University Press, 2005.

———. "The Limits of Experimentation in Hollywood." In *Lovers of Cinema: The First American Film Avant-Garde, 1919–1925*, ed. Jan-Christopher Horak. Madison: University of Wisconsin Press, 1995, 70–77.

Todd, Janet. *Sensibility: An Introduction*. London: Methuen, 1986.

Tompkins, Jane. *West of Everything: The Inner Life of Westerns*. New York: Oxford University Press, 1992.

Van Doren, Carl. *Contemporary American Novelists, 1900–1920*. New York: Macmillan, 1922.

Vanderbilt, Kermit. *American Literature and the Academy: The Roots, Growth, and Maturity of a Profession*. Philadelphia: University of Pennsylvania Press, 1986.

Veeder, William. *Henry James—the Lessons of the Master: Popular Fiction and Personal Style in the Nineteenth Century*. Chicago: University of Chicago Press, 1975.

Vermillion, Billy Budd. "The Remarriage Plot in the 1910s." *Film History* 13, no. 4 (2001): 359–71.

Vidor, King. *King Vidor*. Interviewed by Nancy Dowd and David Shepard. A Directors Guild of America Oral History. Metuchen, NJ: Director's Guild of America/Scarecrow Press, 1988.

———. *A Tree Is a Tree*. New York: Harcourt, Brace and Company, 1952.

Walcutt, Charles Child. *American Literary Naturalism, A Divided Stream*. Minneapolis: University of Minnesota Press, 1956.

Waller, Gregory A. *Main Street Amusements: Movies and Commercial Entertainment in a Southern City, 1896–1930*. Washington, DC: Smithsonian Institution Press, 1995.

———, ed. *Moviegoing in America*. Oxford: Blackwell Publishers, 2002.

Walpole, Hugh. *Joseph Conrad*. New York: Henry Holt, 1916.

Walsh, Raoul. "Interview" by Olivier Eyquem, Michael Henry, and Jacques Saada. In *Raoul Walsh*, ed. Phil Hardy. Colchester, England: Vineyard Press Ltd, for the Edinburgh Film Festival, 1974, 31–49.

White, Percy W. "Stage Terms." *American Speech* 1, no. 8 (May 1926): 436–37.

Wilson, Edmund. *The American Earthquake: A Documentary of the Twenties and Thirties.* New York: Doubleday, 1958.

———. "The Seven Low-Brow Arts." *Dial* (September 1924): 244–50.

———. *The Shores of Light: A Literary Chronicle of the Twenties and Thirties.* New York: Farrar, Straus & Giroux, 1952.

Winchell, Walter. "A Primer of Broadway Slang: An Initiate Reveals Some of the Mysteries of the Much Quoted Theatrical Idiom." *Vanity Fair* (November 1927): 67, 132, 134.

———. "Your Broadway and Mine." New York *Graphic* (October 4, 1928).

Winter, William. *The Wallet of Time: Containing Personal, Biographical and Critical Reminiscence of the American Theatre.* New York: Moffat, Yard & Company, 1913.

Wood, Charles W. "With the Bunk Left Out." *Collier's* (November 17, 1923): 31.

Filmography

This filmography gives minimal identifying information for every film referred to in this book. For the vast majority of American-produced feature-length films, more detailed information is available in *The American Film Institute Catalog of Feature Films Produced in the United States,* published in book form by the University of California Press, Berkeley, California, and available online from Chadwyck-Healey. For all films produced in a country other than the United States, the country of origin is given.

The Affairs of Anatol. Famous Players–Lasky for Paramount, d. Cecil B. DeMille, September 25, 1921.
After Midnight. Metro-Goldwyn-Mayer Pictures, d. Monta Bell, August 20, 1927.
After the Show. Famous Players–Lasky for Paramount, d. William C. deMille, October 9, 1921.
The Air Circus. Fox Film Corp., d. Howard Hawks, September 30, 1928.
Alias Jimmy Valentine. Peerless Pictures for World Film Corp., d. Maurice Tourneur, February 22, 1915.
Amarilly of Clothes-Line Alley. Mary Pickford Film Corp. for Famous Players–Lasky Corp.: Artcraft Pictures, d. Marshall A. Neilan, March 11, 1918.
The Angel of Broadway. De Mille Pictures for Pathé Exchange, d. Lois Weber, October 3, 1927.
Ankles Preferred. Fox Film Corp., d. J. G. Blystone, February 27, 1927.
Anna Boleyn. Germany, Union Film–UFA, d. Ernst Lubitsch, December 3, 1920. U.S. release as *Deception,* April 1921.
Anna Christie. Thomas H. Ince Corp. for Associated First National Pictures, d. John Griffith Wray, November 28, 1923.
Anna Christie. Metro-Goldwyn-Mayer Pictures, d. Clarence Brown, February 21, 1930.
April Showers. Preferred Pictures, d. Tom Forman, October 21, 1923.
The Arab. Metro-Goldwyn Pictures, d. Rex Ingram, July 21, 1924.

Arabian Love. Fox Film Corp., d. Jerome Storm, April 9, 1922.

Ashes of Vengeance. Norma Talmadge Film Co. for Associated First National Pictures, d. Frank Lloyd, August 18, 1923.

At the Stage Door. R-C Pictures, d. William Christy Cabanne, December 11, 1921.

The Average Woman. C. C. Burr Pictures, d. William Christy Cabanne, March 1, 1924.

Babbitt. Warner Brothers Pictures, d. Harry Beaumont, June 15, 1924.

Back Pay. Cosmopolitan Productions for Paramount Pictures, d. Frank Borzage, January 8, 1922.

Barbed Wire. Paramount Famous Lasky Corp., d. Rowland V. Lee, August 6, 1927.

Bardelys, the Magnificent. Metro-Goldwyn-Mayer Pictures, d. King Vidor, September 30, 1926.

The Battle of the Sexes. Art Cinema Corp. for United Artists, d. D. W. Griffith, October 12, 1928.

Beau Brummel. Warner Brothers Pictures, d. Harry Beaumont, March 30, 1924.

Beau Geste. Famous Players–Lasky for Paramount Pictures, d. Herbert Brenon, August 25, 1926.

The Beauty Prize. Metro-Goldwyn Pictures, d. Lloyd Ingraham, December 22, 1924.

Becky. Cosmopolitan Productions for Metro-Goldwyn-Mayer Distributing Corp., d. John P. McCarthey, November 12, 1927.

Behind the Front. Famous Players–Lasky for Paramount Pictures, d. Edward Sutherland, February 22, 1926.

Bella Donna. Famous Players–Lasky for Paramount Pictures, d. George Fitzmaurice, April 1, 1923.

The Beloved Brute. Vitagraph Co. of America, d. J. Stuart Blackton, November 9, 1924.

The Beloved Rogue. Feature Productions for United Artists, d. Alan Crosland, March 12, 1927.

Ben-Hur. Metro-Goldwyn-Mayer Pictures, d. Fred Niblo, December 30, 1925.

Beside the Bonnie Brier Bush. United Kingdom, Famous Players–Lasky British Producers for Paramount Pictures, d. Donald Crisp, November 1921. U.S. release as *The Bonnie Brier Bush*, November 23, 1921.

The Big Parade. Metro-Goldwyn-Mayer Pictures, d. King Vidor, November 5, 1925.

The Birth of a Nation. D. W. Griffith Corp. for Epoch Producing Corp., d. D. W. Griffith, February 8, 1915.

Black Oxen. Frank Lloyd Productions for Associated First National Pictures, d. Frank Lloyd, December 29, 1924.

Blind Husbands. Universal Film Manufacturing Co. for Universal: Universal–Jewel Production de Luxe, d. Erich von Stroheim, December 7, 1919.

Blood and Sand. Famous Players–Lasky for Paramount Pictures, d. Fred Niblo, August 5, 1922.

The Blue Bird. Famous Players–Lasky Corp.: Artcraft Pictures, d. Maurice Tourneur, March 31, 1918.

La Bohème. Metro-Goldwyn-Mayer Pictures, d. King Vidor, February 24, 1926.

The Bonnie Brier Bush. See *Beside the Bonnie Brier Bush.*

Broadway After Dark. Warner Brothers Pictures, d. Monta Bell, May 31, 1924.

Broadway Nights. Robert Kane Productions for First National Pictures, d. Joseph C. Boyle, May 15, 1927.

Broken Blossoms. D. W. Griffith for United Artists Corp., d. D. W. Griffith, October 20, 1919.

The Broken Doll. American Biograph for General Film Co., d. D. W. Griffith, October 17, 1910.

Bucking Broadway. Universal Film Manufacturing Co.: A Harry Carey Production, d. Jack [John] Ford, December 24, 1917.

Burning Words. Universal Pictures, d. Stuart Paton, May 27, 1923.

The Busher. Thomas H. Ince Corp for Famous Players–Lasky Corp.: Paramount Pictures, d. Jerome Storm, May 18, 1919.

Cabiria. Italy, Itala Films, d. Piero Fosco [Giovanni Pastrone], April 11, 1914.

Camille. Nazimova Productions for Metro Pictures, d. Ray C. Smallwood, September 26, 1921.

Camille. Norma Talmadge Productions for First National Pictures, d. Fred Niblo, April 21, 1927.

Captain Lash. Fox Film Corp., d. John Blystone, January 6, 1929.

Captain Salvation. Cosmopolitan Productions for Metro-Goldwyn-Mayer Distributing Corp., d. John S. Robertson, May 14, 1927.

Carmen. Fox Film Corp., d. Raoul Walsh, November 1, 1915.

Carmen. Jesse L. Lasky Feature Play Co. for Paramount Pictures, d. Cecil B. DeMille, November 1, 1915.

The Champ. Metro-Goldwyn-Mayer Corp., d. King Vidor, November 21, 1931.

Chickie. First National Pictures, d. John Frances Dillon, May 10, 1925.

Children of Divorce. Famous Players–Lasky for Paramount Pictures, d. Frank Lloyd, April 2, 1927.

Children of Jazz. Famous Players–Lasky for Paramount Pictures, d. Jerome Storm, July 8, 1923.

City Girl. Fox Film Corp., d. F. W. Murnau, February 16, 1930.

Classified. Corinne Griffith Productions for First National Pictures, d. Alfred Santell, October 11, 1925.

The Closed Gate. Sterling Pictures, d. Phil Rosen, June 1, 1927.

The Cock-Eyed World. Fox Film Corp., d. Raoul Walsh, August 3, 1929.

The College Widow. Warner Brothers Pictures, d. Archie L. Mayo, October 15, 1927.

Come Across. Universal Pictures, d. Ray Taylor, June 30, 1929.

Condemned. Samuel Goldwyn, Inc., for United Artists, d. Wesley Ruggles, November 3, 1929.

The Conquering Power. Metro Pictures, d. Rex Ingram, July 8, 1921.

The Cop and the Anthem. Vitagraph Company of America for General Film Co., d. Thomas R. Mills, May 1917.

A Corner in Wheat. American Biograph Co., d. D. W. Griffith, December 13, 1909.

The Country Doctor. American Biograph Co., d. D. W. Griffith, July 8, 1909.

The Covered Wagon. Famous Players–Lasky for Paramount Pictures, d. James Cruze, March 16, 1923.

The Crowd. Metro-Goldwyn-Mayer Pictures, d. King Vidor, February 18, 1928.

Dancing Mothers. Famous Players–Lasky for Paramount Pictures, d. Herbert Brenon, March 1, 1926.

The Dark Angel. Samuel Goldwyn Productions for First National Pictures, d. George Fitzmaurice, September 27, 1925.

The Dawn Patrol. First National Pictures, d. Howard Hawks, July 10, 1930.

Deception. See *Anna Boleyn.*

The Docks of New York. Paramount Famous Players Lasky Corp., d. Josef von Sternberg, September 29, 1928.

Don Juan. Warner Brothers Pictures, d. Alan Crosland, August 6, 1926.

Don't Call Me Little Girl. Realart Pictures, d. Joseph Henabery, June 1921.

Don't Change Your Husband. Famous Players–Lasky for Paramount Pictures, d. Cecil B. DeMille, January 26, 1919.

Don't Tell the Wife. Warner Brothers Pictures, d. Paul Stein, January 22, 1927.

The Dragnet. Paramount Famous Players Lasky Corp., d. Josef von Sternberg, May 26, 1928.

Dream Street. D. W. Griffith, Inc., for United Artists, d. D. W. Griffith, April 12, 1921.

Dressed to Kill. Fox Film Corp., d. Irving Cummings, March 18, 1928.

The Duchess of Buffalo. Constance Talmadge Productions for First National Pictures, d. Sidney A. Franklin, August 8, 1926.

Dynamite. Metro-Goldwyn-Mayer Pictures, d. Cecil B. DeMille, December 13, 1929.

The Eagle. Art Finance Corp. for United Artists, d. Clarence Brown, November 8, 1925.

East Lynne. Hugo Ballin Productions for W. W. Hodkinson Corp., d. Hugo Ballin, March 1921.

East of Suez. Famous Players–Lasky for Paramount Pictures, d. Raoul Walsh, January 12, 1925.

The Enemies of Women. Cosmopolitan Productions for Goldwyn Distributing Corp., d. Alan Crosland, April 15, 1923.

Exchange of Wives. Metro-Goldwyn-Mayer Pictures, d. Hobart Henley, October 23, 1925.

The Exciters. Famous Players–Lasky, d. Maurice Campbell, June 3, 1923.

The Fair Co-Ed. Metro-Goldwyn-Mayer Pictures, d. Sam Wood, October 15, 1927.

The Far Country. Universal-International Pictures, d. Anthony Mann, February 12, 1955.

The Far Cry. First National Pictures, d. Silvano Balboni, February 14, 1926.

The Fast Set. Famous Players–Lasky for Paramount Pictures, d. William C. deMille, October 20, 1924.

Fazil. Fox Film Corp., d. Howard Hawks, June 4, 1928.

The First Year. Fox Film Corp., d. Frank Borzage, January 24, 1926.

Flaming Youth. Associated First National Pictures, d. John Francis Dillon, November 12, 1923.

Flesh and the Devil. Metro-Goldwyn-Mayer Pictures, d. Clarence Brown, December 25, 1926.

Flower of Night. Famous Players–Lasky for Paramount Pictures, d. Paul Bern, October 18, 1925.

The Fool. Fox Film Corp., d. Harry Millarde, November 15, 1925.

Foolish Wives. Universal Film Manufacturing Co., d. Erich von Stroheim, January 11, 1922.

The Footlight Ranger. Fox Film Corp., d. Scott Dunlap, January 14, 1923.

For You, My Boy. Rubicon Pictures, d. William L. Roubert, July 15, 1923.

Forbidden. Lois Weber Productions for Universal Film Manufacturing Co.: Universal Jewel, d. Lois Weber and Phillips Smalley, September 8, 1919.

Forbidden Fruit. Famous Players–Lasky for Paramount Pictures, d. Cecil B. DeMille, January 23, 1921.

Forbidden Paradise. Famous Players–Lasky for Paramount Pictures, d. Ernst Lubitsch, November 16, 1924.

The Forbidden Woman. De Mille Pictures for Pathé Exchange, d. William C. deMille, October 29, 1927.

The Four Horsemen of the Apocalypse. Metro Pictures, d. Rex Ingram, March 6, 1921.

French Dressing. First National Pictures, d. Allan Dwan, December 10, 1927.

The Gangsters and the Girl. KayBee for Mutual Film Corporation, d. Scott Sidney, August 1914.

A Gentleman of Paris. Paramount Famous Lasky Corp., d. Harry D'Abbadie D'Arrast, October 1, 1927.

The Girl from Woolworth's. First National Pictures, d. William Beaudine, October 27, 1929.

A Girl in Every Port. Fox Film Corp., d. Howard Hawks, February 26, 1928.

Going Straight. Fine Arts Film Co. for Triangle Film Corp., d. Chester M Franklin and Sidney A. Franklin, June 4, 1916.

The Gold Diggers. Warner Brothers Pictures, d. Harry Beaumont, September 22, 1923.

The Golden Bed. Famous Players–Lasky, d. Cecil B. DeMille, January 19, 1925.

The Good Provider. Cosmopolitan Productions for Paramount Pictures, d. Frank Borzage, April 2, 1922.

Goodness Gracious, or, Movies as They Shouldn't Be. Vitagraph Company of America, d. James Young, February 7, 1914.

The Grand Duchess and the Waiter. Famous Players–Lasky for Paramount Pictures, d. Malcolm St. Clair, February 8, 1926.

Grandma's Boy. Hal Roach Studio for Associated Exhibitors, d. Fred Newmeyer, May 20, 1922.

Graustark. Joseph M. Schenck Productions for First National Pictures, d. Dimitri Buchowetski, August 30, 1925.

The Great Love. D. W. Griffith for Famous Players–Lasky Corp.: Artcraft Pictures, d. D. W. Griffith, August 12, 1918.
The Greatest Thing in Life. D. W. Griffith for Famous Players–Lasky Corp.: Artcraft Pictures, d. D. W. Griffith, December 8, 1918.
Greed. Metro-Goldwyn Pictures, d. Erich von Stroheim, January 26, 1925.
Hail the Woman. Thomas H. Ince Productions for Associated Producers, d. John Griffith Wray, November 28, 1921.
Hallelujah. Metro-Goldwyn Pictures, d. King Vidor, August 20, 1929.
Happiness. Metro Pictures, d. King Vidor, March 9, 1924.
Hard-Boiled Haggerty. First National Pictures, d. Charles Brabin, August 21, 1927.
The Heart of Humanity. Universal Film Manufacturing Co.: Universal Jewel, d. Allen Holubar, February 15, 1919.
Hearts of Oak. Fox Film Corp., d. John Ford, October 5, 1924.
Hearts of the World. D. W. Griffith, d. D. W. Griffith, March 12, 1918.
Hearts of Youth. Fox Film Corp., d. Tom Miranda and Millard Webb, May 1921.
Hell's Angels. Caddo Co. for United Artists, d. Howard Hughes, May 27, 1930.
Her Night of Romance. Constance Talmadge Productions for First National Pictures, d. Sidney A. Franklin, October 1924.
Her Sister from Paris. Joseph M. Schenck Productions for First National Pictures, d. Sidney A. Franklin, August 2, 1925.
The Hired Man. Thomas H. Ince Productions for Famous Players–Lasky Corp.: Paramount Pictures, d. Victor L. Schertzinger, January 28, 1918.
His Buddy's Wife. Associated Exhibitors, d. Tom Terriss, October 4, 1925.
His Children's Children. Famous Players–Lasky for Paramount Pictures, d. Sam Wood, November 4, 1923.
His Glorious Night. Metro-Goldwyn-Mayer Pictures, d. Lionel Barrymore, September 28, 1929.
His Hour. Louis B. Mayer Productions for Metro-Goldwyn Distributing Corp., d. King Vidor, September 29, 1924.
His Supreme Moment. Samuel Goldwyn Productions for First National Pictures, d. George Fitzmaurice, May 3, 1925.
Hogan's Alley. Warner Brothers Pictures, d. Roy Del Ruth, December 12, 1925.
Home. Lois Weber Productions for Universal Film Manufacturing Co.: Universal Jewel, d. Lois Weber, August 31, 1919.
Home Stuff. Metro Pictures, d. Albert Kelley, June 16, 1921.
The Hoodlum. Mary Pickford Co. for First National Exhibitors Circuit, d. Sidney A. Franklin, September 1, 1919.
Hook and Ladder No. 9. R-C Pictures for FBO Pictures, d. F. Harmon Weight, November 13, 1927.
Hot for Paris. Fox Film Corp., d. Raoul Walsh, December 22, 1929.
Hot Pepper. Fox Film Corp., d. John Blystone, January 15, 1933.
Hotel Imperial. Famous Players–Lasky for Paramount Pictures, d. Mauritz Stiller, January 1, 1927.

The House of Youth. Regal Pictures for Producers Distributing Corp., d. Ralph Ince, October 19, 1924.

Humoresque. Cosmopolitan Productions and International Film Service Co. for Famous Players–Lasky Corp.: Paramount Artcraft Pictures, d. Frank Borzage, September 19, 1920.

Husband Hunters. Tiffany Productions, d. John G. Adolfi, January 15, 1927.

Hush. Equity Pictures for Jans Film Service, d. Harry Garson, February 1921.

Ibáñez' Torrent. Cosmopolitan Pictures for Metro-Goldwyn-Mayer Distributing Corp., d. Monta Bell, February 8, 1926.

In a Moment of Temptation. R-C Pictures for Film Booking Offices of America, d. Philip Carle, September 18, 1927.

Intolerance. D. W. Griffith for Wark Producing Corp., d. D. W. Griffith, September 5, 1916.

Irene. First National Pictures, d. Alfred E. Green, February 21, 1926.

Is Love Everything? Garsson Enterprises for Associated Exhibitors, d. William Christy Cabanne, November 30, 1924.

Is Matrimony a Failure? Famous Players–Lasky for Paramount Pictures, d. James Cruze, April 2, 1922.

Isn't Life Wonderful. United Artists, d. D. W. Griffith, December 1, 1924.

It. Famous Players–Lasky for Paramount Pictures, d. Clarence Badger, February 5, 1927.

Joanna. Edwin Carewe Productions for First National Pictures, d. Edwin Carewe, December 6, 1925

Journey's End. Tiffany-Gainsborough Productions, d. James Whale, April 8, 1930.

The Jungle. All Star Feature Corp., d. August Thomas, George Henry Irving and John H. Pratt, May 25, 1914.

Just Gold. American Biograph Co. for General Film Co., d. D. W. Griffith, May 24, 1913.

The Kid. Charles Chaplin Productions for Associated First National Pictures, d. Charles Chaplin, February 6, 1921.

Kiki. Norma Talmadge Productions for First National Pictures, d. Clarence Brown, April 4, 1926.

Kindling. Jesse L. Lasky Feature Play Co. for Paramount Pictures Corp., d. Cecil B. DeMille, July 12, 1915.

The King on Main Street. Famous Players–Lasky for Paramount Pictures, d. Monta Bell, October 17, 1925.

Kiss Me Again. Warner Brothers Pictures, d. Ernst Lubitsch, August 1, 1925.

The Knockout. First National Pictures, d. Lambert Hillyer, August 23, 1925.

Knockout Reilly. Famous Players–Lasky for Paramount Pictures, d. Malcolm St. Clair, April 16, 1927.

Laddie. Gene Stratton Porter Productions for Film Booking Offices of America, d. James Leo Meehan, September 26, 1926.

Ladies Must Live. Mayflower Photoplay Corp. for Paramount Pictures, d. George Loane Tucker, October 30, 1921.

The Lady. Norma Talmadge Productions for First National Pictures, d. Frank Borzage, February 8, 1925.

Lady Windemere's Fan. Warner Brothers Pictures, d. Ernst Lubitsch, December 26, 1925.

The Last of Mrs. Cheyney. Metro-Goldwyn-Mayer Pictures, d. Sidney A. Franklin, July 6, 1929.

The Last of the Mohicans. Maurice Tourneur Productions for Associated Producers, Inc., d. Maurice Tourneur, November 21, 1920.

Lazybones. Fox Film Corp. d. Frank Borzage, November 6, 1925.

Let Not Man Put Asunder. Vitagraph Co. of America, d. J. Stuart Blackton, February 1924.

Life's Whirlpool. World Film Corp., d. Barry O'Neil, January 10, 1916.

Lightnin'. Fox Film Corp., d. John Ford, August 23, 1925.

Lily of the Dust. Famous Players–Lasky for Paramount Pictures, d. Dimitri Buchowetski, August 24, 1924.

The Little American. Mary Pickford Film Corp. for Artcraft Pictures Corp., d. Cecil B. DeMille, July 2, 1917.

The Little Church Around the Corner. Warner Brothers Pictures, d. William A. Seiter, March 18, 1923.

The Little Grey Mouse. Fox Film Corp., d. James P. Hogan, October 31, 1920.

Lonesome. Universal Pictures, d. Paul Fejös, September 30, 1928.

Lord Jim. Famous Players–Lasky for Paramount Pictures, d. Victor Fleming, December 14, 1925.

Lorna Doone. Thanhouser Film Corp., d. Theodore Marston, June 1911.

Lorna Doone. American Biograph Co., d. J. Farrell MacDonald, April 1915.

Lorna Doone. Thomas H. Ince Corp for Associated First National Pictures, d. Maurice Tourneur, October 1, 1922.

Love. Metro-Goldwyn-Mayer Pictures, d. Edmund Goulding, November 29, 1927.

Love of Women. Interlocutory Films for Selznick Distributing Corp., d. Whitman Bennett, June 30, 1924.

Love's Greatest Mistake. Famous Players–Lasky for Paramount Pictures, d. Edward Sutherland, February 13, 1927.

Loves of Carmen. Fox Film Corp, d. Raoul Walsh, September 4, 1927.

Lucky Star. Fox Film Corp. d. Frank Borzage, August 18, 1929.

Mad Love. See *Sappho.*

Madame Dubarry. Germany, Projektions–A.G. 'Union,' d. Ernst Lubitsch, September 18, 1919. U.S. release as *Passion*, December 17, 1920.

Main Street. Warner Brothers Pictures, d. Harry Beaumont, April 25, 1923.

Mama's Affair. Constance Talmadge Film Co. for Associated First National Pictures, d. Victor Fleming, January 1921.

Man Crazy. Charles R. Rogers Productions for First National Pictures, d. John Francis Dillon, November 27, 1927.

The Man from Nevada. J. P. McGowan Productions for Syndicate Pictures, d. J. P. McGowan, August 1929.

The Man of Stone. Selznick Pictures for Select Pictures, d. George Archainbaud, November 10, 1921.

The Manicure Girl. Famous Players–Lasky for Paramount Pictures, d. Frank Tuttle, July 6, 1925.

A Man's Mate. Fox Film Corp., d. Edmund Mortimer, March 16, 1924.
Mantrap. Famous Players–Lasky for Paramount Pictures, d. Victor Fleming, July 18, 1926.
Mare Nostrum. Metro-Goldwyn-Mayer Pictures, d. Rex Ingram, February 15, 1926.
Marianne. Cosmopolitan Productions for Metro-Goldwyn-Mayer Distributing Corp., d. Robert Z. Leonard, August 24, 1929.
The Marriage Circle. Warner Brothers Pictures, d. Ernst Lubitsch, February 3, 1924.
The Marriage Whirl. Corinne Griffith Productions for First National Pictures, d. Alfred Santell, July 19, 1925.
Men Without Women. Fox Film Corp., d. John Ford, January 31, 1930.
The Merry Widow. Metro-Goldwyn-Mayer Pictures, d. Erich von Stroheim, August 26, 1925.
Mine to Keep. Bryant Washburn Productions for Grand-Asher Distributing Corp., d. Ben Wilson, August 20, 1923.
The Mirage. Regal Pictures for Producers Distributing Corp, d. George Archainbaud, December 28, 1924.
Miss Lulu Bett. Famous Players–Lasky for Paramount Pictures, d. William C. deMille, November 13, 1921.
M'liss. Pickford Film Corp. for Famous Players–Lasky Corp. Artcraft Pictures, d. Marshall Neilan, May 13, 1918.
Molly O'. Mack Sennett–Mabel Normand Productions/Associated Producers for Associated First National Pictures, d. F. Richard Jones, November 20, 1921.
Monsieur Beaucaire. Famous Players–Lasky for Paramount Pictures, d. Sidney Olcott, August 18, 1924.
The Music Master. Fox Film Corp., d. Allan Dwan, January 23, 1927.
The Naked Spur. Metro-Goldwyn-Mayer Corp., d. Anthony Mann, February 6, 1953.
Name the Man. Goldwyn Pictures for Goldwyn-Cosmopolitan Distributing Corp., d. Victor Seastrom [Sjöström], January 15, 1924.
Nanook of the North. Revillon Frères for Pathé Exchange, d. Robert Flaherty, June 11, 1922.
Naughty Baby. First National Pictures, d. Mervyn Leroy, January 19, 1929.
The New Klondike. Famous Players–Lasky for Paramount Pictures, d. Lewis Milestone, March 15, 1926.
The New York Idea. Realart Pictures Corp, d. Herbert Blaché, November 27, 1920.
The Night of Love. Samuel Goldwyn, Inc., for United Artists, d. George Fitzmaurice, January 22, 1927.
No Place to Go. Henry Hobart Productions for First National Pictures, d. Mervyn Leroy, October 10, 1927.
The Nth Commandment. Cosmopolitan Productions for Paramount Pictures, d. Frank Borzage, March 18, 1923.
Old Loves and New. Sam E. Rork Productions for First National Pictures, d. Maurice Tourneur, April 11, 1926.

The Old Swimmin' Hole. Charles Ray Productions for Associated First National Pictures, d. Joseph De Grasse, February 1921.

Old Wives for New. Famous Players–Lasky Corp. for Paramount Pictures: Artcraft Pictures, d. Cecil B. DeMille, June 16, 1918.

One Stolen Night. Vitagraph Co. of America, d. Robert Ensminger, January 29, 1923.

Open All Night. Famous Players–Lasky for Paramount Pictures, d. Paul Bern, October 13, 1924.

Orchids and Ermine. John McCormick Productions for First National Pictures, d. Alfred Santell, March 6, 1927.

Orphans of the Storm. D. W. Griffith, Inc., for United Artists, d. D. W. Griffith, June 22, 1922.

Our Dancing Daughters. Cosmopolitan Productions for Metro-Goldwyn-Mayer Distributing Corp., d. Harry Beaumont, September 1, 1928.

Our Modern Maidens. Metro-Goldwyn-Mayer Pictures, d. Jack Conway, August 24, 1929.

Over the Hill to the Poorhouse. Fox Film Corp., d. Harry Millarde, September 17, 1920.

The Painted Flapper. Chadwick Pictures, d. John Gorman, October 15, 1924.

A Pair of Silk Stockings. Select Pictures Corp., d. Walter Edwards, July 20, 1918.

Paradise for Two. Famous Players–Lasky for Paramount Pictures, d. Gregory La Cava, January 23, 1927.

Passers-By. J. Stuart Blackton Feature Pictures, inc., for Pathé Exchange, Inc., d. J. Stuart Blackton, June 20, 1920.

Passion. See *Madame Dubarry.*

Passionate Youth. Truart Film Corp., d. Dallas M. Fitzgerald, June 28, 1925.

The Patent Leather Kid. First National Pictures, d. Alfred Santell, September 1, 1927.

Paying the Price. Columbia Pictures, d. David Selman, April 5, 1927.

The Perfect Flapper. Associated First National Pictures, d. John Francis Dillon, May 25, 1924.

The Plastic Age. B. P. Schulberg Productions, d. Wesley Ruggles, December 15, 1925.

The Plaything of Broadway. Realart Pictures, d. Jack Dillon, February 1921.

Pollyanna. Mary Pickford Co. for United Artists, d. Paul Powell, January 18, 1920.

The Price of a Good Time. Lois Weber Productions for Universal Film Manufacturing Co.: Universal Jewel, d. Lois Weber and Phillips Smalley, November 4, 1917.

Pride of the Force. Rayart Pictures, d. Duke Worne, September 11, 1925.

Prodigal Daughters. Famous Players–Lasky for Paramount Pictures, d. Sam Wood, April 15, 1923.

Proud Flesh. Metro-Goldwyn Pictures, d. King Vidor, April 27, 1925.

Prudence on Broadway. Triangle Film Corp., d. Frank Borzage, July 6, 1919.

Prunella. Famous Players–Lasky Corp for Paramount Pictures, d. Maurice Tourneur, May 27, 1918.

Public Enemy. Warner Bros. Pictures, Inc., d. William A. Wellman, May 15,
1931.
Queen Christina. Metro-Goldwyn-Mayer Corp., d. Rouben Mamoulian,
February 9, 1934.
The Racket. Caddo Co., for Paramount Famous Players Lasky Corp., d. Lewis
Milestone, June 30, 1928.
Ranch Life in the Great South-West. Selig Polyscope Co. for General Film
Co., d. Otis Turner and Frank Boggs, July 31, 1910.
Rebecca of Sunnybrook Farm. Mary Pickford Corp. for Artcraft Pictures, d.
Marshall Neilan, September 22, 1917.
Regeneration. Fox Film Corp., d. Raoul Walsh, September 13, 1915.
Reno. Goldwyn Pictures for Goldwyn-Cosmopolitan Distributing Corp., d.
Rupert Hughes, December 1923.
The Rescue. Samuel Goldwyn, Inc., for United Artists, d. Herbert Brenon,
January 12, 1929.
Rich but Honest. Fox Film Corp., d. Albert Ray, May 22, 1927.
Rio Bravo. Armada Productions for Warner Bros., d. Howard Hawks, March
18, 1959.
The River. Fox Film Corp., d. Frank Borzage, December 22, 1928.
Rolled Stockings. Paramount Famous Lasky Corp., d. Richard Rosson, June
18, 1927.
Romance. United Artists Corp., d. Chet Withey, May 30, 1920.
A Romance of Happy Valley. D. W. Griffith for Famous Players–Lasky Corp.:
Artcraft Pictures, d. D. W. Griffith, January 26, 1919.
Romola. Inspiration Pictures for Metro-Goldwyn Distributing Corp., d.
Henry King, August 30, 1925.
Rosita. Mary Pickford Co. for United Artists, d. Ernst Lubitsch, September 3,
1923.
Rouged Lips. Metro Pictures, d. Harold Shaw, August 20, 1923.
Sadie Thompson. Gloria Swanson Productions for United Artists, d. Raoul
Walsh, January 7, 1928.
A Sainted Devil. Famous Player–Lasky for Paramount Pictures, d. Joseph
Henabery, November 17, 1924.
Sally, Irene and Mary. Metro-Goldwyn-Mayer Pictures, d. Edmund Gould-
ing, December 27, 1925.
Salome. Nazimova Productions for Allied Producers and Distributors, d.
Charles Bryant, December 31, 1922.
The Salvation Hunters. Academy Photoplays for United Artists, d. Josef von
Sternberg, February 7, 1925.
Sappho. Germany, Projektions–A.G. 'Union,' d. Dimitri Buchowetzki, Sep-
tember 9, 1921. U.S. release as *Mad Love*, March 8, 1923.
Scarface. The Caddo Co. for United Artists, d. Howard Hawks, April 9, 1932.
The Scarlet Empress. Paramount Productions, d. Josef von Sternberg, Septem-
ber 15, 1924.
The Scarlet Letter. Metro-Goldwyn-Mayer Pictures, d. Victor Seastrom
[Sjöström], August 9, 1926.
7th Heaven. Fox Film Corp., d. Frank Borzage, May 6, 1927.

The Shakedown. Universal Pictures: Universal Jewel Pictures, d. William
    Wyler, March 10, 1929.
The Sheik. Famous Players–Lasky for Paramount Pictures, d. George Melford,
    October 30, 1921.
The Shield of Honor. Universal Pictures: Universal Jewel Pictures, d. Emory
    Johnson, December 10, 1927.
Shoulder Arms. Charles Chaplin for First National, d. Charles Chaplin, Octo-
    ber 20, 1918.
The Sign on the Door. Norma Talmadge Productions for Associated First
    National Pictures, d. Herbert Brenon, May 1921.
Singin' in the Rain. Metro-Goldwyn-Mayer Corp., d. Stanley Donen and
    Gene Kelly, March 27, 1952.
The Single Standard. Metro-Goldwyn-Mayer Pictures, d. John S. Robertson,
    July 29, 1929.
A Slave of Fashion. Metro-Goldwyn-Mayer Pictures, d. Hobart Henley,
    August 23, 1925.
Smilin' Through. Norma Talmadge Productions for Associated First National
    Pictures, d. Sidney A. Franklin, February 13, 1922.
Smilin' Through. Metro-Goldwyn-Mayer Corp., d. Frank Borzage, October
    1941.
The Snob. Metro-Goldwyn-Mayer Pictures, d. Monta Bell, November 3,
    1924.
So This Is Paris. Warner Brothers Pictures, d. Ernst Lubitsch, July 31, 1926.
A Son of the Sahara. Edwin Carewe Productions for Associated First National
    Pictures, d. Edwin Carewe, April 13, 1924.
The Son of the Sheik. Feature Productions for United Artists, d. George Fitz-
    maurice, July 9, 1926.
The Song of Love. Norma Talmadge Productions for Associated First National
    Pictures, d. Chester M. Franklin and Frances Marion, December 24, 1923.
Sorrell and Son. Feature Productions for United Artists, d. Herbert Brenon,
    November 12, 1927.
Souls for Sables. Tiffany Productions, d. James C. McKay, September 14, 1925.
The Spaniard. Famous Players–Lasky for Paramount Pictures, d. Raoul
    Walsh, May 4, 1925.
The Spanish Dancer. Famous Players–Lasky for Paramount Pictures, d. Her-
    bert Brenon, October 7, 1923.
Speakeasy. Fox Film Corp., d. Benjamin Stoloff, March 24, 1929.
Speed. Banner Productions, d. Edward J. Le Saint, April 26, 1925.
Speed Madness. Hercules Film Productions, d. Bruce Mitchell, October 3,
    1925.
The Spoilers. Selig Polyscope Co., d. Colin Campbell, April 11, 1914.
The Spoilers. Jesse D. Hampton Productions for Goldwyn Distributing Corp.,
    d. Lambert Hillyer, August 5, 1923.
The Sporting Venus. Metro-Goldwyn Pictures, d. Marshall Neilan, April 13,
    1925.
The Squaw Man. Jesse L. Lasky Feature Play Co., d. Cecil B. DeMille, Febru-
    ary 15, 1914.

The Squaw Man. Famous Players–Lasky Corp.: Artcraft Pictures, d. Cecil B.
  DeMille, December 15, 1918.
Stark Love. Paramount Famous Lasky Corp., d. Karl Brown, February 28,
  1927.
Stella Dallas. Samuel Goldwyn, Inc., for United Artists, d. Henry King,
  November 16, 1925.
Die Strasse. Germany, Stern Film for Hansa–Filmverleih, d. Karl Grune,
  November 29, 1923. U.S. release as *The Street,* September 1927.
The Street. See *Die Strasse.*
Street Angel. Fox Film Corp., d. Frank Borzage, April 9, 1928.
Suds. Mary Pickford Co. for United Artists, d. Jack Dillon, June 27, 1920.
Sunrise—a Song of Two Humans. Fox Film Corp., d. F. W. Murnau, Septem-
  ber 23, 1927.
Swim, Girl, Swim. Paramount Famous Lasky Corp., d. Clarence Badger, Sep-
  tember 3, 1927.
The Taxi Dancer. Metro-Goldwyn-Mayer Pictures, d. Harry Millarde, Febru-
  ary 5, 1927.
The Temptress. Cosmopolitan Productions for Metro-Goldwyn-Mayer Dis-
  tributing Corp., d. Fred Niblo, October 3, 1926.
The Ten Commandments. Famous Players–Lasky for Paramount Pictures, d.
  Cecil B. DeMille, December 21, 1923.
Tess of the Storm Country. Famous Players Film Co., d. Edwin Stanton Porter,
  March 20, 1914.
Tess of the Storm Country. Mary Pickford Co. for United Artists, d. John S.
  Robertson, November 12, 1922.
Tessie. Arrow Pictures, d. Dallas M. Fitzgerald, September 18, 1925.
The Thirteenth Juror. Universal Pictures: Universal Jewel, d. Edward
  Laemmle, November 13, 1927.
Three Hours. Corinne Griffith Productions for First National Pictures, d.
  James Flood, March 5, 1927.
Three Sinners. Paramount Famous Lasky Corp., d. Rowland V. Lee, April 14,
  1928.
Three Weeks. Goldwyn Pictures for Goldwyn-Cosmopolitan Distributing
  Corp., d. Alan Crosland, February 10, 1924.
To Please One Woman. Lois Weber Productions for Famous Players–Lasky
  Corp.: Paramount Pictures, d. Lois Weber, December 19, 1920.
Tomorrow's Love. Famous Players–Lasky for Paramount Pictures, d. Paul
  Bern, January 5, 1925.
The Torrent. See *Ibañez' Torrent.*
The Tower of Lies. Metro-Goldwyn-Mayer Pictures, d. Victor Seastrom
  [Sjöström], October 11, 1925.
True Heart Susie. D. W. Griffith for Famous Players–Lasky Corp.: Artcraft
  Pictures, d. D. W. Griffith, June 1, 1919.
Twelve Miles Out. Metro-Goldwyn-Mayer Pictures, d. Jack Conway, July 9,
  1927.
Two Arabian Knights. Caddo Co. for United Artists, d. Lewis Milestone,
  October 22, 1927.

Two-Faced Woman. Metro-Goldwyn-Mayer Corp. for Loew's Inc., d. George Cukor, November 1941.

The Unbeliever. Thomas A. Edison, Inc.: Perfection Pictures for George Kleine System, February 1918.

Underworld. Paramount Famous Lasky Corp., d. Josef von Sternberg, August 20, 1927.

Uneasy Payments. R-C Pictures for Film Booking Offices of America, d. David Kirkland, January 19, 1927.

Upstairs and Down. Selznick Pictures Corp. for Select Pictures Corp.: Star Series Attraction, d. Charles Giblyn, June 8, 1919.

Varieté. Germany, Universum Film A.G., d. E. A. Dupont, November 16, 1925. U.S. release as *Variety,* June 1926.

Variety. See *Varieté.*

Victory. Maurice Tourneur Productions, Inc., for Famous Players–Lasky Corp.: Paramount-Artcraft Pictures, d. Maurice Tourneur, December 7, 1919.

The Virginian. Jesse L. Lasky Feature Play Co. for Paramount Pictures Corp., d. Cecil B. DeMille, September 7, 1914.

The Virginian. B. P. Schulberg Productions for Preferred Pictures, d. Tom Forman, September 30, 1923.

The Virginian. Paramount Famous Lasky Corp., d. Victor Fleming, November 9, 1929.

Way Down East. D. W. Griffth Inc. for United Artists, d. D. W. Griffith, September 3, 1920.

We Moderns. John McCormick Productions for First National Pictures, d. John Francis Dillon, November 15, 1925.

What Fools Men. First National Pictures, d. George Archainbaud, September 13, 1925.

What Price Glory. Fox Film Corp., d. Raoul Walsh, November 13, 1926.

What Price Glory. Twentieth Century-Fox Film Corp., d. John Ford, July 25, 1952.

When a Man Loves. Warner Brothers Pictures, d. Alan Crosland, February 3, 1927.

Where East Is East. Metro-Goldwyn-Mayer Pictures, d. Tod Browning, May 4, 1929.

The White Desert. Metro-Goldwyn Pictures, d. Reginald Barker, May 4, 1925.

White Man. B. P. Schulberg Productions, d. Louis Gasnier, November 1, 1924.

The White Sister. Inspiration Pictures for Metro Pictures, d. Henry King, September 5, 1923.

Why Change Your Wife? Famous Players–Lasky Corp.: A Paramount-Artcraft Special, d. Cecil B. DeMille, May 2, 1920.

Wife of the Centaur. Metro-Goldwyn Pictures, d. King Vidor, December 1, 1924.

A Wife's Awakening. Robertson-Cole Co. for R-C Pictures, d. Louis Gasnier, September 25, 1921.

Wild and Woolly. Douglas Fairbanks Pictures Corp. for Artcraft Pictures Corp., d. John Emerson, June 24, 1917.

Wild Geese. Tiffany-Stahl Productions, d. Phil Stone, November 15, 1927.

The Wild Goose. Cosmopolitan Productions/Famous Players–Lasky for Paramount Pictures, d. Albert Capellani, June 5, 1921.

Wild Orchids. Metro-Goldwyn-Mayer Pictures, d. Sidney A. Franklin, February 23, 1929.

The Wild Party. Paramount Famous Lasky Corp., d. Dorothy Arzner, April 6, 1929.

The Wind. Metro-Goldwyn-Mayer Corp., d. Victor Seastrom [Sjöström], November 23, 1928.

Wine of Youth. Metro-Goldwyn Pictures, d. King Vidor, August 10, 1924.

Wings. Paramount Famous Lasky Corp., d. William A. Wellman, August 1927.

The Winning of Barbara Worth. Samuel Goldwyn, Inc., for United Artists, d. Henry King, October 14, 1926.

The Woman Disputed. United Artists, d. Henry King and Sam Taylor, September 1928.

A Woman of Affairs. Metro-Goldwyn-Mayer Pictures, d. Clarence Brown, December 15, 1928.

A Woman of Paris. United Artists, d. Charles Chaplin, October 1, 1923.

A Woman of the World. Famous Players–Lasky for Paramount Pictures, d. Malcolm St. Clair, December 28, 1925.

The Woman on Trial. Paramount Famous Lasky Corp., d. Mauritz Stiller, September 25, 1927.

Woman's Place. Joseph M. Schenck Productions for Associated First National Pictures, d. Victor Fleming, October 17, 1921.

Women Love Diamonds. Metro-Goldwyn-Mayer Pictures, d. Edmund Goulding, February 12, 1927.

Women of All Nations. Fox Film Corp., d. Raoul Walsh, May 31, 1931.

The World at Her Feet. Paramount Famous Lasky Corp., d. Luther Reed, May 14, 1927.

Worldly Goods. Trem Carr Productions for Continental Talking Pictures, d. Phil Rosen, August 1, 1930.

Young Nowheres. First National Pictures, d. Frank Lloyd, October 1, 1929.

Index

Text:	10/13 Aldus
Display:	Aldus
Compositor:	BookComp, Inc.
Printer and Binder:	Sheridan Books, Inc.